[1] Maurice Merleau-Ponty, *Structure of Behavior* or *Phenomenolog[y]* *Perception*, in *Basic writings*, ed. Thomas Baldwin (NY: Rou[tledge] 2004), 119.

[2] Ibid., 120.

or

[2] Merleau-Ponty, *Basic writings*, 99.

Stanford Encyc. of Philosophy, "_____," Merleau-Ponty,

(accessed)

MAURICE **MERLEAU-PONTY** basic writings

Merleau-Ponty was a pivotal figure in twentieth-century French philosophy. He helped to bring the phenomenological method of the German philosophers – Husserl and Heidegger – to France and instigated a new wave of interest in this approach. His influence extended well beyond the boundaries of philosophy and can be seen in theories of politics, psychology, art and language.

This is the first volume to bring together a comprehensive selection of Merleau-Ponty's writing. Sections from the following are included:

The Primacy of Perception   *The Structure of Behavior*
The Phenomenology of Perception   *The Prose of the World*
The Visible and the Invisible   *Sense and Non-sense*
The Adventures of the Dialectic

In a substantial introduction Thomas Baldwin provides a critical discussion of the main themes of Merleau-Ponty's philosophy, connecting it to subsequent philosophical debates and setting it in the context of the ideas of Bergson, Husserl, Heidegger and Sartre. Each text is also prefaced with an explanation which sets it in its context in Merleau-Ponty's work; and there are extensive suggestions for further reading to enable students to pursue the issues raised by Merleau-Ponty. Thus the book provides the ideal materials for students studying Merleau-Ponty for the first time.

Thomas Baldwin is a Professor of Philosophy at the University of York. Recent publications include *The Cambridge History of Philosophy 1870–1945* (2003), and *Contemporary Philosophy: Philosophy in English since 1945* (2001); other publications include *G. E. Moore* (Routledge, 1990).

MAURICE
MERLEAU-
PONTY

basic writings

edited by **thomas baldwin**

Routledge
Taylor & Francis Group

LONDON AND NEW YORK

First published 2004
by Routledge
2 Park Square, Milton Park, Abingdon, Oxon, OX14 4RN

Simultaneously published in the USA and Canada
by Routledge
270 Madison Ave, New York, NY 10016

Reprinted 2007

Routledge is an imprint of the Taylor & Francis Group, an informa business

Editorial matter © 2004 Thomas Baldwin

Typeset in Celeste and Helvetica Neue
by RefineCatch Ltd, Bungay, Suffolk
Printed and bound in Great Britain by TJ International Ltd, Padstow, Cornwall

British Library Cataloguing in Publication Data
A catalogue record for this book is available from the British Library

Library of Congress Cataloging in Publication Data
A catalogue record for this book has been requested

ISBN10: 0-415-31586-7 (hbk)
ISBN10: 0-415-31587-5 (pbk)

ISBN13: 978-0-415-31586-9 (hbk)
ISBN13: 978-0-415-31587-6 (pbk)

CONTENTS

ACKNOWLEDGEMENTS

Selections from *The Structure of Behavior* by Maurice Merleau-Ponty. Copyright © 1963 by Beacon Press; originally published in French under the title *La Structure du comportement*, copyright © 1942 by Presses Universitaires de France. Reprinted by permission of Beacon Press, Boston, USA.

Selections from *Phenomenology of Perception* by Maurice Merleau-Ponty.
Copyright © Routledge (Routledge Kegan Paul 1962); originally published under the title *Phénoménologie de la perception*, © Editions Gallimard, Paris, 1945. Reprinted by permission of Taylor & Francis and Editions Gallimard.

Selection from *The Prose of the Word* by Maurice Merleau-Ponty.
Edited by Claude Lefort. Translated by John O'Neill. Evanston: Northwestern University Press, 1973. Originally published in French as *La Prose du monde*. Copyright © 1969 by Editions Gallimard. English translation copyright © 1973 by Northwestern University Press.

Selection from *The Visible and the Invisible* by Maurice Merleau-Ponty.
Edited by Claude Lefort. Translated by Alphonso Lingis. Evanston: Northwestern University Press, 1968. Originally published in French as *Le Visible et l'invisible*. Copyright © 1964 by editions Gallimard. English translation copyright © 1968 by Northwestern University Press.

EDITOR'S NOTE

References are to English translations of Merleau-Ponty's works and are set out as follows:

PP: *The Phenomenology of Perception.* In '(*PP* 346 [403])' the first number gives the page(s) of the original edition of this (London: Routledge and Kegan Paul, 1962); the second number, in square brackets, gives the page(s) of the new Routledge Classics edition (London: Routledge, 2002). The original translation was by Colin Smith; this was substantially revised in 1974 by Forrest Williams for the sixth impression of the original edition. A few further changes have been introduced in the Routledge Classics edition, and it is this text that is used here. Page numbers for the French text (*Phénoménologie de la perception*, Paris: Gallimard, 1945) are not given here, but it is useful to note that the page numbers in the Routledge Classics translation are a good guide to those in the French text (of which there is, fortunately, only one edition at the time of writing). In addition, where a passage referred to in the Introduction is reprinted later in this book, the citation includes, first, the page number in this book, and second, the page number in *PP*. Thus '(p. X; *PP* 104 [119])' refers to a passage that occurs on page X of this book, page 104 of the 1962 edition, and page 119 of the 2002 edition.

SB: *The Structure of Behavior.* In this case there is only one edition of the English translation (Boston, MA: Beacon, 1963). As before, where a passage referred to in the Introduction is included in this book, the citation includes, first, the page number in this book, and second, the page number in *SB*. So '(p. X; *SB* 171–2)' refers to a passage that occurs on page X of this book and pages 171–2 of *SB*.

References to passages from other texts by Merleau-Ponty are to translations as specified in the notes.

EDITOR'S INTRODUCTION

Life: Maurice Merleau-Ponty (1908–61)

Merleau-Ponty's father died while he was still a small child and, along with his brother and sister, he was brought up in Paris by his widowed mother, to whom he remained very close. This period seems to have been one of exceptional happiness and intimacy, and he carried the memory of it throughout his life:

> It is at the present time that I realize that the first twenty-five years of my life were a prolonged childhood, destined to be followed by a painful break leading eventually to independence. If I take myself back to those years as I actually lived them and as I carry them within me, my happiness at that time cannot be explained in terms of the sheltered atmosphere of the parental home; the world itself was more beautiful, things were more fascinating.
>
> (*PP* 346 [403])

After attending lycée, Merleau-Ponty gained admission to the École Normale Superièure (where he briefly encountered Sartre, though without getting to know him). He graduated in 1930 and went to teach at a lycée in Beauvais; in 1935 he returned to Paris to a junior position at the École Normale. During this period he was working on his doctoral thesis, which became his first book, *The Structure of Behavior*, published during the German occupation in 1942. In 1939–40 Merleau-Ponty had served briefly in the French army as a second lieutenant, but after demobilisation he returned to his teaching position and he wrote his major work *The Phenomenology of Perception* during the war; it was published after the liberation in 1945.

In 1945 Merleau-Ponty helped Sartre found the influential periodical *Les Temps Modernes*; they edited it together until 1950, when their different political judgements made continued collaboration impossible.[1] Meanwhile Merleau-Ponty's academic career progressed quickly. In 1945 he was appointed a professor at Lyon; in 1950 he became Professor of Psychology at the Sorbonne in Paris; and then in 1952 he was appointed to the most prestigious position for a French philosopher, the chair in philosophy at the Collège de France, and he held this position until his unexpected early death in 1961. But after his death his reputation in France declined quickly as French philosophers turned away from French existential phenomenology to the study of German philosophy, especially to the works of Heidegger and the 'masters of suspicion', Marx, Nietzsche and Freud. Elsewhere, however, and especially in the United States, his former pupils preserved his reputation, and more recently within the analytic tradition there has been a growth of interest in his writings, especially his account of intentionality and of the role of the body in perception.

In this introduction I attempt to describe the central themes of his two completed monographs, *The Structure of Behavior* and *The Phenomenology of Perception*, and to say a bit about their general significance. At the end of it I discuss briefly the relationship between Merleau-Ponty's thought and that of some other philosophers: Bergson, Husserl, Heidegger and Sartre. Later in the book each selection from Merleau-Ponty's works is prefaced by a brief discussion and in that context I say a little about some of his later, posthumously published, writings.

The Structure of Behavior (1942)

The central thesis of this book is that neither the methodology of the natural sciences ('realism') nor that of an abstract rational psychology ('intellectualism') provides a satisfactory explanatory framework for the understanding of behaviour, both animal and human. Instead, behaviour can be understood only within a distinctive 'existential' context that situates the subject, animal or human, in its world and identifies the structures of its behaviour in the light of the subject's 'body', its bodily way of making sense of its world. Merleau-Ponty further holds that these structures can themselves be identified only as structures within the perceived world of an embodied subject; so the project of understanding behaviour is inseparable from an account of the phenomenology of perception. When the matter is expressed in this way, it is easy to see how Merleau-Ponty's first book prepares the way for his second one. But the arguments of the first book can, and should, be identified and appraised on their own merits.

Merleau-Ponty starts by criticising the hypothesis that reflex psychology shows how behaviour can be thought of as in principle explicable by neuro-physiological connections that link behaviour to the effects of past and present environment. He argues persuasively that the then current theories of Pavlov, Watson and other behaviourists are unsatisfactory; in making his case, Merleau-Ponty draws extensively on the work of the gestalt theorists (Wertheimer, Kohler, Koffka) to show that perception and action have complex 'forms' (*Gestalten*) that cannot be constructed from 'atomic' reflex connections. It is not worth returning here to the details of these long-superseded psychological debates, but it is important to note Merleau-Ponty's invocation here of the work of the gestalt psychologists, especially their insistence on the role of forms in perception. He does not, however, endorse the alternative neuro-physiological theories that the gestalt psychologists propounded to account for the role of these forms; for he holds that their approach is blinded by their 'realist' presuppositions, and that it is only phenomenology that provides a theoretical framework adequate for this psychology (see *PP* 50–1 n. 1 [58–9 n. 45]).

Merleau-Ponty's thought here is radical and far-reaching: he holds that the notion of 'form' can be given a very wide application and then used to indicate both what is wrong with 'realism' and why phenomenology provides a fundamental source of insight. We can best approach this via his critique of realism. To appreciate this we need to distinguish between the reductionist thesis that the fundamental principles of physics provide an adequate explanatory framework for all events and processes, and a weaker thesis, which I shall call 'scientism', that even if reductionism fails, the standard causal methodology of the physical sciences is that which is appropriate for explanatory inquiries of all kinds. Merleau-Ponty clearly invokes gestalt psychology to argue against reductionism in psychology; but he also argues against the scientism of the gestalt theorists themselves. Thus his critique of realism is a critique of scientism, and not just reductionism.

Merleau-Ponty's most striking criticism of scientism is that it is unsatisfactory in its own terms, within the domain of physics. He makes this criticism because he thinks that physical processes are subject to general equilibrium conditions that are themselves a kind of 'form' that cannot be encompassed within standard causal methodology

(*SB* 137–9). It is not easy at first to understand what Merleau-Ponty is driving at here, since the standard methodology of the physical sciences allows for field equations, and it can seem that Merleau-Ponty is just criticising a naive and superseded conception of physics. But in fact Merleau-Ponty places his emphasis on the notion of physical law, with the suggestion that realism cannot account for the status of physical laws of nature; and this does make rather more sense, since empiricists at least notoriously find it difficult to deal with 'the idea of necessary connexion'. It is not obvious that Merleau-Ponty's suggestion that physical laws are dependent upon perceptible forms is really defensible; but this is Merleau-Ponty's claim: 'reference to a sensible or historical given is not a provisional imperfection; it is essential to physical knowledge. . . . Laws have meaning only as a means of conceptualising the perceived world'. So physics is not a closed system, and we should recognise 'that the universe of naturalism has not been able to become self-enclosed, and that perception is not a fact of nature' (*SB* 145).

This conclusion is of fundamental importance to Merleau-Ponty: perception, he holds, is so fundamental to our ways of making sense of the world that it cannot itself be just a fact within the world, and certainly not just 'a fact of nature'. This conclusion is incipiently idealist: perception cannot be a fact of nature precisely because it plays a crucial role in constituting nature, since the forms, structures or laws that we find in nature are there only as aspects of a perceived world. Exactly what form of idealism is here in question is, however, a delicate matter. Merleau-Ponty twice quotes Hegel's early philosophy with approval (*SB* 161–2, 210, though the passages comes straight from one of Jean Hyppolite's essays to which Merleau-Ponty refers,[2] so it is not clear how far Merleau-Ponty had studied Hegel himself), and there are indeed some similarities at this point between Merleau-Ponty's position and Hegel's philosophy of nature. Furthermore, as we shall see, Merleau-Ponty describes the relationship between the forms characteristic of the three main different orders – physical, vital and human – as 'dialectical', with a manifestly Hegelian intent. Nonetheless Hegel would have regarded Merleau-Ponty's emphasis on the role of perception in his account of the status and identification of these forms as excessively subjectivist; hence it is Kant's transcendental idealism, rather than Hegel's absolute idealism, that is a better model for Merleau-Ponty's position.

Merleau-Ponty does indeed appear to endorse a position of this kind. His discussion is often elusive but towards the end of the book he writes, 'Speaking generally, it seems that we are rejoining the critical attitude. ... A reversal of perspective is produced *vis-à-vis* adult consciousness: the historical becoming which prepared it was not *before* it, it is only *for* it; the time during which it progressed is no longer the time *of* its constitution, but a time which it constitutes' (*SB* 206). Hence he remarks, concerning this discussion, 'It leads, as we have just said, to the transcendental attitude. This is the first conclusion we have to draw from the preceding chapters.' As will be obvious from the passage quoted here, however, it is no straightforward Kantian position that Merleau-Ponty affirms. The general gestalt principles such as that of figure and ground that Merleau-Ponty invokes are less abstract than Kant's a priori forms of intuition and, in the first instance, are supposed to function as structures of the lived world of ordinary experience, rather than of the objective world of the natural sciences. Another point of difference concerns our belief in the existence of others and our understanding of language: Merleau-Ponty affirms that our attitudes here are informed by a priori forms (pp. 55–6; *SB* 171–2), but he acknowledges these are not a priori conditions for the possibility of objective knowledge. So his 'transcendental' (or 'critical') attitude is not altogether that of the *Critique of Pure Reason*; and in fact he himself remarks (*SB* 206 n. 41) that Kant's discussion in the *Critique of Judgement* serves as a better model for his approach. This must be a reference to the conception of 'reflective' judgement which Kant employs here to elucidate the way in which in aesthetic and teleological judgement we introduce a priori concepts such as 'beauty' and 'purpose' without taking them from some prior analysis of the possibilities of objective judgement, as applies to the categories of the understanding. So it is this conception of reflective judgement that is to be a model for Merleau-Ponty's transcendental attitude (see also p. 74; *PP* xvii [xix]).

A crucial point for Merleau-Ponty is that the idealist position needs to be worked out in a way that does not detach the subject of perception altogether from the world and thereby end up treating the world and his own body merely as objects for consciousness. This is the 'intellectualist' position, which is, in its own way, just as unsatisfactory as the realist position. It fails to account for the structure of perceptual experience, for the fact that we see things from a point of view that is located in space and moves around within it, and equally the fact that things manifest themselves to us only in time, through a series of partial appearances that can be continued indefinitely. Indeed according to Merleau-Ponty it is natural for us to misunderstand these facts by interpreting them as the causal dependence of experience upon the world.

But although this misunderstanding is the fundamental error of realist accounts of perception, it arises from an 'authentic phenomenon' (*SB* 216), namely that things are only ever perceived in partial profile. This phenomenon indicates that we are not an abstract, absolute, consciousness, but in some way inserted into the world of space and time, and, according to Merleau-Ponty, it is our embodiment that realises this insertion. So Merleau-Ponty's transcendental idealism is not that of a 'pure' subject of consciousness; instead it is an idealism which gives a special status to the body as that for which there is a perceived world: 'In this way our analyses have indeed led us to the ideality of the body' (*SB* 210).

In his subsequent writings this is a theme to which Merleau-Ponty returns again and again. In *The Structure of Behavior* it is developed and discussed in the context of a discussion of the relationship between the three main 'orders' of being: the physical, the vital and the human. I have already discussed his idealist conception of laws of nature, which is central to his account of the physical order. The 'vital' order comprises organisms, and their distinctive mark is precisely that they are capable of behaviour, that is to say bodily movements with a significance in relation to the structure of their perceived world. Thus for Merleau-Ponty gestalt psychology again has direct application, and its importance is initially that it separates the vital order from the physical order without the need to invoke Bergson's *élan vital* or any other special vital force: 'the idea of *signification* permits conserving the category of life without the hypothesis of a vital force' (*SB* 155). Merleau-Ponty's thought is that in so far as organisms are capable of perception and movement their relationship to their environment is structured with respect to their own forms of perception in a way which cannot be encompassed from within physical science alone: 'the organism itself measures the action of things upon it and itself delimits its milieu by a circular process which is without analogy in the physical world' (*SB* 148).

There is clearly much here that is contentious; contemporary theories of artificial intelligence and computational psychology suggest that one can construct physical systems that are at least analogous to organisms in respect of their capacity for perception and action. But that issue cannot be pursued here; in the present context the point to note is, as ever, the central role and status of the perceived forms that enter into biological explanations. For if, as Merleau-Ponty holds, perception is not a fact of nature because it is that which gives form to nature, then indeed it will follow that explanations that invoke perceived forms draw on a resource that is not available within standard scientific methodology. Hence Merleau-Ponty uses this point to draw a conclusion with respect to biology that is similar to that made before concerning physics: 'the object of biology cannot be grasped without the unities of signification which a consciousness grasps and sees unfolding within it' (*SB* 161). As before, it is not just reductionism, but scientism, that is Merleau-Ponty's target.

The human order is often distinguished from the vital order by reference to the role of culture, a second nature, in human life and thus by the irreducibility of the human to the natural sciences including biology. Merleau-Ponty does not reject this characterisation; but he holds that it rests on something more fundamental: the capacity to set aside the immediate significance of one's environment in order to find new solutions to one's problems, and this capacity, he holds, essentially involves a relationship to that which is merely possible: 'These acts of the human dialectic all reveal the same essence: the capacity of orienting oneself in relation to the possible, to the mediate, and not in relation to a limited milieu' (p. 59; *SB* 175–6). The importance of this capacity is that by liberating the understanding from the immediate demands of their situation it makes it possible for humans to step back from that situation and gain knowledge of the world: 'the knowledge of a truth is substituted for the experience of an immediate reality' (p. 60; *SB* 176). Among other things this kind of knowledge makes natural science possible; but, as we have seen, it is Merleau-Ponty's central thesis that this is not the fundamental type of knowledge. Instead it is but 'a derived mode of consciousness' (*SB* 199) and

> The analysis of the act of knowing leads to the idea of a constituting or naturizing thought which internally subtends the characteristic structure of objects. In order to indicate both the intimacy of objects to the subject and the presence in them of solid structures which distinguish them from appearances, they will be called phenomena'; and philosophy, to the extent that it adheres to this theme, becomes a phenomenology, that is, an inventory of consciousness as milieu of the universe.
>
> (*SB* 199)

So it is the constituting thoughts studied by phenomenology, and not the scientific methods beloved of realists, that provide the proper subject matter for philosophical inquiry into knowledge.

Having distinguished these three orders and their characteristic features, Merleau-Ponty faces the question as to how they connect, especially in humans, since, being physical organisms, they belong to all three orders. Merleau-Ponty is emphatic in rejecting the dualist solution that sees man as compounded of a rational soul and a physical body (the fact that one would need a quasi-Platonic tripartite structure to encompass all three orders just makes this line of thought more obviously untenable). Instead he draws on Hegel to propose that the relationship between the three orders is 'dialectical': explanations in psychology somehow draw on the characteristic features of lower-order processes of biology and physics but do so in a way that modifies their application without contradicting the relevant science.

Merleau-Ponty sets out his position in the following passage: 'Mind is not a specific difference which would be added to vital or psychological being in order to constitute a man. Man is not a rational animal. The appearance of reason does not leave a sphere of self-enclosed instincts in man. . . . Either mind is nothing, or it constitutes a real and not an ideal transformation of man. Because it is not a new sort of being but a new form of unity, it cannot stand by itself' (*SB* 181). This position is clearly a form of 'emergentism', which relies on 'new forms of unity' to enable higher-order explanations to emerge by transcending the lower-order systems.[3] But just how things are to be guaranteed to fit together is not clearly explained. I suspect, however, that Merleau-Ponty's idealist perspective helps here. For this perspective implies that, instead of being the most fundamental order of being, the physical order is all-encompassing only because it is the most abstract; indeed the hierarchy of orders should be inverted so that, for human life, we start from the concrete forms of explanation in which 'mind' plays a part, and then progressively abstract details as we consider humans as organisms or physical systems. Merleau-Ponty's idealist conception of the body helps here too; for because he thinks of the body as our way of being in the world he regards it as the bearer of the complex dialectic that gives structure to our behaviour: it is 'the acquired dialectical soil upon which a higher "formation" is accomplished' (*SB* 210). So, again, there is no question of somehow making space for higher-order explanations of bodily processes which, on the face of it, should be describable and explicable in terms of physics, the fundamental natural science; for according to Merleau-Ponty the realist's presumption of the priority of physics as a 'closed' science is mistaken. Instead it provides only the most abstract characterisation of the body, which needs to be enriched and transcended in the fuller descriptions provided by biology, psychology and the human sciences.

I do not pretend that by thus inverting priorities the issue of the harmony of the different orders of explanation is resolved. Indeed the network of positions Merleau-Ponty advances in *The Structure of Behavior* plainly raises a host of questions. Most of these should be postponed, since Merleau-Ponty develops his positions further in *The Phenomenology of Perception*, whose motivation, in the light of the discussion so far, will be apparent. But there are a couple of issues to be briefly mentioned here before moving on.

One is just the absence of any reference to evolutionary theory. Contemporary philosophy of biology treats evolutionary theory as the distinctive mark of biological science, as opposed to the physical sciences, and to the extent that Merleau-Ponty fails to address the question of the significance of evolutionary theory he remains silent on one of the fundamental questions in this area that is directly relevant to the debates about the status of biology he addresses. In my judgement, however, this omission does not undermine the interest of Merleau-Ponty's book; one can even speculate about the ways in which he might have used his 'dialectical' approach to explanation to encompass the historical dimension to biology that evolutionary theory brings. The combination of Hegelian metaphysics with evolutionary theory is, after all, a familiar feature of late nineteenth-century philosophy (*pace* Hegel himself). Perhaps it was this very familiarity that led Merleau-Ponty to say nothing on the topic.

The other issue I want to address briefly is Merleau-Ponty's critique of realism, in particular his thesis that because perception gives form to nature it cannot itself be a fact of nature (*SB* 145). This claim recurs in *The Phenomenology of Perception*, where it is nicely captured by means of an allusion to Valéry's metaphor for consciousness as the 'flaw' in the great diamond that purports to be the complete world (pp. 127–8; *PP* 207 [241]). As we shall see, however, in this later book Merleau-Ponty directs his critical attention rather more to the 'intellectualist' position that he also rejects. So it is worth briefly considering at this stage the effectiveness of Merleau-Ponty's critical discussion of realism. The tricky issue here is that of the relationship between epistemology and metaphysics, and in reflecting on it it is useful to separate two lines of thought, one concerning subjectivity, the other the role of the a priori.

One element of Merleau-Ponty's discussion starts from the fact that perceptual consciousness has an irreducible subjective element which cannot enter the perceived world, as in the familiar thought that the eye does not appear within its own visual world. The connections between perception and belief imply that our own subjective consciousness is similarly absent, in the first instance, from the world as we believe it to be. But it does not follow that, on further reflection, we cannot be quite properly led to regard our own perceptions and beliefs as further facts within the world, whose relationship to the structure of the world is in principle amenable to the same kinds of explanation that we employ when considering the perceptions and beliefs of others. We have only to acknowledge that there is nothing special about our own situation, except that it gives rise to our own inalienable subjective 'point of view' from which we cannot detach ourselves. In this sense, therefore, we can be legitimately led to regard perception and belief, including our own, as 'a fact of nature'. Thus there is no direct route from the undeniable subjectivity of epistemology to idealist metaphysics.

But, as the earlier discussion indicates, Merleau-Ponty's position rests primarily on the existence and role of a priori principles in perception and belief. It is these principles that underpin his talk of 'constitution' and his 'transcendental attitude', and that he takes to be inconsistent with a realist metaphysics. But is there really an inconsistency here? Kant plainly thought that there is not, that transcendental idealism was consistent with an empirical realism that even included a thoroughgoing determinism. Arguably, however, Kant's position involves only a weak interpretation of the realist claim, as a claim concerning appearances only and not 'things-in-themselves', and scientific realists, at least, would not be satisfied with this result. But more recently Wilfred Sellars has argued in a different way that there is no essential inconsistency here. On the one hand, a priori principles belong to the 'space of reasons'; they are fundamental norms for belief and an essential ingredient of epistemology, even a pragmatic one. Scientific realism, on the other hand, concerns the 'world of causes', and need not undermine a normative epistemology even when it seeks to make sense of its existence from within a causal, naturalistic, standpoint.[4] There would only be a conflict here if the scientific, naturalistic perspective were to imply that the very idea of beliefs with intentional content is illusory. Some philosophers have indeed argued for this 'eliminativist' thesis,[5] and perhaps Merleau-Ponty has to be interpreted as agreeing with them (though reversing the argument to draw a very different conclusion, namely the unacceptability of its realist premises). But their arguments are by no means unquestionable, and Sellars, for one, certainly rejected them. Thus Sellars's work shows how to construct a defensible position which combines respect for an a priori contribution to epistemology with a robustly realist metaphysics.

Having thus used Sellars to call into question the basis for

Merleau-Ponty's transcendental attitude, I should add that there are many other differences between Merleau-Ponty and Sellars where my sympathies lie largely with Merleau-Ponty. In particular, Sellars distinguishes sharply between thought and perception, and holds that only the former is genuinely intentional; the appearance of intentionality in the case of perception is, Sellars holds, a mere illusion that we need to shed in order to abandon 'the myth of the given'.[6] But Merleau-Ponty's use of gestalt psychology, and his discussions of the phenomenology of perception, show that there is nothing illusory about the intentionality of perception; instead it is the fundamental form of intentionality. So on this point Sellars was mistaken, and his criticisms of 'the myth of the given' need to be reconstructed if they are to be reused.

The Phenomenology of Perception (1945)

Merleau-Ponty ends *The Structure of Behavior* by calling for a philosophy that 'inverts the natural movement of consciousness' in order to uncover the ways in which the real world is constituted in perception (*SB* 220). He opens *The Phenomenology of Perception* with a famous preface, which asks 'What is phenomenology?' (pp. 63–78; *PP* vii–xxi [vii–xxiv]) and answers that phenomenology is precisely a philosophy that will achieve this result; phenomenological reflection, he says, 'steps back to watch the forms of transcendence fly up like sparks from a fire; it slackens the intentional threads which attach us to the world and thus brings them to our notice' (p. 70; *PP* xiii [xv]). In doing this, philosophy brings to our attention the ways in which we are 'condemned', not to freedom, as Sartre had declared in *Being and Nothingness* (p. 439), but to 'meaning' (p. 76; *PP* xix [xxii]). For philosophy will make it apparent to us that the structure of our life is subtended by a multiplicity of ways in which we give it meaning and thereby constitute the worlds – natural, social, sexual, historical – in which we live. As such, philosophy will provide a 'genealogy of being' (*PP* 54 [63]), which will, like a work of art, bring to expression for the first time the truth about being (p. 77; *PP* xx [xxiii]).

Not surprisingly this phenomenological project is contrasted with faith in scientific realism (usually called 'empiricism' here). Merleau-Ponty asserts that science provides only an 'abstract and derivative' schematization of the world, which rests on more familiar beliefs about the world that science itself seeks to discredit (p. 65; *PP* ix [x]). By contrast, he maintains, it is one of the tasks of phenomenology to make explicit 'the prescientific life of consciousness which alone endows scientific operations with meaning and to which these latter always refer back' (*PP* 58–9 [68]). These programmatic claims are reminiscent of the conception of science to be found in Schlick's writings, which was persuasively criticised by Carnap, Neurath, Popper and other critics of the idea of an observation language uncontaminated by theory. Thus on the face of it, Merleau-Ponty seems to be here committing himself to a problematic foundationalist epistemology and theory of language; to 'the myth of the given', indeed, as Sellars would say. I shall return to this issue.

In *The Phenomenology of Perception*, however, rather more critical attention is directed against 'intellectualism', or 'analytical reflection'.[7] This is the idealist view that we have to get altogether outside the world, to a transcendental subject, an 'inner self' or a 'pure Ego', in order to find something which can use the resources of reason and abstract intuition to make sense of experience and thereby give meaning to a world in which it ends up locating itself as a mere 'empirical' self. As representatives of this position Merleau-Ponty takes leading figures from pre-war French philosophy, such as Alain (the pseudonym of Emile-Auguste Chartier), L. Brunschvicg and P. Lachièze-Rey; he sometimes also associates Husserl with this position (e.g. *PP* 60 n. 1 [70 n. 12]) despite noting the ways in which Husserl's writings also diverge from it (p. 125 n. 1; *PP* 121 n. 5 [140 n. 54]): I discuss later the delicate question of the extent to which Merleau-Ponty differentiates his existential phenomenology from Husserl's 'transcendental phenomenology').

Against this position, Merleau-Ponty argues that by detaching the subject of experience altogether from the world, the intellectualist fails to do justice to the structure of experience. He cannot account for the necessity that our visual experience yields only partial profiles of things seen from a point of view (p. 81; *PP* 68–9 [78–9]), nor that in tactile experience we experience ourselves actually touching things (*PP* 91–2 [105]). More generally the intellectualist cannot account for the 'ambiguities' of experience, exemplified both by the familiar gestalt figures (*PP* 47–50 [54–9]) and, more radically, by the ways in which the significance of our acts, feelings and thoughts remains indeterminate (p. 96; *PP* 85 [98], 169 [196]). Equally, the intellectualist cannot account for the way in which our body seems to provide the structure for sense-experience when, according to the intellectualist, it is just another object within the world (*PP* 90–1 [103–4]). This is most strikingly seen in cases of bodily disorder as a result of which our experience is radically altered in ways that are not intelligible without reference to the body's contribution to experience (pp. 113–18; *PP* 121–5 [138–43]). And as the book progresses,

Merleau-Ponty adds further criticisms: most notably that the intellectualist position makes it impossible to understand how there can be other thinkers (p. 148; *PP* 349 [407]), how we can mistake ourselves (p. 179; *PP* 380 [442]), and how we are both vulnerable to sceptical doubts and yet able to respond to them (*PP* 344 [401]).

The position opposed both to the 'empiricist' and 'intellectualist' positions is, of course, Merleau-Ponty's own phenomenology, which seeks to unravel the phenomena given in perception in such a way as to reveal the role of our bodily existence in giving meaning to the world we perceive, and thereby to all forms of consciousness. Such a position rejects the empiricist's determination to explain everything by reference to facts encountered within the world without inquiring how these facts come to be intelligible to us. But equally it repudiates the intellectualist's belief that the meaning of these facts has to be found altogether outside the world in a pure stream of experience that alone has 'absolute' being. The dialectic of Merleau-Ponty's position is that existential phenomenology is the 'synthesis' that transcends the opposition between these equally unsatisfactory positions, empiricism and intellectualism. There is no question, however, that Merleau-Ponty's position is in fact a good deal closer to intellectualism than empiricism, and a theological analogy can be used to show the overall relationship between the positions here.[8] The empiricist position is comparable to that of the atheist who thinks that in so far as life has a meaning it lies wholly in this world and can be identified without reference to any non-natural, or theological, facts; the intellectualist position is comparable to that of the theist who thinks that only a wholly transcendent God can give meaning to life; and the existential phenomenologist is comparable to those who believe that the meaning of life shows the presence in this world of an immanent deity. This third position is of course also a form of theism, which in the terms of the analogy is comparable to idealism. So the intellectualist and the existential phenomenologist are both idealists, and the difference between them is comparable to that between upholders of transcendent as opposed to immanent conceptions of God; that is, it is just the question as to whether the subject is 'transcendent', an absolute pure Ego altogether beyond the world, or 'immanent', somehow present within the world to which it gives meaning.[9]

After the Preface Merleau-Ponty sets himself to the task of accomplishing the philosophical project he gives himself there of making 'the ever-renewed experiment in making its own beginning' (p. 71; *PP* xiv [xv–xvi]). In the first part of the book his aim, therefore, is to explain why such a philosophy requires a return to 'phenomena' and what this involves. The traditional, and obvious, starting place for such a philosophy is with our own sense-experience, and Merleau-Ponty indeed wants us to reflect on this, but to understand better what it involves. So he begins from one all-too-familiar account of it, in terms of the notion of 'sensation' as it occurs in seventeenth-century philosophy (e.g. Locke). He argues persuasively that, at least as considered in the context of talk of sensations as simple ideas of colour, this notion lacks application. For sense-experience is always more or less inchoate perception, and perception is essentially perception of things in a world; the gestalt-ist 'figure/ground' contrast is an a priori structure of sense-experience (*PP* 22 [26]). Thus experience is not a mosaic of simple ideas which we somehow organise or interpret as representations of the world; it is, on the contrary, the appearance of things in a world. So in returning to experience, the philosopher's task must be 'to rediscover phenomena, the layer of living experience through which other people and things are first given to us, the system "Self-others-things" as it comes into being' (*PP* 57 [66]).

Thus far Merleau-Ponty's discussion is compatible with a common-sense direct realist account of perception, as, typically, the perception of things in space. But the passage quoted just now continues with the insistence that the philosopher's task is also 'to reawaken perception and foil its trick of allowing us to forget it as a fact and as perception in the interest of the object which it presents to us' (*PP* 57 [66]). This now takes us away from common sense; for Merleau-Ponty's claim is that prior to the objective world that common sense unreflectively takes for granted, there is a phenomenal field in which phenomena take shape as the appearances of things, other people and so on. It is in the nature of perceptual experience to forget this phenomenal field, for phenomena themselves always direct us beyond themselves to the things they present, the things of which they are the appearances. Nonetheless, if we want to return to the beginning, the foundation, of our understanding of the world, we need to reawaken this 'preobjective' experience, the phenomenal field, in order to understand how our familiar conception of the world, 'the system Self-others-things', is manifested within experience.

It is not easy, I think, to know quite how to place Merleau-Ponty's discussion of this matter. As he makes clear, he draws a good deal on the work of the gestalt psychologists, and his discussion is in part a sum-mary of some of their views; hence as far as this goes he appears to be just advancing a thesis which is psychological in content. But it would be 'psychologism' to suppose that a psychological thesis of this kind can by itself establish a philosophical conclusion, and Merleau-Ponty is himself quite clear in repudiating any such psychologism. But the anxiety that Merleau-Ponty's phenomenology is in the end a sophisticated form of psychologism is one to which I shall return. For the moment, however, we can note that at the end of this section, having acknowledged that his discussion so far has been partly motivated by psychological considerations ('Thus we could begin neither without psychology nor with psychology alone', *PP* 63 [73]), he announces that subsequent argument 'decisively transforms the phenomenal field into a transcendental one' (*PP* 63 [74]).

This talk of transformation into a 'transcendental field', and thus to a genuinely philosophical theme, is of course linked to transcendental idealism; and in the next section of the book Merleau-Ponty begins to develop this theme through a discussion of the status of the body. He aims to show how the conception of the body as simply an object within the world fails to do justice to the body's contribution to our experience of the world, and thus how we should learn to recognise our own body as a 'phenomenal body', as something that by playing an active role in our experience of the world is apt to fill the role of transcendental subject. So the question of the status of the body has a special position in this dialectic: Merleau-Ponty's thought is that 'the body, by withdrawing from the objective world, will carry with it the intentional threads linking it to its surrounding and finally reveal to us the perceiving subject as the perceived world' (p. 84; *PP* 72 [83][10]).

In the initial discussions of the status of the body Merleau-Ponty summarises the critical arguments against realism and intellectualism set out in *The Structure of Behavior*. He also includes a long discussion of the phantom limb phenomenon (see pp. 87–100; *PP* 76–89 [88–102]), which he takes to show the inadequacies of both the realist's reliance on causal categories and the intellectualist's appeal to the rational structure of consciousness in order to explain the behaviour of patients with a phantom limb. In place of these inadequate approaches he urges the existential perspective of our bodily being-in-the-world. For taking this as a starting point, it is then possible to interpret the phantom limb as a case in which the patient's remaining, but stunted, neural network keeps alive the patient's bodily memory of habitual kinaesthetic sensation. As a result the patient's body has a 'repressed' memory of the severed limb – a shattered arm, say – which is liable to be awakened by unreflective experience of the world as one in which things are available to be picked up. In this way, as Merleau-Ponty puts it 'the phenomenon of the phantom limb is absorbed into that of repression' (p. 94; *PP*

82–3 [95]). No doubt there is now more to be said about these cases in the light of advances in neurophysiology. But Merleau-Ponty's discussion remains subtle and insightful; it shows well how existential phenomenology can draw on a range of resources to illuminate these puzzling cases.[11]

Merleau-Ponty then moves on to discuss a different case of someone with a psychological disorder: the case of a German soldier, Schneider, who had suffered a brain injury from a shell splinter during the First World War. Schneider was studied in detail after the war by the German psychologists A. Gelb and K. Goldstein, and Merleau-Ponty draws extensively on these studies in *The Phenomenology of Perception*, most particularly in an extended discussion of some peculiarities in Schneider's body-image and capacity for bodily movement. Schneider can readily perform complex habitual movements, such as those involved in making and mending clothes; but he cannot perform any 'abstract' movements, e.g. he cannot just point his arm in a specified direction, nor can he locate unseen points of contact on his body. Merleau-Ponty begins by characterising Schneider's disorder as one in which he has retained a sense of his 'phenomenal body', which is manifested in his capacity for perception and habitual movement, but lost his sense of his body as something objectively located in space and available for 'gratuitous and free spatial thought' (p. 108; *PP* 104 [119]). Merleau-Ponty connects this latter deficit with the loss of a sense of the range of possible movements that are normally available to us, which is also manifested in his inability to engage in play-acting (p. 120; *PP* 135 [156]). Thus far the contrast is drawn in terms that are reminiscent of the distinction Merleau-Ponty drew in *The Structure of Behavior* between the vital and the human orders, whereby the distinctive essence of the latter is 'the capacity of orienting oneself in relation to the possible' (p. 59; *SB* 176). In *The Structure of Behavior* Merleau-Ponty had held that this capacity is important because it is crucial to the existence of human culture, and, in effect, he takes the same view here, maintaining that it provides us with an ability to creatively reorganise the structure of our world and then retain this reorganised structure as a cultural 'sediment' within our experience of the world. Hence, he suggests, the lack of this ability accounts for the impoverished world in which Schneider appears to live:

> The essence of consciousness is to provide itself with one or several worlds, to bring into being its own thoughts *before* itself, as if they were things, and it demonstrates its vitality indivisibly by

outlining these landscapes for itself and then by abandoning them. The world-structure, with its two stages of sedimentation and spontaneity, is at the core of consciousness, and it is in the light of a levelling-down of the world' that we shall succeed in understanding Schneider's intellectual, perceptual and motor disturbances, without assimilating them to each other.

(*PP* 130 [150])

This 'levelling-down of the world' that afflicts Schneider is to be connected also to a diminution in his capacity for a distinctive personal life, and it is here that Merleau-Ponty locates the 'seat' of his disorder:

It is this existential basis of intelligence which is affected, much more than intelligence itself, for, as we have shown, Schneider's general intelligence is intact. . . . Beneath the intelligence as an anonymous function or a categorial process, a personal core has to be recognised, which is the patient's being, his power of existing. It is here that the illness has its seat.

(p. 119; *PP* 134 [155])

Merleau-Ponty then explains more clearly what he has in mind as 'this existential basis of intelligence':

the life of consciousness – cognitive life, the life of desire or perceptual life – is subtended by an intentional arc' which projects round about us our past, our future, our human setting, our physical, ideological and moral situation, or rather which results from our being situated in all these respects. It is this intentional arc which brings about the unity of the senses, of intelligence, of sensibility and motility. And it is this which goes limp' in illness.

(p. 120–1; *PP* 136 [157])

So Schneider's case is used by Merleau-Ponty to bring into relief this basic form of intentionality which, in normal life, draws on the 'sediments' of meaning we have retained from our creative activities to make apparent to us the possibilities inherent in the various dimensions of our situation and thereby 'subtend' the kind of ordinary personal life that Schneider can no longer enjoy. Merleau-Ponty goes on to say that this basic structure of intentionality is 'motility'[12] (p. 122; *PP* 137 [158]), by which he seems to mean a capacity for action (so that its characteristic expression is 'I can', – p. 122; *PP* 137 [159]). This seems to me an oversimplification in the light of Schneider's manifold deficits and the role of the 'intentional arc' as set out in the passage quoted above. But what he has in mind, I think, is, first, that this is a kind of intentionality that is manifested in our ordinary, immediate, perceptions, feelings and actions, rather than our reflective thoughts, and, second, that as such it is inseparable from the ways in which our body relates us to our world; it informs the functioning of our sense-organs, our body-image and capacity for movement, and draws upon our memory, which is somehow activated through our body. Thus Merleau-Ponty ends this long discussion of Schneider's case with a conclusion in which he sets out what is, in effect, the main thesis of the book:

> Bodily experience forces us to acknowledge an imposition of meaning which is not the work of a universal constituting consciousness, a meaning which clings to certain contents. My body is that meaningful core[13] which behaves like a general function, and which nevertheless exists, and is susceptible to disease.
>
> (p. 124; *PP* 147 [170])

In much of the rest of the book Merleau-Ponty extends and applies this thesis by arguing that our experience of the natural world, of others, of history, even of ourselves draws upon this basic 'bodily' intentionality. In each case, he argues, our capacity for these basic modes of thought rests upon unreflective but meaningful relationships that draw upon our condition as essentially embodied subjects. Later in this book I shall say more about Merleau-Ponty's treatment of these topics when I introduce the relevant selections from his work. What I want to do now, in drawing this general introduction to *The Phenomenology of Perception* to a close, however, is to revisit the issue of 'psychologism' since it is so crucial to an assessment of the book's significance.

One might well say that Merleau-Ponty's discussion of Schneider's case, fascinating though it is, remains fundamentally a contribution to psychology, an exploration of deep structures that are implicit within our familiar capacities for thought and action, much as Chomsky's work on syntax has led him to postulate, as an empirical psycholinguistic hypothesis, the existence of an innate universal grammar or an I-language.[14] It is clear that Merleau-Ponty would reject this judgement: while allowing that his discussion connects with debates in psychology, he would maintain that his conclusion has a 'transcendental' significance in so far as it concerns 'the imposition of meaning'. It is supposed to reveal to us the way in which the body acts as the 'constituting' subject of our being in the world: as 'a natural self and, as it were, the subject of perception' (p. 126; *PP* 206 [239]). In effect he would deny that the alternatives, psychological or philosophical, are exclusive. On the contrary, he would say, once we understand ourselves properly, we will recognise that our psychology is ineluctably philosophical (a theologian will make comparable claims about the alternatives, psychological or religious; for if man really is made in the image of God then it is as such that he is best understood).

More, however, needs to be said to vindicate the claim that Merleau-Ponty's thesis concerning the deep, bodily, intentionality that the discussion of Schneider's case reveals is of philosophical as well as psychological import. One line of argument that Merleau-Ponty's discussion invites is that his thesis about this bodily imposition of meaning constitutes the basis for an idealist, or at least anti-realist, theory of meaning which fills out the sketchy immanentist idealism whose possibility I characterised only analogically earlier. A position of this kind certainly seems implicit in Merleau-Ponty's discussion of the status of ordinary things such as tables, where he endorses Berkeley's thesis that 'we cannot conceive anything that is not perceived or perceptible' (p. 139; *PP* 320 [373]) and goes on to reject the illusions of 'objective thinking' that lead us to regard such things as existing altogether independently of us; the truth is that 'in reality all things are concretions of a setting' (p. 139; *PP* 320 [374]). Later in the book he puts to himself the objection to this thesis that will be raised by common-sense realism: 'To our assertion above that there is no world without an Existence that sustains its structure, it might have been retorted that the world nevertheless preceded man' (*PP* 432 [502]), and his reply to this objection shows clearly the nature and role of his anti-realist theory of meaning:

> For what precisely is meant by saying that the world existed before any human consciousness? An example of what is meant is that the earth originally issued from a primitive nebula from which the combination of conditions necessary for life was absent. But every one of these words, like every equation in physics, presupposes *our* pre-scientific experience of the world, and this reference to the world in which we *live* goes to make up the proposition's valid meaning. Nothing will ever bring home to my comprehension what a nebula that no one sees could possibly be.
>
> (*PP* 432 [502])

This passage brings into focus the issue mentioned earlier: Merleau-Ponty's commitment to a foundationalist theory of meaning which ties the meaning of our words, even 'nebula', back to some 'pre-scientific experience' in such a way that the 'valid meaning' of sentences about nebulas includes a reference to the pre-scientific life-world. It seems to me that this is a position that can no longer command serious assent. The dialectic which runs from the Viennese 'protocol sentence' debate through Quine's discussion of the analytic/synthetic distinction to the discussions of natural kind terms initiated by Putnam and Kripke comprehensively undermines any such theory of meaning. Even though we may rely on ordinary pre-scientific experience to help fix the reference of terms like 'nebula', this method of reference fixing is just a ladder we climb before we dispose of it. The meaning, or reference (there is no significant distinction in this case), of 'nebula' is a type of stellar system, and in coming to understand what nebulas are one also learns that the existence of nebulas is wholly independent of that of human beings, and indeed of any intelligent consciousness. So the realist, having noted Merleau-Ponty's dependence upon this untenable theory of meaning, can pass on unmoved.

Is there a better way to fill out Merleau-Ponty's position, as philosophical and not just psychological? One proposal would be to take it as an epistemological thesis, to the effect that there is a fundamental bodily 'imposition of belief' that is an essential precondition for any explicit justification for belief. There is no doubt that Merleau-Ponty does hold a position of this kind: he writes of 'an *opinion* which is not a provisional form of knowledge destined to give way later to an absolute form', an opinion which is 'primary' in the double sense of 'original' and 'fundamental' (pp. 195–6; *PP* 396-7 [461]). This 'primary' opinion or 'primordial faith' (p. 208; *PP* 409 [475]) is inherent in the 'participation in the world' inherent in our bodily perceptions, and it is in the context of characterising it that Merleau-Ponty makes the famous claim that 'All consciousness is, in some measure, perceptual consciousness' (p. 194; *PP* 395 [459]). But in thinking about this suggestion there are then two issues to be faced: first, does it fare any better than the previous approach which relied on the untenable theory of meaning discussed above? Does it not bring with it a similarly untenable foundationalist epistemology? Second, how far does this epistemological approach do justice to Merleau-Ponty's project, in particular to his emphasis upon our primary bodily being in the world?

On the first issue it is natural at first to regard Merleau-Ponty's sharp distinction between the 'objective thinking' and 'phenomenal experience' as bringing with it a commitment to an epistemological foundation that is uninfected by 'objective thinking' or scientific theory; and, as with the theory of meaning discussed earlier, this would not be a commitment to be welcomed. There is no such foundation. But in this case I doubt that one can pin such a commitment on Merleau-Ponty (he repudiates the suggestions that his conception of foundation is empiricist or one in which that which is founded is derived from its foundation: p. 193; *PP* 394 [458]), and there is a different way of taking his remarks. This introduction is not the place to enter into details, but the alternative position I have in mind is that sketched by Wittgenstein, using very different idioms, in his late notes *On Certainty*.[15] For Wittgenstein here affirms the primacy of practice in showing our commitment to a 'common-sense' view of the world that is prior to any reflective method we have for justifying our beliefs; but he does not suggest that this common-sense view is unchallengeable in detail, nor indeed that our common sense is uninfected by our scientific beliefs. The involuntary beliefs inherent in our ways of acting make us certain of the existence of a world in ways which in practice 'stand fast' for us; but all our beliefs about the world are in principle open to revision. Thus Wittgenstein's remarks indicate that there is a tenable, indeed attractive, modest form of practical foundationalism, which is similar in spirit to Merleau-Ponty's 'primordial faith' and which avoids the familiar objections to traditional foundationalist positions.

The second issue raised above, however, cannot be similarly managed. Although there is, as I have indicated, an epistemological strand to Merleau-Ponty's position, it would be a major distortion of his position to represent him as advancing a thesis which is, in the end, fundamentally epistemological. Instead he is clearly advancing a thesis about the way in which some kind of deep intentionality is embedded in our perceptions and actions, an intentionality that underpins the overt intentionality of judgement and other conscious thoughts. Thus to defend Merleau-Ponty against the charge of psychologism we need to see how this is a philosophical thesis, and not just a psychological one. The way to do this is to recognise, first, that the concept of intentionality always brings with it normative considerations, since in characterising a psychological state in intentional terms, as directed to an 'object' of some kind, it is implied that there is a way in which the state can be appraised as inaccurate, incorrect, or inappropriate; and, second, that the question of the legitimacy of this kind of normative appraisal of psychological states is philosophical. It is a question of the philosophy of psychology, not psychology itself. So if we locate

Merleau-Ponty's investigations here, we are on the way to a more productive philosophical interpretation of his position than the idealist and the epistemological ones considered before.

On this interpretation, then, the significance of the conclusion of Merleau-Ponty's discussion of Schneider's case is that intentionality, and thus normativity, enters into the understanding of behaviour in a rather different way from that which one might at first have supposed. For whereas we normally think of normativity as involving guidance by rules laid down in advance that specify what is correct or not, the normativity inherent in Merleau-Ponty's practical intentionality cannot be thought of as guided in this way; instead it is a kind of unguided, or 'blind', practice which is nonetheless informed by normative considerations; the bodily 'imposition of meaning' must allow for possibility of mistakes, for visual phenomena that are illusory and for bodily movements that are misdirected. So Merleau-Ponty's conclusion is to be interpreted as the thesis that guidance by explicit rules set out in definitions rests upon practices that involve the blind following of rules.

At this point it will be clear to those familiar with Wittgenstein's *Philosophical Investigations*[16] that I am suggesting that we can use Wittgenstein's 'rule-following' considerations to provide a preliminary way of thinking about Merleau-Ponty's position. We can link intentionality to 'rule-following', and then use Wittgenstein's discussion of the necessity for blind rule-following as a way of substantiating Merleau-Ponty's conception of a practical intentionality that underpins our ordinary consciousness. But there is no need to reduce Merleau-Ponty's position to that of Wittgenstein; indeed one can use Merleau-Ponty's discussion to extend Wittgenstein's. Schneider's case, for example, can be taken to indicate that the capacity for rule-following is susceptible to disease, with serious implications for the life of anyone thus affected. Hence a Wittgensteinian approach can respect the psychological import of Merleau-Ponty's discussion while also helping to elucidate its philosophical significance.

But exactly what philosophical significance it has is a matter requiring further consideration. Because of the connections between psychological intentionality and linguistic meaning, the issues raised by Merleau-Ponty's book, under this interpretation of it, have implications well beyond the philosophy of psychology; it is the theory of meaning, broadly conceived, that is revealed as the subject of the book, surely rightly. Notoriously there have been those who have argued that, when considered in the context of the theory of meaning, the rule-following considerations themselves have the kind of anti-realist implications I rejected when discussing the first interpretation of Merleau-Ponty's position.[17] But few now take this view, though there remains disagreement about what alternative is to be preferred. It would not be sensible to enter this dispute here, except to note that Wittgenstein's own emphasis on the role of social practices in underpinning rule-following activities provides a ready context for substantiating Merleau-Ponty's famous thesis that 'transcendental subjectivity is a revealed subjectivity, revealed to itself and to others, and is for that reason an inter-subjectivity' (p. 160; *PP* 361 [421]). But my main aim here is not to urge any particular view on this matter, but to encourage fresh thinking about Merleau-Ponty's book.

Merleau-Ponty and other philosophers

Merleau-Ponty frequently alludes to the writings of other philosophers. I have already mentioned how he draws on works by Kant and Hegel; he also frequently discusses Descartes and Malebranche. But because of the complexity of the positions advanced by these philosophers, and their intellectual distance from Merleau-Ponty, it would not be sensible to discuss here his intellectual relationship with them. In the case of the French philosophers of the previous generation whose work he also discusses frequently, Alain, Brunschvicg and Lachièze-Rey, a different reason applies, namely that their work is now largely unknown, at least in the English-speaking world (probably unjustly – Brunschvicg's work certainly merits attention). Hence I shall just discuss briefly the intellectual relationship between Merleau-Ponty and four other twentieth-century philosophers: Bergson, Husserl, Heidegger and Sartre.

Henri Bergson (1859–1941)

Bergson held the chair of philosophy at the Collège de France from 1900 until 1921, and when Merleau-Ponty was appointed to the same chair in 1952 he devoted much of his inaugural lecture 'In praise of philosophy' to a discussion of Bergson's philosophy. But Merleau-Ponty never said much about the connections between Bergson's work and his own.[18] Yet there certainly appear to be important points of contact, particularly in respect of Bergson's most straightforwardly philosophical work *Matière et Mémoire* (1896) (*Matter and Memory*). For Bergson begins here by declaring that he seeks to develop a position that is intermediate between realism and idealism, and that the key concept on which he will rely in doing so is that of an 'image'. As he explains and then uses this concept, it is obvious that it occupies very much the role of 'phenomenon' in the context of Merleau-Ponty's attempt to steer a course between realism and intellectualism. Further, Bergson immediately goes on to assert that, for each of us, there is one image that is fundamental, namely our own living body: for each of us, this image, our own body, is experienced both as a centre of consciousness, especially perception, and also as a centre of action. Again, once 'image' has become 'phenomenon', the resemblance between Bergson's position and Merleau-Ponty's account of the 'phenomenal' body is very striking.

Of course there are differences. Merleau-Ponty rejects Bergson's conception of the *élan vital* which is supposed to explain the creativity of evolution, and he has no sympathy for Bergson's non-conceptual 'intuitions'.[19] But sometimes he appears to disagree with Bergson just for the sake of it. For example, in a long footnote in *The Phenomenology of Perception* (pp. 100–1 n. 2; 78–9 n. 2 [91 n. 19]) Merleau-Ponty complains that Bergson never really gets beneath objective conceptions of the body, perception and time to the phenomenal world. Once one takes on board Bergson's conception of the body as an image, of perception as but the starting point of action, and of time as a personal *durée*, however, it is hard not to feel that the shadow cast by Bergson's very intellectual proximity has led Merleau-Ponty to accentuate the differences between them.

Edmund Husserl (1859–1938)

No one could suggest that Merleau-Ponty accentuated the differences between himself and Husserl; on the contrary, in *The Phenomenology of Perception* Merleau-Ponty repeatedly invokes Husserl's authority for his own thoughts, and seems at times to represent himself as merely Husserl's disciple.

The background to this intellectual relationship (which was not a personal relationship – Merleau-Ponty never met Husserl) goes back to Merleau-Ponty's early work on gestalt psychology. As his discussion in *The Structure of Behavior* makes clear, Merleau-Ponty first came to Husserl's phenomenology because it seemed to provide a better way of exploring the implications of gestalt psychology than was provided by the 'realist' theories of the gestalt psychologists themselves. In writing this book shortly after Husserl's death Merleau-Ponty drew on those of Husserl's main works of phenomenology that had by then been published (*Ideas I, Formal and Transcendental Logic, Cartesian Meditations*[20]). Before completing *The Phenomenology of Perception*, however, he also took the opportunity to consult Husserl's then unpublished works, which had been rescued from Germany and brought to Louvain by Father Von Breda, including in particular the complete text of *The Crisis of European Sciences* and *Ideas II*.[21] Merleau-Ponty clearly found himself in broad agreement with Husserl's treatment of natural science in *The Crisis*; but it was the second text which he found electrifying (he is said to have found reading it 'une expérience presque voluptueuse'[22]).

This is not the place for a detailed comparison between *Ideas II* and *The Phenomenology of Perception*, but it is worth mentioning a few points.[23] Husserl's subtitle is 'Studies in the phenomenology of constitution' and in successive sections he discusses the constitution of, respectively, 'material nature' ('things'), 'animal nature' (which is largely concentrated on 'man'), and 'the spiritual world' (in which he concentrates on 'persons'). In the course of this discussion Husserl is led to assign increasing importance to the body, and in doing so he distinguishes between two concepts: *Körper* (the body as a physical system) and *Leib* (the living body). It is the latter that is given a prominent role both as the expression of 'spirit', the personal self, and also as the vehicle for the human psyche ('soul'). Indeed there is a chapter (section II, chapter 3) entitled 'The constitution of psychic reality through the Body' (*Leib*), in which Husserl explores the body's fundamental role in perception and action. He argues that the body is 'constituted originarily' through the sense of touch (*Ideas II*, p. 158), and concludes that '*a human being's total consciousness is in a certain sense . . . bound to the Body*' (*Ideas II*, p. 160). It is easy to see how Merleau-Ponty would have been excited by passages of this kind, and natural to surmise how he may have refined his own thoughts in the course of studying them. For the theme of 'constitution' runs through *The Phenomenology of Perception*, and the role of the 'phenomenal' body, Husserl's *Leib*, is central to Merleau-Ponty's account (Husserl's *Körper* is of course Merleau-Ponty's 'objective' body).

Yet there are differences. Husserl ends up giving priority to man as a 'spirit', or person, over man as a 'psyche'. Indeed, although the conception of the latter is dependent upon the living body, *Leib*, Husserl places its study, psychology, firmly within the natural sciences. For Merleau-Ponty these matters are organised in a different way: psychology cannot be a natural science, and the living, phenomenal, body is in fact the subject that enables us to sustain whatever personal existence we enjoy. Behind these differences there is a more fundamental disagreement: for Husserl, the phenomenological study of constitution is, ultimately, grounded in the transcendental-phenomenological reduction and the correlative conception of the stream of consciousness as *'absolute subject'* (*Ideas II*, p. 180), for which the 'totality of nature' is constituted, including human bodies which are just 'indices of lawful regulations of bodily appearances' (*Ideas II*, p. 180). For Merleau-Ponty, by contrast, there is no such absolute subject, and in so far as Husserl invokes this conception he is, therefore, among those whom Merleau-Ponty criticizes in his discussions of 'intellectualism' and 'analytical reflection'. Merleau-Ponty tends to signal this disagreement only in occasional footnotes, but there is one other way in which he makes it apparent. In his preface to *The Phenomenology of* Perception he refers to St Augustine's famous Platonist epigram that we should 'return to ourselves' to find 'the inner man' who is the habitation of truth, and comments 'Truth does not "inhabit" only "the inner man", or more accurately, there is no inner man' (p. 67; *PP* xi [xii]). Merleau-Ponty does not add, no doubt because he did not think it necessary, that Husserl had ended his *Cartesian Meditations* by quoting the very same Augustinian epigram, but with evident approval.

Martin Heidegger (1889–1976)

Right at the start of *The Phenomenology of Perception* (p. 64; *PP* vii [viii]) Merleau-Ponty remarks that 'the whole of *Sein und Zeit* springs from an indication given by Husserl'. Thus Merleau-Ponty indicates clearly where his loyalties lie in the vexed question of how far Heidegger's philosophy is indebted to the work of his teacher, Husserl. And careful study of *Ideas II*, which Husserl sent to Heidegger in 1925, does indeed suggest that there was at least greater overlap between their views than Heidegger was later inclined to acknowledge publicly. In particular, the similarities between Husserl's description of 'the personalistic attitude' and Heidegger's account of *Dasein*'s being-in-the-world are at times very striking (e.g. Husserl introduces a conception of 'authentic' motivation: *Ideas II*, p. 232, and later contrasts this with the situation in which I follow others and just do as 'one' (*Das man*) does: *Ideas II*, p. 282).

But the issue here is not the question of Heidegger's debt to Husserl, but Merleau-Ponty's attitude to Heidegger's work, in particular *Sein und Zeit* (*Being and Time*).[24] There are many obvious connections: Merleau-Ponty writes of 'existence' and 'being-in-the-world' (*être-au-monde*) in much the way that Heidegger does (which differs from Husserl's use of these phrases). Where Heidegger maintains that *Dasein* is something whose being as being-in-the-world is antecedent to the distinction between 'subject' and 'object' Merleau-Ponty makes a similar point, though in a different idiom, by his repudiation of Husserl's Augustinian call for a return to 'the inner man', and his insistence, on the contrary that 'man is in the world (*au monde*)' (p. 67; *PP* xi [xii]). One especially striking similarity concerns their attitude to Descartes's famous *Cogito ergo sum*: Heidegger remarks that this slogan needs to be 'turned around' as *Sum ergo cogito* in the sense that *Sum* – my being in the world – is prior to *cogito* – my ability to have thoughts about things within the world (*Being and Time* 254). Merleau-Ponty says something very similar: 'In the proposition: "I think, I am", the two assertions are to be equated . . . Nevertheless we must be clear about the meaning of this equivalence: it is not the "I am" which is pre-eminently contained in the "I think" . . . but conversely the "I think", which is re-integrated into the transcending process of the "I am", and consciousness into existence' (p. 182; *PP* 383 [446]). There is also one area where Merleau-Ponty makes explicit his dependence on Heidegger, namely in his discussion of time. Merleau-Ponty takes over Heidegger's conception of temporality as a fundamental structure of our being, as an *ek-stase* (p. 83: *PP* 70 [81]; Merleau-Ponty employs Heidegger's neologism) whereby our life is a present that looks towards a future that it intends while acknowledging a past that it was.[25] Indeed the agreement concerns not just this characterisation of time, but also its fundamental importance; just as for Heidegger 'temporality' is supposed to be 'the meaning of the Being of that entity which we call "Dasein"' (*BT* 38), Merleau-Ponty affirms that 'time is the foundation and measure of our spontaneity . . . because we are the upsurge of time' (*PP* 428 [497]).

These points suffice to show a deep concurrence between the philosophical standpoints adopted in *Being and Time* and *The Phenomenology of Perception*. Yet there are also major differences: Merleau-Ponty does not show any great interest either in the general question of the meaning of Being that Heidegger seeks to raise or in the questions about authenticity, death and anticipatory resoluteness that dominate the second half of *Being and Time*. By contrast Heidegger avoids all talk of 'intentionality' and says little about the detailed structure of perception and action that Merleau-Ponty discusses so illuminatingly.

So although their philosophical conceptions of human life are broadly similar, they employ this conception for very different ends.

Jean-Paul Sartre (1905–80)

The names 'Sartre' and 'Merleau-Ponty' are inseparably linked in accounts of twentieth-century French philosophy. They actively collaborated in the early post-war period in the running of *Les Temps Modernes* until they fell out over the Korean War, and this disagreement brought out into the open deeper political disagreements.[26] Merleau-Ponty had started off in 1945 as a Marxist dedicated to the cause of Soviet Communism,[27] but then found himself unable to maintain his support for Stalin's regime, especially in the light of the emerging news of Stalin's vast network of prison labour camps. By contrast Sartre had started off in 1945 as a theoretical Marxist unwilling to subject himself to the discipline required by membership of the Communist Party. By 1952, however, his hatred for the bourgeoisie had led him to commit himself to the Communist Party. Though this commitment lasted only until the Russian invasion of Hungary in 1956, most of Sartre's philosophical thought thereafter was dominated by his Marxism, whereas Merleau-Ponty's interests were drawn increasingly away from Marx to thinkers such as Max Weber.[28]

What is important here, however, is the issue of the relationship between their two main works of philosophy, Sartre's *Being and Nothingness* (1943) and *The Phenomenology of Perception* (1945). During the 1930s Sartre had been engaged on the project of writing a critique (provisionally entitled *Le Psyche*) of the conception of psychology as a natural science. Like many of Sartre's projects, he never brought this one to completion, though one part was published as his *Sketch for a Theory of the Emotions*,[29] and in *Being and Nothingness*[30] Sartre summarises the main idea of it in his discussion of 'Psychic temporality' (part two, chapter 2, section III, pp. 161–70), where he argues that scientific psychology has been guided by an illusory conception of the psyche as an inner space to be studied alongside the physical world.

This critical thesis will have been entirely congenial to Merleau-Ponty. In place of the psyche so conceived, however, Sartre introduces in *Being and Nothingness* a conception of consciousness that he characterises as follows: 'Consciousness has nothing substantial, it is pure "appearance" in the sense that it exists only to the degree to which it appears' (*BN* xxxii). Sartre summarises this as the thesis that the being of consciousness is 'being-for-itself' and he then contrasts this with 'the being of this table, this package of tobacco, of the lamp, more generally the being of the world which is implied by consciousness' (*BN* xxxviii). These are things which exist for consciousness as objects of consciousness, and 'the being of that which *appears* does not exist *only* in so far as it appears' (*BN* xxxviii); instead 'The transphenomenal being of what exists for consciousness is itself in itself' (*BN* xxxviii). So their being is being-in-itself. Having set up the issue in this way, Sartre then devotes the bulk of *Being and Nothingness* to a study of 'the connection between the two regions of being which we have discovered' (*BN* 3) or, in other terms, to a study of the 'the original relation of consciousness to being' (*BN* 105). For reasons that are never satisfactorily explained, Sartre opts to use the anachronistic idioms of a Hegelian logic of negation to develop his account of this 'original relation', whose bewildering conclusion is that 'the For-itself, in fact, is nothing but the pure nihilation of the In-itself; it is like a hole of being at the heart of Being' (*BN* 617). It is not worth attempting here to clarify this answer, in so far as this is possible at all.[31] For the point that will be obvious by now is that Sartre's approach to philosophy, and the language he uses to frame his discussion, are wholly antithetical to those employed by Merleau-Ponty. After all, Merleau-Ponty had argued in *The Structure of Behavior* (a work to which Sartre does not allude once in *Being and Nothingness*) that 'in the experience of behavior, I effectively surpass the alternatives of the for-itself and the in-itself' (p. 48; *SB* 126). So he must have been astonished to find Sartre laying out his account of human life in terms of just these alternatives.

One result is that in *The Phenomenology of Perception* there are several places where Merleau-Ponty implicitly indicates his radical rejection of Sartre's approach through his use of the terminology of 'in-itself'/'for-itself' to identify positions he rejects (e.g. *PP* 213 [247]). But in the final chapter, on 'Freedom', Merleau-Ponty comes out into the open to deliver a devastating critique of Sartre's conception of freedom as the essence of consciousness (I say more about this when introducing this chapter; see p. 209). So although Merleau-Ponty alludes from time to time to the phenomenological insights to be found in Sartre's book, the basic difference between them is stark: *The Phenomenology of Perception* is a consistent and deeply thought out work of existential phenomenology, whereas *Being and Nothingness* combines phenomenological insights with a traditional conception of consciousness in a discussion which is crippled by Sartre's decision to employ a

Hegelian logic that is wholly inadequate to the task of philosophical argument.

Notes

1 Sartre's long essay about Merleau-Ponty describes their collaboration and eventual parting: 'Merleau-Ponty vivant', *Les Temps Modernes* 17 (1961), pp. 304–76; trans. B. Eisler, as 'Merleau-Ponty', in *Situations*, New York: G. Braziller, 1965, pp. 227–326.

2 Jean Hyppolite 'Vie et prise de conscience de la vie dans la philosophie hégélienne d'Iena', *Revue de Métaphysique et de Morale*, 1938; trans. J. O'Neill, as 'The concept of life and consciousness of life in Hegel's Jena philosophy', in J. Hyppolite, *Studies on Marx and Hegel*, New York: Basic Books, 1969, pp. 3–21.

3 The basic idea of 'emergence' can be found in C. Lloyd Morgan, *Emergent Evolution*, London: Macmillan, 1923.

4 See 'Philosophy and the scientific image of man', in Wilfred Sellars, *Science, Perception and Reality*, London: Routledge and Kegal Paul, 1963, pp. 1–40.

5 Most notably W. V. Quine, whose notorious 'indeterminacy of translation' thesis is supposed to yield this conclusion; see *Word and Object*, Cambridge, MA: MIT Press, 1960, p. 221. I criticise Quine's argument in *Contemporary Philosophy: Philosophy in English since 1945*, Oxford: Oxford University Press, 2001, ch. 4.

6 See 'Empiricism and the philosophy of mind,' in Sellars, *Science, Perception and Reality*, pp. 127–96.

7 This phrase is not an ideal translation of Merleau-Ponty's *analyse reflexive*. 'Reflective analysis' would have been better; but here as elsewhere I stick with the published translation.

8 Merleau-Ponty was brought up as a Roman Catholic, and although he rejected this faith for much of his adult life his discussion often uses theological imagery.

9 Ever since Kant it has, unfortunately, been important to distinguish positions that invoke 'transcendent' beings, such as a God who stands altogether outside of space and time, from positions that invoke a 'transcendental' attitude in so far as they accept that there is an a priori contribution to knowledge or experience. Merleau-Ponty's existential phenomenology exemplifies a transcendental attitude but repudiates any transcendent self or subject. But matters are further complicated by the fact that Husserl uses the phrase 'transcendental phenomenology' to describe his own position and includes the conception of a 'pure', i.e. transcendent, Ego in characterising it. So although Merleau-Ponty's phenomenology exemplifies a transcendental attitude it is not a form of transcendental phenomenology in Husserl's sense.

10 The last phrase here ('and finally reveal to us the perceiving subject as the perceived world') is to be understood in terms of the thesis that our bodily being is being-in-the-world. Merleau-Ponty later gives a fuller statement of this thesis: '*Insofar* as, when I reflect on the essence of subjectivity, I find it bound up with that of the body and that of the world, this is because my existence as subjectivity is merely one with my existence as a body and

with the existence of the world, and because the subject that I am, when taken concretely, is inseparable from this body and this world' (p. 208; *PP* 408 [475]).

11 One can compare Merleau-Ponty's discussion here with that by Oliver Sacks in *The Man who Mistook his Wife for a Hat*, London: Duckworth, 1985, esp. ch. 6.

12 The French here is actually *motorité*; but 'motority' has the wrong connotations in English.

13 The French here is *noyau*, which might be better translated here as 'nucleus'.

14 See N. Chomsky, *Knowledge of Language*, New York: Praeger, 1986.

15 L. Wittgenstein, *On Certainty*, Oxford: Blackwell, 1969.

16 L. Wittgenstein, *Philosophical Investigations*, Oxford: Blackwell, 1953, esp. § 219.

17 The classic text here is S. Kripke, *Wittgenstein on Rules and Private Language*, Oxford: Blackwell, 1982.

18 His only extended discussion is 'Bergson in the making' (1959) in his *Signs*, trans. R. McCleary, Evanston, IL: Northwestern University Press, 1964, pp. 182–91.

19 See Merleau-Ponty's discussion in his *The Visible and the Invisible*, trans. A. Lingis, Evanston, IL: Northwestern University Press, 1968, pp. 122ff.

20 'Ideen I', *Jahrbuch für Philosophie und phänomenologische Forschung*, 1 (1913), pp. 1–323; repr. as *Husserliana* III, The Hague: Martinus Nijhof, 1950; trans. F. Kersten, *Ideas I*, The Hague: Martinus Nijhof, 1983. 'Formale und transzendentale Logik', *Jahrbuch für Philosophie und phänomenologische Forschung*, 10 (1929), pp. 1–298; repr. as *Husserliana* XVII, The Hague: Martinus Nijhof, 1974; trans. D. Cairns, *Formal and Transcendental Logic*, The Hague: Martinus Nijhof, 1969. *Méditations cartésiennes*, Paris: Colin, 1931; repr. (German text) as *Husserliana* I, The Hague: Martinus Nijhof, 1950; trans. D. Cairns, *Cartesian Meditations*, The Hague: Martinus Nijhof, 1973.

21 'Die Krisis der europäischen Wissenschaften', *Husserliana* VI, The Hague: Martinus Nijhof, 1954; trans. D. Carr, *The Crisis of European Sciences*, Evanston, IL: Northwestern University Press, 1968. 'Ideen II', *Husserliana* IV, The Hague: Martinus Nijhof, 1952; trans. R. Rojciewicz and A. Schuwer, *Ideas II*, The Hague: Martinus Nijhof, 1989.

22 'Translators' introduction' to *Ideas II*, p. xvi.

23 In his essay on Husserl, 'The philosopher and his shadow' (in *Signs*, trans. McCleary, pp. 159–81), Merleau-Ponty gives most attention to *Ideas II*.

24 Martin Heidegger, *Sein und Zeit*, Tübingen: Max Niemayer, 1927; trans. J. Macquarrie and E. Robinson, as *Being and Time*, Oxford: Blackwell, 1973.

25 In McTaggart's influential terminology, Heidegger and Merleau-Ponty are protagonists of an 'A-series' conception of time; unfortunately they do not discuss whether this is not inherently contradictory, as McTaggart held; see 'The unreality of time', *Mind* 17 (1908), pp. 457–74.

26 Merleau-Ponty published a bad-tempered criticism of Sartre, 'Sartre and ultrabolshevism' in *Les Aventures de la dialectique*, Paris: Gallimard, 1955; trans. J. Bien as *The Adventures of the Dialectic*, Evanston, IL: Northwestern University Press, 1973. Simone de Beauvoir responded in kind in 'Merleau-Ponty et le pseudo-sartrisme', *Les Temps Modernes* 10 (1955), 2072–122.

27 See *Humanisme et Terreur*, Paris: Gallimard, 1947; trans. J. O'Neill as *Humanism and Terror*, Boston, MA: Beacon, 1969.
28 As in the essay 'The crisis of the understanding' included here (pp. 326–45).
29 *Esquisse d'une théorie de l'émotion*, Paris: Hermann, 1939; trans. P. Mairet, as *Sketch for a Theory of the Emotions*, London: Methuen, 1962.
30 J.-P. Sartre, *L'Être et le néant*, Paris: Gallimard, 1943; trans. Hazel Barnes as *Being and Nothingness*, London: Methuen, 1958. In citations from this translation page numbers are from the 1969 edition, whose title is abbreviated as *BN*.
31 Merleau-Ponty attempts this task in chapter 2 of *The Visible and the Invisible*. He argues persuasively that in so far as Sartre's position is intelligible it is untenable.

PART ONE – MERLEAU-PONTY'S PROSPECTUS OF HIS WORK

This text is taken from The Primacy of Perception *(ed. J. Edie, Evanston, IL: Northwestern University press, 1964, pp. 3–11). It is a translation by A. B. Dallery of an article originally published as 'Un inédit de Maurice Merleau-Ponty' in* Revue de Métaphysique et de Morale *4 (1962), pp. 401–9, where it was preceded by the following introductory note by M. Guerolt:*

> *The text given below was sent to me by Merleau-Ponty at the time of his candidacy to the Collège de France, when I was putting together a report of his qualifications for presentation to the assembly of professors. In this report Merleau-Ponty traces his past and future as a philosopher in a continuous line, and outlines the perspectives of his future studies from* L'Origine de la vérité *to* L'Homme transcendental. *In reading these unpublished and highly interesting pages, one keenly regrets the death which brutally interrupted the élan of a profound thought in full possession of itself and about to fulfil itself in a series of original works which would have been landmarks in contemporary French philosophy.*

As this note shows, Merleau-Ponty wrote this prospectus late in 1952 or early 1953. In the first half he gives an interesting summary of his own views about The Structure of Behavior *and* The Phenomenology of Perception. *He then sets out his plans for the future, which centre on the articulation of a new theory of truth, to be combined with a study of expression and, ultimately, a theory of history. Finally he hopes to return to the theme of perception, but this time to find there a new way of thinking about 'transcendental man' and thence 'the principle of an ethics'. It was an ambitious programme, and, as Guerolt observes, left incomplete at his death. The studies originally conceived under the title* L'Origine de la vérité *to lead to a theory of truth were reorganized in 1959 under the new working title* Le Visible et l'invisible (The Visible and the Invisible) *and were published as such posthumously in 1964, from which one chapter is included in this volume ('The intertwining – the chiasm', pp. 248–71). The studies of expression were intended to form a book to be called* Introduction à la prose du monde. *Merleau-Ponty abandoned this book in 1952, though he then published parts of it as essays. After Merleau-Ponty's death, however, the abandoned text was published in 1969 as* La Prose du Monde (The Prose of the World), *and one chapter from this book is included in this volume ('The algorithm and the mystery of language', pp. 235–46). Finally, although Merleau-Ponty does not seem to have embarked on an extended study of history of the kind envisaged in this prospectus, the idea of history is central to several of the essays he gathered together in 1955 in the volume* The Adventures of the Dialectic, *especially the essay 'The crisis of understanding', which is included in this volume (pp. 326–45).*

We never cease living in the world of perception, but we go beyond it in critical thought – almost to the point of forgetting the contribution of perception to our idea of truth. For critical thought encounters only *bare propositions* which it discusses, accepts or rejects. Critical thought has broken with the naive evidence of *things*, and when it affirms, it is because it no longer finds any means of denial. However necessary this activity of verification may be, specifying criteria and demanding from our experience its credentials of validity, it is not aware of our contact with the perceived world which is simply there before us, beneath the level of the verified true and the false. Nor does critical thought even define the positive steps of thinking or its most valid accomplishments.

My first two works sought to restore the world of perception. My works in preparation aim to show how communication with others, and thought, take up and go beyond the realm of perception which initiated us to the truth.

The perceiving mind is an incarnated mind. I have tried, first of all, to re-establish the roots of the mind in its body and in its world, going against doctrines which treat perception as a simple result of the action of external things on our body as well as against those which insist on the autonomy of consciousness. These philosophies commonly forget – in favor of a pure exteriority or of a pure interiority – the insertion of the mind in corporeality, the ambiguous relation which we entertain with our body and, correlatively, with perceived things. When one attempts, as I have in *The Structure of Behavior*, to trace out, on the basis of modern psychology and physiology, the relationships which obtain between the perceiving organism and its milieu one clearly finds that they are not those of an automatic machine which needs an outside agent to set off its pre-established mechanisms. And it is equally clear that one does not account for the facts by superimposing a pure, contemplative consciousness on a thinglike body. In the conditions of life – if not in the laboratory – the organism is less sensitive to certain isolated physical and chemical agents than to the constellation which they form and to the whole situation which they define. Behaviors reveal a sort of prospective activity in the organism, as if it were oriented toward the meaning of certain elementary situations, as if it entertained familiar relations with them, as if there were an "*a priori* of the organism," privileged conducts and laws of internal equilibrium which predisposed the organism to certain relations with its milieu. At this level there is no question yet of a real self-awareness or of intentional activity. Moreover, the organism's prospective capability is exercised only within defined limits and depends on precise, local conditions.

The functioning of the central nervous system presents us with similar paradoxes. In its modern forms, the theory of cerebral localizations has profoundly changed the relation of function to substrate. It no longer assigns, for instance, a pre-established mechanism to each perceptual behavior. "Coordinating centers" are no longer considered as storehouses of "cerebral traces," and their functioning is qualitatively different from one case to another, depending on the chromatic nuance to be evoked and the perceptual structure to be realized. Finally, this functioning reflects all the subtlety and all the variety of perceptual relationships.

The perceiving organism seems to show us a Cartesian mixture of the soul with the body. Higher-order behaviors give a new meaning to the life of the organism, but the mind here disposes of only a limited freedom; it needs simpler activities in order to stabilize itself in durable institutions and to realize itself truly as mind. Perceptual behavior emerges from these relations to a situation and to an environment which are not the workings of a pure, knowing subject.

In my work on the *Phenomenology of Perception* we are no longer present at the emergence of perceptual behaviors; rather we install ourselves in them in order to pursue the analysis of this exceptional relation between the subject and its body and its world. For contemporary psychology and psychopathology the body is no longer merely *an object in the world*, under the purview of a separated spirit. It is on the side of the subject; it is our *point of view on the world*, the place where the spirit takes on a certain physical and historical situation. As Descartes once said profoundly, the soul is not merely in the body like a pilot in his ship; it is wholly intermingled with the body. The body, in turn, is wholly animated, and all its functions contribute to the perception of objects – an activity long considered by philosophy to be pure knowledge.

We grasp external space through our bodily situation. A 'corporeal or postural schema' gives us at every moment a global, practical, and implicit notion of the relation between our body and things, of our hold on them. A system of possible movements, or "motor projects" radiates from us to our environment. Our body is not in space like things; it inhabits or haunts space. It applies itself to space like a hand to an instrument, and when we wish to move about we do not move the body as we move an object. We transport it without instruments as if by magic, since it is ours and because through it we have direct access to space. For us the body is much more than an instrument or a means; it is our expression in the world, the visible form of our intentions. Even our most secret affective movements, those most deeply tied to the humoral infrastructure, help to shape our perception of things.

Now if perception is thus the common act of all our motor and affective functions, no less than the sensory, we must rediscover the structure of the perceived world through a process similar to that of an archaeologist. For the structure of the perceived world is buried under the sedimentations of later knowledge. Digging down to the perceived world, we see that sensory qualities are not opaque, indivisible "givens," which are simply exhibited to a remote consciousness – a favorite idea of classical philosophy. We see too that colors (each surrounded by an affective atmosphere which psychologists have been able to study and define) are themselves different modalities of our co-existence with the world. We also find that spatial forms or distances are not so much relations between different points in objective space as they are relations between these points and a central perspective – our body. In short, these relations are different ways for external stimuli to test, to solicit, and to vary our grasp on the world, our horizontal and vertical anchorage in a place and in a here-and-now. We find that perceived things, unlike geometrical objects, are not bounded entities whose laws of construction we possess *a priori*, but that they are open, inexhaustible systems which we recognize through a certain style of development, although we are never able, in principle, to explore them entirely, and even though they never give us more than profiles and perspectival views of themselves. Finally, we find that the perceived world, in its turn, is not a pure object of thought without fissures or lacunae; it is, rather, like a universal style shared in by all perceptual beings. While the world no doubt co-ordinates these perceptual beings, we can never presume that its work is finished. Our world, as Malebranche said, is an "unfinished task."

If we now wish to characterize a subject capable of this perceptual experience, it obviously will not be a self-transparent thought, absolutely present to itself without the interference of its body and its history. The perceiving subject is not this absolute thinker; rather, it functions according to a natal pact between our body and the world, between ourselves and our body. Given a perpetually new natural and historical situation to control, the perceiving subject undergoes a continued birth; at each instant it is something new. Every incarnate subject is like an open notebook in which we do not yet know what will be written. Or it is like a new language; we do not know what works it will accomplish but only that, once it has appeared, it cannot fail to say little or much, to have a history and a meaning. The very productivity or freedom of human life, far from denying our situation, utilizes it and turns it into a means of expression.

This remark brings us to a series of further studies which I have undertaken since 1945 and which will definitively fix the philosophical significance of my earlier works while they, in turn, determine the route and the method of these later studies.

I found in the experience of the perceived world a new type of relation between the mind and truth. The evidence of the perceived thing lies in its concrete aspect, in the very texture of its qualities, and in the equivalence among all its sensible properties – which caused Cézanne to say that one should be able to paint even odors. Before our undivided existence the world is true; it exists. The unity, the articulations of both are intermingled. We experience in it a truth which shows through and envelops us rather than being held and circumscribed by our mind.

Now if we consider, above the perceived world, the field of knowledge properly so called – i.e., the field in which the mind seeks to possess the truth, to define its objects itself, and thus to attain to a universal wisdom, not tied to the particularities of our situation – we must ask: Does not the realm of the perceived world take on the form of a simple appearance? Is not pure understanding a new source of knowledge, in comparison with which our perceptual familiarity with the world is only a rough, unformed sketch? We are obliged to answer these questions first with a theory of truth and then with a theory of intersubjectivity, both of which I have already touched upon in essays such as "Cézanne's Doubt," "Metaphysics and the Novel," and, on the philosophy of history, in *Humanism and Terror* (1947). But the philosophical foundations of these essays are still to be rigorously elaborated. I am now working on two books dealing with a theory of truth.

It seems to me that knowledge and the communication with others which it presupposes not only are original formations with respect to the perceptual life but also they preserve and continue our perceptual life even while transforming it. Knowledge and communication sublimate rather than suppress our incarnation, and the characteristic operation of the mind is in the movement by which we recapture our corporeal existence and use it to symbolize instead of merely to co-exist. This metamorphosis lies in the double function of our body. Through its "sensory fields" and its whole organization the body is, so to speak, predestined to model itself on the natural aspects of the world. But as an active body capable of gestures, of expression, and finally of language, it turns back on the world to signify it. As the observation of apraxics shows, there is in man, superimposed upon actual space with its self-identical points, a "virtual space" in which the spatial values that a point *would receive* (for any other position of our corporal co-ordinates) are also recognized. A system of correspondence is established between our spatial situation and that of others, and each one comes to symbolize all the others. This insertion of our factual situation as a particular case within the system of other possible situations begins as soon as we *designate* a point in space with our finger. For this pointing gesture, which animals do not understand, supposes that we are already installed in virtual space – at the end of the line prolonging our finger in a centrifugal and cultural space. This mimic usage of our body is not yet a conception, since it does not cut us off from our corporeal situation; on the contrary, it assumes all its meaning. It leads us to a concrete theory of the mind which will show the mind in a relationship of reciprocal exchange with the instruments which it uses, but uses only while rendering to them what it has received from them, and more.

In a general way expressive gestures (in which the science of physiognomy sought in vain for the sufficient signs of emotional states) have a univocal meaning only with respect to the situation which they underline and punctuate. But like phonemes, which have no meaning by themselves, expressive gestures have a diacritical value: they announce the constitution of a symbolical system capable of redesigning an

---

infinite number of situations. They are a first language. And recipro-
cally language can be treated as a gesticulation so varied, so precise, so
systematic, and capable of so many convergent expressions [recoupe-
ments] that the internal structure of an utterance can ultimately agree
only with the mental situation to which it responds and of which it
becomes an unequivocal sign. The meaning of language, like that of
gestures, thus does not lie in the elements composing it. The meaning is
their common intention, and the spoken phrase is understood only if
the hearer, following the "verbal chain," goes beyond each of its links
in the direction that they all designate together.

It follows that even solitary thought does not cease using the language which supports it, rescues it from the transitory, and throws it
back again. Cassirer said that thought was the "shuttlecock" of language.
It also follows that perhaps, taken piece by piece, language does not yet
contain its meaning, that all communication supposes in the listener a
creative re-enactment of what is heard. Language leads us to a thought
which is no longer ours alone, to a thought which is presumptively
universal, though this is never the universality of a pure concept which
would be identical for every mind. It is rather the call which a situated
thought addresses to other thoughts, equally situated, and each one
responds to the call with its own resources. An examination of the
domain of algorithm would show there too, I believe, the same strange
function which is at work in the so-called inexact forms of language.
Especially when it is a question of conquering a new domain for
exact thought, the most formal thought is always referred to some
qualitatively defined mental situation from which it extracts a meaning
only by applying itself to the configuration of the problem. The transformation is never a simple analysis, and thought is never more than
relatively formal.

Since I intend to treat this problem more fully in my work L'Origine
de la vérité, I have approached it less directly in a partially written book
dealing with literary language. In this area it is easier to show that
language is never the mere clothing of a thought which otherwise possesses itself in full clarity. The meaning of a book is given, in the first
instance, not so much by its ideas as by a systematic and unexpected
variation of the modes of language, of narrative, or of existing literary
forms. This accent, this particular modulation of speech – if the expression is successful – is assimilated little by little by the reader, and it gives
him access to a thought to which he was until then indifferent or even
opposed. Communication in literature is not the simple appeal on the
part of the writer to meanings which would be part of an *a priori* of

the mind; rather, communication arouses these meanings in the mind through enticement and a kind of oblique action. The writer's thought does not control his language from without; the writer is himself a kind of new idiom, constructing itself, inventing ways of expression, and diversifying itself according to its own meaning. Perhaps poetry is only that part of literature where this autonomy is ostentatiously displayed. All great prose is also a re-creation of the signifying instrument, henceforth manipulated according to a new syntax. Prosaic writing, on the other hand, limits itself to using, through accepted signs, the meanings already accepted in a given culture. Great prose is the art of capturing a meaning which until then had never been objectified and of rendering it accessible to everyone who speaks the same language. When a writer is no longer capable of thus founding a new universality and of taking the risk of communicating, he has outlived his time. It seems to me that we can also say of other institutions that they have ceased to live when they show themselves incapable of carrying on a poetry of human relations – that is, the call of each individual freedom to all the others.

Hegel said that the Roman state was the prose of the world. I shall entitle my book *Introduction à la prose du monde*. In this work I shall elaborate the category of prose beyond the confines of literature to give it a sociological meaning.

For these studies on expression and truth approach, from the epistemological side, the general problem of human interrelations – which will be the major topic of my later studies. The linguistic relations among men should help us understand the more general order of symbolic relations and of institutions, which assure the exchange not only of thoughts but of all types of values, the co-existence of men within a culture and, beyond it, within a single history. Interpreted in terms of symbolism, the concept of history seems to escape the disputes always directed to it because one ordinarily means by this word – whether to accept it or to reject it – an external Power in the name of which men would be dispossessed of consciousness. History is no more external to us than language. There *is* a history of thought: the succession of the works of the spirit (no matter how many detours we see in it) is really a single experience which develops of itself and in whose development, so to speak, truth capitalizes itself. In an analogous sense we can say that there is a history of humanity or, more simply, *a* humanity. In other words, granting all the periods of stagnation and retreat, human relations are able to grow, to change their avatars into lessons, to pick out the truth of their past in the present, to eliminate certain mysteries which render them opaque and thereby make themselves more translucent.

The idea of a single history or of a logic of history is, in a sense, implied in the least human exchange, in the least social perception. For example, anthropology supposes that civilizations very different from ours are comprehensible to us, that they can be situated in relation to ours and vice-versa, that all civilizations belong to the same universe of thought, since the least use of language implies an idea of truth. Also we can never pretend to dismiss the adventures of history as something foreign to our present action, since even the most independent search for the most abstract truth has been and is a factor of history (the only one, perhaps, that we are sure is not disappointing). All human acts and all human creations constitute a single drama, and in this sense we are all saved or lost together. Our life is essentially universal.

But this methodological rationalism is not to be confused with a dogmatic rationalism which eliminates historical contingency in advance by supposing a "World Spirit" (Hegel) behind the course of events. If it is necessary to say that there is a total history, a single tissue tying together all the enterprises of simultaneous and successive civilizations, all the results of thought and all the facts of economics, it must not be in the guise of a historical idealism or materialism – one handing over the government of history to thought; the other, to matter. Because cultures are just so many coherent systems of symbols and because in each culture the modes of work, of human relations, of language and thought, even if not parallel at every moment, do not long remain separated, cultures can be compared and placed under a common denominator. What makes this connection of meaning between each aspect of a culture and all the rest, as between all the episodes of history, is the permanent, harmonious thought of this plurality of beings who recognize one another as "*semblables*," (alike) even when some seek to enslave others, and who are so commonly situated that adversaries are often in a kind of complicity.

Our inquiries should lead us finally to a reflection on this *transcendental man*, or this "natural light" common to all, which appears through the movement of history – to a reflection on this Logos which gives us the task of vocalizing a hitherto mute world. Finally, they should lead us to a study of the Logos of the perceived world which we encountered in our earliest studies in the evidence of things. Here we rejoin the classical questions of metaphysics, but by following a route which removes from them their character as *problems* – that is to say, as difficulties which could be solved cheaply through the use of a few metaphysical entities constructed for this purpose. The notions of Nature and Reason, for instance, far from explaining the metamorphoses which we have observed from perception up to the more complex modes of human exchange, make them incomprehensible. For by relating them to separated principles, these notions mask a constantly experienced moment, the moment when an existence becomes aware of itself, grasps itself, and expresses its own meaning.

The study of perception could only teach us a "bad ambiguity," a mixture of finitude and universality, of interiority and exteriority. But there is a "good ambiguity" in the phenomenon of expression, a spontaneity which accomplishes what appeared to be impossible when we observed only the separate elements, a spontaneity which gathers together the plurality of monads, the past and the present, nature and culture into a single whole. To establish this wonder would be metaphysics itself and would at the same time give us the principle of an ethics.

PART TWO – SELECTIONS FROM *THE STRUCTURE OF BEHAVIOR*

In extracting these passages from the translation of Merleau-Ponty's book I have removed most of his footnotes, since they are references to works of psychology in German and French which will be inaccessible to most readers of this volume; but I have retained an important note to the introduction and I give details of two relevant works of psychology in the section 'Further Reading' at the end of this book.

INTRODUCTION (*SB* 3–5)

Merleau-Ponty sets out his initial agenda, that of confronting traditional conceptions of psychology with the challenge of providing a satisfactory account of behaviour (animal or human). In the revealing footnote he declares that he intends to use the notion of 'existence' to resolve the difficulties inherent in traditional conceptions of behaviour.

Our goal is to understand the relations of consciousness and nature: organic, psychological or even social. By nature we understand here a multiplicity of events external to each other and bound together by relations of causality.

With respect to physical nature, critical thought brings a well-known solution to this problem: reflection reveals that physical analysis is not a decomposition into real elements and that causality in its actual meaning is not a productive operation. There is then no physical nature in the sense we have just given to this word; there is nothing in the world which is foreign to the mind. The world is the ensemble of objective relations borne by consciousness. It can be said that physics, in its development, justifies *de facto* this philosophy. One sees it employing mechanical, dynamic or even psychological models indifferently, as if, liberated from ontological pretensions, it were indifferent to the classical antimonies of mechanism and dynamism which imply a nature in itself.

The situation is not the same in biology. In fact the discussions concerning mechanism and vitalism remain open. The reason for this is probably that analysis of the physico-mathematical type progresses very slowly in this area and, consequently, that our picture of the organism is still for the most part that of a material mass *partes extra partes*. Under these conditions biological thought most frequently remains realistic, either by juxtaposing separated mechanisms or by subordinating them to an entelechy.

As for psychology, critical thought leaves it no other resource than to be in part an "analytical psychology" which would discover judgment present everywhere in a way parallel to analytical geometry, and for the rest, a study of certain bodily mechanisms. To the extent that it has attempted to be a natural science, psychology has remained faithful to realism and to causal thinking. At the beginning of the century, materialism made the "mental" a particular sector of the real world: among events existing in themselves (*en soi*), some of them in the brain also had the property of existing for themselves (*pour soi*). The counter mentalistic thesis posited consciousness as a productive cause or as a thing: first it was the realism of "states of consciousness" bound together by causal relations, a second world parallel and analogous to the "physical world" following the Humean tradition; then, in a more refined psychology, it was the realism of "mental energy" which substituted a multiplicity of fusion and interpenetration, a flowing reality, for the disconnected mental facts. But consciousness remained the analogue of a force. This was clearly seen when it was a question of explaining its action on the body and when, without being able to eliminate it the necessary "creation of energy" was reduced to a minimum, the universe of physics was indeed taken as a reality in itself in which consciousness was made to appear as a second reality. Among psychologists consciousness was distinguished from beings of nature as one thing from another thing, by a certain number of *characteristics*. The mental fact, it was said, *is* unextended, known all at once. More recently the doctrine of Freud applies metaphors of energy to consciousness and accounts for conduct by the interaction of forces or tendencies.

Thus, among contemporary thinkers in France, there exist side by side a philosophy, on the one hand, which makes of every nature an objective unity constituted vis-à-vis consciousness and, on the other, sciences which treat the organism and consciousness as two orders of reality and, in their reciprocal relation, as "effects" and as "causes." Is the solution to be found in a pure and simple return to critical thought? And once the criticism of realistic analysis and causal thinking has been made, is there nothing justified in the naturalism of science – nothing which, "understood" and transposed, ought to find a place in a transcendental philosophy?

We will come to these questions by starting "from below" and by an analysis of the notion of behavior. This notion seems important to us because, taken in itself, it is neutral with respect to the classical distinctions between the "mental" and the "physiological" and thus can give us the opportunity of defining them anew.[1] It is known that in Watson, following the classical antinomy, the negation of consciousness as "internal reality" is made to the benefit of physiology; behavior is reduced to the sum of reflexes and conditioned reflexes between which no intrinsic connection is admitted. But precisely this atomistic interpretation fails even at the level of the theory of the reflex (Chapter 1) and all the more so in the psychology – even the objective psychology – of higher levels of behavior (Chapter 2), as Gestalt theory has clearly shown. By going through behaviorism, however, one gains at least in being able to introduce consciousness, not as psychological reality or as cause, but as structure. It will remain for us to investigate (Chapter 3) the meaning and the mode of existence of these structures.

Note

1   One says of a man or of an animal that he behaves; one does not say it of an acid, an electron, a pebble or a cloud except by metaphor. In the present work we have attempted to elucidate directly the notion of behavior and not to follow its development in American psychology. We will justify briefly this direct procedure by calling to mind the ideological disorder in which the notion of behavior has been developed in the country of its origin. As is shown in the recent work of Tilquin (Le Behaviorisme, origine et développement de la psychologie de réaction en Amérique, Paris: Vrin, 1942) – which comes to us at the moment when ours is in galley proofs – the notion of behavior had a difficult time making its way among philosophies which did not succeed in conceptualizing it. Even with its principal initiator, Watson, it found only an insufficient philosophical

articulation. It was said that behavior was not localized in the central nervous system (A. Tilquin, *Le Behaviorisme*, pp. 72 and 103), that it resides between the individual and the environment (*ibid.*, p. 34), that consequently the study of behavior can be made without a word about physiology (*ibid.*, e.g., p. 107), and finally that it is concerned with a stream of activity which the living being projects around itself (*ibid.*, pp. 180 and 351) affecting the stimuli of a characteristic sense (*ibid.*, p. 346). But what is healthy and profound in this intuition of behavior – that is, the vision of man as perpetual debate and "explanation" with a physical and social world – found itself compromised by an impoverished philosophy. In reaction against the shadows of psychological intimacy, behaviorism for the most part seeks recourse only in a physiological or even a physical explanation, without seeing that this amounts to putting behavior back into the nervous system. In our opinion (which is not that of Tilquin), when Watson spoke of behavior he had in mind what others have called *existence*; but the new notion could receive its philosophical status only if causal or mechanical thinking were abandoned for dialectical thinking.

CHAPTER 2: HIGHER FORMS OF BEHAVIOR

CONCLUSION (*SB* 124–8)

Merleau-Ponty explains that a satisfactory account of behaviour requires an approach that avoids the familiar alternatives of reducing it to bodily movements that are treated as causally explicable through interaction with the physical environment or regarding it as the expression of a pure consciousness guided by rational connections that are independent of their bodily expression. Instead behaviour is a fundamental category that surpasses the alternatives of the physical (en soi) and conscious thought (pour soi), and is to be understood in the light of a theory of 'form' (Gestalt).

The preceding chapters teach us not only not to explain the higher by the lower, as they say, but also not to explain the lower by the higher. Traditionally, lower or mechanical reactions which, like physical events, are functions of antecedent conditions and thus unfold in objective time and space are distinguished from "higher" reactions which do not depend on stimuli, taken materially, but rather on the meaning of the situation, and which appear therefore to presuppose a "view" of this situation, a prospection, and to belong no longer to the order of the in-itself (*en soi*) but to the order of the for-itself (*pour soi*). Both of these orders are transparent for the mind: the first is transparent for the mode of thinking in physics and is like the external order in which events govern each other from the outside; the second is transparent for reflective consciousness and is like the internal order in which that which takes place always depends upon an intention. *Behavior*, inasmuch as it has a structure, is not situated in either of these two orders. It does not unfold in objective time and space like a series of physical events; each moment does not occupy one and only one point of time; rather, at the decisive moment of learning, a "now" stands out from the series of "nows," acquires a particular value and summarizes the groupings which have preceded it as it engages and anticipates the future of the behavior; this "now" transforms the singular situation of the experience into a typical situation and the effective reaction into an aptitude. From this moment on behavior is detached from the order of the in-itself (*en soi*) and becomes the projection outside the organism of a *possibility* which is internal to it. The world, inasmuch as it harbors living beings, ceases to be a material plenum consisting of juxtaposed parts; it opens up at the place where behavior appears.

Nothing would be served by saying that it is we, the spectators, who mentally unite the elements of the situation to which behavior is addressed in order to make them meaningful, that it is we who project into the exterior the intentions of our thinking, since we would still have to discover what it is, what kind of phenomenon is involved upon which this *Einfühlung* rests, what is the sign which invites us to anthropomorphism. Nor would anything be served by saying that behavior "is conscious" and that it reveals to us, as its other side, a being for-itself (*pour soi*) hidden behind the visible body. The gestures of behavior, the intentions which it traces in the space around the animal, are not directed to the true world or pure being, but to being-for-the-animal, that is, to a certain milieu characteristic of the species; they do not allow the showing through of a consciousness, that is, a being whose whole essence is to know, but rather a certain manner of treating the world, of "being-in-the-world" or of "existing." A consciousness, according to Hegel's expression, is a "penetration in being," and here we have nothing yet but an opening up. The chimpanzee, which physically can stand upright but in all urgent cases reassumes the animal posture, which can assemble boxes but gives them only a tactile equilibrium, in this way manifests a sort of adherence to the here and now, a short and heavy manner of existing. Gelb and Goldstein's patient, who no longer has the "intuition" of numbers, no longer "understands" analogies and no longer "perceives" simultaneous wholes, betrays a weakness, a lack of density and vital amplitude, of which the cognitive disorders are only the secondary expression. It is only at the level of symbolic conduct, and more exactly at the level of exchanged speech, that foreign existences (at the same time as our own, moreover) appear to us as ordered to the true world; it is only at this level that, instead of seeking to insinuate his stubborn norms, the subject of behavior "de-realizes himself" and becomes a genuine *alter ego*. And yet the constitution of the other person as another I is never completed since his utterance, even having become a pure phenomenon of expression, always and indivisibly remains expressive as much of himself as of the truth.

There is, then, no behavior which certifies a pure consciousness behind it, and the other person is never given to me as the exact equivalent of myself thinking. In this sense it is not only to animals that consciousness must be denied. The supposition of a *foreign conscious-ness* immediately reduces the world which is given to me to the status of a private spectacle; the world is broken up into a multiplicity of "repre-sentations of the world" and can no longer be anything but the meaning which they have in common, or the invariant of a system of monads. But in fact I am aware of perceiving the world as well as behavior which, caught in it, intends numerically one and the same world, which is to say that, in the experience of behavior, I effectively surpass the alterna-tive of the for-itself (*pour soi*) and the in-itself (*en soi*). Behaviorism, solipsism, and "projective" theories all accept that behavior is given to me like something spread out in front of me. But to reject consciousness in animals in the sense of pure consciousness, the *cogitatio*, is not to make them automatons without interiority. The animal, to an extent which varies according to the integration of its behavior, is certainly *another existence*; this existence is perceived by everybody; we have described it; and it is a phenomenon which is independent of any notional theory concerning the soul of brutes. Spinoza would not have spent so much time considering a drowning fly if this behavior had not offered to the eye something other than a fragment of extension; the theory of animal machines is a "resistance" to the phenomenon of behavior. Therefore this phenomenon must still be conceptualized. The structure of behavior as it presents itself to perceptual experience is neither thing nor consciousness; and it is this which renders it opaque to the mind.

The object of the preceding chapters was not only to establish that behavior is irreducible to its alleged parts. If we had had nothing other in view, instead of this long inductive research – which can never even be finished, since behaviorism can always invent other mechanical models with regard to which the discussion will have to be recom-menced – a moment of reflection would have provided us with a certi-tude in principle. Does not the *cogito* teach us once and for all that we would have no knowledge of any *thing* if we did not first have a knowledge of our thinking and that even the escape into the world and the resolution to ignore interiority or to never leave things, which is the essential feature of behaviorism, cannot be formulated without being transformed into consciousness and without presupposing existence for-itself (*pour soi*)? Thus behavior is constituted of relations; that is, it is conceptualized and not in-itself (*en soi*), as is every other object moreover; this is what reflection would have shown us. But by following this short route we would have missed the essential feature of the phenomenon, the paradox which is constitutive of it: behavior is not a thing, but neither is it an idea. It is not the envelope of a pure consciousness and, as the witness of behavior, I am not a pure consciousness. It is precisely this which we wanted to say in stating that behavior is a form.

Thus, with the notion of "form," we have found the means of avoiding the classical antitheses in the analysis of the "central sector" of behavior as well as in that of its visible manifestations. More generally, this notion saves us from the alternative of a philosophy which juxtaposes externally associated terms and of another philosophy which discovers relations which are intrinsic to thought in all phenomena. But precisely for this reason the notion of form is ambiguous. Up until now it has been introduced by physical examples and defined by characteristics which made it appropriate for resolving problems of psychology and physiology. Now this notion must be understood in itself, without which the philosophical significance of what precedes would remain equivocal.

CHAPTER 3: THE PHYSICAL ORDER; THE VITAL ORDER; THE HUMAN ORDER

INTRODUCTION (*SB* 129–32), THE HUMAN ORDER (*SB* 168–76), CONCLUSION (*SB* 184)

In the introduction to this chapter Merleau-Ponty sketches his account of the distinctive feature of organisms ('the vital order'), namely the fact that their behaviour is always a response to their species-specific world or environment. He then suggests that this fact about them is to be understood in terms of the notion of a 'form', which is elucidated at the start of the next selection as an element within the perceptual field: forms are inherently 'configurations' within sensory fields. He then discusses the relationship between these perceptual forms and traditional a priori concepts and argues that the role of forms in human life has to be understood by reference to the distinctive feature of 'the human order'. Although this is usually identified in terms of the role of culture as a 'second nature' for man, Merleau-Ponty argues that what is more fundamental is the capacity to 'orient oneself' in relation to that which is merely possible. Finally, in the conclusion of the chapter Merleau-Ponty affirms the 'ideality' of the forms that are character-istic of the physical, vital and human orders, and infers from this that their relationship is not simply one of the emergence of increasingly complex causal structures, but 'dialectical' in that, being in some sense 'ideas', these forms make reference to the work of consciousness. However, Merleau-Ponty ends here with a series of questions, rather than assertions. In the fourth and final chapter of The Structure of Behavior *('The relations of the soul and the body and the problem of perceptual consciousness') he argues that these questions can only be answered by reconsidering the phenomenology of perception and the body's place at the heart of perception. But since these issues are discussed again in* The Phenomenology of Perception *this earlier discussion is not included here.*

Introduction

Pavlov's reflexology treats behavior as if it were a thing, inserts and resorbs it into the tissue of events and relations of the universe. When we tried to define the variables on which behavior actually depends, we found them, not in the stimuli taken as events of the physical world, but in relations which are not contained in the latter – from the relation which is established between two nuances of gray to the functional relations of instrument to goal and the relations of mutual expression in symbolic conduct. Gray G1 and gray G2 are part of nature, but not the "pair" of colors constituted by the organism in their regard and which it "recognizes" in another ensemble in which the absolute colors are different. On analysis, the equivocal notion of stimulus separates into two: it includes and confuses the physical event as it is in itself, on the one hand, and the situation as it is "for the organism," on the other, with only the latter being decisive in the reactions of the animal. Against behaviorism, it has been established that the "geographical environ-ment" and the "behavioral environment" cannot be identified. In the hierarchy of species, the efficacious relations at each level define an *a priori* of this species, a manner of elaborating the stimuli which is proper to it; thus the organism has a distinct reality which is not substantial but structural.

Science is not therefore dealing with organisms as the completed modes of a unique world (*Welt*), as the abstract parts of a whole in which the parts would be most perfectly contained. It has to do with a series of "environments" and "milieu" (*Umwelt, Merkwelt, Gegenwelt*) in which the stimuli intervene according to what they signify and what they are worth for the typical activity of the species considered. In the same manner the reactions of an organism are not edifices constructed from elementary movements, but gestures gifted with an internal unity. Like that of stimulus, the notion of response separates into "geographical behavior" – the sum of the movements actually executed by the animal in their objective relation with the physical world; and behavior properly so called – these same movements considered in their internal articulation and as a kinetic melody gifted with a meaning. The time necessary for a rat to get out of a labyrinth and the number of errors which it commits are determinations which belong to its geographical behavior and which may sometimes have more, sometimes less value than its behavior properly so called. It may happen that an act which is not being guided by the essential traits of the situation will encounter them by chance, as when a cat pulls a piece of meat toward itself while playing with a string; and inversely, it may happen that a movement which is in fact fruitless will be a "good" error, as when a chimpanzee, in order to reach a distant object, pushes a stick toward it with the aid of a second stick which it holds in its hand.

One cannot discern in animal behavior something like a first layer of reactions which would correspond to the physical and chemical properties of the world and to which an acquired significance would subsequently be attached by the transference of reflexogenic powers. In an organism, experience is not the recording and fixation of certain actually accomplished movements: it builds up aptitudes, that is, the general power of responding to situations of a certain type by means of varied reactions which have nothing in common but the meaning. Reactions are not therefore a sequence of events; they carry within themselves an immanent intelligibility.

Situation and reaction are linked internally by their common participation in a structure in which the mode of activity proper to the organism is expressed. Hence they cannot be placed one after the other as cause and effect: they are two moments of a circular process. Everything which impedes the activity of the animal also eliminates the reflexogenic power of certain stimuli, cuts them off from its "sensory universe." "The relation of the internal world to the external world of the animal cannot be understood as that of a key with its lock." If behavior is a "form," one cannot even designate in it that which depends on each one of the internal and external conditions taken separately, since their variations will be expressed in the form by a global and indivisible effect. Behavior would not be an effect of the physical world, either in the crude sense of productive causality or even in the sense of the relation of function to variable. The original character of a physiological field beyond the physical field – a system of directed forces – in which it has its place, of a second "system of stresses and strains" which alone determines actual behavior in a decisive manner, will have to be acknowledged. Even if we take symbolic behavior and its proper characteristics fully into account there would be reason for introducing a third field which, by nominal definition, we will call mental field. Are we not brought back to the classical problems which behaviorism tried to eliminate by leveling behavior to the unique plane of physical causality?

It is here that the notion of form would permit a truly new solution. Equally applicable to the three fields which have just been defined, it would integrate them as three types of structures by surpassing the antimonies of materialism and mentalism, of materialism and vitalism. Quantity, order and value or signification, which pass respectively for the properties of matter, life and mind, would no longer be but the dominant characteristic in the order considered and would become universally applicable categories. Quantity is not a negation of quality, as if the equation for a circle negated circular form, of which on the contrary it attempts to be a rigorous expression. Often, the quantitative relations with which physics is concerned are only the formulae for certain distributive processes: in a soap bubble as in an organism, what happens at each point is determined by what happens at all the others. But this is the definition of order.

There is therefore no reason whatsoever for refusing objective value to this category in the study of the phenomena of life, since it has its place in the definition of physical systems. . . .

The human order
It is here that the notion of "form" will permit us to continue the analysis. The form is a visible or sonorous configuration (or even a configuration which is prior to the distinction of the senses) in which the sensory value of each element is determined by its function in the whole and varies with it. The thresholds of chromatic perception are different for the same spot of color depending on whether it is perceived as "figure" or "ground." This same notion of form will permit us to describe the mode of existence of the primitive objects of perception.

They are lived as realities, we have said, rather than known as true objects.

Certain states of adult consciousness permit us to comprehend this distinction. For the player in action the football field is not an "object," that is, the ideal term which can give rise to an indefinite multiplicity of perspectival views and remain equivalent under its apparent transformations. It is pervaded with lines of force (the "yard lines"; those which demarcate the "penalty area") and articulated in sectors (for example, the "openings" between the adversaries) which call for a certain mode of action and which initiate and guide the action as if the player were unaware of it. The field itself is not given to him, but present as the immanent term of his practical intentions; the player becomes one with it and feels the direction of the "goal," for example, just as immediately as the vertical and the horizontal planes of his own body. It would not be sufficient to say that consciousness inhabits this milieu. At this moment consciousness is nothing other than the dialectic of milieu and action. Each maneuver undertaken by the player modifies the character of the field and establishes in it new lines of force in which the action in turn unfolds and is accomplished, again altering the phenomenal field.

But one might be tempted to say that these characteristics pose no special problems. That perception is first a perception of human actions or of use-objects would be explained simply by the actual presence of people and artifacts in the child's milieu. That perception reaches objects only through words would be the effect of language as a social phenomenon. That social structures are carried over into the knowledge of nature itself by perception would be only one further argument in favor of a sociology of knowledge. Finally, that perception opens on a reality which solicits our action rather than on a truth, an object of knowledge, would result from the reverberation in consciousness of its motor accompaniment. In other words, we would have brought to light the social and physiological determinants of perception; we would have described, not an original form of consciousness, but the social or kinesthetic contents which are imposed on it by the existence of the body or the integration into a society and which would not oblige us to modify our conception of its proper structure. On the contrary, we propose to show that the descriptive dimension of nascent perception demands a reformulation of the notion of consciousness.

The simple *de facto* presence of other human beings and of use-objects or cultural objects in the infantile milieu cannot explain the forms of primitive perception as a cause explains its effect. Consciousness is not comparable to a plastic material which would receive its privileged structure from the outside by the action of a sociological or physiological causality. If these structures were not in some way prefigured in the consciousness of the child, the use-object or the "other" would be expressed in it only by constructions of sensation, a progressive interpretation of which would slowly disengage the human meaning. If language did not encounter some predisposition for the act of speech in the child who hears speaking, it would remain for him a sonorous phenomenon among others for a long time; it would have no power over the mosaic of sensations possessed by infantile consciousness; one could not understand how it could play the guiding role which psychologists agree in granting to it in the constitution of the perceived world. In other words, it cannot be in virtue of the fact that it *exists* around the child that the human world can immediately acquire a privileged importance in infantile consciousness; it is in virtue of the fact that the consciousness of the child, who sees human objects used and begins to use them in his turn, is capable of discovering immediately in these acts and in these objects the intention of which they are the visible testimony. To use a human object is always more or less to embrace and assume for one's self the meaning of the work which produced it.

It is not a question of upholding the absurd thesis of an innateness of these fundamental structures of conduct. Aside from the fact that innatism accords poorly with the facts – the influence of the milieu in the formation of the mind is sufficiently evident; it is clear that a child who had never seen an article of clothing would not know how to act with clothing; nor would he be able to speak or to envisage other persons if he had always been absolutely alone – it bypasses the difficulty: it limits itself to putting the contents which empiricism derives from external experience "in" consciousness, that is, in brief, to putting them in an internal experience. Rather, the child would understand the human meaning of bodies and of use-objects or the signifying value of language before any logical elaboration because he himself would sketch the acts which give their meaning to words and gestures. It is evident that this is not a solution: we have already seen that the child understands attitudes which he has never had the occasion of assuming; above all, it is difficult to see why these attitudes – actualized in him in the form of innate structures and presented to him in an internal view – would be more immediately understood than when they are given to him in a view from the outside.

Whether the child contemplates their external and visual appearance or whether he grasps their motor actualization in his own body, the question still remains of knowing how an irreducible unity of meaning is apprehended through these materials. Beyond the artificial opposition between the innate and the acquired, therefore, it is a question of describing the emergence of an indecomposable signification in the moment of experience itself: whether it be precocious or retarded, internal or external, motor or sensory. For a child, language which is understood or simply sketched, the appearance of a face or that of a use-object, must from the beginning be the sonorous, motor or visual envelope of a significative intention coming from another. The organization and the sense of understood language can be very minimal at first; it will be the inflection of the voice, the intonation, which will be understood rather than the verbal material. But from the beginning the sonorous phenomena – whether I speak or another speaks – will be integrated into the structure: expression-expressed; the face – whether I touch my own or I see that of another – will be integrated into the structure: alter-ego.

In other words, as soon as nascent consciousness is taken as the object of analysis one realizes that it is impossible to apply to it the celebrated distinction between *a priori* form and empirical content. Reduced to what is incontestable about it, the *a priori* is that which cannot be conceived part by part and must be conceptualized all at once as an indecomposable essence; the *a posteriori*, on the contrary, designates what can be constructed vis-à-vis thought, piece by piece, by an assembling of external parts. The essence of Kantianism is to admit only two types of experiences as possessing an *a priori* structure: that of a world of external objects, that of states of the inner sense; and to relate all other specifications of experience, for example, linguistic consciousness or consciousness of other persons, to the variety of *a posteriori* contents. Thus, a word can be only a sonorous phenomenon, a moment of external experience to which a signification, that is, a concept, is secondarily adjoined and associated. Another person can consist only of the coordination of a multitude of phenomena of external experience subsumed under a concept which is taken from the inner sense.

The fact that Kant has gone beyond the empiricist notion of the association of states by discovering consciousness as the condition of this association does not change the fact that the relation of meaning to word remains a conceptualized contiguity, the act of speaking, a banal conceptual operation accompanied by a phonation mechanism which is contingent with regard to it. Finally, it does not change the fact that another person remains a derived notion by means of which I coordinate certain aspects of external experience.

But child psychology precisely proposes the enigma of a linguistic consciousness and a consciousness of others which is almost pure and which is prior to that of sonorous and visual phenomena – as is sufficiently shown by the magical and animistic beliefs of the child. Speech and other persons, therefore, cannot derive their meaning from a systematic interpretation of sensory phenomena and the "multiple given." They are indecomposable structures and in that sense are *a priori*. But a double consequence with regard to the definition of consciousness follows from this. Since the distinction between sensible content and *a priori* structure is a secondary distinction – justified in the universe of natural objects known by adult consciousness, but impossible in infantile consciousness – and since there do exist "material *a priori*," the conception of consciousness which we must formulate is profoundly modified. It is no longer possible to define it as a universal function for the organization of experience which would impose on all its objects the conditions of logical and physical existence which are those of a universe of articulated objects and which would owe its specifications only to the variety of its contents. There will be sectors of experience which are irreducible to each other.

At the same time that one abandons the notion of the "multiple given" as the source of all specifications one will doubtless be obliged to abandon the notion of mental activity as the principle of all coordinations. Indeed, as soon as one refuses to separate the relation from the different concrete structures which appear in experience, it is no longer possible to found all relation on the activity of the "epistemological subject"; and, at the same time as the perceived world is fragmented into discontinuous "regions," consciousness is divided into different types of acts of consciousness. In particular, the fact that primitive perception is, as it were, haunted by human presence and lacunary for all the rest obliges us to accept the fact that "others," although they may be reached in adults through "sensations" or "images," can also be known by means of very impoverished representational contents: therefore, there must be several ways for consciousness to intend its object and several sorts of intentions in it. To possess and contemplate a "representation" and to coordinate a mosaic of sensations – these are special attitudes which cannot account for all the life of consciousness and which probably apply to its more primitive modes, as a translation applies to a text. Desire could be related to the object desired, will to the object willed, fear to the object feared, without this reference – even if it always includes a cognitive nucleus – being reduced to the relation of representation to represented. Acts of thought would not be alone in having a signification, of containing in them the prescience of what they are seeking; there would be a sort of blind recognition of the object desired by the desire, and of the good by the will. This is the means by which a person can be "given" to a child as the pole of his desires and fears before the long work of interpretation which would arrive at the person as a conclusion from a universe of representations. This is also the means by which confused sensory ensembles can nevertheless be very precisely identified as the bases of certain human intentions. It may happen that, in entering a room, we perceive a poorly localized disorder before discovering the reason for this impression: for example, the asymmetrical position of a picture frame. In entering an apartment we can perceive the character of those who live there without being capable of justifying this impression by an enumeration of remarkable details, and certainly well before having noted the color of the furniture. To actualize these justifications ahead of time in the form of "latent content" or "unconscious knowing" is to postulate that nothing is accessible to consciousness which is not present to it in the form of representation or content.

The implicit conception of consciousness to which these remarks lead will have to be made more precise. What we have said is sufficient to show that the possession of a representation or the exercise of a judgment is not coextensive with the life of consciousness. Rather, consciousness is a network of significative intentions which are sometimes clear to themselves and sometimes, on the contrary, lived rather than known. Such a conception will permit us to link consciousness with action by enlarging our idea of action. Human action can be reduced to vital action only if one considers the intellectual analysis by which it passes for a more ingenious *means* of achieving animal ends. But it is this completely external relation of end and means which becomes impossible from the point of view which we are adopting. It imposes itself as long as consciousness is defined by the possession of certain "representations," for then the consciousness of the act is necessarily reduced to representation of its goal on the one hand and possibly to that of the bodily mechanisms which assure its execution on the other. The relation of means to end can be only external under these conditions.

But if, as we have just said, representative consciousness is only one of the forms of consciousness and if this latter is defined more generally by reference to an object – whether it be willed, desired, loved, or represented – the felt movements will be linked together by a practical intention which animates them, which makes of them a directed melody; and it becomes impossible to distinguish the goal and the means as separable elements, impossible to treat human action as another solution to the problems which instinct resolves: if the problems were *the same*, the solutions would be identical. An analysis of the immanent meaning of action and its internal structure is substituted for an analysis of the goals of action and their means.

From this new point of view one realizes that, although all actions permit an adaptation to life, the word "life" does not have the same meaning in animality and humanity; and the conditions of life are defined by the proper essence of the species. Doubtless, clothing and houses serve to protect us from the cold; language helps in collective work and in the analysis of the "unorganized mass." But the act of dressing becomes the act of adornment or also of modesty and thus reveals a new attitude toward oneself and others. Only men see that they are nude. In the house that he builds for himself, man projects and realizes his preferred values. Finally, the act of speaking expresses the fact that man ceases to adhere immediately to the milieu, that he elevates it to the status of spectacle and takes possession of it mentally by means of knowledge properly so called.

The conception which we are outlining will also allow us to integrate into consciousness the coefficient of reality which psychologists seek to introduce from the outside when they speak of a "reality function" or of a feeling of present reality. Consciousness of reality cannot be reduced to the reverberation in us of a motor accompaniment of our thoughts. And it is difficult to see how the adjunction of kinesthetic contents (which recalls the mental alchemy of associationism) could be sufficient to constitute the spectacle of a real world in which consciousness grasps itself as involved. There is a motor accompaniment of our thoughts without any doubt, but how the brute existence which it is supposed to make us feel is related to the perceived object must still be explained; clearly something in the visual spectacle itself must solicit this transfer. The fact is that every alteration of individual existences in consciousness manifests itself in a modification of the concrete appearance of the objects. A schizophrenic says: "See these roses; my wife would have found them beautiful; for me, they are a pile of leaves, petals, thorns and stems." The same thing is true of the "reality function" as of "reflex nativism," which thinks it is explaining the precocious perception of space by basing it on the fact of our becoming conscious of certain localizing reflexes, and of the classical theories, which would engender visual space from tactile space.

All of these hypothetical constructions presuppose what they want to explain since how and according to what criteria consciousness recognizes the correspondent of such and such a tactile or motor given in this or that visual given, for example, must still be explained – which implies finally a visual and even an inter-sensory organization of space. Likewise, awareness of an individual existence is not explained by the coupling of judgments which concern only an object of thought with a motor accompaniment charged with transforming the object into reality. It is in the phenomenal dimension of the perceived and in its intrinsic meaning that the existential index must be found, since *it is this* which appears to be real.

But this lived consciousness does not exhaust the human dialectic. What defines man is not the capacity to create a second nature – economic, social or cultural – beyond biological nature; it is rather the capacity of going beyond created structures in order to create others. And this movement is already visible in each of the particular products of human work. A nest is an object which has a meaning only in relation to the possible behavior of the organic individual; if a monkey picks a branch in order to reach a goal, it is because it is able to confer a functional value on an object of nature. But monkeys scarcely succeed at all in constructing instruments which would serve only for preparing others; we have seen that, having become a stick for the monkey, the tree branch is eliminated as such – which is the equivalent of saying that it is never possessed as an instrument in the full sense of the word. Animal activity reveals its limits in the two cases: it loses itself in the real transformations which it accomplishes and cannot reiterate them. For man, on the contrary, the tree branch which has become a stick will remain precisely a tree-branch-which-has-become-a-stick, the same *thing* in two different functions and visible *for him* under a plurality of aspects.

This power of choosing and varying points of view permits man to create instruments, not under the pressure of a *de facto* situation, but for a virtual use and especially in order to fabricate others. The meaning of human work therefore is the recognition, beyond the present milieu, of a world of things visible for each "I" under a plurality of aspects, the taking possession of an indefinite time and space; and one could easily show that the signification of speech or that of suicide and of the revolutionary act is the same. These acts of the human dialectic all reveal the same essence: the capacity of orienting onself in relation to the possible, to the mediate, and not in relation to a limited milieu; they all reveal what we called above, with Goldstein, the categorial attitude. Thus, the human dialectic is ambiguous: it is first manifested by the social or cultural structures, the appearance of which it brings about and in which it imprisons itself. *But its use-objects and its cultural objects would not be what they are if the activity which brings about their appearance did not also have as its meaning to reject them and to surpass them.*

Correlatively, perception, which until now has appeared to us to be the assimilation of consciousness into a cradle of institutions and a narrow circle of human "milieus," can become, especially by means of art, perception of a "universe." The knowledge of a truth is substituted for the experience of an immediate reality. "Man is a being who has the power of elevating to the status of objects the centers of resistance and reaction of his milieu . . . among which animals live entranced." But the knowledge of a universe will already be prefigured in lived perception, just as the negation of all the milieus is prefigured in the work which creates them. More generally, the life of consciousness outside of self which we have described above, on the one hand, and, on the other, the consciousness of self and of a universe, which we are reaching now – in Hegelian terms, consciousness in-itself (*en soi*) and consciousness in-and-for-itself (*en et pour soi*) – cannot be purely and simply juxtaposed. The problem of perception lies completely in this duality. . . .

Conclusion

In the preceding chapters we have considered the birth of behavior in the physical world and in an organism; that is, we have pretended to know nothing of man by reflection and have limited ourselves to developing what was implied in the scientific representation of his behavior. Aided by the notion of structure or form, we have arrived at the conclusion that both mechanism and finalism should be rejected and that the "physical," the "vital" and the "mental" do not represent three powers of being, but three dialectics. Physical nature in man is not subordinated to a vital principle, the organism does not conspire to actualize an idea, and the mental is not a motor principle *in* the body; but what we call nature is already consciousness of nature, what we call life is already consciousness of life and what we call mental is still an object vis-à-vis consciousness. Nevertheless, while establishing the ideality of the physical form, that of the organism, and that of the "mental," and *precisely because we did it*, we could not simply superimpose these three orders; not being a new substance, each of them had to be conceived as a retaking and a "new" structuration of the preceding one. From this comes the double aspect of the analysis which both liberated the higher from the lower and founded the former on the latter. It is this double relation which remains obscure and which now induces us to situate our results with respect to the classical solutions and in particular with respect to critical idealism. At the beginning we considered consciousness as a region of being and as a particular type of behavior. Upon analysis one finds it presupposed everywhere as the place of ideas and everywhere interconnected as the integration of existence. What then is the relation between consciousness as universal milieu and consciousness enrooted in the subordinated dialectics? Must the point of view of the "outside spectator" be abandoned as illegitimate to the benefit of an unconditioned reflection?

PART THREE – SELECTIONS FROM *THE PHENOMENOLOGY OF PERCEPTION*

As before, in extracting these passages from the translation of Merleau-Ponty's text I have omitted most of Merleau-Ponty's footnotes, since they mainly provide references to works of psychology and philosophy in French and German that have never been translated into English and are unlikely to be accessible to most readers of this book; I mention the most important of them in the works mentioned in the section 'Further Reading' at the end of this book. I have, however, retained the notes in which Merleau-Ponty adds something substantive to his discussion. I have also taken the liberty of breaking up Merleau-Ponty's text by inserting some section headings. These headings come from Merleau-Ponty's own description of the contents of the book, which, as is normal in French books, occurs right at the end of Phénoménologie de la perception (pp. 527–31). This material has never been included in an English translation of the book; but it provides very helpful signposts to guide the reader through Merleau-Ponty's long discussions. It is easy to work out from the original French text where these headings should occur, since Merleau-Ponty wrote very long paragraphs, often running over several pages, and as a general rule each heading in the description of contents fits where there is a break in these long paragraphs (the matter is less obvious from the English translation because the translator decided to break up Merleau-Ponty's long paragraphs into shorter ones). Anyone who has ever used Merleau-Ponty's text, or its translation, will, I think, appreciate the presence of these headings since they make it much easier to locate passages to which one wishes to return. In a few cases I have abbreviated Merleau-Ponty's headings, where they would otherwise make a statement whose length is excessive for its role as a heading.[1])

1 *For a full description and translation of Merleau-Ponty's table of contents, see D. Gurrière, 'Table of contents of "Phenomenology of Perception": translation and pagination',* Journal of the British Society for Phenomenology *10 (1979), pp. 65–9.*

PREFACE (*PP* vii–xxi [vii–xxiv])

This dense preface is not divided into sections with the new headings, since Merleau-Ponty did not provide any. Merleau-Ponty here sets out his own answer to the question 'What is phenomenology?', and thereby gives what is in effect a summary of the book. Phenomenology is to be, first of all, an attempt to 'reawaken' the basic experience of that world which precedes science and cannot be supplanted by science since it is this pre-scientific world that science seeks to rationalise and explain. Because the emphasis here is on the object of this basic experience, the pre-scientific world, phenomenology is not an idealist return to consciousness of our familiar world. Indeed there cannot be a complete return to consciousness, that is, a complete 'reduction' of the world. For there is no 'inner' self unrelated to a world: man is inescapably in the world. Thus phenomenology is the attempt to articulate the 'operative intentionality' that is antecedent to conscious thought of the world and thereby bring 'truth into being' by standing back from the intentional threads that normally bind us to the world.

What is phenomenology? It may seem strange that this question has still to be asked half a century after the first works of Husserl. The fact remains that it has by no means been answered. Phenomenology is the study of essences; and according to it, all problems amount to finding definitions of essences: the essence of perception, or the essence of consciousness, for example. But phenomenology is also a philosophy which puts essences back into existence, and does not expect to arrive at an understanding of man and the world from any starting point other than that of their 'facticity'. It is a transcendental philosophy which places in abeyance the assertions arising out of the natural attitude, the better to understand them; but it is also a philosophy for which the world is always 'already there' before reflection begins – as an inalienable presence; and all its efforts are concentrated upon re-achieving a direct and primitive contact with the world, and endowing that contact with a philosophical status. It is the search for a philosophy which shall be a 'rigorous science', but it also offers an account of space, time and the world as we 'live' them. It tries to give a direct description of our experience as it is, without taking account of its psychological origin and the causal explanations which the scientist, the historian or the sociologist may be able to provide. Yet Husserl in his last works mentions a 'genetic phenomenology' and even a 'constructive phenomenology'. One may try to do away with these contradictions by making a distinction between Husserl's and Heidegger's phenomenologies; yet the whole of *Sein und Zeit* springs from an indication given by Husserl and amounts to no more than an explicit account of the 'natürlicher Weltbegriff' or the 'Lebenswelt' which Husserl, towards the end of his life, identified as the central theme of phenomenology, with the result that the contradiction reappears in Husserl's own philosophy. The reader pressed for time will be inclined to give up the idea of covering a doctrine which says everything, and will wonder whether a philosophy which cannot define its scope deserves all the discussion which has gone on around it, and whether he is not faced rather by a myth or a fashion.

Even if this were the case, there would still be a need to understand the prestige of the myth and the origin of the fashion, and the opinion of the responsible philosopher must be that *phenomenology can be practised and identified as a manner or style of thinking, that it existed as a movement before arriving at complete awareness of itself as a philosophy.* It has been long on the way, and its adherents have discovered it in every quarter, certainly in Hegel and Kierkegaard, but equally in Marx, Nietzsche and Freud. A purely linguistic examination of the texts in question would yield no proof; we find in texts only what we put into them, and if ever any kind of history has suggested the interpretations which should be put on it, it is the history of philosophy. We shall find in ourselves, and nowhere else, the unity and true meaning of phenomenology. It is less a question of counting up quotations than of determining and expressing in concrete form this *phenomenology for ourselves* which has given a number of present-day readers the impression, on reading Husserl or Heidegger, not so much of encountering a new philosophy as of recognizing what they had been waiting for. Phenomenology is accessible only through a phenomenological method. Let us, therefore, try systematically to bring together the celebrated phenomenological themes as they have grown spontaneously together in life. Perhaps we shall then understand why phenomenology has for so long remained at an initial stage, as a problem to be solved and a hope to be realized.

It is a matter of describing, not of explaining or analysing. Husserl's first directive to phenomenology, in its early stages, to be a 'descriptive psychology', or to return to the 'things themselves', is from the start a rejection of science. I am not the outcome or the meeting-point of numerous causal agencies which determine my bodily or psychological make-up. I cannot conceive myself as nothing but a bit of the world, a mere object of biological, psychological or sociological investigation. I cannot shut myself up within the realm of science. All my knowledge of the world, even my scientific knowledge, is gained from my own particular point of view, or from some experience of the world without which the symbols of science would be meaningless. The whole universe of science is built upon the world as directly experienced, and if we want to subject science itself to rigorous scrutiny and arrive at a precise assessment of its meaning and scope, we must begin by reawakening the basic experience of the world of which science is the second-order expression. Science has not and never will have, by its nature, the same significance *qua* form of being as the world which we perceive, for the simple reason that it is a rationale or explanation of that world. I am, not a 'living creature' nor even a 'man', nor again even 'a consciousness' endowed with all the characteristics which zoology, social anatomy or inductive psychology recognize in these various products of the natural or historical process – I am the absolute source, my existence does not stem from my antecedents, from my physical and social environment; instead it moves out towards them and sustains them, for I alone bring into being for myself (and therefore into being in the only sense that the word can have for me) the tradition which I elect to carry on, or the horizon whose distance from me would be abolished – since that distance is not one of its properties – if I were not there to scan it with my gaze. Scientific points of view, according to which my existence is a moment of the world's, are always both naïve and at the same time dishonest, because they take for granted, without explicitly mentioning it, the other point of view, namely that of consciousness, through which from the outset a world forms itself round me and begins to exist for me. To return to things themselves is to return to that world which precedes knowledge, of which knowledge always *speaks*, and in relation to which every scientific schematization is an abstract and derivative sign-language, as is geography in relation to the countryside in which we have learnt beforehand what a forest, a prairie or a river is.

This move is absolutely distinct from the idealist return to consciousness, and the demand for a pure description excludes equally the procedure of analytical reflection on the one hand, and that of scientific explanation on the other. Descartes and particularly Kant *detached* the subject, or consciousness, by showing that I could not possibly apprehend anything as existing unless I first of all experienced myself as existing in the act of apprehending it. They presented consciousness, the absolute certainty of my existence for myself, as the condition of there being anything at all; and the act of relating as the basis of relatedness. It is true that the act of relating is nothing if divorced from the spectacle of the world in which relations are found; the unity of consciousness in Kant is achieved simultaneously with that of the world. And in Descartes methodical doubt does not deprive us of anything, since the whole world, at least in so far as we experience it, is reinstated in the *Cogito*, enjoying equal certainty, and simply labelled 'thought of . . .' But the relations between subject and world are not strictly bilateral: if they were, the certainty of the world would, in Descartes, be immediately given with that of the *Cogito*, and Kant would not have talked about his 'Copernican revolution'. Analytical reflection starts from our experience of the world and goes back to the subject as to a condition of possibility distinct from that experience, revealing the all-embracing synthesis as that without which there would be no world. To this extent it ceases to remain part of our experience and offers, in place of an account, a reconstruction. It is understandable, in view of this, that Husserl, having accused Kant of adopting a 'faculty psychologism', should have urged, in place of a noetic analysis which bases the world on the synthesizing activity of the subject, his own '*noematic reflection*' which remains within the object and, instead of begetting it, brings to light its fundamental unity.

The world is there before any possible analysis of mine, and it would be artificial to make it the outcome of a series of syntheses which link, in the first place sensations, then aspects of the object corresponding to different perspectives, when both are nothing but products of analysis, with no sort of prior reality. Analytical reflection believes that it can trace back the course followed by a prior constituting act and arrive, in the 'inner man' – to use Saint Augustine's expression – at a constituting power which has always been identical with that inner self. Thus reflection is carried away by itself and installs itself in an impregnable subjectivity, as yet untouched by being and time. But this is very ingenuous, or at least it is an incomplete form of reflection which loses sight of its own beginning. When I begin to reflect my reflection bears upon an unreflective experience; moreover my reflection cannot be unaware of itself as an event, and so it appears to itself in the light of a truly creative act, of a changed structure of consciousness, and yet it has to recognize, as having priority over its own operations, the world which is given to the subject because the subject is given to himself. The real has to be described, not constructed or formed. Which means that I cannot put perception into the same category as the syntheses represented by judgements, acts or predications. My field of perception is constantly filled with a play of colours, noises and fleeting tactile sensations which I cannot relate precisely to the context of my clearly perceived world, yet which I nevertheless immediately 'place' in the world, without ever confusing them with my daydreams. Equally constantly I weave dreams round things. I imagine people and things whose presence is not incompatible with the context, yet who are not in fact involved in it: they are ahead of reality, in the realm of the imaginary. If the reality of my perception were based solely on the intrinsic coherence of 'representations', it ought to be for ever hesitant and, being wrapped up in my conjectures on probabilities, I ought to be ceaselessly taking apart misleading syntheses, and reinstating in reality stray phenomena which I had excluded in the first place. But this does not happen. The real is a closely woven fabric. It does not await our judgement before incorporating the most surprising phenomena, or before rejecting the most plausible figments of our imagination. Perception is not a science of the world, it is not even an act, a deliberate taking up of a position; it is the background from which all acts stand out, and is presupposed by them. The world is not an object such that I have in my possession the law of its making; it is the natural setting of, and field for, all my thoughts and all my explicit perceptions. Truth does not 'inhabit' only 'the inner man',[1] or more accurately, there is no inner man, man is in the world, and only in the world does he know himself. When I return to myself from an excursion into the realm of dogmatic common sense or of science, I find, not a source of intrinsic truth, but a subject destined to the world.

All of which reveals the true meaning of the famous phenomenological reduction. There is probably no question over which Husserl spent more time – or to which he more often returned, since the 'problematic of reduction' occupies an important place in his unpublished work. For a long time, and even in recent texts, the reduction is presented as the return to a transcendental consciousness before which the world is spread out and completely transparent, quickened through and through by a series of apperceptions which it is the philosopher's task to reconstitute on the basis of their outcome. Thus my sensation of redness is *perceived as* the manifestation of a certain redness experienced, this in turn as the manifestation of a red surface, which is the manifestation of a piece of red cardboard, and this finally is the manifestation or outline of a red thing, namely this book. We are to understand, then, that it is the apprehension of a certain *hylè*, as indicating a phenomenon of a higher degree, the *Sinngebung*, of active meaning-giving operation which may be said to define consciousness, so that the world is nothing but 'world-as-meaning', and the phenomenological reduction is idealistic, in the sense that there is here a transcendental idealism which treats the world as an indivisible unity of value shared by Peter and Paul, in which their perspectives blend. 'Peter's consciousness' and 'Paul's consciousness' are in communication, the perception of the world 'by Peter' is not Peter's doing any more than its perception 'by Paul' is Paul's doing; in each case it is the doing of pre-personal forms of consciousness, whose communication raises no problem, since it is demanded by the very definition of consciousness, meaning or truth. In so far as I am a consciousness, that is, in so far as something has meaning for me, I am neither here nor there, neither Peter nor Paul; I am in no way distinguishable from an 'other' consciousness, since we are immediately in touch with the world and since the world is, by definition, unique, being the system in which all truths cohere. A logically consistent transcendental idealism rids the world of its opacity and its transcendence. The world is precisely that thing of which we form a representation, not as men or as empirical subjects, but in so far as we are all one light and participate in the One without destroying its unity. Analytical reflection knows nothing of the problem of other minds, or of that of the world, because it insists that with the first glimmer of consciousness there appears in me theoretically the power of reaching some universal truth, and that the other person, being equally without thisness, location or body, the Alter and the Ego are one and the same in the true world which is the unifier of minds. There is no difficulty in understanding how *I* can conceive the Other, because the I and consequently the Other are not conceived as part of the woven stuff of phenomena; they have validity rather than existence. There is nothing hidden behind these faces and gestures, no domain to which I have no access, merely a little shadow which owes its very existence to the light. For Husserl, on the contrary, it is well known that there is a problem of other people, and the *alter ego* is a paradox. If the other is truly for himself alone, beyond his being for me, and if we are for each other and not both for God, we must necessarily have some appearance for each other. He must and I must have an outer appearance, and there must be, besides the perspective of the For Oneself – my view of myself and the other's of himself – a perspective of For Others – my view of others and theirs of me. Of course, these two perspectives, in each one of us, cannot be simply juxtaposed, *for in that case it is not I that the other would see, nor he that I should see.* I must be the exterior that I present to others, and the body of the other must be the other himself. This paradox and the dialectic of the Ego and the Alter are possible only provided that the Ego and the Alter Ego are defined by their situation and are not freed from all inherence; that is, provided that philosophy does not culminate in a return to the self, and that I discover by reflection not only my presence to myself, but also the possibility of an 'outside spectator'; that is, again, provided that at the very moment when I experience my existence – at the ultimate extremity of reflection – I fall short of the ultimate density which would place me outside time, and that I discover within myself a kind of internal weakness standing in the way of my being totally individualized: a weakness which exposes me to the gaze of others as a man among men or at least as a consciousness among consciousnesses. Hitherto the *Cogito* depreciated the perception of others, teaching me as it did that the I is accessible only to itself, since it defined *me* as the thought which I have of myself, and which clearly I am alone in having, at least in this ultimate sense. For the 'other' to be more than an empty word, it is necessary that my existence should never be reduced to my bare awareness of existing, but that it should take in also the awareness that *one* may have of it, and thus include my incarnation in some nature and the possibility, at least, of a historical situation. The *Cogito* must reveal me in a situation, and it is on this condition alone that transcendental subjectivity can, as Husserl puts it, *be* an intersubjectivity. As a meditating Ego, I can clearly distinguish from myself the world and things, since I certainly do not exist in the way in which things exist. I must even set aside from myself my body understood as a thing among things, as a collection of physico-chemical processes. But even if the *cogitatio*, which I thus discover, is without location in objective time and space, it is not without place in the phenomenological world. The world, which I distinguished from myself as the totality of things or of processes linked by causal relationships, I rediscover 'in me' as the permanent horizon of all my *cogitationes* and as a dimension in relation to which I am constantly situating myself. The true *Cogito* does not define the subject's existence in terms of the thought he has of existing, and furthermore does not convert the indubitability of the world into the indubitability of thought about the world, nor finally does it replace the world itself by the world as meaning. On the contrary it recognizes my thought itself as an inalienable fact, and does away with any kind of idealism in revealing me as 'being-in-the-world'.

It is because we are through and through compounded of relationships with the world that for us the only way to become aware of the fact is to suspend the resultant activity, to refuse it our complicity (to look at it *ohne mitzumachen*, as Husserl often says), or yet again, to put it 'out of play'. Not because we reject the certainties of common sense and a natural attitude to things – they are, on the contrary, the constant theme of philosophy – but because, being the presupposed basis of any thought, they are taken for granted, and go unnoticed, and because in order to arouse them and bring them to view, we have to suspend for a moment our recognition of them. The best formulation of the reduction is probably that given by Eugen Fink, Husserl's assistant, when he spoke of 'wonder' in the face of the world. Reflection does not withdraw from the world towards the unity of consciousness as the world's basis; it steps back to watch the forms of transcendence fly up like sparks from a fire; it slackens the intentional threads which attach us to the world and thus brings them to our notice; it alone is consciousness of the world because it reveals that world as strange and paradoxical. Husserl's transcendental is not Kant's and Husserl accuses Kant's philosophy of being 'worldly', because it *makes use* of our relation to the world, which is the motive force of the transcendental deduction, and makes the world immanent in the subject, instead of *being filled with wonder* at it and conceiving the subject as a process of transcendence towards the world. All the misunderstandings with his interpreters, with the existentialist 'dissidents' and finally with himself, have arisen from the fact that in order to see the world and grasp it as paradoxical, we must break with our familiar acceptance of it and, also, from the fact that from this break we can learn nothing but the unmotivated upsurge of the world. The most important lesson which the reduction teaches us is the impossibility of a complete reduction. This is why Husserl is constantly re-examining the possibility of the reduction. If we were absolute mind, the reduction would present no problem. But since, on the contrary, we are in the world, since indeed our reflections are carried out in the temporal flux on to which we are trying to seize (since they *sich einströmen*, as Husserl says), there is no thought which embraces all our thought. The philosopher, as the unpublished works declare, is a perpetual beginner, which means that he takes for granted nothing that men, learned or otherwise, believe they know. It means also that philosophy itself must not take itself for granted, in so far as it may have managed to say something true; that it is an ever-renewed experiment in making its own beginning; that it consists wholly in the description of this beginning, and finally, that radical reflection amounts to a consciousness of its own dependence on an unreflective life which is its initial situation, unchanging, given once and for all. Far from being, as has been thought, a procedure of idealistic philosophy, phenomenological reduction belongs to existential philosophy: Heidegger's 'being-in-the-world' appears only against the background of the phenomenological reduction.

A misunderstanding of a similar kind confuses the notion of the 'essences' in Husserl. Every reduction, says Husserl, as well as being transcendental is necessarily eidetic. That means that we cannot subject our perception of the world to philosophical scrutiny without ceasing to be identified with that act of positing the world, with that interest in it which delimits us, without drawing back from our commitment which is itself thus made to appear as a spectacle, without passing from the *fact* of our existence to its *nature*, from the Dasein to the Wesen. But it is clear that the essence is here not the end, but a means, that our effective involvement in the world is precisely what has to be understood and made amenable to conceptualization, for it is what polarizes all our conceptual particularizations. The need to proceed by way of essences does not mean that philosophy takes them as its object, but, on the contrary, that our existence is too tightly held in the world to be able to know itself as such at the moment of its involvement, and that it requires the field of ideality in order to become acquainted with and to prevail over its facticity. The Vienna Circle, as is well known, lays it down categorically that we can enter into relations only with meanings. For example, 'consciousness' is not for the Vienna Circle identifiable with what we are. It is a complex meaning which has developed late in time, which should be handled with care, and only after the many meanings which have contributed, throughout the word's semantic development, to the formation of its present one have been made explicit. Logical positivism of this kind is the antithesis of Husserl's thought. Whatever the subtle changes of meaning which have ultimately brought us, as a linguistic acquisition, the word and concept of consciousness, we enjoy direct access to what it designates. For we have the experience of ourselves, of that consciousness which we are, and it is on the basis of this experience that all linguistic connotations are assessed, and precisely through it that language comes to have any meaning at all for us. 'It is that as yet dumb experience . . . which we are concerned to lead to the pure expression of its own meaning.' Husserl's essences are destined to bring back all the living relationships of experience, as the fisherman's net draws up from the depths of the ocean quivering fish and sea weed. Jean Wahl is therefore wrong in saying that 'Husserl separates essences from existence'. The separated essences are those of language. It is the office of language to cause essences to exist in a state of separation which is in fact merely apparent, since through language they still rest upon the antepredicative life of consciousness. In the silence of primary consciousness can be seen appearing not only what words mean, but also what things mean: the core of primary meaning round which the acts of naming and expression take shape.

Seeking the essence of consciousness will therefore not consist in developing the *Wortbedeutung* of consciousness and escaping from existence into the universe of things said; it will consist in rediscovering my actual presence to myself, the fact of my consciousness which is in the last resort what the word and the concept of consciousness mean. Looking for the world's essence is not looking for what it is as an idea once it has been reduced to a theme of discourse; it is looking for what it is as a fact for us, before any thematization. Sensationalism 'reduces' the world by noticing that after all we never experience anything but states of ourselves. Transcendental idealism too 'reduces' the world since, in so far as it guarantees the world, it does so by regarding it as thought or consciousness of the world, and as the mere correlative of our knowledge, with the result that it becomes immanent in consciousness and the aseity of things is thereby done away with. The eidetic reduction is, on the other hand, the determination to bring the world to light as it is before any falling back on ourselves has occurred, it is the ambition to make reflection emulate the unreflective life of consciousness. I aim at and perceive a world. If I said, as do the sensationalists, that we have here only 'states of consciousness', and if I tried to distinguish my perceptions from my dreams with the aid of 'criteria', I should overlook the phenomenon of the world. For if I am able to talk about 'dreams' and 'reality', to bother my head about the distinction between imaginary and real, and cast doubt upon the 'real', it is because this distinction is already made by me before any analysis; it is because I have an experience of the real as of the imaginary, and the problem then becomes one not of asking how critical thought can provide for itself secondary equivalents of this distinction, but of making explicit our primordial knowledge of the 'real', of describing our perception of the world as that upon which our idea of truth is forever based. We must not, therefore, wonder whether we really perceive a world, we must instead say: the world is what we perceive. In more general terms we must not wonder whether our self-evident truths are real truths, or whether, through some perversity inherent in our minds, that which is self-evident for us might not be illusory in relation to some truth in itself. For in so far as we talk about illusion, it is because we have identified illusions, and done so solely in the light of some perception which at the same time gave assurance of its own truth. It follows that doubt, or the fear of being mistaken, testifies as soon as it arises to our power of unmasking error, and that it could never finally tear us away from truth. We are in the realm of truth and it is 'the experience of truth' which is self-evident. To seek the essence of perception is to declare that perception is, not presumed true, but defined as access to truth. So, if I now wanted, according to idealistic principles, to base this *de facto* self-evident truth, this irresistible belief, on some absolute self-evident truth, that is, on the absolute clarity which my thoughts have for me; if I tried to find in myself a creative thought which bodied forth the framework of the world or illumined it through and through, I should once more prove unfaithful to my experience of the world, and should be looking for what makes that experience possible instead of looking for what it is. The self-evidence of perception is not adequate thought or apodeictic self-evidence. The world is not what I think, but what I live through. I am open to the world, I have no doubt that I am in communication with it, but I do not possess it; it is inexhaustible. 'There is a world', or rather: 'There is the world'; I can never completely account for this ever-reiterated assertion in my life. This facticity of the world is what constitutes the *Weltlichkeit der Welt*, what causes the world to be the world; just as the facticity of the *cogito* is not an imperfection in itself, but rather what assures me of my existence. The eidetic method is the method of a phenomenological positivism which bases the possible on the real.

We can now consider the notion of intentionality, too often cited as the main discovery of phenomenology, whereas it is understandable only through the reduction. 'All consciousness is consciousness of something'; there is nothing new in that. Kant showed, in the *Refutation of Idealism*, that inner perception is impossible without outer perception, that the world, as a collection of connected phenomena, is anticipated in the consciousness of my unity, and is the means whereby I come into being as a consciousness. What distinguishes intentionality from the Kantian relation to a possible object is that the unity of the world, before being posited by knowledge in a specific act of identification, is 'lived' as ready-made or already there. Kant himself shows in the *Critique of Judgement* that there exists a unity of the imagination and the understanding and a unity of subjects *before the object*, and that, in experiencing the beautiful, for example, I am aware of a harmony between sensation and concept, between myself and others, which is itself without any concept. Here the subject is no longer the universal thinker of a system of objects rigorously interrelated, the positing power who subjects the manifold to the law of the understanding, in so far as he is to be able to put together a world – he discovers and enjoys his own nature as spontaneously in harmony with the law of the understanding. But if the subject has a nature, then the hidden art of the imagination must condition the categorial activity. It is no longer merely the aesthetic judgement, but knowledge too which rests upon this art, an art which forms the basis of the unity of consciousness and of consciousness.

Husserl takes up again the *Critique of Judgement* when he talks about a teleology of consciousness. It is not a matter of duplicating human consciousness with some absolute thought which, from outside, is imagined as assigning to it its aims. It is a question of recognizing consciousness itself as a project of the world, meant for a world which it neither embraces nor possesses, but towards which it is perpetually directed – and the world as this pre-objective individual whose imperious unity decrees what knowledge shall take as its goal. This is why Husserl distinguishes between intentionality of act, which is that of our judgements and of those occasions when we voluntarily take up a position – the only intentionality discussed in the *Critique of Pure Reason* – and operative intentionality (*fungierende Intentionalität*), or that which produces the natural and antepredicative unity of the world and of our life, being apparent in our desires, our evaluations and in the landscape we see, more clearly than in objective knowledge, and furnishing the text which our knowledge tries to translate into precise language. Our relationship to the world, as it is untiringly enunciated within us, is not a thing which can be any further clarified by analysis; philosophy can only place it once more before our eyes and present it for our ratification.

Through this broadened notion of intentionality, phenomenological 'comprehension' is distinguished from traditional 'intellection', which is confined to 'true and immutable natures', and so phenomenology can become a phenomenology of origins. Whether we are concerned with a thing perceived, a historical event or a doctrine, to 'understand' is to take in the total intention – not only what these things are for representation (the 'properties' of the thing perceived, the mass of 'historical facts', the 'ideas' introduced by the doctrine) – but the unique mode of existing expressed in the properties of the pebble, the glass or the piece of wax, in all the events of a revolution, in all the thoughts of a philosopher. It is a matter, in the case of each civilization, of finding the Idea in the Hegelian sense, that is, not a law of the physico-mathematical type, discoverable by objective thought, but that formula which sums up some unique manner of behaviour towards others, towards Nature, time and death: a certain way of patterning the world which the historian should be capable of seizing upon and making his own. These are the *dimensions* of history. In this context there is not a human word, not a gesture, even one which is the outcome of habit or absent-mindedness, which has not some meaning. For example, I may have been under the impression that I lapsed into silence through weariness, or some minister may have thought he had uttered merely an appropriate platitude, yet my silence or his words immediately take on a significance, because my fatigue or his falling back upon a ready-made formula are not accidental, for they express a certain lack of interest, and hence some degree of adoption of a definite position in relation to the situation.

When an event is considered at close quarters, at the moment when it is lived through, everything seems subject to chance: one man's ambition, some lucky encounter, some local circumstance or other appears to have been decisive. But chance happenings offset each other, and facts in their multiplicity coalesce and show up a certain way of taking a stand in relation to the human situation, reveal in fact an *event* which has its definite outline and about which we can talk. Should the starting point for the understanding of history be ideology, or politics, or religion, or economics? Should we try to understand a doctrine from its overt content, or from the psychological make-up and the biography of its author? We must seek an understanding from all these angles simultaneously, everything has meaning, and we shall find this same structure of being underlying all relationships. All these views are true provided that they are not isolated, that we delve deeply into history and reach the unique core of existential meaning which emerges in each perspective. It is true, as Marx says, that history does not walk on its head, but it is also true that it does not think with its feet. Or one should say rather that it is neither its 'head' not its 'feet' that we have to worry about, but its body. All economic and psychological explanations of a doctrine are true, since the thinker never thinks from any starting point but the one constituted by what he is. Reflection even on a doctrine will be complete only if it succeeds in linking up with the doctrine's history and the extraneous explanations of it, and in putting back the causes and meaning of the doctrine in an existential structure. There is, as Husserl says, a 'genesis of meaning' (*Sinngenesis*), which alone, in the last resort, teaches us what the doctrine 'means.' Like understanding, criticism must be pursued at all levels, and naturally, it will be insufficient, for the refutation of a doctrine, to relate it to some accidental event in the author's life: its significance goes beyond, and there is no pure accident in existence or in co-existence, since both absorb random events and transmute them into the rational.

Finally, as it is indivisible in the present, history is equally so in its sequences. Considered in the light of its fundamental dimensions, all periods of history appear as manifestations of a single existence, or as episodes in a single drama – without our knowing whether it has an ending. Because we are in the world, we are *condemned to meaning*, and we cannot do or say anything without its acquiring a name in history.

Probably the chief gain from phenomenology is to have united extreme subjectivism and extreme objectivism in its notion of the world or of rationality. Rationality is precisely measured by the experiences in which it is disclosed. To say that there exists rationality is to say that perspectives blend, perceptions confirm each other, a meaning emerges. But it should not be set in a realm apart, transposed into absolute Spirit, or into a world in the realist sense. The phenomenological world is not pure being, but the sense which is revealed where the paths of my various experiences intersect, and also where my own and other people's intersect and engage each other like gears. It is thus inseparable from subjectivity and intersubjectivity, which find their unity when I either take up my past experiences in those of the present, or other people's in my own. For the first time the philosopher's thinking is sufficiently conscious not to anticipate itself and endow its own results with reified form in the world. The philosopher tries to conceive the world, others and himself and their interrelations. But the meditating Ego, the 'impartial spectator' (*uninteressierter Zuschauer*) do not rediscover an already given rationality, they 'establish themselves', and establish it, by an act of initiative which has no guarantee in being, its justification resting entirely on the effective power which it confers on us of taking our own history upon ourselves.

The phenomenological world is not the bringing to explicit

expression of a pre-existing being, but the laying down of being. Philosophy is not the reflection of a pre-existing truth, but, like art, the act of bringing truth into being. One may well ask how this creation is *possible*, and if it does not recapture in things a pre-existing Reason. The answer is that the only pre-existent Logos is the world itself, and that the philosophy which brings it into visible existence does not begin by being *possible*; it is actual or real like the world of which it is a part, and no explanatory hypothesis is clearer than the act whereby we take up this unfinished world in an effort to complete and conceive it. Rationality is not a *problem*. There is behind it no unknown quantity which has to be determined by deduction, or, beginning with it, demonstrated inductively. We witness every minute the miracle of related experiences, and yet nobody knows better than we do how this miracle is worked, for we are ourselves this network of relationships. The world and reason are not problematical. We may say, if we wish, that they are mysterious, but their mystery defines them: there can be no question of dispelling it by some 'solution', it is on the hither side of all solutions. True philosophy consists in relearning to look at the world, and in this sense a historical account can give meaning to the world quite as 'deeply' as a philosophical treatise. We take our fate in our hands, we become responsible for our history through reflection, but equally by a decision on which we stake our life, and in both cases what is involved is a violent act which is validated by being performed.

Phenomenology, as a disclosure of the world, rests on itself, or rather provides its own foundation. All knowledge is sustained by a 'ground' of postulates and finally by our communication with the world as primary embodiment of rationality. Philosophy, as radical reflection, dispenses in principle with this resource. As, however, it too is in history, it too exploits the world and constituted reason. It must therefore put to itself the question which it puts to all branches of knowledge, and so duplicate itself infinitely, being, as Husserl says, a dialogue or infinite meditation, and, in so far as it remains faithful to its intention, never knowing where it is going. The unfinished nature of phenomenology and the inchoative atmosphere which has surrounded it are not to be taken as a sign of failure, they were inevitable because phenomenology's task was to reveal the mystery of the world and of reason. If phenomenology was a movement before becoming a doctrine or a philosophical system, this was attributable neither to accident, nor to fraudulent intent. It is as painstaking as the works of Balzac, Proust, Valéry or Cézanne – by reason of the same kind of attentiveness and wonder, the same demand for awareness, the same will to seize the meaning of the world or of history as that meaning comes into being. In this way it merges into the general effort of modern thought.

Note

1   In te redi; in interiore homine habitat veritas (Saint Augustine).

PART I: THE BODY
INTRODUCTION (*PP* 67–72 [77–83])

In the introductory section, subtitled 'Experience and objective thought.
The problem of the body' Merleau-Ponty begins by characterising our
experience of the perspectival nature of vision, which naturally guides us
to its objects and leads us to form the conception of them as things
transcending our varied perceptions of them. Thus we are led down the
path of 'objective thought' to think of our perceptions as the products
of causal interaction between these things and our bodies, which are
themselves to be thought of merely as things located in objective
space. Against this natural tendency Merleau-Ponty seeks to reawaken
the 'ante-predicative knowledge' we have of our body, and, by showing
the inadequacy of any purely objective conception of it, to show
likewise the inadequacy of any purely objective conception of the world.

Experience and objective thought: the problem of the body

Our perception ends in objects, and the object once constituted, appears
as the reason for all the experiences of it which we have had or could
have. For example, I see the next-door house from a certain angle, but it
would be seen differently from the right bank of the Seine, or from the
inside, or again from an aeroplane: the house *itself* is none of these
appearances; it is, as Leibnitz said, the flat projection of these perspectives and of all possible perspectives, that is, the perspectiveless position
from which all can be derived, the house seen from nowhere. But what
do these words mean? Is not to see always to see from somewhere? To
say that the house itself is seen from nowhere is surely to say that it is

invisible! Yet when I say that I see the house with my own eyes, I am saying something that cannot be challenged: I do not mean that my retina and crystalline lens, my eyes as material organs, go into action and cause me to see it: with only myself to consult, I can know nothing about this. I am trying to express in this way a certain manner of approaching the object, the 'gaze' in short, which is as indubitable as my own thought, as directly known by me. We must try to understand how vision can be brought into being from somewhere without being enclosed in its perspective.

To see an object is either to have it on the fringe of the visual field and be able to concentrate on it, or else respond to this summons by actually concentrating upon it. When I do concentrate my eyes on it, I become anchored in it, but this coming to rest of the gaze is merely a modality of its movement: I continue inside one object the exploration which earlier hovered over them all, and in one movement I close up the landscape and open the object. The two operations do not fortuitously coincide: it is not the contingent aspects of my bodily make-up, for example the retinal structure, which force me to see my surroundings vaguely if I want to see the object clearly. Even if I knew nothing of rods and cones, I should realize that it is necessary to put the surroundings in abeyance the better to see the object, and to lose in background what one gains in focal figure, because to look at the object is to plunge oneself into it, and because objects form a system in which one cannot show itself without concealing others. More precisely, the inner horizon of an object cannot become an object without the surrounding objects becoming a horizon, and so vision is an act with two facets. For I do not identify the detailed object which I now have with that over which my gaze ran a few minutes ago, by expressly comparing these details with a memory of my first general view. When, in a film, the camera is trained on an object and moves nearer to it to give a close-up view, we can *remember* that we are being shown the ash tray or an actor's hand, we do not actually identify it. This is because the screen has no horizons. In normal vision, on the other hand, I direct my gaze upon a sector of the landscape, which comes to life and is disclosed, while the other objects recede into the periphery and become dormant, while, however, not ceasing to be there. Now, with them, I have at my disposal their horizons, in which there is implied, as a marginal view, the object on which my eyes at present fall. The horizon, then, is what guarantees the identity of the object throughout the exploration; it is the correlative of the impending power which my gaze retains over the objects which it has just surveyed, and which it already has over the fresh details which it is about to discover. No distinct memory and no explicit conjecture could fill this rôle: they would give only a probable synthesis, whereas my perception presents itself as actual. The object-horizon structure, or the perspective, is no obstacle to me when I want to see the object: for just as it is the means whereby objects are distinguished from each other, it is also the means whereby they are disclosed. To see is to enter a universe of beings which *display themselves*, and they would not do this if they could not be hidden behind each other or behind me. In other words: to look at an object is to inhabit it, and from this habitation to grasp all things in terms of the aspect which they present to it. But in so far as I see those things too, they remain abodes open to my gaze, and, being potentially lodged in them, I already perceive from various angles the central object of my present vision. Thus every object is the mirror of all others. When I look at the lamp on my table, I attribute to it not only the qualities visible from where I am, but also those which the chimney, the walls, the table can 'see'; but the back of my lamp is nothing but the face which it 'shows' to the chimney. I can therefore see an object in so far as objects form a system or a world, and in so far as each one treats the others round it as spectators of its hidden aspects and as guarantee of the permanence of those aspects. Any seeing of an object by me is instantaneously reiterated among all those objects in the world which are apprehended as co-existent, because each of them is all that the others 'see' of it. Our previous formula must therefore be modified; the house itself is not the house seen from nowhere, but the house seen from everywhere. The completed object is translucent, being shot through from all sides by an infinite number of present scrutinies which interesect in its depths leaving nothing hidden.

What we have just said about the spatial perspective could equally be said about the temporal. If I contemplate the house attentively and with no thought in my mind, it has something eternal about it, and an atmosphere of torpor seems to be generated by it. It is true that I see it from a certain point in my 'duration', but it is the same house that I saw yesterday when it was a day younger; it is the same house that either an old man or a child might behold. It is true, moreover, that age and change affect it, but even if it should collapse tomorrow, it will remain for ever true that it existed today: each moment of time calls all the others to witness; it shows by its advent 'how things were meant to turn out' and 'how it will all finish'; each present permanently underpins a point of time which calls for recognition from all the others, so that the object is seen at all times as it is seen from all directions and by the same means, namely the structure imposed by a horizon. The present still holds on to the immediate past without positing it as an object, and since the immediate past similarly holds its immediate predecessor, past time is wholly collected up and grasped in the present. The same is true of the imminent future which will also have its horizon of imminence. But with my immediate past I have also the horizon of futurity which surrounded it, and thus I have my actual present seen as the future of that past. With the imminent future, I have the horizon of past which will surround it, and therefore my actual present as the past of that future. Thus, through the double horizon of retention and protention, my present may cease to be a factual present quickly carried away and abolished by the flow of duration, and become a fixed and identifiable point in objective time.

But, once more, my human gaze never *posits* more than one facet of the object, even though by means of horizons it is directed towards all the others. It can never come up against previous appearances or those presented to other people otherwise than through the intermediary of time and language. If I conceive in the image of my own gaze those others which, converging from all directions, explore every corner of the house and define it, I have still only a harmonious and indefinite set of views of the object, but not the object in its plenitude. In the same way, although my present draws into itself time past and time to come, it possesses them only in intention, and even if, for example, the consciousness of my past which I now have seems to me to cover exactly the past as it was, the past which I claim to recapture is not the real past, but my past as I now see it, perhaps after altering it. Similarly in the future I may have a mistaken idea about the present which I now experience. Thus the synthesis of horizons is no more than a presumptive synthesis, operating with certainty and precision only in the immediate vicinity of the object. The remoter surrounding is no longer within my grasp; it is no longer composed of still discernible objects or memories; it is an anonymous horizon now incapable of bringing any precise testimony, and leaving the object as incomplete and open as it is indeed, in perceptual experience. Through this opening, indeed, the substantiality of the object slips away. If it is to reach perfect density, in other words if there is to be an absolute object, it will have to consist of an infinite number of different perspectives compressed into a strict co-existence, and to be presented as it were to a host of eyes all engaged in one concerted act of seeing. The house *has its* water pipes, *its* floor, perhaps its cracks which are insidiously spreading in the thickness of its ceilings. We never see them, but it *has them* along with its chimneys and windows which we can see. We shall forget our present perception of the house: every time we are able to compare our memories with the objects to which they refer, we are surprised, even allowing for other sources of error, at the changes which they owe to their own duration. But we still believe that there is a truth about the past; we base our memory on the world's vast Memory, in which the house has its place as it really was on that day, and which guarantees its *being* at this moment. Taken in itself – and as an object it demands to be taken thus – the object has nothing cryptic about it; it is completely displayed and its parts co-exist while our gaze runs from one to another, its present does not cancel its past, nor will its future cancel its present. The positing of the object therefore makes us go beyond the limits of our actual experience which is brought up against and halted by an alien being, with the result that finally experience believes that it extracts all its own teaching from the object. It is this *ek-stase*[1] of experience which causes all perception to be perception of something.

Obsessed with being, and forgetful of the perspectivism of my experience, I henceforth treat it as an object and deduce it from a relationship between objects. I regard my body, which is my point of view upon the world, as one of the objects of that world. My recent awareness of my gaze as a means of knowledge I now repress, and treat my eyes as bits of matter. They then take their place in the same objective space in which I am trying to situate the external object and I believe that I am producing the perceived perspective by the projection of the objects on my retina. In the same way I treat my own perceptual history as a result of my relationships with the objective world; my present, which is my point of view on time, becomes one moment of time among all the others, my duration a reflection or abstract aspect of universal time, as my body is a mode of objective space. In the same way, finally, if the objects which surround the house or which are found in it remained what they are in perceptual experience, that is, acts of seeing conditioned by a certain perspective, the house would not be posited as an autonomous being. Thus the positing of one single object, in the full sense, demands the compositive bringing into being of all these experiences in one act of manifold creation. Therein it exceeds perceptual experience and the synthesis of horizons – as the notion of a *universe*, that is to say, a completed and explicit totality, in which the relationships are those of reciprocal determination, exceeds that of a *world*, or an open and indefinite multiplicity of relationships which are of reciprocal implication. I detach myself from my experience and pass to the *idea*. Like the object, the idea purports to be the same for everybody, valid in all times and places, and the individuation of an object in an objective point of time and space finally appears as the expression of a universal positing power. I am no longer concerned with my body, nor with time, nor with the world, as I experience them in antepredicative knowledge, in the inner communion that I have with them. I now refer to my body only as an idea, to the universe as idea, to the idea of space and the idea of time. Thus 'objective' thought (in Kierkegaard's sense) is formed – being that of common sense and of science – which finally causes us to lose contact with perceptual experience, of which it is nevertheless the outcome and the natural sequel. The whole life of consciousness is characterized by the tendency to posit objects, since it is consciousness, that is to say self-knowledge, only in so far as it takes hold of itself and draws itself together in an indentifiable object. And yet the absolute positing of a single object is the death of consciousness, since it congeals the whole of existence, as a crystal placed in a solution suddenly crystallizes it.

We cannot remain in this dilemma of having to fail to understand either the subject or the object. We must discover the origin of the object at the very centre of our experience; we must describe the emergence of being and we must understand how, paradoxically, there is *for us* an *in-itself*. In order not to prejudge the issue, we shall take objective thought on its own terms and not ask it any questions which it does not ask itself. If we are led to rediscover experience behind it, this shift of ground will be attributable only to the difficulties which objective thought itself raises. Let us consider it then at work in the constitution of our body as object, since this is a crucial moment in the genesis of the objective world. It will be seen that one's own body evades, even within science itself, the treatment to which it is intended to subject it. And since the genesis of the objective body is only a moment in the constitution of the object, the body, by withdrawing from the objective world, will carry with it the intentional threads linking it to its surrounding and finally reveal to us the perceiving subject as the perceived world.

Note

1   Active transcendence of the subject in relation to the world. The author uses either the French word *extase*, or Heidegger's form *ek-stase*. The latter is the one used throughout this translation (Translator's note).

CHAPTER 1: THE BODY AS OBJECT AND MECHANISTIC PHYSIOLOGY (*PP* 73–89 [84–102])

In Chapter 1 Merleau-Ponty discusses the phenomenon of the 'phantom limb' and argues that this cannot be understood properly within the constraints of an objective, physiological, conception of the body. It demands the existential perspective of ourselves as agents with a repressed bodily memory of our previous, undamaged, being in the world. Merleau-Ponty enriches his discussion of this case by means of an illuminating comparison with the psychoanalytic conception of repression, and his discussion of this is indicative of the way in which he seeks to appropriate psychoanalytic insights while rejecting the quasi-scientific Freudian theory of the unconscious.

Neural physiology itself goes beyond causal thinking

The definition of the object is, as we have seen, that it exists *partes extra partes*, and that consequently it acknowledges between its parts, or between itself and other objects only external and mechanical relationships, whether in the narrow sense of motion received and transmitted, or in the wider sense of the relation of function to variable. Where it was desired to insert the organism in the universe of objects and thereby close off that universe, it was necessary to translate the functioning of the body into the language of the *in-itself* and discover, beneath behaviour, the linear dependence of stimulus and receptor, receptor and *Empfinder*. It was of course realized that in the circuit of behaviour new particular forms emerge, and the theory of specific nervous energy, for example, certainly endowed the organism with the power of transforming the physical world. But in fact it attributed to the nervous systems the occult power of creating the different structures of our experience, and whereas sight, touch and hearing are so many ways of gaining access to the object, these structures found themselves transformed into compact qualities derived from the local distinction between the organs used. Thus the relationship between stimulus and perception could remain clear and objective, and the psycho-physical event was of the same kind as the causal relations obtaining 'in the world'. Modern physiology no longer has recourse to these pretences. It no longer links the different qualities of one and the same sense, and the data of different senses, to distinct material instruments. In reality injuries to centres and even to conductors are not translated into the loss of certain qualities of sensation or of certain sensory data, but into loss of differentiation in the function. We have already discussed this: wherever the seat of the injury in the sensory routes and whatever its origin, one observes, for example, a decay of sensitivity to colour; at the beginning, all colours are affected, their basic shade remaining the same, but their saturation decreasing; then the spectrum is simplified and reduced to four colours: yellow, green, blue, crimson, and indeed all short-wave colours tend towards a kind of blue, all long-wave colours towards a kind of yellow, vision being liable, moreover, to vary from moment to moment, according to degree of fatigue. Finally a mono-chrome stage in grey is reached, although favourable conditions (con-trast, long exposure) may momentarily bring back dichromic sight. The progress of the lesion in the nervous tissue does not, therefore, destroy, one after another, ready-made sensory contents, but makes the active differentiation of stimuli, which appears to be the essential function of the nervous system, increasingly unreliable. In the same way, in the case of non-cortical injury to the sense of touch, if certain contents (temper-atures) are more easily destroyed and are the first to disappear, this is not because a determinate region, lost to the patient, enables us to feel heat and cold, since the specific sensation will be restored if a suf-ficiently extensive stimulus is applied; it is rather that the sensation succeeds in taking its typical form only under a more energetic stimu-lus. Central lesions seem to leave qualities intact; on the other hand they modify the spatial organization of data and the perception of objects. This is what had led to the belief in specialized gnosic centres for the localization and interpretation of qualities. In fact, modern research shows that central lesions have the effect in most cases of raising the chronaxies, which are increased to two or three times their normal strength in the patient. The excitation produces its effects more slowly, these survive longer, and the tactile perception of roughness, for example, is jeopardized in so far as it presupposes a succession of cir-cumscribed impressions or a precise consciousness of the different posi-tions of the hand. The vague localization of the stimulus is not explained by the destruction of a localizing centre, but by the reduction to a uni-form level of sensations, which are no longer capable of organizing themselves into a stable grouping in which each of them receives a univocal value and is translated into consciousness only by a limited change. Thus the excitations of one and the same sense differ less by reason of the material instrument which they use than in the way in which the elementary stimuli are spontaneously organized among themselves, and this organization is the crucial factor both at the level of sensible 'qualities' and at that of perception. It is this, and not the specific energy of the nervous apparatus examined, which causes an excitant to give rise to a tactile or thermic sensation. If a given area of skin is several times stimulated with a hair, the first perceptions are clearly distinguished and localized each time at the same point. As the stimulus is repeated, the localization becomes less precise, perception widens in space, while at the same time the sensation ceases to be specific: it is no longer a contact, but a feeling of burning, at one moment cold and at the next hot. Later still the patient thinks the stimulus is moving and describing a circle on his skin. Finally nothing more is felt. It follows that the 'sensible quality', the spatial limits set to the percept, and even the presence or absence of a perception, are not *de facto* effects of the situation outside the organism, but represent the way in which it meets stimulation and is related to it. An excitation is not perceived when it strikes a sensory organ which is not 'attuned' to it. The function of the organism in receiving stimuli is, so to speak, to 'conceive' a certain form of excitation. The 'psychophysical event' is therefore no longer of the type of 'worldly' causality, the brain becomes the seat of a process of 'patterning' which intervenes even before the cortical stage, and which, from the moment the nervous system comes into play, confuses the relations of stimulus to organism. The excitation is seized and reorganized by transversal functions which make it *resemble* the perception which it is *about to* arouse. I cannot envisage this form which is traced out in the nervous system, this exhibiting of a structure, as a set of processes in the third person, as the transmission of movement or as the determination of one variable by another. I cannot gain a removed knowledge of it. In so far as I guess what it may be, it is by abandoning the body as an object, *partes extra partes*, and by going back to the body which I experience at this moment, in the manner, for example, in which my hand moves round the object it touches, anticipating the stimuli and itself tracing out the form which I am about to perceive. I cannot understand the function of the living body except by enacting it myself, and except in so far as I am a body which rises towards the world.

The phenomenon of the phantom limb

Thus exteroceptivity demands that stimuli be given a shape; the consciousness of the body invades the body, the soul spreads over all its parts, and behaviour overspills its central sector. But one might reply that this 'bodily experience' is itself a 'representation', a 'psychic fact', and that as such it is at the end of a chain of physical and physiological events which alone can be ascribed to the 'real body'. Is not my body, exactly as are external bodies, an object which acts on receptors and finally gives rise to the consciousness of the body? Is there not an 'interoceptivity' just as there is an 'exteroceptivity'? Cannot I find in the body message-wires sent by the internal organs to the brain, which are installed by nature to provide the soul with the opportunity of feeling its body? Consciousness of the body, and the soul, are thus repressed. The body becomes the highly polished machine which the ambiguous notion of behaviour nearly made us forget. For example, if, in the case of a man who has lost a leg, a stimulus is applied, instead of to the leg, to the path from the stump to the brain, the subject will feel a phantom leg, because the soul is immediately linked to the brain and to it alone.

What has modern physiology to say about this? Anaesthesia with cocaine does not do away with the phantom limb, and there are cases of phantom limbs without amputation as a result of brain injury. Finally the imaginary limb is often found to retain the position in which the real arm was at the moment of injury: a man wounded in battle can still feel in his phantom arm the shell splinters that lacerated his real one. Is it then necessary to abandon the 'peripheral theory' in favour of a 'central theory'? But a central theory would get us no further if it added no more to the peripheral conditions of the imaginary limb than cerebral symptoms. For a collection of cerebral symptoms could not represent the relationships in consciousness which enter into the phenomenon. It depends indeed on 'psychic' determinants. An emotion, a circumstance which recalls those in which the wound was received, creates a phantom limb in subjects who had none. It happens that the imaginary arm is enormous after the operation, but that it subsequently shrinks and is absorbed into the stump 'as the patient consents to accept his mutilation'. The phenomenon of the phantom limb is here elucidated by that of anosognosia,[1] which clearly demands a psychological explanation. Subjects who systematically ignore their paralysed right hand, and hold out their left hand when asked for their right, refer to their paralysed arm as 'a long, cold snake', which rules out any hypothesis of real anaesthesia and suggests one in terms of the refusal to recognize their deficiency. Must we then conclude that the phantom limb is a memory, a volition or a belief, and, failing any physiological explanation, must we provide a psychological explanation for it? But no psychological explanation can overlook the fact that the severance of the nerves to the brain abolishes the phantom limb.

What has to be understood, then, is how the psychic determining factors and the physiological conditions gear into each other: it is not clear how the imaginary limb, if dependent on physiological conditions and therefore the result of a third person causality, can *in another context* arise out of the personal history of the patient, his memories, emotions and volitions. For in order that the two sets of conditions might together bring about the phenomenon, as two components bring about a resultant, they would need an identical point of application or a common ground, and it is difficult to see what ground could be common to 'physiological facts' which are in space and 'psychic facts' which are nowhere: or even to objective processes like nervous influxes which belong to the realm of the *in-itself*, and *cogitationes* such as acceptance and refusal, awareness of the past, and emotion, which are of the order of the *for-itself*. A hybrid theory of the phantom limb which found a place for both sets of conditions may, then, be valid as a statement of the known facts; but it is fundamentally obscure. The phantom limb is not the mere outcome of objective causality; no more is it a *cogitatio*. It could be a mixture of the two only if we could find a means of linking the 'psychic' and the 'physiological', the 'for-itself' and the 'in-itself', to each other to form an articulate whole, and to contrive some meeting-point for them: if the third person processes and the personal acts could be integrated into a common middle term.

Existence is between the 'psychic' and the 'physiological'
In order to describe the belief in the phantom limb and the unwillingness to accept mutilation, writers speak of a 'driving into the unconscious' or 'an organic repression' These un-Cartesian terms force us to form the idea of an organic thought through which the relation of the 'psychic' to the 'physiological' becomes conceivable. We have already met elsewhere, in the case of substitutions, phenomena which lie outside the alternatives of psychic and physiological, of final and mechanistic causes. When the insect, in the performance of an instinctive act, substitutes a sound leg for one cut off, it is not, as we saw, that a stand-by device, set up in advance, is automatically put into operation and substituted for the circuit which is out of action. But neither is it the case that the creature is aware of an aim to be achieved, using its limbs as various means, for in that case the substitution ought to occur every time the act is prevented, and we know that it does not occur if the leg is merely tied. The insect simply continues to belong to the same world and moves in it with all its powers. The tied limb is not replaced by the

free one, because it continues to count in the insect's scheme of things, and because the current of activity which flows towards the world still passes through it. There is in this instance no more choice than in the case of a drop of oil which uses all its strength to solve in practical terms the maximum and minimum problem which confronts it. The difference is simply that the drop of oil adapts itself to given external forces, while the insect itself projects the norms of its environment and itself lays down the terms of its vital problem; but here it is a question of an *a priori* of the species and not a personal choice. Thus what is found behind the phenomenon of substitution is the impulse of being-in-the-world, and it is now time to put this notion into more precise terms. When we say that an animal *exists*, that it *has* a world, or that it *belongs* to a world, we do not mean that it has a perception or objective consciousness of that world. The situation which unleashes instinctive operations is not entirely articulate and determinate, its total meaning is not possessed, as is adequately shown by the mistakes and the blindness of instinct. It presents only a practical significance; it asks for only bodily recognition; it is experienced as an 'open' situation, and 'requires' the animal's movements, just as the first notes of a melody requires a certain kind of resolution, without its being known in itself, and it is precisely what allows the limbs to be substituted for each other, and to be of equal value before the self-evident demands of the task. In so far as it anchors the subject to a certain 'environment', is 'being-in-the-world' something like 'attention to life' in Bergson or 'the function of the real' in P. Janet? Attention to life is the awareness we experience of 'nascent movements' in our bodies. Now reflex movements, whether adumbrated or executed, are still only objective processes whose course and results consciousness can observe, but in which it is not involved.[2] In fact the reflexes themselves are never blind processes: they adjust themselves to a 'direction' of the situation, and express our orientation towards a 'behavioural setting' just as much as the action of the 'geographical setting' upon us. They trace out from a distance the structure of the object without waiting for its point by point stimulation. It is this global presence of the situation which gives a meaning to the partial stimuli and causes them to acquire importance, value or existence for the organism. The reflex does not arise from objective stimuli, but moves back towards them, and invests them with a meaning which they do not possess taken singly as psychological agents, but only when taken as a situation. It causes them to exist as a situation, it stands in a 'cognitive' relation to them, which means that it shows them up as that which it is destined to confront. The reflex, in so far as it opens itself to the meaning of a situation, and perception; in so far as it does not first of all posit an object of knowledge and is an intention of our whole being, are modalities of a *pre-objective view* which is what we call being-in-the-world. Prior to stimuli and sensory contents, we must recognize a kind of inner diaphragm which determines, infinitely more than they do, what our reflexes and perceptions will be able to aim at in the world, the area of our possible operations, the scope of our life. Some subjects can come near to blindness without changing their 'world': they can be seen colliding with objects everywhere, but they are not aware of no longer being open to visual qualities, and the structure of their conduct remains unmodified. Other patients, on the other hand, lose their world as soon as its contents are removed; they abandon their habitual way of life even before it has become impossible, making themselves into premature invalids and breaking their vital contact with the world before losing sensory contact with it. There is, then, a certain consistency in our 'world', relatively independent of stimuli, which refuses to allow us to treat being-in-the-world as a collection of reflexes – a certain energy in the pulsation of existence, relatively independent of our voluntary thoughts, which prevents us from treating it as an *act* of consciousness. It is because it is a preobjective view that being-in-the-world can be distinguished from every third person process, from every modality of the *res extensa*, as from every *cogitatio*, from every first person form of knowledge – and that it can effect the union of the 'psychic' and the 'physiological'.

Ambiguity of the phantom limb

Let us return now to the problem with which we began. Anosognosia and the phantom limb lend themselves neither to a physiological nor to a psychological explanation, nor yet to a mixture of the two, though they can be related to the two sets of conditions. A physiological explanation would account for anosognosia and the phantom limb as the straightforward suppression or equally straightforward persistence of 'interoceptive' stimulations. According to this hypothesis, anosognosia is the absence of a fragment of representation which ought to be given, since the corresponding limb is there; the phantom limb is the presence of part of the representation of the body which should not be given, since the corresponding limb is not there. If one now gives a psychological account of the phenomena, the phantom limb becomes a memory, a positive judgement or a perception, while anosognosia becomes a bit of forgetfulness, a negative judgement or a failure to perceive. In the first case the phantom limb is the actual presence of a representation, anosognosia the actual absence of a representation. In the second case the phantom limb is the representation of an actual presence, whereas anosognosia is the representation of an actual absence. In both cases we are imprisoned in the categories of the objective world, in which there is no middle term between presence and absence. In reality the anosognosic is not simply ignorant of the existence of his paralysed limb: he can evade his deficiency only because he knows where he risks encountering it, just as the subject, in psychoanalysis, knows what he does not want to face, otherwise he would not be able to avoid it so successfully. We do not understand the absence or death of a friend until the time comes when we expect a reply from him and when we realize that we shall never again receive one; so at first we avoid asking in order not to have to notice this silence; we turn aside from those areas of our life in which we might meet this nothingness, but this very fact necessitates that we intuit them. In the same way the anosognosic leaves his paralysed arm out of account in order not to have to feel his handicap, but this means that he has a preconscious knowledge of it. It is true that in the case of the phantom limb the subject appears to be unaware of the mutilation and relies on his imaginary limb as he would on a real one, since he tries to walk with his phantom leg and is not discouraged even by a fall. But he can describe quite well, in spite of this, the peculiarities of the phantom leg, for example its curious motility, and if he treats it in practice as a real limb, this is because, like the normal subject, he has no need, when he wants to set off walking, of a clear and articulate perception of his body: it is enough for him to have it 'at his disposal' as an undivided power, and to sense the phantom limb as vaguely involved in it. The consciousness of the phantom limb remains, then, itself unclear. The man with one leg feels the missing limb in the same way as I feel keenly the existence of a friend who is, nevertheless, not before my eyes; he has not lost it because he continues to allow for it, just as Proust can recognize the death of his grandmother, yet without losing her, as long as he can keep her on the horizon of his life. The phantom arm is not a representation of the arm, but the ambivalent presence of an arm. The refusal of mutilation in the case of the phantom limb, or the refusal of disablement in anosognosia are not deliberate decisions, and do not take place at the level of positing consciousness which takes up its position explicitly after considering various possibilities. The will to have a sound body or the rejection of an infirm one are not formulated for themselves; and the awareness of the amputated arm as present or of the disabled arm as absent is not of the kind: 'I think that . . .'

This phenomenon, distorted equally by physiological and psychological explanations, is, however, understood in the perspective of being-in-the-world. What it is in us which refuses mutilation and disablement is an *I* committed to a certain physical and inter-human world, who continues to tend towards his world despite handicaps and amputations and who, to this extent, does not recognize them *de jure*. The refusal of the deficiency is only the obverse of our inherence in a world, the implicit negation of what runs counter to the natural momentum which throws us into our tasks, our cares, our situation, our familiar horizons. To have a phantom arm is to remain open to all the actions of which the arm alone is capable; it is to retain the practical field which one enjoyed before mutilation. The body is the vehicle of being in the world, and having a body is, for a living creature, to be intervolved in a definite environment, to identify oneself with certain projects and be continually committed to them. In the self-evidence of this complete world in which manipulatable objects still figure, in the force of their movement which still flows towards him, and in which is still present the project of writing or playing the piano, the cripple still finds the guarantee of his wholeness. But in concealing his deficiency from him, the world cannot fail simultaneously to reveal it to him: for if it is true that I am conscious of my body *via* the world, that it is the unperceived term in the centre of the world towards which all objects turn their face, it is true for the same reason that my body is the pivot of the world: I know that objects have several facets because I could make a tour of inspection of them, and in that sense I am conscious of the world through the medium of my body. It is precisely when my customary world arouses in me habitual intentions that I can no longer, if I have lost a limb, be effectively drawn into it, and the utilizable objects, precisely in so far as they present themselves as utilizable, appeal to a hand which I no longer have. Thus are delimited, in the totality of my body, regions of silence. The patient therefore realizes his disability precisely in so far as he is ignorant of it, and is ignorant of it precisely to the extent that he knows of it. This paradox is that of all being in the world: when I move towards a world I bury my perceptual and practical intentions in objects which ultimately appear prior to and external to those intentions, and which nevertheless exist for me only in so far as they arouse in me thoughts or volitions. In the case under consideration, the ambiguity of knowledge amounts to this: our body comprises as it were two distinct layers, that of the habit-body and that of the body at this moment. In the first appear manipulatory movements which have disappeared from the second, and the problem how I can have the sensation of still possessing a limb which I no longer have amounts to finding out how the habitual body can act as guarantee for the body at this moment. How can I perceive objects as manipulatable when I can no longer manipulate them? The manipulatable must have ceased to be what I am now manipulating, and become what *one* can manipulate; it must have ceased to be a thing *manipulatable for me* and become a thing *manipulatable in itself.* Correspondingly, my body must be apprehended not only in an experience which is instantaneous, peculiar to itself and complete in itself, but also in some general aspect and in the light of an impersonal being.

'Organic repression' and the body as an inborn complex

In that way the phenomenon of the phantom limb is absorbed into that of repression, which we shall find throwing some light on it. For repression, to which psycho-analysis refers, consists in the subject's entering upon a certain course of action – a love affair, a career, a piece of work – in his encountering on this course some barrier, and, since he has the strength neither to surmount the obstacle nor to abandon the enterprise, he remains imprisoned in the attempt and uses up his strength indefinitely renewing it in spirit. Time in its passage does not carry away with it these impossible projects; it does not close up on traumatic experience; the subject remains open to the same impossible future, if not in his explicit thoughts, at any rate in his actual being. One present among all presents thus acquires an exceptional value; it displaces the others and deprives them of their value as authentic presents. We continue to be the person who once entered on this adolescent affair, or the one who once lived in this parental universe. New perceptions, new emotions even, replace the old ones, but this process of renewal touches only the content of our experience and not its structure. Impersonal time continues its course, but personal time is arrested. Of course this fixation does not merge into memory; it even excludes memory in so far as the latter spreads out in front of us, like a picture, a former experience, whereas this past which remains our true present does not leave us but remains constantly hidden behind our gaze instead of being displayed before it. The traumatic experience does not survive as a representation in the mode of objective consciousness and as a 'dated' moment; it is of its essence to survive only as a manner of being and with a certain degree of generality. I forgo my constant power of providing myself with 'worlds' in the interest of one of them, and for that very reason this privileged world loses its substance and eventually becomes no more than *a certain dread*. All repression is, then, the transition from first person existence to a sort of abstraction of that existence, which lives on a former experience, or rather on the memory of having had the memory, and so on, until finally only the essential form remains. Now as an advent of the impersonal, repression is a universal phenomenon, revealing our condition as incarnate beings by relating it to the temporal structure of being in the world. To the extent that I have 'sense organs', a 'body', and 'psychic functions' comparable with other men's, each of the moments of my experience ceases to be an integrated and strictly unique totality, in which details exist only in virtue of the whole; I become the meeting point of a host of 'causalities'. In so far as I inhabit a 'physical world', in which consistent 'stimuli' and typical situations recur – and not merely the historical world in which situations are never exactly comparable – my life is made up of rhythms which have not their *reason* in what I have chosen to be, but their *condition* in the humdrum setting which is mine. Thus there appears round our personal existence a margin of *almost* impersonal existence, which can be practically taken for granted, and which I rely on to keep me alive; round the human world which each of us has made for himself is a world in general terms to which one must first of all belong in order to be able to enclose oneself in the particular context of a love or an ambition. Just as we speak of repression in the limited sense when I retain through time one of the momentary worlds through which I have lived, and make it the formative element of my whole life – so it can be said that my organism, as a prepersonal cleaving to the general form of the world, as an anonymous and general existence, plays, beneath my personal life, the part of an *inborn complex*. It is not some kind of inert thing; it too has something of the momentum of existence. It may even happen when I am in danger that my human situation abolishes my biological one, that my body lends itself without reserve to action.[3] But these moments can be no more than moments,[4] and for most of the time personal existence represses the organism without being able either to go beyond it or to renounce itself; without, in other words, being able either to reduce the organism to its existential self, or itself to the organism. While I am overcome by some grief and wholly given over to my distress, my eyes already stray in front of me, and are drawn, despite everything, to some shining object, and thereupon resume their autonomous existence. Following upon that minute into which we wanted to compress our whole life, time, or at least, prepersonal time, begins once more to flow, carrying away, if not our resolution, at least the heartfelt emotions which sustained it. Personal existence is intermittent and when this tide turns and recedes, decision can henceforth endow my life with only an artificially induced significance. The fusion of soul and body in the act, the sublimation of biological into personal exist-ence, and of the natural into the cultural world is made both possible and precarious by the temporal structure of our experience. Every pres-ent grasps, by stages, through its horizon of immediate past and near future, the totality of possible time; thus does it overcome the dispersal of instants, and manage to endow our past itself with its definitive meaning, re-integrating into personal existence even that past of all pasts which the stereotyped patterns of our organic behaviour seem to suggest as being at the origin of our volitional being. In this context even reflexes have a meaning, and each individual's style is still visible in them, just as the beating of the heart is felt as far away as the body's periphery. But this power naturally belongs to all presents, the old no less than the new. Even if we claim to have a better understanding of our past than it had of itself, it can always reject our present judgement and shut itself up in its own autonomous self-evidence. It necessarily does so in so far as I conceive it as a former present. Each present may claim to solidify our life, and indeed that is what distinguishes it as the present. In so far as it presents itself as the totality of being and fills an instant of consciousness, we never extricate ourselves completely from it, time never completely closes over it and it remains like a wound through which our strength ebbs away. It can now be said that, *a fortiori*, the specific past, which our body is, can be recaptured and taken up by an individual life only because that life has never transcended it, but secretly nourishes it, devoting thereto part of its strength, because its present is still that past. This can be seen in cases of illness in which bodily events become the events of the day. What enables us to centre our existence is also what prevents us from centring it completely, and the anonymity of our body is inseparably both freedom and servitude. Thus, to sum up, the ambiguity of being-in-the-world is translated by that of the body, and this is understood through that of time.

We shall return later to the question of time. Let it merely be noted for the moment that starting with this central phenomenon the rela-tionships between the 'psychic' and the 'physiological' become con-ceivable. Why can the memories recalled to the one-armed man cause the phantom arm to appear? The phantom arm is not a recollection, it is a quasi-present and the patient feels it now, folded over his chest, with no hint of its belonging to the past. Nor can we suppose that the image of an arm, wandering through consciousness, has joined itself to the stump: for then it would not be a 'phantom', but a renascent perception. The phantom arm must be that same arm, lacerated by shell splinters, its visible substance burned or rotted somewhere, which appears to haunt the present body without being absorbed into it. The imaginary arm is, then, like repressed experience, a former present which cannot decide to recede into the past. The memories called up before the patient induce in him a phantom limb, not as an image in associationism summons up another image, but because any memory reopens time lost to us and invites us to recapture the situation evoked. Intellectual memory, in Proust's sense, limits itself to a description of the past, a past as idea, from which it extracts 'characteristics' or communicable meaning rather than discovering a structure. But it would not be memory if the object which it constructs were not still held by a few intentional threads to the horizon of the lived-through past, and to that past itself as we should rediscover it if we were to delve beyond these horizons and reopen time. In the same way, if we put back emotion into being-in-the-world, we can understand how it can be the origin of the phantom limb. To feel emotion is to be involved in a situation which one is not managing to face and from which, nevertheless, one does not want to escape. Rather than admit failure or retrace one's steps, the subject, caught in this existential dilemma, breaks in pieces the objective world which stands in his way and seeks symbolical satisfaction in magic acts.[5] The ruin of the objective world, abandonment of true action, flight into a self-contained realm are conditions favouring the illusion of those who have lost a limb in that it too presupposes the erasure of reality. In so far as memory and emotion can call up the phantom limb, this is not comparable to the action of one *cogitatio* which necessitates another *cogitatio*, or that of one condition bringing about its consequence. It is not that an ideal causality here superimposes itself on a physiological one, it is that an existential attitude motivates another and that memory, emotion and phantom limb are equivalents in the context of being in the world.

Now why does the severing of the afferent nerves banish the phantom limb? In the perspective of being in the world this fact means that the impulses arriving from the stump keep the amputated limb in the circuit of existence. They establish and maintain its place, prevent it from being abolished, and cause it still to count in the organism. They keep empty an area which the subject's history fills, they enable the latter to build up the phantom, as structural disturbances allow the content of psychosis to form into delirium. From our point of view, a sensori-motor circuit is, within our comprehensive being in the world, a relatively autonomous current of existence. Not that it always brings to our total being a separable contribution, but because under certain circumstances it is possible to bring to light constant responses to stimuli which are themselves constant. The question is, therefore, how the refusal of the deficiency, which is a total attitude of our existence, needs for its expression such a highly specialized modality as a sensori-motor circuit, and why our being-in-the-world, which provides all our reflexes with their meaning, and which is thus their basis, nevertheless delivers itself over to them and is finally based upon them. Indeed, as we have shown elsewhere, sensori-motor circuits are all the more clearly marked as one is concerned with more integrated existences, and the reflex in its pure state is to be found only in man, who has not only a setting (*Umwelt*), but also a world (*Welt*).

From the existential point of view, these two facts, which scientific induction contents itself with setting side by side, are linked internally and are understood in the light of one and the same idea. If man is not to be embedded in the matrix of that syncretic setting in which animals lead their lives in a sort of *ek-stase*, if he is to be aware of a world as the common reason for all settings and the theatre of all patterns of behaviour, then between himself and what elicits his action a distance must be set, and, as Malebranche put it, forms of stimulation from outside must henceforth impinge on him 'respectfully'; each momentary situation must cease to be, for him, the totality of being, each particular response must no longer fill his whole field of action. Furthermore, the elaboration of these responses, instead of occurring at the centre of his existence, must take place on the periphery and finally the responses themselves must no longer demand that on each occasion some special position be taken up, but they must be outlined once and for all in their generality. Thus it is by giving up part of his spontaneity, by becoming involved in the world through stable organs and pre-established circuits that man can acquire the mental and practical space which will theoretically free him from his environment and allow him to *see* it. And provided that even the realization of an objective world is set in the realm of existence, we shall no longer find any contradiction between it and bodily conditioning: it is an inner necessity for the most integrated existence to provide itself with an habitual body. What allows us to link to each other the 'physiological' and the 'psychic', is the fact that, when reintegrated into existence, they are no longer distinguishable respectively as the order of the *in-itself*, and that of the *for-itself*, and that they are both directed towards an intentional pole or towards a world. Probably the two histories never quite coincide: one is common-place and cyclic, the other may be open and unusual, and it would be necessary to keep the term 'history' for the second order of phenomena if history were a succession of events which not only have a meaning, but furnish themselves with it. However, failing a true revolution which breaks up historical categories so far valid, the figure in history does not create his part completely: faced with typical situations he takes typical decisions and Nicholas II, repeating the very words of Louis XVI, plays the already written part of established power in face of a new power. His decisions translate the *a priori* of a threatened prince as our reflexes translate a specific *a priori*. These stereotypes, moreover, are not a des-tiny, and just as clothing, jewellery and love transfigure the biological needs from which they arise, in the same way within the cultural world the historical *a priori* is constant only for a given phase and provided that the balance of *forces* allows the same *forms* to remain. So history is neither a perpetual novelty, nor a perpetual repetition, but the *unique* movement which creates stable forms and breaks them up. The organ-ism and its monotonous dialectical processes are therefore not alien to history and as it were inassimilable to it. Man taken as a concrete being is not a psyche joined to an organism, but the movement to and fro of existence which at one time allows itself to take corporeal form and at others moves towards personal acts. Psychological motives and bodily occasions may overlap because there is not a single impulse in a living body which is entirely fortuitous in relation to psychic intentions, not a single mental act which has not found at least its germ or its general outline in physiological tendencies. It is never a question of the incomprehensible meeting of two causalities, nor of a collision between the order of causes and that of ends. But by an imperceptible twist an organic process issues into human behaviour, an instinctive act changes direction and becomes a sentiment, or conversely a human act becomes torpid and is continued absent-mindedly in the form of a reflex. Between the psychic and the physiological there may take place exchanges which almost always stand in the way of defining a mental disturbance as psychic *or* somatic. The disturbance described as somatic produces, on the theme of the organic accident, tentative psychic commentaries, and the 'psychic' trouble confines itself to elaborating the human signifi-cance of the bodily event. A patient feels a second person implanted in his body. He is a man in half his body, a woman in the other half. How are we to distinguish in this symptom the physiological causes and psychological motives? How are we to associate the two explanations and how imagine any point at which the two determinants meet? 'In symptoms of this kind, the psychic and the physical are so intimately linked that it is unthinkable to try to complete one of these functional domains by the other, and that both must be subsumed under a third . . . (We must) . . . move on from knowledge of psychological and physiological facts to a recognition of the animic event as a vital process inherent in our existence'. Thus, to the question which we were asking, modern physiology gives a very clear reply: the psycho-physical event can no longer be conceived after the model of Cartesian physiology and as the juxtaposition of a process in itself and a *cogitatio*. The union of soul and body is not an amalgamation between two mutually external terms, subject and object, brought about by arbitrary decree. It is enacted at every instant in the movement of existence. We found existence in the body when we approached it by the first way of access, namely through physiology. We may therefore at this stage examine this first result and make it more explicit, by questioning existence this time on its own nature, which means, by having recourse to psychology.

Notes

1 Failure or refusal on the patient's part to recognize the existence of a disease or disability (Translator's note).

2 When Bergson stresses the unity of perception and action and invents, for its expression, the term 'sensory-motor process', he is clearly seeking to involve consciousness in the world. But if feeling is representing a quality to oneself, and if movement is changing one's position in the objective world, then between sensation and movement, even taken in their nascent state, no *compromise* is possible, and they are distinct from each other as are the *for-itself* and the *in-itself*. Generally speaking, Bergson saw that the body and the mind communicate with each other through the medium of time, that to be a mind is to stand above time's flow and that to have a body is to have a present. The body, he says, is an instantaneous section made in the becoming of consciousness (*Matière et Mémoire*, p. 150). But the body remains for him what we have called the objective body; consciousness remains knowledge; time remains a successive 'now', whether it 'snowballs upon itself' or is spread in spatialized time. Bergson can therefore only compress or expand the series of 'present moments'; he never reaches the unique movement whereby the three dimensions of time are constituted, and one cannot see why duration is squeezed into a present, or why consciousness becomes involved in a body and a world.

As for the 'function of the real', P. Janet *uses* it as an existential notion. This is what enables him to sketch out a profound theory of emotion as the collapse of our customary being, and a flight from our world. (Cf. for example the interpretation of the fit of hysterics, *De l'Angoisse à l'Extase*, T. II, pp. 450 and ff.) But this theory of emotion is not followed out and, as J.-P. Sartre shows, it conflicts, in the writings of P. Janet, with a mechanistic conception rather close to that of James: the collapse of our existence into emotion is treated as a mere *derivation* from psychological forces, and the emotion itself as the consciousness of this process expressed in the third person, so that there is no longer reason to look for a meaning in the emotional behaviour which is the result of the blind momentum of the tendencies, and we return to dualism. (Cf. J.-P. Sartre, *Sketch for a Theory of the Emotions.*) P. Janet, moreover, treats psychological tension – that is, the movement whereby we spread our 'world' before us – expressly as a representative hypothesis; so he is far from considering it in general terms as the concrete essence of man, though he does so implicitly in particular analyses.

3 Thus Saint-Exupéry, above Arras, with shells bursting all round him, can no longer feel as a thing distinct from him his body which shortly before seemed to escape him: 'It is as if my life were given to me every second, as if my life became every moment more keenly felt. I live. I am alive. I am still alive. I am always alive. I am now nothing but a source of life.' *Pilote de Guerre*, p. 174.

4 'But it is true that, in the course of my life, when not in the grip of urgency, when my meaning is not at stake, I can see no more serious problems than those raised by my body.' A. de Saint-Exupéry, *Pilote de Guerre*, p. 169.

5 Cf. J.-P. Sartre, *Sketch for a Theory of the Emotions.*

FROM CHAPTER 3: THE SPATIALITY OF ONE'S OWN BODY AND MOTILITY (*PP* 98–109 [112–25], 120–7 [138–47], 134–9 [155–61], 146–7 [169–70])

Merleau-Ponty begins Chapter 3 by introducing the concept of the 'body-image'. He argues that this cannot be understood simply as a region within the context of normal objective space; instead, for each of us, our body-image, or body-space, is to be understood as a background to our practical capacity to organise our bodily movements. He then extends his argument by introducing the case of Schneider, a German soldier wounded in the First World War, whose strange disabilities were recorded and studied by the German psychologists A. Gelb and K. Goldstein. Schneider can undertake habitual 'concrete' actions such as swatting a mosquito which is biting him; but when asked to perform apparently similar 'abstract' actions, such as pointing to a place on his body which is being touched, he has somehow to activate the appropriate region, to induce 'quiverings of the skin'. Merleau-Ponty's preliminary suggestion is that what underlies this difference is Schneider's inability to engage in non-serious, hypothetical, courses of action. He then discusses, and rejects, Goldstein's suggestion that this is to be explained by his 'loss of visual content' (this discussion is not reproduced here); likewise, he argues, Schneider's problem cannot be explained in terms of a loss of a power of 'consciousness', at least where this is thought of as a completely rational faculty. Instead, he argues, we need a 'genetic phenomenology' which will enable us to identify a domain of 'motility' which falls between pure thought and blind causation. Merleau-Ponty claims that this domain comprises a kind of basic intentionality which normally supports the life of consciousness by projecting other times and other possibilities around us, thereby constituting our basic being in the world. It is this basic intentionality which has 'gone limp' in the case of Schneider, whose impaired situation precisely reveals our normal bodily 'imposition of meaning'.

The body image

Let us first of all describe the spatiality of my own body. If my arm is resting on the table I should never think of saying that it is *beside* the ash-tray in the way in which the ash-tray is beside the telephone. The outline of my body is a frontier which ordinary spatial relations do not cross. This is because its parts are inter-related in a peculiar way: they are not spread out side by side, but enveloped in each other. For example, my hand is not a collection of points. In cases of allocheiria,[1] in which the subject feels in his right hand stimuli applied to his left hand, it is impossible to suppose that each of the stimulations changes its spatial value on its own account. The various points on the left hand are transferred to the right as relevant to a total organ, a hand without parts which has been suddenly displaced. Hence they form a system and the space of my hand is not a mosaic of spatial values. Similarly my whole body for me is not an assemblage of organs juxtaposed in space. I am in undivided possession of it and I know where each of my limbs is through a *body image* in which all are included. But the notion of body image is ambiguous, as are all notions which make their appearance at turning points in scientific advance. They can be fully developed only through a reform of methods. At first, therefore, they are used only in a sense which falls short of their full sense, and it is their immanent development which bursts the bounds of methods hitherto used. 'Body image' was at first understood to mean a *compendium* of our bodily experience, capable of giving a commentary and meaning to the internal impressions and the impression of possessing a body at any moment. It was supposed to register for me the positional changes of the parts of my body for each movement of one of them, the position of each local stimulus in the body as a whole, an account of the movements performed at every instant during a complex gesture, in short a continual translation into visual language of the kinaesthetic and articular impressions of the moment. When the term body image was first used, it was thought that nothing more was being introduced than a convenient name for a great many associations of images, and it was intended merely to convey the fact that these associations were firmly established and constantly ready to come into play. The body image was supposed gradually to show itself through childhood in proportion as the tactile, kinaesthetic and articular contents were associated among themselves or with visual contents, and more easily evoked them. Its physiological representation could then be no more than a focus of images in the classical sense. Yet in the use made of it by psychologists, it is clear that the body image does not fit into this associationist definition. For example, in order that the body image may elucidate allocheiria, it is not enough that each sensation of the left hand should take its place among generic images of all parts of the body acting in association to form around the left hand, as it were, a superimposed *sketch* of the body; these associations must be constantly subject to a unique law, the spatiality of the body must work downwards from the whole to the parts, the left hand and its position must be implied in a comprehensive bodily *purpose* and must originate in that purpose, so that it may at one stroke not only be superimposed on or cleave to the right hand, but actually become the right hand. When we try to elucidate the phenomenon of the phantom limb by relating it to the body image of the subject, we add to the accepted explanations, in terms of cerebral tracks and recurrent sensations, only if the body image, instead of being the residue of habitual cenesthesis, becomes the law of its constitution. If a need was felt to introduce this new word, it was in order to make it clear that the spatial and temporal unity, the intersensory or the sensorimotor unity of the body is, so to speak, *de jure*, that it is not confined to contents actually and fortuitously associated in the course of our experience, that it is in some way anterior to them and makes their association possible. We are therefore feeling our way towards a second definition of the body image: it is no longer seen as the straightforward result of associations established during experience, but a total awareness of my posture in the intersensory world, a 'form' in the sense used by Gestalt psychology. But already this second definition too is superseded by the analyses of the psychologists. It is inadequate to say that my body is a form, that is to say a phenomenon in which the totality takes precedence over the parts. How is such a phenomenon possible? Because a form, compared to the mosaic of a physico-chemical body or to that of 'cenesthesis', is a new type of existence. The fact that the paralysed limb of the anosognosic no longer counts in the subject's body image, is accounted for by the body image's being neither the mere copy nor even the global awareness of the existing parts of the body, and by its active integration of these latter only in proportion to their value to the organism's projects. Psychologists often say that the body image is *dynamic*. Brought down to a precise sense, this term means that my body appears to me as an attitude directed towards a certain existing or possible task. And indeed its spatiality is not, like that of external objects or like that of 'spatial sensations', a *spatiality of position*, but a *spatiality of situation*. If I stand in front of my desk and lean on it with both hands, only my hands are stressed and the whole of my body trails behind them like the tail of a comet. It is not that I am unaware of the whereabouts of my shoulders or back, but these are simply swallowed up in the position of my hands, and my whole posture can be read so to speak in the pressure they exert on the table. If I stand holding my pipe in my closed hand, the position of my hand is not determined discursively by the angle which it makes with my forearm, and my forearm with my upper arm, and my upper arm with my trunk, and my trunk with the ground. I know indubitably where my pipe is, and thereby I know where my hand and my body are, as primitive man in the desert is always able to take his bearings immediately without having to cast his mind back, and add up distances covered and deviations made since setting off. The word 'here' applied to my body does not refer to a determinate position in relation to other positions or to external co-ordinates, but the laying down of the first co-ordinates, the anchoring of the active body in an object, the situation of the body in face of its tasks. Bodily space can be distinguished from external space and envelop its parts instead of spreading them out, because it is the darkness needed in the theatre to show up the performance, the background of somnolence or reserve of vague power against which the gesture and its aim stand out, the zone of not being *in front of which* precise beings, figures and points can come to light. In the last analysis, if my body can be a 'form' and if there can be, in front of it, important figures against indifferent backgrounds, this occurs in virtue of its being polarized by its tasks, of its *existence towards* them, of its collecting together of itself in its pursuit of its aims; the body image is finally a way of stating that my body is in-the-world.[2] As far as spatiality is concerned, and this alone interests us at the moment, one's own body is the third term, always tacitly understood, in the figure-background structure, and every figure stands out against the double horizon of external and bodily space. One must therefore reject as an abstraction any analysis of bodily space which takes account only of figures and points, since these can neither be conceived nor be without horizons.

It will perhaps be replied that the figure-background structure or the point-horizon structure themselves presuppose the notion of object-ive space; that in order to experience a display of dexterity as a figure *against* the massive background of the body, the hand and the rest of the body must be linked by this relationship of objective spatiality, so that the figure-background structure becomes once again one of the contin-gent contents of the universal form of space. But what meaning could the word 'against' have for a subject not placed by his body face to face with the world? It implies the distinction of a top and a bottom, or an 'orientated space'. When I say that an object is *on* a table, I always mentally put myself either in the table or in the object, and I apply to them a category which theoretically fits the relationship of my body to external objects. Stripped of this anthropological association, the word *on* is indistinguishable from the word 'under' or the word 'beside'. Even if the universal form of space is that without which there would be for us no bodily space, it is not that by which there is one. Even if the form is not the *setting in which*, but the *means whereby* the content is posited, it is not the sufficient means of this act of positing as far as bodily space is concerned, and to this extent the bodily content remains, in relation to it, something opaque, fortuitous and unintelligible. The only solution along this road would be to acknowledge that the body's spatiality has no meaning of its own to distinguish it from objective spatiality, which would do away with the content as a phenomenon and hence with the problem of its relation to form. But can we pretend to discover no distinctive meaning in the words 'on', 'under', 'beside', or in the dimensions of orientated space? Even if analysis discovers in all these relationships the universal relation of externality, the self-evidentness of top and bottom, right and left, for the person who has his being in space, prevents us from treating all these distinctions as nonsense, and suggests to us that we should look beneath the explicit meaning of definitions for the latent meaning of experiences. The rela-tionships between the two spaces would therefore be as follows: as soon as I try to posit bodily space or bring out its meaning I find nothing in it but intelligible space. But at the same time this intelligible space is not extracted from orientated space, it is merely its explicit expression, and, when separated from that root has no meaning whatsoever. The truth is that homogeneous space can convey the meaning of orientated space only because it is from the latter that it has received that meaning. In so far as the content can be really subsumed under the form and can appear as the content *of* that form, it is because the form is accessible only through the content. Bodily space can really become a fragment of objective space only if within its individuality as bodily space it contains the dialectical ferment to transform it into universal space. This is what we have tried to express by saying that the point-horizon structure is the foundation of space. The horizon or background would not extend beyond the figure or round about it, unless they partook of the same kind of being as the figure, and unless they could be converted into points by a transference of the gaze. But the point-horizon structure can teach me what a point is only in virtue of the maintenance of a hither zone of corporeality from which to be seen, and round about it indeterminate horizons which are the counterpart of this seeing. The multiplicity of points or 'heres' can in the nature of things be constituted only by a chain of experiences in which on each occasion one and no more of them is presented as an object, and which is itself built up in the heart of this space. And finally, far from my body's being for me no more than a fragment of space, there would be no space at all for me if I had no body.

Analysis of motility in the light of Schneider's case from Gelb and Goldstein

If bodily space and external space form a practical system, the first being the background against which the object as the goal of our action may stand out or the void in front of which it may *come to light*, it is clearly in action that the spatiality of our body is brought into being, and an analysis of one's own movement should enable us to arrive at a better understanding of it. By considering the body in movement, we can see better how it inhabits space (and, moreover, time) because movement is not limited to submitting passively to space and time, it actively assumes them, it takes them up in their basic significance which is obscured in the commonplaceness of established situations. We should like to analyse closely an example of morbid motility which clearly shows the fundamental relations between the body and space.

A patient whom traditional psychiatry would class among cases of psychic blindness is unable to perform 'abstract' movements with his eyes shut; movements, that is, which are not relevant to any actual situation, such as moving arms and legs to order, or bending and straightening a finger. Nor can he describe the position of his body or even his head, or the passive movements of his limbs. Finally, when his head, arm or leg is touched, he cannot identify the point on his body; he cannot distinguish two points of contact on his skin even as much as three inches apart; and he cannot recognize the size or shape of objects placed against his body. He manages the abstract movements only if he is allowed to watch the limb required to perform them, or to go through preparatory movements involving the whole body. The localization of stimuli, and recognition of objects by touch also become possible with the aid of the preparatory movements. Even when his eyes are closed, the patient performs with extraordinary speed and precision the movements needed in living his life, provided that he is in the habit of performing them: he takes his handkerchief from his pocket and blows his nose, takes a match out of a box and lights a lamp. He is employed in the manufacture of wallets and his production rate is equal to three quarters of that of a normal workman. He can even without any preparatory movement, perform these 'concrete' movements to order. In the same patient, and also in cerebellar cases, one notices a dissociation of the act of pointing from reactions of taking or grasping: the same subject who is unable to point to order to a part of his body, quickly moves his hand to the point where a mosquito is stinging him. Concrete movements and acts of grasping therefore enjoy a privileged position for which we need to find some explanation.

'Concrete movement'

Let us examine the question more closely. A patient, asked to point to some part of his body, his nose for example, can only manage to do so if he is allowed to take hold of it. If the patient is set the task of interrupting the movement before its completion, or if he is allowed to touch his nose only with a wooden ruler, the action becomes impossible. It must therefore be concluded that 'grasping' or 'touching', even for the body, is different from 'pointing'. From the outset the grasping movement is magically at its completion; it can begin only by anticipating its end, since to disallow taking hold is sufficient to inhibit the action. And it has to be admitted that a point on my body can be present to me as one to be taken hold of without being given in this anticipated grasp as a point to be indicated. But how is this possible? If I know where my nose is when it is a question of holding it, how can I not know where it is when it is a matter of pointing to it? It is probably because knowledge of where something is can be understood in a number of ways. Traditional psychology has no concept to cover these varieties of consciousness of place because consciousness of place is always, for such psychology, a positional consciousness, a representation, *Vor-stellung*, because as such it gives us the place as a determination of the objective world and because such a representation either is or is not, but, if it is, yields the object to us quite unambiguously and as an end identifiable through all its appearances. Now here, on the other hand, we have to create the concepts necessary to convey the fact that bodily space may be given to me in an intention to take hold without being given in an intention to know. The patient is conscious of his bodily space as the matrix of his habitual action, but not as an objective setting; his body is at his disposal as a means of ingress into a familiar surrounding, but not as the means of expression of a gratuitous and free spatial thought. When ordered to perform a concrete movement, he first of all repeats the order in a questioning tone of voice, then his body assumes the general position required for the task; finally he goes through the movement. It is noticeable that the whole body is involved in it, and that the patient never cuts it down, as a normal subject would, to the strict minimum. To the military salute are added the other external marks of respect. To the right hand pantomime of combing the hair is added, with the left, that of holding a mirror; when the right hand pretends to knock in a nail, the left pretends to hold the nail. The explanation is that the order is taken quite seriously and that the patient manages to perform these concrete movements to order only provided that he places himself mentally in the actual situation to which they correspond. The normal subject, on giving, to order, a military salute, sees in it no more than an experimental situation, and therefore restricts the movement to its most important elements and does not throw himself into it. He is using his body as a means to play acting; he finds it entertaining to pretend to be a soldier; he escapes from reality in the rôle of the soldier just as the actor slips his real body into the 'great phantom' of the character to be played. The normal man and the actor do not mistake imaginary situations for reality, but extricate their real bodies from the living situation to make them breathe, speak and, if need be, weep in the realm of imagination. This is what our patient is no longer able to do. In the course of living, he says 'I experience the movements as being a result of the situation, of the sequence of events themselves; myself and my movements are, so to speak, merely a link in the whole process and I am scarcely aware of any voluntary initiative ... It all happens independently of me.' In the same way, in order to make a movement to order he places himself 'in the affective situation as a whole, and it is from this that the movement flows, as in real life'. If his performance is interrupted and he has the experimental situation recalled to him, all his dexterity disappears. Once more kinetic initiative becomes impossible, the patient must first of all 'find' his arm, 'find', by the preparatory movements, the gesture called for, and the gesture itself loses the melodic character which it presents in ordinary life, and becomes manifestly a collection of partial movements strung laboriously together. I can therefore take my place, through the medium of my body as the potential source of a certain number of familiar actions, in my environment conceived as a set of *manipulanda* and without, moreover, envisaging my body or my surrounding as objects in the Kantian sense, that is, as systems of qualities linked by some intelligible law, as transparent entities, free from any attachment to a specific place or time, and ready to be named or at least pointed out. There is my arm seen as sustaining familiar acts, my body as giving rise to determinate action having a field or scope known to me in advance, there are my surroundings as a collection of possible points upon which this bodily action may operate, – and there is, furthermore, my arm as a mechanism of muscles and bones, as a contrivance for bending and stretching, as an articulated object, the world as a pure spectacle into which I am not absorbed, but which I contemplate and point out. As far as bodily space is concerned, it is clear that there is a knowledge of place which is reducible to a sort of co-existence with that place, and which is not simply nothing, even though it cannot be conveyed by a description or even by the mute reference of a gesture. A patient of the kind discussed above, when stung by a mosquito, does not need to look for the place where he has been stung. He finds it straight away, because for him there is no question of locating it in relation to axes of co-ordinates in objective space, but of reaching with his phenomenal hand a certain painful spot on his phenomenal body, and because between the hand as a scratching potentially and the place stung as a spot to be scratched a directly experienced relationship is presented in the natural system of one's own body. The whole operation takes place in the domain of the phenomenal; it does not run through the objective world, and only the spectator, who lends his objective representation of the living body to the acting subject, can believe that the sting is perceived, that the hand moves in objective space, and consequently find it odd that the same subject should fail in experiments requiring him to point things out. Similarly the subject, when put in front of his scissors, needle and familiar tasks, does not need to look for his hands or his fingers, because they are not objects to be discovered in objective space: bones, muscles and nerves, but potentialities already mobilized by the perception of scissors or needle, the central end of those 'intentional threads' which link him to the objects given. It is never our objective body that we move, but our phenomenal body, and

abstract → concrete

there is no mystery in that, since our body, as the potentiality of this or that part of the world, surges towards objects to be grasped and perceives them.[3] In the same way the patient has no need to look for a theatre of action and a space in which to deploy these concrete movements: the space is given to him in the form of the world at this moment; it is the piece of leather 'to be cut up'; it is the lining 'to be sewn'. The bench, scissors, pieces of leather offer themselves to the subject as poles of action; through their combined values they delimit a certain situation, an open situation moreover, which calls for a certain mode of resolution, a certain kind of work. The body is no more than an element in the system of the subject and his world, and the task to be performed elicits the necessary movements from him by a sort of remote attraction, as the phenomenal forces at work in my visual field elicit from me, without any calculation on my part, the motor reactions which establish the most effective balance between them, or as the conventions of our social group, or our set of listeners, immediately elicit from us the words, attitudes and tone which are fitting. Not that we are trying to conceal our thoughts or to please others, but because we are literally what others think of us and what our world is. In the concrete movement the patient has a positing awareness neither of the stimulus nor of his reaction: quite simply he is his body and his body is the potentiality of a certain world.

'Abstract movement'

What, on the other hand, happens in experiments in which the patient fails? If a part of his body is touched and he is asked to locate the point of contact, he first of all sets his whole body in motion and thus narrows down the problem of location, then he comes still nearer by moving the limb in question, and the process is completed in the form of quiverings of the skin in the neighbourhood of the point touched. If the subject's arm is extended horizontally, he cannot describe its position until he has performed a set of pendular movements which convey to him the arm position in relation to the trunk, that of the forearm to the rest of the arm, and that of the trunk in relation to the vertical. In the case of passive movement, the subject feels that there is movement but cannot say of what kind and in what direction. Here again he resorts to active movements. The patient concludes that he is lying down from the pressure of the mattress on his back, or that he is standing from the pressure of the ground on his feet. If the two points of a compass are placed on his hand, he can distinguish them only if he is allowed to rotate his hand, and bring first one and then the other point into contact with his skin. If letters or figures are traced out on his hand, he identifies them only provided that he can himself move his hand, and it is not the movement of the point on his hand which he perceives, but conversely the movement of his hand in relation to the point. This is proved by tracing on his left hand normal letters, which are never recognized, then the mirrored image of the same letters, which is immediately understood. The mere touching of a paper rectangle or oval gives rise to no recognition, whereas the subject recognizes the figures if he is allowed to make exploratory movements to 'spell out' the shapes, to spot their 'characteristics' and to identify the object on this basis. How are we to co-ordinate this set of facts and how are we to discover by means of it what function, found in the normal person, is absent in the patient? There can be no question of simply transferring to the normal person what the deficient one lacks and is trying to recover. Illness, like childhood and 'primitive' mentality, is a complete form of existence and the procedures which it employs to replace normal functions which have been destroyed are equally pathological phenomena. It is impossible to deduce the normal from the pathological, deficiencies from the substitute functions, by a mere change of the sign. We must take substitutions as substitutions, as allusions to some fundamental function that they are striving to make good, and the direct image of which they fail to furnish. The genuine inductive method is not a 'differential method'; it consists in correctly reading phenomena, in grasping their meaning, that is, in treating them as modalities and variations of the subject's total being. We observe that when the patient is questioned about the position of his limbs or of a tactile stimulus, he tries, by means of preparatory movements, to make his body into an object of present perception. Asked about the shape of an object in contact with his body, he tries to trace it out himself by following the outline of the object. Nothing would be more misleading than to suppose the normal person adopting similar procedures, differing merely in being shortened by constant use. The kind of patient under consideration sets out in search of these explicit perceptions only in order to provide a substitute for a certain mutual presence of body and object which is a datum of normal experience and which we still have to reconstitute. It is true that even in the normal person the perception of the body and of objects in contact with the body is vague when there is no movement. The fact remains that the normal person can, in the absence of any movements, always distinguish a stimulus applied to his head from one applied to his body. Are we to suppose that excitations felt as coming either from outside or from one's own body have brought into play, in that person, 'kinaesthetic residua' which take the place of actual movements? But then how could data supplied by the sense of touch arouse 'kinaesthetic residua' of a determinate kind unless they carried within themselves some characteristic which enables them to do so, unless they themselves, in other words, had some well defined or obscure spatial significance? At least we can say that the normal subject can immediately 'come to grips' with his body. He enjoys the use of his body not only in so far as it is involved in a concrete setting, he is in a situation not only in relation to the tasks imposed by a particular job, he is not open merely to real situations; for, over and above all this, his body is correlated with pure stimuli devoid of any practical bearing; he is open to those verbal and imaginary situations which he can choose for himself or which may be suggested to him in the course of an experiment. His body, when touched, is not presented to him as a geometrical outline in which each stimulus occupies an explicit position, and Schneider's disease lies precisely in his need, in order to find out where he is being touched, to convert the bodily area touched into a shape. But each stimulus applied to the body of the normal person arouses a kind of 'potential movement', rather than an actual one; the part of the body in question sheds its anonymity, is revealed, by the presence of a particular tension, as a certain power of action within the framework of the anatomical apparatus. In the case of the normal subject, the body is available not only in real situations into which it is drawn. It can turn aside from the world, apply its activity to stimuli which affect its sensory surfaces, lend itself to experimentation, and generally speaking take its place in the realm of the potential. It is because of its confinement within the actual that an unsound sense of touch calls for special movements designed to localize stimuli, and for the same reason the patient substitutes, for tactile recognition and perception, a laborious decoding of stimuli and deduction of objects. For a key, for instance, to appear as such in my tactile experience, a kind of fulness of touch is required, a tactile field in which local impressions may be co-ordinated into a shape just as notes are mere stepping-stones in a melody; and that very viscosity of tactile data which makes the body dependent upon actual situations reduces the object to a collection of successive 'characteristics', perception to an abstract account, recognition to a rational synthesis or a plausible conjecture, and strips the object of its carnal presence and facticity. Whereas in the normal person every event related to movement or sense of touch causes consciousness to put up a host of intentions which run from the body as the centre of potential action either towards the body itself or towards the object, in the case of the patient, on the other hand, the tactile impression remains opaque and sealed up. It may well draw the grasping hand towards itself, but does not stand in front of the hand in the manner of a thing which can be pointed out. The normal person *reckons with* the possible, which thus, without shifting from its position as a possibility, acquires a sort of actuality. In the patient's case, however, the field of actuality is limited to what is met with in the shape of a real contact or is related to these data by some explicit process of deduction. . . .

The impossibility of comprehending these phenomena by a reflexive analysis

We cannot explain disturbances in the power of abstract movement in terms of loss of visual contents, nor, consequently, the function of projection in terms of the actual presence of these contents. So one method alone still seems possible: it consists in reconstituting the basic disturbance by going back from the symptoms not to a *cause* which is itself observable, but to a *reason* or intelligible condition of possibility for the state of affairs. It involves treating the human subject as an irresolvable consciousness which is wholly present in every one of its manifestations. If the disturbance is not to be related to the contents, it must be linked to the form of knowledge; if psychology is not empiricist and explicative, it ought to be rationalistic and reflective. In exactly the same way as the act of naming, the act of pointing out presupposes that the object, instead of being approached, grasped and absorbed by the body, is kept at a distance and stands as a picture in front of the patient. Plato still allowed the empiricist the power of pointing a finger at things, but the truth is that even this silent gesture is impossible if *what* is pointed out is not already torn from instantaneous existence and monadic existence, and treated as representative of its previous appearances in me, and of its simultaneous appearances in others, in other words, subsumed under some category and promoted to the status of a concept. If the patient is no longer able to point to some part of his body which is touched, it is because he is no longer a subject face to face with an objective world, and can no longer take up a 'categorial attitude'. In the same way, abstract movement is endangered in so far as it presupposes awareness of an objective, is borne on by that awareness, and is movement for itself. Indeed it is not triggered off by any existing object, but is clearly centrifugal, outlining in space a gratuitous intention which has reference to one's own body, making an object of it instead of going through it to link up with things by means of it. It is, then, diffused with a power of objectification, a 'symbolical function', a 'representative function', a power of 'projection' which is, moreover, already at work in forming 'things'. It consists in treating sense-data as mutually representative, and also collectively representative of an 'eidos'; in giving a meaning to these data, in breathing a spirit into them, in systematizing them, in centring a plurality of experiences round one intelligible core, in bringing to light in them an identifiable unity when seen in different perspectives. To sum up, it consists in placing beneath the flow of impressions an explanatory invariant, and in giving a form to the stuff of experience. Now it is not possible to maintain that consciousness *has* this power, it *is* this power itself. As soon as there is consciousness, and in order that there may be consciousness, there must be something to be conscious of, an intentional object, and consciousness can move towards this object only to the extent that it 'derealizes' itself and throws itself into it, only if it is wholly in this reference to . . . something, only if it is a pure meaning-giving act. If a being is consciousness, he must be nothing but a network of intentions. If he ceases to be definable in terms of the act of sense-giving, he relapses into the condition of a thing, the thing being precisely what does not know, what slumbers in absolute ignorance of itself and the world, what consequently is not a true 'self', i.e. a 'for-itself', and has only a spatio-temporal form of individuation, existence in itself.[4] Consciousness, therefore, does not admit of degree. If the patient no longer exists as a consciousness, he must then exist as a thing. Either movement is movement for itself, in which case the 'stimulus' is not its cause but its intentional object – or else it disintegrates and is dispersed in existence in itself, and becomes an objective process in the body, whose phases are successive but unknown to each other. The special status of concrete movements in illness is explained by seeing them as reflexes in the traditional sense. The patient's hand meets the point on his body where the mosquito has settled because preestablished nerve circuits, not the excitation, control the reaction. Actions performed in the course of his work are preserved because they are dependent upon firmly rooted conditioned reflexes. They persist in spite of psychic deficiencies because they are movements in themselves. The distinction between concrete and abstract movement, between *Greifen* and *Zeigen* comes down to that between the physiological and the psychic, existence in itself and existence for itself.[5]

But we shall see that in reality the first distinction, far from covering also the second, is incompatible with it. Every 'physiological explanation' tends to become generalized. If the grasping action or the concrete movement is guaranteed by some factual connection between each point on the skin and the motor muscles which guide the hand, it is difficult to see why the same nerve circuit communicating a scarcely different movement to the same muscles should not guarantee the gesture of *Zeigen* as it does the movement of *Greifen*. Between the mosquito which pricks the skin and the ruler which the doctor presses on the same spot, the physical difference is not great enough to explain why the grasping movement is possible, but the act of pointing impossible. The two 'stimuli' are really distinguishable only if we take into account their affective value or biological meaning, and the two responses cease to merge into one another only if we consider the *Zeigen* and the *Greifen* as two ways of relating to the object and two types of being in the world. But this is precisely what cannot be done once we have reduced the living body to the condition of an object. If it is once conceded that it may be the seat of third person processes, nothing in behaviour can be reserved for consciousness. Both gestures and movements, employing as they do the same organ-objects, the same nerve-objects, must be given their place on the map of interiorless processes, and inserted in the compactly woven stuff of 'physiological conditions'. Does not the patient who, in doing his job, moves his hand towards a tool lying on the table, displace the segments of his arm exactly as he would have to do to perform the abstract movement of extending it? Does not an everyday gesture involve a series of muscular contractions and innervations? It is therefore impossible to set limits to physiological explanation. In another way it is impossible also to set limits to consciousness. If we relate the act of pointing to consciousness, if once the stimulus can cease to be the cause of the reaction and become its intentional object, it becomes inconceivable that it should ever function as a pure cause or that the movement should ever be blind. For if 'abstract' movements are possible, in which consciousness of the starting and finishing points is present, we must at every moment in our life know where our body is without having to look for it as we look for an object moved from its place during our absence. Even 'automatic' movements must therefore announce themselves to our consciousness, which means that there never occur, in our bodies, movements in themselves. And if all objective space is for intellectual consciousness only, we must recognize the categorial attitude even in the movement of grasping itself. Like physiological causality, arrival at self-awareness has nowhere to start. We must either reject physiological explanation or admit that it is all-inclusive – either deny consciousness or accept it as comprehensive. We cannot relate certain movements to bodily mechanism and others to consciousness. The body and consciousness are not mutually limiting, they can be only parallel. Any physiological explanation becomes generalized into mechanistic physiology, any achievment of self-awareness into intellectualist psychology, and mechanistic physiology or intellectualist psychology bring behaviour down to the same uniform level and wipe out the distinction between abstract and concrete movement, between *Zeigen* and *Greifen*. This distinction can survive only if there are *several ways for the body to be a body, several ways for consciousness to be consciousness*. As long as the body is defined in terms of existence in-itself, it functions uniformly like a mechanism, and as long as the mind is defined in terms of pure existence for-itself, it knows only objects arrayed before it. The distinction between abstract and concrete movement is therefore not to be confused with that between body and consciousness; it does not belong to the same reflective dimension, but finds its place only in the behavioural dimension. Pathological phenomena introduce variations before our eyes in something which is not the pure awareness of an object. Any diagnosis, like that of intellectualist psychology, which sees here a collapse of consciousness and the freeing of automatism, or again that of an empiricist psychology of contents, would leave the fundamental disturbance untouched.

The existential ground of the symbolic function

The intellectualist analysis, here as everywhere, is less false than abstract. It is true that the 'symbolic function' or the 'representative function' underlies our movements, but it is not a final term for analysis. It too rests on a certain groundwork. The mistake of intellectualism is to make it self-subsistent, to remove it from the stuff in which it is realized, and to recognize in us, as a non-derivative entity, an undistanced presence in the world. For, using this consciousness, an entirely transparent consciousness, this intentionality which admits of no degrees of more or less, as a starting point, everything that separates us from the real world – error, sickness, madness, in short incarnation – is reduced to the status of mere appearance. Admittedly intellectualism does not bring consciousness into being independently of its material. For example it takes great care not to introduce behind the word, the action and the perception, any 'symbolic consciousness' as the common and numerically sole form of linguistic, perceptual and motor material. There is no 'general symbolic faculty', says Cassirer, and analytical reflection does not seek to establish between pathological phenomena relating to perception, language and action a 'community in being', but a 'community in meaning'. Just because it has finally gone beyond causal thought and realism, intellectualist psychology would be able to see the meaning or essence of illness, and recognize a unity of consciousness which is not evident on the plane of being, and which is vouched for, in its own eyes, on the plane of truth. But the distinction between community in being and community in sense, the conscious passage from the existential order to the order of value and the transvaluation which allows meaning and value to be declared autonomous are, for practical purposes, equivalent to an abstraction, since, from the point of view finally adopted, the variety of phenomena becomes insignificant and incomprehensible. If consciousness is placed outside being, the latter cannot breach it, the empirical variety of consciousnesses – morbid, primitive, childlike consciousness, the consciousness of others – cannot be taken seriously, there is nothing to be known or understood, one thing alone makes sense: the pure essence of consciousness. None of these consciousnesses could fail to effect the *Cogito*. The lunatic, *behind* his ravings, his obsessions and lies, *knows that he* is raving, that he is allowing himself to be haunted by an obsession, that he is lying, in short he *is* not mad, *he thinks he is*. All is then for the best and insanity is only perversion of the will. The analysis of the meaning of illness, once it ends with the symbolic function, identifies all disorders as the same, uniting aphasia, apraxia and agnosia and perhaps even has no way of distinguishing them from schizophrenia.[6] It then becomes understandable that doctors and psychologists should decline the invitation to intellectualism and fall back, for want of anything better, on the attempts at causal explanation which at least have the merit of taking into account what is peculiar to illness, and to each form of it, and which by this means give at any rate the illusion of possessing actual knowledge. Modern pathology shows that there is no strictly elective disturbance, but it shows equally that each one is coloured by the sector of behaviour which it principally attacks. Even if all aphasia, when closely observed, is seen to involve disturbances of both gnosic[7] and praxic kinds; if all apraxia[8] involves linguistic and perceptual disturbances, and all agnosia[9] disturbances of language and action, the fact remains that the core of these disorders is here to be found in the domain of language, there in that of perception, and elsewhere in that of action. When we invoke in all these cases the symbolic function, we are, it is true, characterizing the structure common to the different derangements, but this structure should not be separated from the stuff through which on each occasion it is realized, if not electively, at least in great measure. After all Schneider's trouble was not initially meta-physical, for it was a shell splinter which wounded him at the back of the head. The damage to his sight was serious, but it would be ridiculous, as we have said, to explain all the other deficiencies in terms of the visual one as their cause; but no less ridiculous to think that the shell splinter directly struck symbolic consciousness. It was through his sight that Mind in him was impaired.

Until some means has been discovered whereby we can link the origin and the essence or meaning of the disturbance; until some definition is found for a *concrete essence*, a *structure* of illness which shall express both its generality and its particularity, until phenomenology becomes genetic phenomenology, unhelpful reversions to causal thought and naturalism will remain justified. Our problem therefore becomes clearer. The task for us is to conceive, between the linguistic, perceptual and motor contents and the form given to them or the symbolic function which breathes life into them, a relationship which shall be neither the reduction of form to content, nor the subsuming of content under an autonomous form. We need to understand both how Schneider's complaint everywhere overshoots particular contents – visual, tactile and motor – of his experience, and how it nevertheless attacks the symbolic function only through the specially chosen material provided by sight. The senses and one's own body generally present the mystery of a collective entity which, without abandoning its thisness and its individuality, puts forth beyond itself meanings capable of providing a framework for a whole series of thoughts and experiences. Although Schneider's trouble affects motility and thought as well as perception, the fact remains that what it damages, particularly in the domain of thought, is his power of apprehending simultaneous wholes, and in the matter of motility, that, so to speak, of taking a bird's-eye view of movement and projecting it outside himself. It is then in some sense mental space and practical space which are destroyed or impaired, and the words themselves are a sufficient indication of the visual origin of the disturbance. Visual trouble is not the cause of the other disturbances, particularly that directly affecting thought. But neither is it a mere consequence of them. Visual contents, moreover, are not the cause of the function of projection, but neither is sight a mere opportunity given to Mind to bring into play a power in itself unconditioned. Visual contents are taken up, utilized and sublimated to the level of thought by a symbolical power which transcends them, but it is on the basis of sight that this power can be constituted. The relationship between matter and form is called in phenomenological terminology a relationship of

Fundierung: the symbolic function rests on the visual as on a ground; not that vision is its cause, but because it is that gift of nature which Mind was called upon to make use of beyond all hope, to which it was to give a fundamentally new meaning, yet which was needed, not only to be incarnate, but in order to be at all. Form integrates within itself the content until the latter finally appears as a mere mode of form itself, and the historical stages leading up to thought as a ruse of Reason disguised as Nature. But conversely, even in its intellectual sublimation, content remains in the nature of a radical contingency, the initial establishment or foundation[10] of knowledge and action, the first laying hold of being or value, whose concrete richness will never be finally exhausted by knowledge and action, and whose spontaneous method they will ceaselessly reapply. This dialectic of form and content is what we have to restore, or rather, since 'reciprocal action' is as yet only a compromise with causal thought, and a contradictory principle, we have to describe the circumstances under which this contradiction is conceivable, which means existence, the perpetual re-ordering of fact and hazard by a reason non-existent before and without those circumstances. . . .

The intentional arc

. . . It is this existential basis of intelligence which is affected, much more than intelligence itself, for, as we have shown, Schneider's general intelligence is intact: his replies are slow, never meaningless, but those of a mature, thinking man who takes an interest in the doctor's experiments. Beneath the intelligence as an anonymous function or as a categorial process, a personal core has to be recognized, which is the patient's being, his power of existing. It is here that the illness has its seat. Schneider would still like to arrive at political or religious opinions, but knows that it is useless to try. 'He must now be content. with large-scale beliefs, without the power to express them.' He never sings or whistles of his own accord. We shall see later that he never takes any initiative sexually. He never goes out for a walk, but always on an errand, and he never recognizes Professor Goldstein's house as he passes it 'because he did not go out with the intention of going there'. Just as he needs, by means of preparatory movements, to be able to 'take a grip' on his own body before performing movements when they are not mapped out ahead in a familiar situation, – so, a conversation with another person does not constitute for him a situation significant in itself, and requiring extempore replies. He can speak only in accordance with a plan drawn up in advance: 'He cannot fall back on the inspiration of the moment in order to find the ideas required in response to a complex stage of the conversation, and this is true whether it is a question of new or old points of view.' There is in his whole conduct something meticulous and serious which derives from the fact that he is incapable of play-acting. To act is to place oneself for a moment in an imaginary situation, to find satisfaction in changing one's 'setting'. The patient, on the other hand, cannot enter into a fictitious situation without converting it into a real one: he cannot tell the difference between a riddle and a problem. In his case, the possible situation at every moment is so narrow that two sectors of the environment not having anything in common for him cannot simultaneously form a situation. If one talks to him he cannot hear the sound of another conversation in the next room; if a dish is brought and placed on the table, he does not stop to wonder where the dish comes from. He states that one can see only in the direction in which one is looking, and only objects at which one is looking. Future and past are for him only 'shrunken' extensions of the present. He has lost 'our power of looking according to the temporal vector'. He cannot take a bird's-eye view of his past and unhesitatingly rediscover it by going from the whole to the parts: he rebuilds it, starting with a fragment which has kept its meaning and which provides him with a 'supporting-point'. Since he complains of the weather, he is asked if he feels better in winter. He replies: 'I can't say now, I can't say anything at the moment'. Thus all Schneider's troubles are reducible to a unity, but not the abstract unity of the 'representative function': he is 'tied' to actuality, he 'lacks liberty', that concrete liberty which comprises the general power of putting oneself into a situation. Beneath intelligence as beneath perception, we discover a more fundamental function, 'a vector mobile in all directions like a searchlight, one through which we can direct ourselves towards anything, in or outside ourselves, and display a form of behaviour in relation to that object'. Yet the analogy of the searchlight is inadequate, since it presupposes given objects on to which the beam plays, whereas the nuclear function to which we refer, before bringing objects to our sight or knowledge, makes them exist in a more intimate sense, for us. Let us therefore say rather, borrowing a term from other works, that the life of consciousness – cognitive life, the life of desire or perceptual life – is subtended by an 'intentional arc' which projects round about us our past, our future, our human setting, our physical, ideological and moral situation, or rather which results in our being situated in all these respects. It is this intentional arc which brings about the unity of the senses, of intelligence, of sensibility and motility. And it is this which 'goes limp' in illness.

The study of a pathological case, then, has enabled us to glimpse a new mode of analysis – existential analysis – which goes beyond the traditional alternatives of empiricism and rationalism, of explanation and introspection. If consciousness were a collection of mental facts each disturbance should be elective. If it were a 'representative function', a pure power of signification, it could be or not be (and with it everything else), but it could not cease to be having once been, or become sick, that is, deteriorate. If, in short, it is a projective activity, which leaves objects all round it, like traces of its own acts, but which nevertheless uses them as springboards from which to leap towards other spontaneous acts, then it becomes understandable that any 'content' deficiency should have its repercussions on the main body of experience and open the door to its disintegration, that any pathological degeneration should affect the whole of consciousness – and that nevertheless the derangement should on each occasion attack a certain 'side' of consciousness, that in each case certain symptoms should dominate the clinical picture of the disease, and, in short, that consciousness should be vulnerable and able to receive the illness into itself. In attacking the 'visual sphere', illness is not limited to destroying certain contents of consciousness, 'visual representations' or sight literally speaking; it affects sight in the figurative sense, of which the former is no more than the model or symbol – the power of 'looking down upon' (*überschauen*) simultaneous multiplicities, a certain way of positing the object or being aware. However, as this type of consciousness is only the sublimation of sensory vision, as it is schematized constantly within the dimensions of the visual field, albeit endowing them with a new meaning, it will be realized that this general function has its psychological roots. Consciousness freely develops its visual data beyond their own specific significance; it uses them for the expression of its spontaneous acts, as semantic evolution clearly shows in loading the terms intuition, self-evidence and natural light with increasingly rich meaning. But conversely, not one of these terms, in the final sense which history has given them, is understandable without reference to the structures of visual perception. Hence one cannot say that man sees because he is Mind, nor indeed that he is Mind because he sees: to see as a man sees and to be Mind are synonymous. In so far as consciousness is consciousness of something only by allowing its furrow to trail behind it, and in so far as, in order to conceive an object one must rely on a previously constructed 'world of thought', there is always some degree of depersonalization at the heart of consciousness. Hence the principle of an intervention from outside: consciousness may be ailing, the world of its thoughts may collapse into fragments, – or rather, as the 'contents' dissociated by the illness did not appear in the rôle of parts in normal consciousness and served only as stepping-stones to significances which outstrip them, consciousness can be seen trying to hold up its superstructures when their foundations have given way, aping its everyday processes, but without being able to come by any intuitive realization, and without being able to conceal the particular deficiency which robs them of their complete significance. It is in the same way theoretically understandable that mental illness may, in its turn, be linked with some bodily accident; consciousness projects itself into a physical world and has a body, as it projects itself into a cultural world and has its habits: because it cannot be consciousness without playing upon significances given either in the absolute past of nature or in its own personal past, and because any form of lived experience tends towards a certain generality whether that of our habits or that of our 'bodily functions'.

The intentionality of the body

These elucidations enable us clearly to understand motility as basic intentionality. Consciousness is in the first place not a matter of 'I think that' but of 'I can'.[11] Schneider's motor trouble cannot, any more than his visual deficiency, be reduced to any failure of the general function of representation. Sight and movement are specific ways of entering into relationship with objects and if, through all these experiences, some unique function finds its expression, it is the momentum of existence, which does not cancel out the radical diversity of contents, because it links them to each other, not by placing them all under the control of an 'I think', but by guiding them towards the intersensory unity of a 'world'. Movement is not thought about movement, and bodily space is not space thought of or represented. 'Each voluntary movement takes place in a setting, against a background which is determined by the movement itself. . . . We perform our movements in a space which is not "empty" or unrelated to them, but which on the contrary, bears a highly determinate relation to them: movement and background are, in fact, only artificially separated stages of a unique totality.' In the action of the hand which is raised towards an object is contained a reference to the object, not as an object represented, but as that highly specific thing towards which we project ourselves, near _bodily intentionalit_

which we are, in anticipation, and which we haunt. Consciousness is being towards the thing through the intermediary of the body. A movement is learned when the body has understood it, that is, when it has incorporated it into its 'world', and to move one's body is to aim at things through it; it is to allow oneself to respond to their call, which is made upon it independently of any representation. Motility, then, is not, as it were, a handmaid of consciousness, transporting the body to that point in space of which we have formed a representation beforehand. In order that we may be able to move our body towards an object, the object must first exist for it, our body must not belong to the realm of the 'in-itself'. Objects no longer exist for the arm of the apraxic, and this is what causes it to remain immobile. Cases of pure apraxia in which the perception of space remains unaffected, in which even the 'intellectual notion of the gesture to be made' does not appear to be obscured, and yet in which the patient cannot copy a triangle; cases of constructive apraxia, in which the subject shows no gnosic disturbance except as regards the localization of stimuli on his body, and yet is incapable of copying a cross, a _v_ or an _o_, all prove that the body has its world and that objects or space may be present to our knowledge but not to our body. We must therefore avoid saying that our body is _in_ space, or _in_ time. It _inhabits_ space and time. . . .

. . . Now the body is essentially an expressive space. If I want to take hold of an object, already, at a point of space about which I have been quite unmindful, this power of grasping constituted by my hand moves upwards towards the thing. I move my legs not as things in space two and a half feet from my head, but as a power of locomotion which extends my motor intention downwards. The main areas of my body are devoted to actions, and participate in their value, and asking why common sense makes the head the seat of thought raises the same problem as asking how the organist distributes, through 'organ space', musical significances. But our body is not merely one expressive space among the rest, for that is simply the constituted body. It is the origin of the rest, expressive movement itself, that which causes them to begin to exist as things, under our hands and eyes. Although our body does not impose definite instincts upon us from birth, as it does upon animals, it does at least give to our life the form of generality, and develops our personal acts into stable dispositional tendencies. In this sense our nature is not long-established custom, since custom presupposes the form of passivity derived from nature. The body is our general medium for having a world. Sometimes it is restricted to the actions necessary for the conservation of life, and accordingly it posits around us a

[handwritten note at top: concrete intentionality]

biological world; at other times, elaborating upon these primary actions and moving from their literal to a figurative meaning it manifests through them a core of new significance: this is true of motor habits such as dancing. Sometimes, finally, the meaning aimed at cannot be achieved by the body's natural means; it must then build itself an instrument, and it projects thereby around itself a cultural world. At all levels it performs the same function which is to endow the instant-aneous expressions of spontaneity with 'a little renewable action and independent existence'. Habit is merely a form of this fundamental power. We say that the body has understood and habit has been culti-vated when it has absorbed a new meaning, and assimilated a fresh core of significance. *[handwritten note: habit body is fluid, open to change]*

To sum up, what we have discovered through the study of motility, is a new meaning of the word 'meaning'. The great strength of intel-lectualist psychology and idealist philosophy comes from their having no difficulty in showing that perception and thought have an intrinsic significance and cannot be explained in terms of the external associ-ation of fortuitously agglomerated contents. The *Cogito* was the coming to self-awareness of this inner core. But all meaning was *ipso facto* conceived as an act of thought, as the work of a pure *I*, and although rationalism easily refuted empiricism, it was itself unable to account for the variety of experience, for the element of senselessness in it, for the contingency of contents. Bodily experience forces us to acknowledge an imposition of meaning which is not the work of a universal constituting *[handwritten note: Kant]* consciousness, a meaning which clings to certain contents. My body is that meaningful core which behaves like a general function, and which nevertheless exists, and is susceptible to disease. In it we learn to know that union of essence and existence which we shall find again in perception generally, and which we shall then have to describe more fully.

Notes

1 A disorder of sensation in which sensations are referred to the wrong part of the body (Translator's note).
2 We have already seen that the phantom limb, which is a modality of the body image, is understood in terms of the general movement of being-in-the-world.
3 It is not a question of how the soul acts on the objective body, since it is not on the latter that it acts, but on the phenomenal body. So the question has to be reframed, and we must ask why there are two views of me and of my body: my body for me and my body for others, and how these two systems can exist together. It is indeed not enough to say that the objective body

belongs to the realm of 'for others', and my phenomenal body to that of 'for me', and we cannot refuse to pose the problem of their relations, since the 'for me' and the 'for others' co-exist in one and the same world, as is proved by my perception of an other who immediately brings me back to the condition of an object for him.

4 Husserl has often been credited with this distinction. In fact, it is found in Descartes and Kant. In our opinion Husserl's originality lies beyond the notion of intentionality; it is to be found in the elaboration of this notion and in the discovery, beneath the intentionality of representations, of a deeper intentionality, which others have called existence.

5 Gelb and Goldstein sometimes tend to interpret phenomena in this sense. They have done more than anyone to go beyond the traditional dualism of automatism and consciousness. But they have never named this third term *between* the psychic and the physiological, between the for itself and the in itself to which their analyses always led them and which we call existence. . . .

6 One can indeed imagine an intellectualist interpretation of schizophrenia which would equate the atomistic conception of time and the loss of the future with a collapse of the categorial attitude.

7 *Gnosia*: The perceptive faculty, enabling one to recognize the form and nature of persons and things (Translator's note).

8 *Apraxia*: (i) A disorder of voluntary movement, consisting in a more or less complete incapacity to execute purposeful movements, notwithstanding the preservation of muscular power, sensibility, and co-ordination in general. (ii) A psychomotor defect in which one is unable to apply to its proper use an object which one is nevertheless able to name and the uses of which one can describe (Translator's note).

9 *Agnosia*: Absence of ability to recognize the form and nature of persons and things, or the perceptive faculty (Translator's note).

10 We are translating Husserl's favourite word: *Stiftung*.

11 This term is the usual one in Husserl's unpublished writings.

PART II: THE WORLD AS PERCEIVED

FROM INTRODUCTION (*PP* 206 [239])

Merleau-Ponty summarises the conclusion of the previous part: the body is not an 'object' within the world; on the contrary it is 'as it were, the subject of perception'. The task now is to effect a similar transformation in our conception of the perceived world.

The theory of the body image is, implicitly, a theory of perception. We have relearned to feel our body; we have found underneath the objective and detached knowledge of the body that other knowledge which we have of it in virtue of its always being with us and of the fact that we are our body. In the same way we shall need to reawaken our experience of the world as it appears to us in so far as we are in the world through our body, and in so far as we perceive the world with our body. But by thus remaking contact with the body and with the world, we shall also rediscover ourself, since, perceiving as we do with our body, the body is a natural self and, as it were, the subject of perception.

FROM CHAPTER 1: SENSE-EXPERIENCE (*PP* 207–8 [240–2], 214–7 [248–51], 238–41 [276–80])

Merleau-Ponty begins by rejecting purely objective conceptions of the world and purely subjective conceptions of oneself. On the one hand, we do not ourselves belong within the objective world since perception itself is not a fact within the world; on the other hand, we are not pure subjects either, since our perceptions somehow involve our body in the gradual, perspectival, appearance of the things.

If we turn back to sense-experience itself, however, we find ourselves at the heart of our sensory fields, endowed by our bodily sense-organs with the power to perceive form and thus the appearances of things. Sense-perception is, therefore, our fundamental bodily way of being in the world, neither wholly objective nor wholly subjective. It rests upon a temporal synthesis whereby experience points beyond itself to past and future experiences of things; and in truth our embodied subjectivity is precisely the inherent temporality of sense-perception.

What is the subject of perception?

Objective thought is unaware of the subject of perception. This is because it presents itself with the world ready made, as the setting of every possible event, and treats perception as one of these events. For example, the empiricist philosopher considers a subject *x* in the act of perceiving and tries to describe what happens: *there are* sensations which are the subject's states or manners of being and, in virtue of this, genuine mental things. The perceiving subject is the place where these things occur, and the philosopher describes sensations and their sub-stratum as one might describe the fauna of a distant land – without being aware that he himself perceives, that he is the perceiving subject and that perception as he lives it belies everything that he says of perception in general. For, seen from the inside, perception owes nothing to what we know in other ways about the world, about *stimuli* as physics describes them and about the sense organs as described by biology. It does not present itself in the first place as an event in the world to which the category of causality, for example, can be applied, but as a re-creation or re-constitution of the world at every moment. In so far as we believe in the world's past, in the physical world, in 'stimuli', in the organism as our books depict it, it is first of all because we have present at this moment to us a perceptual field, a surface in contact with the world, a permanent rootedness in it, and because the world ceaselessly assails and beleaguers subjectivity as waves wash round a wreck on the shore. All knowledge takes its place within the horizons opened up by perception. There can be no question of describing perception itself as one of the facts thrown up in the world, since we can never fill up, in the picture of the world, that gap which we ourselves are, and by which it comes into existence for someone, since perception is the 'flaw' in this 'great diamond'.[1] Intellectualism certainly represents a step forward in coming to self-consciousness: that place outside the world at which the empiricist philosopher hints, and in which he tacitly takes up his position in order to describe the event of perception, now receives a name, and appears in the description. It is the transcendental Ego. Through it every empiricist thesis is reversed: the state of consciousness becomes the consciousness of a state, passivity the positing of passivity, the world becomes the correlative of thought about the world and henceforth exists only for a constituting agent. And yet it remains true to say that intellectualism too provides itself with a ready-made world. For the constitution of the world, as conceived by it, is a mere require-ment that to each term of the empiricist description be added the indica-tion 'consciousness of . . .' The whole system of experience – world, own body and empirical self – are subordinated to a universal thinker charged with sustaining the relationships between the three terms. But, since he is not actually involved, these relationships remain what they were in empiricism: causal relations spread out in the context of cosmic events. Now, if one's own body and the empirical self are no more than elements of the system of experience, objects among other objects in the eyes of the true *I*, how can we ever be confused with our body? How can we ever have believed that we saw with our eyes what we in fact grasp through an inspection of the mind; how is it that the world does not present itself to us as perfectly explicit; why is it displayed only grad-ually and never 'in its entirety'? In short, how does it come about that we perceive? We shall understand this only if the empirical self and the body are not immediately objects, in fact only if they never quite become objects, if there is a certain significance in saying that I can see the piece of wax with my eyes, and if correlatively the possibility of absence, the dimension of escape and freedom which reflection opens in the depths of our being, and which is called the transcendental Ego, are not initially given and are never absolutely acquired; if I can never say 'I' absolutely, and if every act of reflection, every voluntary taking up of a position is based on the ground and the proposition of a life of pre-personal consciousness. The subject of perception will remain over-looked as long as we cannot avoid the dilemma of *natura naturata* and *natura naturans*, of sensation as a state of consciousness and as the consciousness of a state, of existence in itself and existence for itself. Let us then return to sensation and scrutinize it closely enough to learn from it the living relation of the perceiver to his body and to his world. . . .

Let us be more explicit. The sentient and the sensible do not stand in relation to each other as two mutually external terms, and sensation is not an invasion of the sentient by the sensible. It is my gaze which subtends colour, and the movement of my hand which subtends the object's form, or rather my gaze pairs off with colour, and my hand with hardness and softness, and in this transaction between the subject of sensation and the sensible it cannot be held that one acts while the other suffers the action, or that one confers significance on the other. Apart from the probing of my eye or my hand, and before my body synchronizes with it, the sensible is nothing but a vague beckoning. 'If a subject tries to experience a specific colour, blue for example, while trying to take up the bodily attitude appropriate to red, an inner conflict results, a sort of spasm which stops as soon as he adopts the bodily attitude corresponding to blue.' Thus a sensible datum which is on the point of being felt sets a kind of muddled problem for my body to solve. I must find the attitude which *will* provide it with the means of becoming determinate, of showing up as blue; I must find the reply to a question which is obscurely expressed. And yet I do so only when I am invited by it, my attitude is never sufficient to make me really see blue or really touch a hard surface. The sensible gives back to me what I lent to it, but this is only what I took from it in the first place. As I contemplate the blue of the sky I am not *set over against* it as an acosmic subject; I do not possess it in thought, or spread out towards it some idea of blue such as might reveal the secret of it, I abandon myself to it and plunge into this mystery, it 'thinks itself within me',[2] I am the sky itself as it is drawn together and unified, and as it begins to exist for itself; my consciousness is saturated with this limitless blue. But, it may be retorted, the sky is not mind and there is surely no sense in saying that it exists for itself. It is indeed true that the geographer's or the astronomer's sky does not exist for itself. But of the sky, as it is perceived or sensed, subtended by my gaze which ranges over and resides in it, and providing as it does the theatre of a certain living pulsation adopted by my body, it can be said that it exists for itself, in the sense that it is not made up of mutually exclusive parts, that each part of the whole is 'sensitive' to what happens in all the others, and 'knows them dynamically'. As for the subject of sensation, he need not be a pure nothingness with no terrestrial weight. That would be necessary only if, like constituting consciousness, he had to be simultaneously omnipresent, coextensive with being, and in process of thinking universal truth. But the spectacle perceived does not partake of pure being. Taken exactly as I see it, it is a moment of my individual history, and since sensation is a reconstitution, it presupposes in me sediments left behind by some previous constitution, so that I am, as a sentient subject, a repository stocked with natural powers at which I am the first to be filled with wonder. I am not, therefore, in Hegel's phrase, 'a hole in being', but a hollow, a fold, which has been made and which can be unmade.[3]

We must stress this point. How have we managed to escape from the dilemma of the *for itself* and the *in itself*, how can perceptual consciousness be saturated with its object, how can we distinguish sensible consciousness from intellectual consciousness? Because: (1) Every perception takes place in an atmosphere of generality and is presented to us anonymously. I cannot say that *I* see the blue of the sky in the sense in which I say that I understand a book or again in which I decide to devote my life to mathematics. My perception, even when seen from the inside, expresses a given situation: I can see blue because I am *sensitive* to colours, whereas personal acts create a situation: I am a mathematician because I have decided to be one. So, if I wanted to render precisely the perceptual experience, I ought to say that *one* perceives in me, and not that I perceive. Every sensation carries within it the germ of a dream or depersonalization such as we experience in that quasi-stupor to which we are reduced when we really try to live at the level of sensation. It is true that knowledge teaches me that sensation would not occur unless my body were in some way adapted to it, for example, that there would be no specific contact unless I moved my hand. But this activity takes place on the periphery of my being. I am no more aware of being the true subject of my sensation than of my birth or my death. Neither my birth nor my death can appear to me as experiences of my own, since, if I thought of them thus, I should be assuming myself to be pre-existent to, or outliving, myself, in order to be able to experience them, and I should therefore not be genuinely thinking of my birth or my death. I can, then, apprehend myself only as 'already born' and 'still alive' – I can apprehend my birth and my death only as prepersonal horizons: I know that people are born and die, but I cannot know my own birth and death. Each sensation, being strictly speaking, the first, last and only one of its kind, is a birth and a death. The subject who experiences it begins and ends with it, and as he can neither precede nor survive himself, sensation necessarily appears to itself in a setting of generality, its origin is anterior to myself, it arises from *sensibility* which has preceded it and which will outlive it, just as my birth and death belong to a natality and a mortality which are anonymous. By means of sensation I am able to grasp, on the fringe of my own personal life and acts, a life of given consciousness from which these latter emerge, the life of my eyes, hands and ears, which are so many natural selves. Each time I experience a sensation, I feel that it concerns not my own being, the one for which I am responsible and for which I make decisions, but another self which has already sided with the world, which is already open to certain of its aspects and synchronized with them. Between my sensation and myself there stands always the thickness of some *primal acquisition* which prevents my experience from being clear of itself. I experience the sensation as a modality of a general existence, one already destined for a physical world and which runs through me without my being the cause of it.

Sensation can be anonymous only because it is incomplete. The person who sees and the one who touches is not exactly myself, because the visible and the tangible worlds are not the world in its entirety. When I see an object, I always feel that there is a portion of being beyond what I see at this moment, not only as regards visible being, but also as regards what is tangible or audible. And not only sensible being, but a depth of the object that no progressive sensory deduction will ever exhaust. In a corresponding way, I am not myself wholly in these operations, they remain marginal. They occur out in front of me, for the self which sees or the self which hears is in some way a specialized self, familiar with only one sector of being, and it is precisely for this reason that eye and hand are able to guess the movement which will fix the perception, thus displaying that foreknowledge which gives them an involuntary appearance.

We may summarize these two ideas by saying that any sensation belongs to a certain *field*. To say that I have a visual field is to say that by reason of my position I have access to and an opening upon a system of beings, visible beings, that these are at the disposal of my gaze in virtue of a kind of primordial contract and through a gift of nature, with no effort made on my part; from which it follows that vision is prepersonal. And it follows at the same time that it is always limited, that around what I am looking at at a given moment is spread a horizon of things which are not seen, or which are even invisible. Vision is a *thought subordinated to a certain field,* and this is what is called a *sense*. When I say that I have senses and that they give me access to the world, I am not the victim of some muddle, I do not confuse causal thinking and reflection, I merely express this truth which forces itself upon reflection taken as a whole: that I am able, being connatural with the world, to discover a sense in certain aspects of being without having myself endowed them with it through any constituting operation.

The perceptual synthesis is temporal

Let us return to the perceptual experience. I perceive this table on which I am writing. This means, among other things, that my act of perception *occupies me*, and occupies me sufficiently for me to be unable, while I am actually perceiving the table, to perceive myself perceiving it. When I want to do this, I cease, so to speak, to use my gaze in order to plunge into the table, I turn my back towards myself who am perceiving, and then realize that my perception must have gone through certain subjective appearances, and interpreted certain of my own 'sensations'; in short it takes its place in the perspective of my individual history. I start from unified experience and from there acquire, in a secondary way, consciousness of a unifying activity when, taking up an analytical attitude, I break up perception into qualities and sensations, and when, in order to recapture on the basis of these the object into which I was in the first place blindly thrown, I am obliged to suppose an act of synthesis which is merely the counterpart of my analysis. My act of perception, in its unsophisticated form, does not itself bring about this synthesis; it takes advantage of work already done, of a general synthesis constituted once and for all, and this is what I mean when I say that I perceive with my body or my senses, since my body and my senses are precisely that familiarity with the world born of habit, that implicit or sedimentary body of knowledge. If my consciousness were at present constituting the world which it perceives, no distance would separate them and there would be no possible discrepancy between them; it would find its way into the world's hidden concatenations, intentionality would carry us to the heart of the object, and simultaneously the percept would lose the thickness conferred by the present, and consciousness would not be lost and become bogged down in it. But what we in fact have is consciousness of an inexhaustible object, and we are sucked into it because, between it and us, there is this latent knowledge which our gaze uses – the possibility of its rational development being a mere matter of presumption on our part – and which remains for ever anterior to our perception. If, as we have said, every perception has something anonymous in it, this is because it makes use of something which it takes for granted. The *person who* perceives is not spread out before himself as a consciousness must be; he has historical density, he takes up a perceptual tradition and is faced with a present. In perception we do not think the object and we do not think ourselves thinking it, we are given over to the object and we merge into this body which is better informed than we are about the world, and about the motives we have and the means at our disposal for synthesizing it. That is why we said with Herder that man *is* a *sensorium commune*. In this primary layer of sense-experience which is discovered only provided that we really coincide with the act of perception and break with the critical attitude, I have the living experience of the unity of the subject and the intersensory unity of the thing, and do not conceive them after the fashion of analytical reflection and science. But what is the unified without unification, what is this object which is not yet an object for someone? Psychological reflection, which posits my act of perception as an event in my personal history, may well be a second order thing. But transcendental reflection, which reveals me as the non-temporal thinker of the object, brings nothing to it which is not already there: it restricts itself to the formulation of what gives significance to 'the table' and 'the chair', what underlies their stable structure and makes my experience of objectivity possible. In short, what is living the unity of the object or the subject, if it is not making it? Even if it be supposed that this unity makes its appearance with the phenomenon of my body, must I not think of it in my body in order to find it there, and must I not effect the synthesis of this phenomenon in order to have the experience of it? We are not trying to derive the *for itself* from the *in itself*, nor are we returning to some form of empiricism; the body to which we are entrusting the synthesis of the perceived world is not a pure datum, a thing passively received. For us the perceptual synthesis is a temporal synthesis, and subjectivity, at the level of perception, is nothing but temporality, and this is what enables us to leave to the subject of perception his opacity and historicity. I open my eyes on to my table, and my consciousness is flooded with colours and confused reflections; it is hardly distinguishable from what is offered to it; it spreads out, through its accompanying body, into the spectacle which so far is not a spectacle of anything. Suddenly, I start to focus my eyes on the table which is not yet there, I begin to look into the distance while there is as yet no depth, my body centres itself on an object which is still only potential, and so disposes its sensitive surfaces as to make it a present reality. I can thus re-assign to its place in the world the something which was impinging upon me, because I can, by slipping into the future, throw into the immediate past the world's first attack upon my senses, and direct myself towards the determinate object as towards a near future. The act of looking is indivisibly prospective, since the object is the final stage of my process of focusing, and retrospective, since it will present itself as preceding its own appearance, as the 'stimulus', the motive or the prime mover of every process since its beginning. The spatial synthesis and the synthesis of the object are based on this unfolding of time. In every focusing movement my body unites present, past and future, it secretes time, or rather it becomes that location in nature where, for the first time, events, instead of pushing each other into the realm of being, project round the present a double horizon of past and future and acquire a historical orientation. There is here indeed the summoning, but not the experience, of an eternal *natura naturans*. My body takes possession of time; it brings into existence a past and a future for a present; it is not a thing, but creates time instead of submitting to it. But every act of focusing must be renewed, otherwise it falls into unconsciousness. The object remains clearly before me provided that I run my eyes over it, free-ranging scope being an essential property of the gaze. The hold which it gives us upon a segment of time, the synthesis which it effects are themselves temporal phenomena which pass, and can be recaptured only in a fresh act which is itself temporal. The claim to objectivity laid by each perceptual act is remade by its successor, again disappointed and once more made. This ever-recurrent failure of perceptual consciousness was foreseeable from the start. If I cannot see the object except by distancing it in the past, this is because, like the first attack launched by the object upon my senses, the succeeding perception equally occupies and expunges my consciousness; it is because this perception will in turn pass away, the subject of perception never being an absolute subjectivity, but being destined to become an object for an ulterior *I*. Perception is always in the mode of the impersonal 'One'. It is not a personal act enabling me to give a fresh significance to my life. The person who, in sensory exploration, gives a past to the present and directs it towards a future, is not myself as an autonomous subject, but myself in so far as I have a body and am able to 'look'. Rather than being a genuine history, perception ratifies and renews in us a 'prehistory'. And that again is of the essence of time: there would be no present, that is to say, no sensible world with its thickness and inexhaustible richness, if perception, in Hegel's words, did not retain a past in the depth of the present, and did not contract that past into that depth. It fails at this moment to realize the synthesis of its object, not because it is the passive recipient of it, as empiricists would have it, but because the unity of the object makes its appearance through the medium of time, and because time slips away as fast as it catches up with itself. It is true that I find, through time, later experiences interlocking with earlier ones and carrying them further, but nowhere do I enjoy absolute possession of myself by myself, since the hollow void of the future is for ever being refilled with a fresh present. There is no related object without relation and without subject, no unity without unification, but every synthesis is both exploded and rebuilt by time which, with one and the same process, calls it into question and confirms it because it produces a new present which retains the past. The duality of *naturata* and *naturans* is therefore converted into a dialectic of constituted and constituting time. If we are to solve the problem which we have set ourselves – that of sensoriality, or finite subjectivity – it will be by thinking about time and showing how it exists only for a subjectivity, since without the latter, the past in itself being no longer and the future in itself being not yet, there would be no time – and how nevertheless this subject is time itself, and how we can say with Hegel that time is the existence of mind, or refer with Husserl to a self-constitution of time.

Notes

1 Cf.   Mes repentirs, mes doutes, mes contraintes
          Sont le défaut de ton grand diamant.
                                    Paul Valéry, *Le Cimetière marin*
                                                (Translator's note)

2 Cf.   Midi là-haut, Midi sans mouvement
          En soi se pense et convient à soi-même.
                                    Paul Valéry, *Le Cimetière marin*
                                                (Translator's note)

3 We have pointed out elsewhere that consciousness seen from outside cannot be a pure *for itself* (*The Structure of Behavior*). We are beginning to see that the same applies to consciousness seen from the inside.

FROM CHAPTER 3: THE THING AND THE NATURAL WORLD (*PP* 317–20 [370–4], 322–7 [375–81])

The things we perceive are unities among phenomena that are experienced as appearances of the same thing. This unity is not that of a substance postulated behind appearances; it is a unity formed by our body's way of organising experience, so that our body takes on the role of 'interlocutor' with the world. It is inherent in this role that the things we perceive should be felt to transcend our perceptions of them; but our bodily intentionality also projects further possibilities around the things that appear to us, and thereby leads us into an 'objective thinking', which is a kind of post-natal forgetfulness that 'severs the links which unite the thing and the embodied subject'. Thus although 'the thing is the outcome of a flow of subjective appearances', we do not experience it as such. Instead it confronts us as something altogether alien, and it takes the genius of a painter such as Cézanne to take us back to a visual 'pre-world' in which things take shape for us.

The thing as a norm of perception

We are now in a position to approach the analysis of the thing as an inter-sensory entity. The thing as presented to sight (the moon's pale disc) or to touch (my skull as I can feel it when I touch it), and which stays the same for us through a series of experiences, is neither a *quale* genuinely subsisting, nor the notion or consciousness of such an objective property, but what is discovered or taken up by our gaze or our movement, a question to which these things provide a fully appropriate reply. The object which presents itself to the gaze or the touch arouses a certain motor intention which aims not at the movements of one's own body, but at the thing itself from which they are, as it were, suspended. And in so far as my hand knows hardness and softness, and my gaze knows the moon's light, it is as a certain way of linking up with the phenomenon and communicating with it. Hardness and softness, roughness and smoothness, moonlight and sunlight, present themselves in our recollection, not pre-eminently as sensory contents, but as certain kinds of symbiosis, certain ways the outside has of invading us and certain ways we have of meeting this invasion, and memory here merely frees the framework of the perception from the place where it originates. If the constants of each sense are thus understood, the question of defining the inter-sensory thing into which they unite as a collection of stable attributes or as the notion of this collection, will not arise. The sensory 'properties' of a thing together constitute one and the same thing, just as my gaze, my touch and all my other senses are together the powers of one and the same body integrated into one and the same action. The surface which I am about to recognize as the surface of the table, when vaguely looked at, already summons me to focus upon it, and demands those movements of convergence which will endow it with its 'true' aspect. Similarly any object presented to one sense calls upon itself the concordant operation of all the others. I see a surface colour because I have a visual field, and because the arrangement of the field leads my gaze to that surface – perceive a thing because I have a field of existence and because each phenomenon, on its appearance, attracts towards that field the whole of my body as a system of perceptual powers. I run through appearances and reach the real colour or the real shape when my experience is at its maximum of clarity, in spite of the fact that Berkeley may retort that a fly would see the same object differently or that a stronger microscope would transform it: these different appearances are for me appearances of a certain true spectacle, that in which the perceived configuration, for a sufficient degree of clarity, reaches its maximum richness. I have visual objects because I have a visual field in which richness and clarity are in inverse proportion to each other, and because these two demands, either of which taken separately might be carried to infinity, when brought together, produce a certain culmination and optimum balance in the perceptual process. In the same way, what I call experience of the thing or of reality – not merely of a reality-for-sight or for-touch, but of an absolute reality – is my full co-existence with the phenomenon, at the moment when it is in every way at its maximum articulation, and the 'data of the different senses' are directed towards this one pole, as my 'aims' as I look through a microscope vacillate about one predominant 'target'. I do not propose to bestow the term 'visual thing' upon a phenomenon which, like areas of colour, presents no maximum visibility through the various experiences which I have of it, or which, like the sky, remote and thin on the horizon, unlocalized and diffuse at the zenith, allows itself to be contaminated by the structures closest to it without setting over against them any configuration of its own. If a phenomenon – for example, a reflection or a light gust of wind – strikes only one of my senses, it is a mere phantom, and it will come near to real existence only if, by some chance, it becomes capable of speaking to my other senses, as does the wind when, for example, it blows strongly and can be seen in the tumult it causes in the surrounding countryside. Cézanne declared that a picture contains within itself even the smell of the landscape. He meant that the arrangement of colour on the thing (and in the work of art, if it catches the thing in its entirety) signifies by itself all the responses which would be elicited through an examination by the remaining senses; that a thing would not have this colour had it not also this shape, these tactile properties, this resonance, this odour, and that the thing is the absolute fullness which my undivided existence projects before itself. The unity of the thing beyond all its fixed properties is not a substratum, a vacant X, an inherent subject, but that unique accent which is to be found in each one of them, that unique manner of existing of which they are a second order expression. For example, the brittleness, hardness, transparency and crystal ring of a glass all translate a single manner of being. If a sick man sees the devil, he sees at the same time his smell, his flames and smoke, because the significant unity 'devil' is precisely that acrid, fire-and-brimstone essence. There is a symbolism in the thing which links each sensible quality to the rest. Heat enters experience as a kind of vibration of the thing; with colour on the other hand it is as if the thing is thrust outside itself, and it is *a priori* necessary that an extremely hot object should redden, for it is its excess of vibration which causes it to blaze forth.[1] The passing of sensory givens before our eyes or under our hands is, as it were, a language which teaches itself, and in which the meaning is secreted by the very structure of the signs, and this is why it can literally be said that our senses question things and that things reply to them. 'The sensible appearance is what reveals (*Kundgibt*), and expresses as such what it is not itself'. We understand the thing as we understand a new kind of behaviour, not, that is, through any intellectual operation of subsumption, but by taking up on our own account the mode of existence which the observable signs adumbrate before us. A form of behaviour outlines a certain manner of treating the world. In the same way, in the interaction of things, each one is characterized by a kind of *a priori* to which it remains faithful in all its encounters with the outside world. The significance of a thing inhabits that thing as the soul inhabits the body: it is not behind appearances. The significance of the ash-tray (at least its total and individual significance, as this is given in perception) is not a certain idea of the ash-tray which co-ordinates its sensory aspects and is accessible to the understanding alone, it animates the ash-tray, and is self-evidently embodied in it. That is why we say that in perception the thing is given to us 'in person', or 'in the flesh'. Prior to and independently of other people, the thing achieves that miracle of expression: an inner reality which reveals itself externally, a significance which descends into the world and begins its existence there, and which can be fully understood only when the eyes seek it in its own location. Thus the thing is correlative to my body and, in more general terms, to my existence, of which my body is merely the stabilized structure. It is constituted in the hold which my body takes upon it; it is not first of all a meaning for the understanding, but a structure accessible to inspection by the body, and if we try to describe the real as it appears to us in perceptual experience, we find it overlaid with anthropological predicates.

The relations between things or aspects of things having always our body as their vehicle, the whole of nature is the setting of our own life, or our interlocutor in a sort of dialogue. That is why in the last analysis we cannot conceive anything which is not perceived or perceptible. As Berkeley says, even an unexplored desert has at least one person to observe it, namely myself when I think of it, that is, when I perceive it in purely mental experience. The thing is inseparable from a person perceiving it, and can never be actually *in itself* because its articulations are those of our very existence, and because it stands at the other end of our gaze or at the terminus of a sensory exploration which invests it with humanity. To this extent, every perception is a communication or a communion, the taking up or completion by us of some extraneous intention or, on the other hand, the complete expression outside ourselves of our perceptual powers and a coition, so to speak, of our body with things. The fact that this may not have been realized earlier is explained by the fact that any coming to awareness of the perceptual world was hampered by the prejudices arising from objective thinking. The function of the latter is to reduce all phenomena which bear witness to the union of subject and world, putting in their place the clear idea of the object as *in itself* and of the subject as pure consciousness. It therefore severs the links which unite the thing and the embodied subject, leaving only sensible qualities to make up our world (to the exclusion of the modes of appearance which we have described), and preferably visual qualities, because these give the impression of being autonomous, and because they are less directly linked to our body and present us with an object rather than introducing us into an atmosphere. But in reality all things are concretions of a setting, and any explicit perception of a thing survives in virtue of a previous communication with a certain atmosphere. . . .

The real as an identity of meaning among the data

However, we have not exhausted the meaning of 'the thing' by defining it as the correlative of our body and our life. After all, we grasp the unity of our body only in that of the thing, and it is by taking things as our starting point that our hands, eyes and all our sense-organs appear to us as so many interchangeable instruments. The body by itself, the body at rest is merely an obscure mass, and we perceive it as a precise and identifiable being when it moves towards a thing, and in so far as it is intentionally projected outwards, and even then this perception is never more than incidental and marginal to consciousness, the centre of which is occupied with things and the world. One cannot, as we have said, conceive any perceived thing without someone to perceive it. But the fact remains that the thing presents itself to the person who perceives it as a thing in itself, and thus poses the problem of a genuine *in-itself-for-us*. Ordinarily we do not notice this because our perception, in the context of our everyday concerns, alights on things sufficiently attentively to discover in them their familiar presence, but not sufficiently so to disclose the non-human element which lies hidden in them. But the thing holds itself aloof from us and remains self-sufficient. This will become clear if we suspend our ordinary preoccupations and pay a metaphysical and disinterested attention to it. It is then hostile and alien, no longer an interlocutor, but a resolutely silent Other, a Self which evades us no less than does intimacy with an outside consciousness. The thing and the world, we have already said, are offered to perceptual communication as is a familiar face with an expression which is immediately understood. But then a face expresses something only through the arrangements of the colours and lights which make it up, the meaning of the gaze being not behind the eyes, but in them, and a touch of colour more or less is all the painter needs in order to transform the facial expression of a portrait. In the work of his earlier years, Cézanne tried to paint the expression first and foremost, and that is why he never caught it. He gradually learned that expression is the language of the thing itself and springs from its configuration. His painting is an attempt to recapture the physiognomy of things and faces by the integral reproduction of their sensible configuration. This is what nature constantly and effortlessly achieves, and it is why the paintings of Cézanne are 'those of a pre-world in which as yet no men existed'. The thing appeared to us above as the goal of a bodily teleology, the norm of our psycho-physiological setting. But that was merely a psychological definition which does not make the full meaning of the thing defined explicit, and which reduces the thing to those experiences in which we encounter it. We now discover the core of reality: a thing is a thing because, whatever it imparts to us, is imparted through the very organization of its sensible aspects. The 'real' is that environment in which each moment is not only in separable from the rest, but in some way synonymous with them, in which the 'aspects' are mutually significatory and absolutely equivalent. This is perfect fulness: it is impossible completely to describe the colour of the carpet without saying that it *is* a carpet, made of wool, and without implying in this colour a certain tactile value, a certain weight and a certain resistance to sound. The thing is an entity of a kind such that the complete definition of one of its attributes demands that of the subject in its entirety: an entity, consequently, the significance of which is indistinguishable from its total appearance. Cézanne again said: 'The outline and the colour are no longer distinct; in proportion as one paints, one outlines, and the more the colour is harmonized, the more definite the outline becomes ... when the colour is at its richest, the form is at its most complete'. With the structure lighting-lighted, background and foreground are possible. With the appearance of the thing, there can at last be univocal forms and positions. The system of appearances, the pre-spatial fields acquire an anchorage and ultimately become a space. But it is not the case that geometrical features alone are merged with colour. The very significance of the thing is built up before our eyes, a significance which no verbal analysis can exhaust, and which merges with the exhibiting of the thing in its self-evidence. Every touch of colour applied by Cézanne must, as E. Bernard says, 'contain the atmosphere, the light, the object, the relief, the character, the outline and the style'. Each fragment of a visible spectacle satisfies an infinite number of conditions, and it is of the nature of the real to compress into each of its instants an infinity of relations. Like the thing, the picture has to be seen and not defined, nevertheless, though it is a small world which reveals itself within the larger one, it cannot lay claim to the same substantiality. We feel that it is put together by design, that in it significance precedes existence and clothes itself in only the minimum of matter necessary for its communication. The miracle of the real world, on the other hand, is that in it significance and existence are one, and that we see the latter lodge itself in no uncertain fashion in the former. In the realm of imagination, I have no sooner formed the intention of seeing than I already believe that I have seen. The imaginary has no depth, and does not respond to our efforts to vary our points of view; it does not lend itself to our observation. We never have a hold upon it. In every perception, on the other hand, it is the material itself which assumes significance and form. If I wait for someone at a door in a poorly lit street, each person who comes out has an indistinct appearance. *Someone* is coming out, and I do not yet know whether I can recognize him as the person I am waiting for. The familiar figure will emerge from this nebulous background as the earth does from a ground mist. The real is distinguishable from our fictions because in reality the significance encircles and permeates matter. Once a picture is torn up, we have in our hands nothing but pieces of daubed canvas. But if we break up a stone and then further break up the fragments, the pieces remaining are still pieces of stone. The real lends itself to unending exploration; it is inexhaustible. This is why objects belonging to man, tools, seem to be placed on the world, whereas things are rooted in a background of nature which is alien to man. For our human existence, the thing is much less a pole which attracts than one which repels. We do not begin by knowing the per-spective aspects of the thing; it is not mediated by our senses, our sensations or our perspectives; we go straight to it, and it is only in a secondary way that we become aware of the limits of our knowledge and of ourselves as knowing. Here is a die; let us consider it as it is presented, in the natural attitude, to a subject who has never wondered about perception, and who lives among things. The die is there, lying in the world. When the subject moves round it, there appear, not *signs*, but sides of the die. He does not perceive projections or even profiles of the die, but he sees the die itself at one time from this side, at another from that, and those appearances which are not yet firmly fixed inter-communicate, run into each other, and all radiate from a central *Würfelhaftigkeit* which is the mystical link between them.

A set of reductions makes its appearance from the moment we take the perceiving subject into account. In the first place I notice that this die is for me only. Perhaps after all people nearby do not see it, and this alone deprives it of some element of its reality; it ceases to be *in itself* in order to become the pole of a personal history. Then I observe that the die is, strictly speaking, presented to me only through sight, and immediately I am left with nothing but the outer surface of the whole die; it loses its materiality, empties itself, and is reduced to a visual structure of form, colour, light and shade. But the form, colour, light and shade are not in a void, for they still retain a point of support, namely the visual thing. Furthermore the visual thing has still a spatial structure which endows its qualitative properties with a particular value: if I learn that the die is merely an illusory one, its colour changes straight away, and it no longer has the same manner of modulating space. All the spatial relations to be found in the die and which are capable of being made explicit, for example the distance from its nearer to its farther face, the 'real' size of the angles, the 'real' direction of its sides, are indivisible in its being as a visible die. It is by way of a third reduction that we pass from the visual thing to the perspective aspect: I observe that the faces of the die cannot all fall beneath my gaze, and that certain of them undergo distortions. Through a final reduction, I arrive ultimately at the sensation which is no longer a property of the thing, or even of the perspective aspect, but a modification of my body. The experience of the thing does not go through all these mediations, and consequently the thing is not presented to a mind which seizes each constituent layer as representative of a higher layer, building it up from start to finish. It exists primarily in its self-evidence, and any attempt to define the thing either as a pole of my bodily life, or as a permanent possibility of sensations, or as a synthesis of appearances, puts in place of the thing itself in its primordial being an imperfect reconstruction of the thing with the aid of bits and pieces of subjective provenance. How are we to understand both that the thing is the correlative of my knowing body, and that it rejects that body?

The thing is 'prior' to man

What is given is not the thing on its own, but the experience of the thing, or something transcendent standing in the wake of one's subjectivity, some kind of natural entity of which a glimpse is afforded through a personal history. If one tried, according to the realistic approach, to make perception into some coincidence with the thing, it would no longer be possible to understand what the perceptual event was, how the subject managed to assimilate the thing, how after coinciding with the thing he was able to consign it to his own history, since *ex hypothesi* he would have nothing of it in his possession. In order to perceive things, we need to live them. Yet we reject the idealism involved in the synthetic view, because it too distorts our lived-through relationship to things. In so far as the perceiving subject synthesizes the percept, he has to dominate and grasp in thought a material of perception, to organize and himself link together, from the inside, all the aspects of the thing, which means that perception ceases to be inherent in an individual subject and a point of view, and that the thing loses its transcendence and opacity. To 'live' a thing is not to coincide with it, nor fully to embrace it in thought. Our problem, therefore, becomes clear. The perceiving subject must, without relinquishing his place and his point of view, and in the opacity of sensation, reach out towards things to which he has, in advance, no key, and for which he nevertheless carries within himself the project, and open himself to an absolute Other which he is making ready in the depths of his being. The thing is not all of a piece, for though the perspective aspects, and the ever-changing flow of appearances, are not explicitly posited, all are at least ready to be perceived and given in non-positing consciousness, to precisely the extent necessary for me to be able to escape from them into the thing. When I perceive a pebble, I am not expressly conscious of knowing it only through my eyes, of enjoying only certain perspective aspects of it, and yet an analysis in these terms, if I undertake it, does not surprise me. Beforehand I knew obscurely that my gaze was the medium and instrument of comprehensive perception, and the pebble appeared to me in the full light of day in opposition to the concentrated darkness of my bodily organs. I can imagine possible fissures in the solid mass of the thing if I take it into my head to close one eye or to think of the perspective. It is in this way that it is true to say that the thing is the outcome of a flow of subjective appearances. And yet I did not actually constitute it, in the sense that I did not actively and through a process of mental inspection posit the interrelations of the many aspects presented to the senses, and the relations of all of them to my different kinds of sensory apparatus. We have expressed this by saying that I perceive with my body. The visual thing appears when my gaze, following the indications offered by the spectacle, and drawing together the light and shade spread over it, ultimately settles on the lighted surface as upon that which the light reveals. My gaze 'knows' the significance of a certain patch of light in a certain context; it understands the logic of lighting. Expressed in more general terms, there is a logic of the world to which my body in its entirety conforms, and through which things of intersensory significance become possible for us. In so far as it is capable of synergy, my body knows the significance, for the totality of my experience, of this or that colour added or subtracted, and the occurrence of any such change is immediately picked out from the object's presentation and general significance. To have senses, sight for example, is to possess that general apparatus, that cast of possible visual relations with the help of which we are able to take up any given visual grouping. To have a body is to possess a universal setting, a schema of all types of perceptual unfolding and of all those inter-sensory correspondences which lie beyond the segment of the world which we are actually perceiving. A thing is, therefore, not actually *given* in perception, it is internally taken up by us, reconstituted and experienced by us in so far as it is bound up with a world, the basic structures of which we carry with us, and of which it is merely one of many possible concrete forms. Although a part of our living experience, it is nevertheless transcendent in relation to our life because the human body, with its habits which weave round it a human environment, has running through it a movement towards the world itself. Animal behaviour aims at an animal setting (*Umwelt*) and centres of resistance (*Widerstand*). If we try to subject it to natural stimuli devoid of concrete significance, we produce neuroses. Human behaviour opens upon a world (*Welt*) and upon an object (*Gegenstand*) beyond the tools which it makes for itself, and one may even treat one's own body as an object. Human life is defined in terms of this power which it has of denying itself in objective thought, a power which stems from its primordial attachment to the world itself. Human life 'understands' not only a certain definite environment, but an infinite number of possible environments, and it understands itself because it is thrown into a natural world.

Note

1 This unity of the sensory experiences rests on their integration in a single life of which they thus become the visible witness and emblem. The perceived world is not only a system of symbols of each sense in terms of the other senses, but also a set of symbols of human life, as is proved by the 'flames' of passion, the 'light' of the spirit and so many other metaphors and myths.

FROM CHAPTER 4: OTHER SELVES AND THE HUMAN WORLD (*PP* 347–65 [405–25])

Merleau-Ponty's account of the constitution of things within the natural world has, deliberately, made no reference to others. But our ordinary experience of things such as roads, cutlery and villages is permeated with references to other people, and Merleau-Ponty now asks, in a Kantian way, how this is possible and, more generally, how we can make sense of there being other subjects just like ourselves.

He starts by arguing that the familiar sense of a difficulty here arises because we are liable to think of the issue from the standpoint of realism or idealism, so that the other must be either just another object within the world or another pure subject who constitutes the world. But neither of these approaches allows for another who is a subject but not me. Merleau-Ponty argues that the way to move beyond these familiar debates is to get behind objective thought to our pre-objective experience of ourselves and the world. For once we have internalized this new conception of our own bodily being in the world, we will be in a position to understand how there can be other similar bodily experiences of the world which are not located mysteriously inside another's body but are expressed through behaviour in just the way that my behaviour expresses my own being.

At this pre-objective level it is not simply that the existence of others becomes conceivable, it becomes manifest through the ways in which we make sense of each other and relate to each other. Language, and especially dialogue, has a special role here, for in a dialogue we 'co-exist through a common world'. Thus Merleau-Ponty rejects the Sartrean thesis that 'being-for-others' is the experience of inescapable master–slave conflict as subjects seek to dominate each other. But he adds that it is important not to exaggerate our understanding of each other in this intersubjective intermonde.

For we recognise each other always as another *subject, someone with whom indifference as well as reciprocity is possible. Hence 'There is here a genuine solipsism rooted in living experience and quite insurmountable.' This limitation enters into the constitution of the social world: we cannot escape from our relatedness to others, but we cannot become one with them. Thus there is here experience of a new form of transcendence: in the social world I acknowledge the presence to me of another subject whose presence to herself I can never experience.*

How is the Other possible?

Just as nature finds its way to the core of my personal life and becomes inextricably linked with it, so behaviour patterns settle into that nature, being deposited in the form of a cultural world. Not only have I a physical world, not only do I live in the midst of earth, air and water, I have around me roads, plantations, villages, streets, churches, implements, a bell, a spoon, a pipe. Each of these objects is moulded to the human action which it serves. Each one spreads round it an atmosphere of humanity which may be determinate in a low degree, in the case of a few footmarks in the sand, or on the other hand highly determinate, if I go into every room from top to bottom of a house recently evacuated. Now, although it may not be surprising that the sensory and perceptual functions should lay down a natural world in front of themselves, since they are prepersonal, it may well seem strange that the spontaneous acts through which man has patterned his life should be deposited, like some sediment, outside himself and lead an anonymous existence as things. The civilization in which I play my part exists for me in a self-evident way in the implements with which it provides itself. If it is a question of an unknown or alien civilization, then several manners of being or of living can find their place in the ruins or the broken instruments which I discover, or in the landscape through which I roam. The cultural world is then ambiguous, but it is already present. I have before me a society to be known. An Objective Spirit dwells in the remains and the scenery. How is this possible? In the cultural object, I feel the close presence of others beneath a veil of anonymity. *Someone* uses the pipe for smoking, the spoon for eating, the bell for summoning, and it is through the perception of a human act and another person that the perception of a cultural world could be verified. How can an action or a human thought be grasped in the mode of the 'one' since, by its very nature, it is a first person operation, inseparable from an *I*? It is easy to reply that the indefinite pronoun is here no more than a vague formula for referring to a multiplicity of *I*'s or even a general *I*. It will be said that I experience a certain cultural environment along with behaviour corresponding to it: faced with the remains of an extinct civilization, I conceive analogically the kind of man who lived in it. But the first need is to know how I experience my own cultural world, my own civilization. The reply will once more be that I see a certain use made by other men of the implements which surround me, that I interpret their behaviour by analogy with my own, and through my inner experience, which teaches me the significance and intention of perceived gestures. In the last resort, the actions of others are, according to this theory, always understood through my own; the 'one' or the 'we' through the 'I'. But this is precisely the question: how can the word 'I' be put into the plural, how can a general idea of the *I* be formed, how can I speak of an *I* other than my own, how can I know that there are other *I*'s, how can consciousness which, by its nature, and as self-knowledge, is in the mode of the *I*, be grasped in the mode of Thou, and through this, in the world of the 'One'? The very first of all cultural objects, and the one by which all the rest exist, is the body of the other person as the vehicle of a form of behaviour. Whether it be a question of vestiges or the body of another person, we need to know how an object in space can become the eloquent relic of an existence; how, conversely, an intention, a thought or a project can detach themselves from the personal subject and become visible outside him in the shape of his body, and in the environment which he builds for himself. The constitution of the other person does not fully elucidate that of society, which is not an existence involving two or even three people, but co-existence involving an indefinite number of consciousnesses. Yet the analysis of the perception of others runs up against a difficulty in principle raised by the cultural world, since it is called upon to solve the paradox of a consciousness seen from the outside, of a thought which has its abode in the external world, and which, therefore, is already subjectless and anonymous compared with mine.

The discovery of perceptual consciousness makes co-existence possible

What we have said about the body provides the beginning of a solution to this problem. The existence of other people is a difficulty and an outrage for objective thought. If the events of the world are, in Lachelier's words, a network of general properties standing at the point of intersection of functional relations which, in principle, enable the analysis of the former to be carried through, and if the body is indeed a province of the world, if it is that object which the biologist talks about, that conjunction of processes analysed in physiological treatises, that collection of organs shown in the plates of books on anatomy, then my experience can be nothing but the dialogue between bare consciousness and the system of objective correlations which it conceives. The body of another, like my own, is not inhabited, but is an object standing before the consciousness which thinks about or constitutes it. Other men, and myself, seen as empirical beings, are merely pieces of mechanism worked by springs, but the true subject has no counterpart, for that consciousness which is hidden in so much flesh and blood is the least intelligible of occult qualities. My consciousness, being co-extensive with what can exist for me, and corresponding to the whole system of experience, cannot encounter, in that system, another consciousness capable of bringing immediately to light in the world the background, unknown to me, of its own phenomena. There are two modes of being, and two only: being in itself, which is that of objects arrayed in space, and being for itself, which is that of consciousness. Now, another person would seem to stand before me as an *in-itself* and yet to exist *for himself*, thus requiring of me, in order to be perceived, a contradictory operation, since I ought both to distinguish him from myself, and therefore place him in the world of objects, and think of him as a consciousness, that is, the sort of being with no outside and no parts, to which I have access merely because that being is myself, and because the thinker and the thought about are amalgamated in him. There is thus no place for other people and a plurality of consciousnesses in objective thought. In so far as I constitute the world, I cannot conceive another consciousness, for it too would have to constitute the world and, at least as regards this other view of the world, I should not be the constituting agent. Even if I succeeded in thinking of it as constituting the world, it would be I who would be constituting the consciousness as such, and once more I should be the sole constituting agent.

But we have in fact learned to shed doubt upon objective thought, and have made contact, on the hither side of scientific representations of the world and the body, with an experience of the body and the world which these scientific approaches do not successfully embrace. My body and the world are no longer objects co-ordinated together by the kind of functional relationships that physics establishes. The system of experience in which they intercommunicate is not spread out before me and ranged over by a constituting consciousness. *I have* the world as an incomplete individual, through the agency of my body as the potentiality of this world, and I have the positing of objects through that of my body, or conversely the positing of my body through that of objects, not in any kind of logical implication, as we determine an unknown size through its objective relations to given sizes, but in a real implication, and because my body is a movement towards the world, and the world my body's point of support. The ideal of objective thought – the system of experience conceived as a cluster of physico-mathematical correlations – is grounded in my perception of the world as an individual concordant with itself, and when science tries to include my body among the relationships obtaining in the objective world, it is because it is trying, in its way, to translate the suturation of my phenomenal body on to the primordial world. At the same time as the body withdraws from the objective world, and forms between the pure subject and the object a third genus of being, the subject loses its purity and its transparency. Objects stand before me and throw on to my retina a certain projection of themselves, and I perceive them. There can no longer be any question of isolating, in my physiological representation of the phenomenon, the retinal images and their cerebral counterpart from the total field, actual and possible, in which they appear. The physiological event is merely the abstract schema of the perceptual event. Nor can one invoke, under the name of mental images, discontinuous perspective views corresponding to the successive retinal images, or finally bring in an 'inspection of the mind' which restores the object beyond the distorting perspectives. We must conceive the perspectives and the point of view as our insertion into the world-as-an-individual, and perception, no longer as a constitution of the true object, but as our inherence in things. Consciousness reveals in itself, along with the sensory fields and with the world as the field of all fields, the opacity of a primary past. If I experience this inhering of my consciousness in its body and its world, the perception of other people and the plurality of consciousnesses no longer present any difficulty. If, for myself who am reflecting on perception, the perceiving subject appears provided with a primordial setting in relation to the world, drawing in its train that bodily thing in the absence of which there would be no other things for it, then why should other bodies which I perceive not be similarly inhabited by consciousnesses? If my consciousness has a body, why should other bodies not 'have' consciousness? Clearly this involves a profound transformation of the notions of body and consciousness. As far as the body is concerned, even the body of another, we must learn to distinguish it from the objective body as set forth in works on physiology. This is not the body which is capable of being inhabited by a consciousness. We must restore to visible bodies those forms of behaviour which are outlined by them and which appear on them, but are not really contained in them.[1] How significance and intentionality could come to dwell in molecular edifices or masses of cells is a thing which can never be made comprehensible, and here Cartesianism is right. But there is, in any case, no question of any such absurd undertaking. It is simply a question of recognizing that the body, as a chemical structure or an agglomeration of tissues, is formed, by a process of impoverishment, from a primordial phenomenon of the body-for-us, the body of human experience or the perceived body, round which objective thought works, but without being called upon to postulate its completed analysis. As for consciousness, it has to be conceived, no longer as a constituting consciousness and, as it were, a pure being-for-itself, but as a perceptual consciousness, as the subject of a pattern of behaviour, as being-in-the-world or existence, for only thus can another appear at the top of his phenomenal body, and be endowed with a sort of 'locality'. Under these conditions the antinomies of objective thought vanish. Through phenomenological reflection I discover vision, not as a 'thinking about seeing', to use Descartes's expression, but as a gaze at grips with a visible world, and that is why for me there can be another's gaze; that expressive instrument called a face can carry an existence, as my own existence is carried by my body, that knowledge-acquiring apparatus. When I turn towards perception, and pass from direct perception to thinking about that perception, I re-enact it, and find at work in my organs of perception a thinking older than myself of which those organs are merely the trace. In the same way I understand the existence of other people. Here again I have only the trace of a consciousness which evades me in its actuality and, when my gaze meets another gaze, I re-enact the alien existence in a sort of reflection. There is nothing here resembling 'reasoning by analogy'. As Scheler so rightly declares, reasoning by analogy presupposes what it is called on to explain. The other consciousness can be deduced only if the emotional expressions of others are compared and identified with mine, and precise correlations recognized between my physical behaviour and my 'psychic events'. Now the perception of others is anterior to, and the condition of, such observations, the observations do not constitute the perception. A baby of fifteen months opens its mouth if I playfully take one of its fingers between my teeth and pretend to bite it. And yet it has scarcely looked at its face in a glass, and its teeth are not in any case like mine. The fact is that its own mouth and teeth, as it feels them from the inside, are immediately, for it, an apparatus to bite with, and my jaw, as the baby sees it from the outside, is immediately, for it, capable of the same intentions. 'Biting' has immediately, for it, an intersubjective significance. It perceives its intentions in its body, and my body with its own, and thereby my intentions in its own body. The observed correlations between my physical behaviour and that of others, my intentions and my pantomime, may well provide me with a clue in the methodical attempt to know others and on occasions when direct perception fails, but they do not teach me the existence of other people. Between my consciousness and my body as I experience it, between this phenomenal body of mine and that of another as I see it from the outside, there exists an internal relation which causes the other to appear as the completion of the system. The possibility of another person's being self-evident is owed to the fact that I am not transparent for myself, and that my subjectivity draws its body in its wake. We said earlier: in so far as the other person resides in the world, is visible there, and forms a part of my field, he is never an Ego in the sense in which I am one for myself. In order to think of him as a genuine *I*, I ought to think of myself as a mere object for him, which I am prevented from doing by the knowledge which I have of myself. But if another's body is not an object for me, nor mine an object for him, if both are manifestations of behaviour, the positing of the other does not reduce me to the status of an object in his field, nor does my perception of the other reduce him to the status of an object in mine. The other person is never quite a personal being, if I myself am totally one, and if I grasp myself as apodeictically self-evident. But if I find in myself, through reflection, along with the perceiving subject, a pre-personal subject given to itself, and if my perceptions are centred outside me as sources of initiative and judgement, if the perceived world remains in a state of neutrality, being neither verified as an object nor recognized as a dream, then it is not the case that everything that appears in the world is arrayed before me, and so the behaviour of other people can have its place there. This world may remain undivided between my perception and his, the self which perceives is in no particularly privileged position which rules out a perceived self; both are, not *cogitationes* shut up in their own immanence, but beings which are outrun by their world, and which consequently may well be outrun by each other. The affirmation of an alien consciousness standing over against mine would immediately make my experience into a private spectacle, since it would no longer be co-extensive with being. The *cogito* of another person strips my own *cogito* of all value, and causes me to lose the assurance which I enjoyed in my solitude of having access to the only being conceivable for me, being, that is, as it is aimed at and constituted by me. But we have learned in individual perception not to conceive our perspective views as independent of each other; we know that they slip into each other and are brought together finally in the thing. In the same way we must learn to find the communication between one consciousness and another in one and the same world. In reality, other people are not included in my perspective of the world because this perspective itself has no definite limits, because it slips spontaneously into the other person's, and because both are brought together in the one single world in which we all participate as anonymous subjects of perception.

Co-existence of psycho-physical subjects in a natural world, and of men in a cultural world

In so far as I have sensory functions, a visual, auditory and tactile field, I am already in communication with others taken as similar psycho-physical subjects. No sooner has my gaze fallen upon a living body in process of acting than the objects surrounding it immediately take on a fresh layer of significance: they are no longer simply what I myself could make of them, they are what this other pattern of behaviour is about to make of them. Round about the perceived body a vortex forms, towards which my world is drawn and, so to speak, sucked in: to this extent, it is no longer merely mine, and no longer merely present, it is present to x, to that other manifestation of behaviour which begins to take shape in it. Already the other body has ceased to be a mere fragment of the world, and become the theatre of a certain process of elaboration, and, as it were, a certain 'view' of the world. There is taking place over there a certain manipulation of things hitherto my property. Someone is making use of my familiar objects. But who can it be? I say that it is another person, a second self, and this I know in the first place because this living body has the same structure as mine. I experience my own body as the power of adopting certain forms of behaviour and a certain world, and I am given to myself merely as a certain hold upon the world: now, it is precisely my body which perceives the body of another person, and discovers in that other body a miraculous prolongation of my own intentions, a familiar way of dealing with the world. Henceforth, as the parts of my body together comprise a system, so my body and the other person's are one whole, two sides of one and the same phenomenon, and the anonymous existence of which my body is the ever-renewed trace henceforth inhabits both bodies simultaneously.[2]

All of which makes another living being, but not yet another man. But this alien life, like mine with which it is in communication, is an open life. It is not entirely accounted for by a certain number of biological or sensory functions. It annexes natural objects by diverting them from their immediate significance, it makes tools for itself, and projects itself into the environment in the shape of cultural objects. The child finds them around him at birth like meteorites from another planet. He appropriates them and learns to use them as others do, because the body image ensures the immediate correspondence of what he sees done and what he himself does, and because in that way the implement is fixed in his mind as a determinate *manipulandum*, and other people as centres of human action. There is one particular cultural object which is destined to play a crucial rôle in the perception of other people: language. In the experience of dialogue, there is constituted between the other person and myself a common ground; my thought and his are interwoven into a single fabric, my words and those of my interlocutor are called forth by the state of the discussion, and they are inserted into a shared operation of which neither of us is the creator. We have here a dual being, where the other is for me no longer a mere bit of behaviour in my transcendental field, nor I in his; we are collaborators for each other in consummate reciprocity. Our perspectives merge into each other, and we co-exist through a common world. In the present dialogue, I am freed from myself, for the other person's thoughts are certainly his; they are not of my making, though I do grasp them the moment they come into being, or even anticipate them. And indeed, the objection which my interlocutor raises to what I say draws from me thoughts which I had no idea I possessed, so that at the same time that I lend him thoughts, he reciprocates by making me think too. It is only retrospectively, when I have withdrawn from the dialogue and am recalling it that I am able to reintegrate it into my life and make of it an episode in my private history, and that the other recedes into his absence, or, in so far as he remains present for me, is felt as a threat. The perception of other people and the intersubjective world are problematical only for adults. The child lives in a world which he unhesitatingly believes accessible to all around him. He has no awareness of himself or of others as private subjectivities, nor does he suspect that all of us, himself included, are limited to one certain point of view of the world. That is why he subjects neither his thoughts, in which he believes as they present themselves, without attempting to link them to each other, nor our words, to any sort of criticism. He has no knowledge of points of view. For him men are empty heads turned towards one single, self-evident world where everything takes place, even dreams, which are, he thinks, in his room, and even thinking, since it is not distinct from words. Others are for him so many gazes which inspect things, and have an almost material existence, so much so that the child wonders how these gazes avoid being broken as they meet. At about twelve years old, says Piaget, the child achieves the *cogito* and reaches the truths of rationalism. At this stage, it is held, he discovers himself both as a point of view on the world and also as called upon to transcend that point of view, and to construct an objectivity at the level of judgement. Piaget brings the child to a mature outlook as if the thoughts of the adult were self-sufficient and disposed of all contradictions. But, in reality, it must be the case that the child's outlook is in some way vindicated against the adult's and against Piaget, and that the unsophisticated thinking of our earliest years remains as an indispensable acquisition underlying that of maturity, if there is to be for the adult one single intersubjective world. My awareness of constructing an objective truth would never provide me with anything more than an objective truth for me, and my greatest attempt at impartiality would never enable me to prevail over my subjectivity (as Descartes so well expresses it by the hypothesis of the malignant demon), if I had not, underlying my judgements, the primordial certainty of being in contact with being itself, if, before any voluntary *adoption of a position* I were not already *situated* in an intersubjective world, and if science too were not upheld by this basic δοξα. With the *cogito* begins that struggle between consciousnesses, each one of which, as Hegel says, seeks the death of the other. For the struggle ever to begin, and for each consciousness to be capable of suspecting the alien presences which it negates, all must necessarily have some common ground and be mindful of their peaceful co-existence in the world of childhood.

The permanent truth of solipsism

But is it indeed other people that we arrive at in this way? What we do in effect is to iron out the I and the Thou in an experience shared by a plurality, thus introducing the impersonal into the heart of subjectivity and eliminating the individuality of perspectives. But have we not, in this general confusion, done away with the alter Ego as well as the Ego? We said earlier that they are mutually exclusive. But this is only because they both lay the same claims, and because the alter Ego follows all the variations of the Ego: if the perceiving *I* is genuinely an *I*, it cannot perceive a different one; if the perceiving subject is anonymous, the other which it perceives is equally so; so when, within this collective consciousness, we try to bring out the plurality of consciousnesses, we shall find ourselves back with the difficulties which we thought we had left behind. I perceive the other person as a piece of behaviour, for example, I perceive the grief or the anger of the other in his conduct, in his face or his hands, without recourse to any 'inner' experience of suffering or anger, and because grief and anger are variations of belonging to the world, undivided between the body and consciousness, and equally applicable to the other person's conduct, visible in his phenomenal body, as in my own conduct as it is presented to me. But then, the behaviour of another person, and even his words, are not that other person. The grief and the anger of another have never quite the same significance for him as they have for me. For him these situations are lived through, for me they are displayed. Or in so far as I can, by some friendly gesture, become part of that grief or that anger, they still remain the grief and anger of my friend Paul: Paul suffers because he has lost his wife, or is angry because his watch has been stolen, whereas I suffer because Paul is grieved, or I am angry because he is angry, and our situations cannot be superimposed on each other. If, moreover, we undertake some project in common, this common project is not one single project, it does not appear in the selfsame light to both of us, we are not both equally enthusiastic about it, or at any rate not in quite the same way, simply because Paul is Paul and I am myself. Although his consciousness and mine, working through our respective situations, may contrive to produce a common situation in which they can communcate, it is nevertheless from the subjectivity of each of us that each one projects this 'one and only' world. The difficulties inherent in considering the perception of other people did not all stem from objective thought, nor do they all dissolve with the discovery of behaviour, or rather objective thought and the uniqueness of the *cogito* which flows from it are not fictions, but firmly grounded phenomena of which we shall have to seek the basis. The conflict between myself and the other does not begin only when we try to *think ourselves into* the other and does not vanish if we reintegrate thought into non-positing consciousness and unreflective living; it is already there if I try to live another's experiences, for example in the blindness of sacrifice. I enter into a pact with the other person, having resolved to live in an interworld in which I accord as much place to others as to myself. But this interworld is still a project of mine, and it would be hypocritical to pretend that I seek the welfare of another *as if it were mine*, since this very attachment to another's interest still has its source in me.

In the absence of reciprocity there is no alter Ego, since the world of the one then takes in completely that of the other, so that one feels disinherited in favour of the other. This is what happens in the case of a couple where there is more love felt on one side than on the other: one throws himself, and his whole life, into his love, the other remains free, finding in this love a merely contingent manner of living. The former feels his being and substance flowing away into that freedom which confronts him, whole and unqualified. And even if the second partner, through fidelity to his vows or through generosity, tries to reciprocate by reducing himself, or herself, to the status of a mere phenomenon in the other's world, and to see himself through the other's eyes, he can succeed only by an expansion of his own life, so that he denies by necessity the equivalence of himself with the other that he is trying to posit. Co-existence must in all cases be experienced on both sides. If neither of us is a constituting consciousness at the moment when we are about to communicate and discover a common world, the question then is: who communicates, and for whom does this world exist? And if someone does communicate with someone else, if the interworld is not an inconceivable *in-itself* and must exist for both of us, then again communication breaks down, and each of us operates in his own private world like two players playing on two chessboards a hundred miles apart. But here the players can still make known their moves to each other by telephone or correspondence, which means that they are in fact participants in the same world. I, on the other hand, share no common ground with another person, for the positing of the other with his world, and the positing of myself with mine are mutually exclusive. Once the other is posited, once the other's gaze fixed upon me has, by inserting me into his field, stripped me of part of my being, it will readily be understood that I can recover it only by establishing relations with him, by bringing about his clear recognition of me, and that my freedom requires the same freedom for others. But first we need to know how it has been possible for me to posit the other. In so far as I am born into the world, and have a body and a natural world, I can find in that world other patterns of behaviour with which my own interweave, as we have explained above. But also in so far as I am born and my existence is already at work and is aware that it is given to itself, it always remains on the hither side of the acts in which it tries to become engaged and which are for ever mere modalities of its own, and particular cases of its insurmountable generality. It is this ground of given existence that is disclosed by the *cogito*: every assertion, every commitment, and even every negation and doubt takes its place in a field open in advance, and testifies to a self contiguous with itself before those particular acts in which it loses contact with itself. This self, a witness to any actual communication, and without which the latter would be ignorant of itself, and would not, therefore, be communication at all, would seem to preclude any solution of the problem of other people. There is here a solipsism rooted in living experience and quite insurmountable. It is true that I do not feel that I am the constituting agent either of the natural or of the cultural world: into each perception and into each judgement I bring either sensory functions or cultural settings which are not actually mine. Yet although I am outrun on all sides by my own acts, and submerged in generality, the fact remains that I am the one by whom they are experienced, and with my first perception there was launched an insatiable being who appropriates everything that he meets, to whom nothing can be purely and simply given because he has inherited his share of the world, and hence carries within him the project of all possible being, because it has been once and for all imprinted in his field of experiences. The generality of the body will never make it clear how the indeclinable *I* can estrange itself in favour of another, since this generality is exactly compensated by the other generality of my inalienable subjectivity. How should I find *elsewhere*, in my perceptual field, such a presence of self to self? Are we to say that the existence of the other person is for me a simple fact? It is in any case a fact *for me*, and it must necessarily be among my own possibilities, and understood or in some way experienced by me in order to be valid as a fact.

After this failure to set limits to solipsism from the outside, are we then to try to outrun it inwardly? It is true that I can recognize only one Ego, but as universal subject I cease to be a finite self, and become an impartial spectator before whom the other person and myself, each as an empirical being, are on a footing of equality, without my enjoying any particular privilege. Of the consciousness which I discover by reflection and before which everything is an object, it cannot be said that it is myself: my self is arrayed before me like any other thing, and my consciousness constitutes it and is not enclosed within it, so that it can without difficulty constitute other (my)selves. In God I can be conscious of others as of myself, and love others as myself. But the subjectivity that we have run up against does not admit of being called God. If reflection reveals myself to me as an infinite subject, we must recognize, at least at the level of appearance, my ignorance of this self which is even more myself than I. I knew it, the reply will be, because I perceived both the other and myself, and because this perception is possible only through him. But if I did already know it, then all books of philosophy are useless. In fact, the truth needs to be revealed. It was, therefore, this finite and ignorant self which recognized God in itself, while God, beyond phenomena, thought about himself since the beginning of time. It is through this shadow that unavailing light manages to be shed on at least something, and thus it is ultimately impossible to bring the shadow into the light; I can never *recognize myself* as God without necessarily denying what I am trying in fact to assert. I might love others as myself in God, but even then my love of God would have to come not from me, and would have to be truly, as Spinoza said, the love which God has for himself through me. So that finally nowhere would there be love of others or indeed others, but one single self-love linked to itself beyond our own lives, and nowise relevant, indeed inaccessible, to us. The act of reflection and love leading to God places the God sought outside the realm of possibility.

Solitude and communication are two faces of the same phenomenon
We are thus brought back to solipsism, and the problem now appears in all its difficulty. I am not God, but merely lay claim to divinity. I escape from every involvement and transcend others in so far as every situation and every other person must be experienced by me in order to exist in my eyes. And yet other people have for me at least an initial significance. As with the gods of polytheism, I have to reckon with other gods, or again, as with Aristotle's God, I polarize a world which I do not create. Consciousnesses present themselves with the absurdity of a multiple solipsism, such is the situation which has to be understood. Since we live through this situation, there must be some way of making it explicit. Solitude and communication cannot be the two horns of a dilemma, but two 'moments' of one phenomenon, since in fact other people do exist for me. We must say of experience of others what we have said elsewhere about reflection: that its object cannot escape it entirely, since we have a notion of the object only through that experience. Reflection must in some way present the unreflected, otherwise we should have nothing to set over against it, and it would not become a problem for us. Similarly my experience must in some way present me with other people, since otherwise I should have no occasion to speak of solitude, and could not begin to pronounce other people inaccessible. What is given and initially true, is a reflection open to the unreflective, the reflective assumption of the unreflective – and similarly there is given the tension of my experience towards another

whose existence on the horizon of my life is beyond doubt, even when my knowledge of him is imperfect. There is more than a vague analogy between the two problems, for in both cases it is a matter of finding out how to steal a march on myself and experience the unreflective as such. How, then, can I who perceive, and who, *ipso facto*, assert myself as universal subject, perceive another who immediately deprives me of this universality? The central phenomenon, at the root of both my subjectivity and my transcendence towards others, consists in my being given to myself. *I am given*, that is, I find myself already situated and involved in a physical and social world – *I am given to myself*, which means that this situation is never hidden from me, it is never round about me as an alien necessity, and I am never in effect enclosed in it like an object in a box. My freedom, the fundamental power which I enjoy of being the subject of all my experiences, is not distinct from my insertion into the world. It is a fate for me to be free, to be unable to reduce myself to anything that I experience, to maintain in relation to any factual situation a faculty of withdrawal, and this fate was sealed the moment my transcendental field was thrown open, when I was born as vision and knowledge, when I was thrown into the world. Against the social world I can always avail myself of my sensible nature, close my eyes, stop up my ears, live as a stranger in society, treat others, ceremonies and institutions as mere arrangements of colour and light, and strip them of all their human significance. Against the natural world I can always have recourse to the thinking nature and entertain doubts about each perception taken on its own. The truth of solipsism is there. Every experience will always appear to me as a particular instance which does not exhaust the generality of my being, and I have always, as Malebranche said, movement left wherewith to go further. But I can fly from being only into being; for example, I escape from society into nature, or from the real world into an imaginary one made of the broken fragments of reality. The physical and social world always functions as a stimulus to my reactions, whether these be positive or negative. I call such and such a perception into question only in the name of a truer one capable of correcting it; in so far as I can deny each thing, it is always by asserting that there is something in general, and this is why we say that thought is a thinking nature, an assertion of being over and above the negation of beings. I can evolve a solipsist philosophy but, in doing so, I assume the existence of a community of men endowed with speech, and I address myself to it. Even the 'indefinite refusal to be anything at all' assumes something which is refused and in relation to which the subject holds himself apart. I must choose between others and myself, it is said. But we choose one *against* the other, and thus assert both. The other person transforms me into an object and denies me, I transform him into an object and deny him, it is asserted. In fact the other's gaze transforms me into an object, and mine him, only if both of us withdraw into the core of our thinking nature, if we both make ourselves into an inhuman gaze, if each of us feels his actions to be not taken up and understood, but observed as if they were an insect's. This is what happens, for instance, when I fall under the gaze of a stranger. But even then, the objectification of each by the other's gaze is felt as unbearable only because it takes the place of possible communication. A dog's gaze directed towards me causes me no embarrassment. The refusal to communicate, however, is still a form of communication. Manifold freedom, the thinking nature, the inalienable core, existence without qualification, which in me and in others mark the bounds of sympathy, do call a halt to communication, but do not abolish it. If I am dealing with a stranger who has as yet not uttered a word, I may well believe that he is an inhabitant of another world in which my own thoughts and actions are unworthy of a place. But let him utter a word, or even make a gesture of impatience, and already he ceases to transcend me: that, then, is his voice, those are his thoughts and that is the realm that I thought inaccessible. Each existence finally transcends the others only when it remains inactive and rests upon its natural difference. Even that universal meditation which cuts the philosopher off from his nation, his friendships, his prejudices, his empirical being, the world in short, and which seems to leave him in complete isolation, is in reality an act, the spoken word, and consequently dialogue. Solipsism would be strictly true only of someone who managed to be tacitly aware of his existence without being or doing anything, which is impossible, since existing is being in and of the world. The philosopher cannot fail to draw others with him into his reflective retreat, because in the uncertainty of the world, he has for ever learned to treat them as *associates*, and because all his knowledge is built on this datum of opinion. Transcendental subjectivity is a revealed subjectivity, revealed to itself and to others, and is for that reason an intersubjectivity. As soon as existence collects itself together and commits itself in some line of conduct, it falls beneath perception. Like every other perception, this one asserts more things than it grasps: when I say that I see the ash-tray over there, I suppose as completed an unfolding of experience which could go on *ad infinitum*, and I commit a whole perceptual future. Similarly, when I say that I know and like someone, I aim, beyond his qualities, at an inexhaustible core which may one day shatter the image that I have formed of him. It is subject to this condition that there are things and 'other people' for us, not as the result of some illusion, but as the result of a violent act which is perception itself.

The social not as an object but as a dimension of my being
We must therefore rediscover, after the natural world, the social world, not as an object or sum of objects, but as a permanent field or dimension of existence: I may well turn away from it, but not cease to be situated relatively to it. Our relationship to the social is, like our relationship to the world, deeper than any express perception or any judgement. It is as false to place ourselves in society as an object among other objects, as it is to place society within ourselves as an object of thought, and in both cases the mistake lies in treating the social as an object. We must return to the social with which we are in contact by the mere fact of existing, and which we carry about inseparably with us before any objectification. Objective and scientific consciousness of the past and of civilizations would be impossible had I not, through the intermediary of my society, my cultural world and their horizons, at least a possible communication with them, and if the place of the Athenian Republic or the Roman Empire were not somewhere marked out on the borders of my own history, and if they were not there as so many individuals to be known, indeterminate but pre-existing, and if I did not find in my own life the basic structures of history. The social is already there when we come to know or judge it. An individualistic or sociological philosophy is a certain perception of co-existence systematized and made explicit. Prior to the process of becoming aware, the social exists obscurely and as a summons. At the end of *Notre Patrie* Péguy finds once again a buried voice which had never ceased to speak, much as we realize on waking that objects have not, during the night, ceased to be, or that someone has been knocking for some time at our door. Despite cultural, moral, occupational and ideological differences, the Russian peasants of 1917 joined the workers of Petrograd and Moscow in the struggle, because they felt that they shared the same fate; class was experienced in concrete terms before becoming the object of a deliberate volition. Primarily the social does not exist as a third person object. It is the mistake of the investigator, the 'great man' and the historian to try to treat it as an object. Fabrice would have liked to see the Battle of Waterloo as one sees a landscape, but found nothing but confused

episodes. Does the Emperor really see it on his map? It reduces itself in his eyes to a general plan by no means free from gaps; why is this regiment not making headway; why don't the reserves come up? The historian who is not engaged in the battle and who sees it from all angles, who brings together a mass of evidence, and who knows what the result was, thinks he has grasped it in its essential truth. But what he gives us is no more than a representation; he does not bring before us the battle itself since the issue was, at the time, contingent, and is no longer so when the historian recounts it, since the deeper causes of defeat and the fortuitous incidents which brought them into play were, in that singular event called Waterloo, equally determining factors, and since the historian assigns to the said singular event its place in the general process of decline of the Empire. The true Waterloo resides neither in what Fabrice, nor the Emperor, nor the historian sees, it is not a determinable object, it is what *comes about* on the fringes of all perspectives, and on which they are all erected.[3] The historian and the philosopher are in search of an objective definition of class or nation: is the nation based on common language or on conceptions of life; is class based on income statistics or on its place in the process of production? It is well known that none of these criteria enables us to decide whether an individual belongs to a nation or a class. In all revolutions there are members of the privileged class who make common cause with the revolutionaries, and members of the oppressed class who remain faithful to the privileged. And every nation has its traitors. This is because the nation and class are neither versions of fate which hold the individual in subjection from the outside nor values which he posits from within. They are modes of co-existence which are a call upon him. Under conditions of calm, the nation and the class are there as stimuli to which I respond only absent-mindedly or confusedly; they are merely latent. A revolutionary situation, or one of national danger, transforms those pre-conscious relationships with class and nation, hitherto merely lived through, into the definite taking of a stand; the tacit commitment becomes explicit. But it appears to itself as anterior to decision.

The problems of transcendence
The problem of the existential modality of the social is here at one with all problems of transcendence. Whether we are concerned with my body, the natural world, the past, birth or death, the question is always how I can be open to phenomena which transcend me, and which

nevertheless exist only to the extent that I take them up and live them; *how the presence to myself (Urpräsenz) which establishes my own limits and conditions every alien presence is at the same time depresentation (Entgegenwärtigung) and throws me outside myself.* Both idealism and realism, the former by making the external world immanent in me, the latter by subjecting me to a causal action, falsify the motivational relations existing between the external and internal worlds, and make this relationship unintelligible. Our individual past, for example, cannot be given to us either on the one hand by the actual survival of states of consciousness or paths traced in the brain, or on the other by a consciousness of the past which constitutes it and immediately arrives at it: in either case we should lack any sense of the past, for the past would, strictly speaking, be present. If anything of the past is to exist for us, it can be only in an ambiguous presence, anterior to any express evocation, like a field upon which we have an opening. It must exist for us even though we may not be thinking of it, and all our recollections must have their substance in and be drawn from this opaque mass. Similarly, if the world were to me merely a collection of things, and the thing merely a collection of properties, I should have no certainties, but merely probabilities, no unchallengeable reality, but merely conditional truths. If the past and the world exist, they must be theoretically immanent – they can be only what I see behind and around me – and factually transcendent – they exist in my life before appearing as objects of my explicit acts. Similarly, moreover, my birth and death cannot be objects of thought for me. Being established in my life, buttressed by my thinking nature, fastened down in this transcendental field which was opened for me by my first perception, and in which all absence is merely the obverse of a presence, all silence a modality of the being of sound, I enjoy a sort of ubiquity and theoretical eternity, I feel destined to move in a flow of endless life, neither the beginning nor the end of which I can experience in thought, since it is my living self who thinks of them, and since thus my life always forestalls and survives itself. Yet this same thinking nature which produces in me a superabundance of being opens the world to me through a perspective, along with which there comes to me the feeling of my contingency, the dread of being outstripped, so that, although I do not manage to encompass my death in thought, I nevertheless live in an atmosphere of death in general, and there is a kind of essence of death always on the horizon of my thinking. In short, just as the instant of my death is a future to which I have not access, so I am necessarily destined never to experience the presence of another person to himself. And yet each other person does exist for me as an unchallengeable style or setting of co-existence, and my life has a social atmosphere just as it has a flavour of mortality.

The true transcendental is the foundation of transcendance

We have discovered, with the natural and social worlds, the truly transcendental, which is not the totality of constituting operations whereby a transparent world, free from obscurity and impenetrable solidity, is spread out before an impartial spectator, but that ambiguous life in which the forms of transcendence have their *Ursprung*, and which, through a fundamental contradiction, puts me in communication with them, and on this basis makes knowledge possible.[4] It will perhaps be maintained that a philosophy cannot be centred round a contradiction, and that all our descriptions, since they ultimately defy thought, are quite meaningless. The objection would be valid if we were content to lay bare, under the term phenomenon or phenomenal field, a layer of prelogical or magical experiences. For in that case we should have to choose between believing the descriptions and abandoning thought, or knowing what we are talking about and abandoning our descriptions. These descriptions must become an opportunity for defining a variety of comprehension and reflection altogether more radical than objective thought. To phenomenology understood as direct description needs to be added a phenomenology of phenomenology. We must return to the *cogito*, in search of a more fundamental *Logos* than that of objective thought, one which endows the latter with its relative validity, and at the same time assigns to it its place. At the level of being it will never be intelligible that the subject should be both *naturans* and *naturatus*, infinite and finite. But if we rediscover time beneath the subject, and if we relate to the paradox of time those of the body, the world, the thing, and other people, we shall understand that beyond these there is nothing to understand.

Notes

1 This task we have tried to perform elsewhere (*The Structure of Behavior* I and II).
2 That is why disturbances affecting a subject's body image can be unearthed by requiring him to point out on the doctor's body the part of his own which is being touched.
3 It would therefore seem that history should be written in the present tense. It is what Jules Romains, for example, did in *Verdun*. Naturally, from the fact that objective thought is incapable of retailing down to the last detail a

present historical situation, we must not conclude that we should live through our history with our eyes closed, as if it were an individual adventure, reject every attempt to put it into perspective, and throw ourselves into action with no guiding principle. Fabrice misses Waterloo, but the reporter is already nearer to the event, for the spirit of adventure leads us astray even more than objective thought. There is a way of thinking, in contact with the event, which seeks its concrete structure. A revolution which is really moving with the march of history can be thought as well as lived.

4 Husserl in his last period concedes that all reflection should in the first place return to the description of the world of living experience (*Lebenswelt*). But he adds that, by means of a second 'reduction', the structures of the world of experience must be reinstated in the transcendental flow of a universal constitution in which all the world's obscurities are elucidated. It is clear, however, that we are faced with a dilemma: either the constitution makes the world transparent, in which case it is not obvious why reflection needs to pass through the world of experience, or else it retains something of that world, and never rids it of its opacity. Husserl's thought moves increasingly in this second direction, despite many throwbacks to the logicist period – as is seen when he makes a problem of rationality, when he allows significances which are in the last resort 'fluid', when he bases knowledge on a basic δοξα.

PART III: BEING-FOR-ITSELF AND BEING-IN-THE-WORLD

CHAPTER 1: THE *COGITO* (PP 369–409 [429–75])

Descartes famously held that we can doubt the existence of the things we think we see, but not our thought that we see them. Merleau-Ponty here takes issue with Descartes. For thought, or self-consciousness, is not an enclosed inner subjective space; instead self-consciousness is consciousness of ourselves as subjects-in-the-world, so consciousness of perception throws us back into the perceived world, and we cannot doubt one without the other. Nor is there anything special about consciousness of perception; our consciousness of our feelings, such as love, is similarly provisional and dependent on our actual feelings.

But does this not make scepticism unavoidable? If Descartes was mistaken in thinking that subjective self-consciousness is immune from doubt, how are sceptical doubts to be halted? Merleau-Ponty suggests that we should look to our propensities to action: our actions manifest a commitment to the world that is antecedent to doubt. He then discusses the case of mathematical truth as a possible objection to this suggestion, as a case in which absolute certainty is attainable without reference to our practical commitment to the perceived world. But he argues that here too there is an implicit dependence upon concepts grounded in our bodily experience of the perceived world (this discussion covers in a condensed way the issues discussed more clearly in the chapter on the 'algorithm' in The Prose of the World, *which is included later, on pp. 235–46).*

He now turns directly to the case of language, which was already implicated in the discussion of mathematical truth. His target here is the thesis that speech is just the 'clothing' of a thought or meaning that is already clear to itself and not dependent upon our bodily experience. As against this thesis

he introduces a distinction that is an application to language of his distinc-
tion between objective thinking and phenomenal experience; in this case it is
a distinction between 'secondary' or 'constituted' speech and 'originating' or
'authentic' speech (elsewhere he describes this as a distinction between
'spoken' and 'speaking' language – le langage parlé *and* le langage parlant*).*
His claim is then that originating speech has a role comparable to phenom-
enal experience in bringing new thoughts to existence. Once expressed these
thoughts retrospectively deny their origins in speech, and we are liable to give
them the status of 'eternal verities' instead. But this is an illusion comparable
to the other illusions of objective thinking.

Returning to his theme of the 'primary opinion' that is inherent in our
being in the world, Merleau-Ponty now affirms that 'all consciousness is, in
some measure, perceptual consciousness'. This is not a reductive empiricist
thesis comparable to Hume's thesis that all our ideas are derived from our
sense-impressions; instead it is just the claim that all our ways of thinking
about the world and ourselves remain rooted in our pre-objective practical
perceptual experiences which give us our fundamental belief in the world.
Finally, Merleau-Ponty comes back to the question of self-consciousness (the
cogito*), and the impression we have of finding absolute certainty here. He*
suggests that this impression arises from the role of language in our ordinary
self-consciousness, since, like perception, language 'promotes its own oblivion'
and thus seems to bring us directly to the truth about ourselves, the apparent
truth of subjective self-consciousness. But phenomenology teaches us to find
beneath the 'spoken' cogito of ordinary self-consciousness a 'tacit' cogito, a
form of subjectivity in which we are present to ourselves merely as a field of
perception in which the possibility of doubt coexists alongside our primary
faith in the world and ourselves.

Interpretation of the cogito *in terms of eternity*

I am thinking of the Cartesian *cogito*, wanting to finish this work,
feeling the coolness of the paper under my hand, and perceiving the
trees of the boulevard through the window. My life is constantly
thrown headlong into transcendent things, and passes wholly outside
me. The *cogito* is either this thought which took shape three centuries
ago in the mind of Descartes, or the meaning of the books he has left
for us, or else an eternal truth which emerges from them, but in any
case is a cultural being of which it is true to say that my thought
strains towards it rather than that it embraces it, as my body, in a
familiar surrounding, finds its orientation and makes its way among
objects without my needing to have them expressly in mind. This

book, once begun, is not a certain set of ideas; it constitutes for me an open situation, for which I could not possibly provide any complex formula, and in which I struggle blindly on until, miraculously, thoughts and words become organized by themselves. *A fortiori* the sensible forms of being which lie around me, the paper under my hand, the trees before my eyes, do not yield their secret to me, rather is it that my consciousness takes flight from itself and, in them, is unaware of itself. Such is the initial situation that realism tries to account for by asserting an actual transcendence and the existence in itself of the world and ideas.

There is, however, no question of justifying realism, and there is an element of final truth in the Cartesian return of things or ideas to the self. The very experience of transcendent things is possible only provided that their project is borne, and discovered, within myself. When I say that things are transcendent, this means that I do not possess them, that I do not circumambulate them; they are transcendent to the extent that I am ignorant of what they are, and blindly assert their bare existence. Now what meaning can there be in asserting the existence of one knows not what? If there can be any truth at all in this assertion, it is in so far as I catch a glimpse of the nature or essence to which it refers, in so far, for instance, as my vision of the tree as a mute *ek-stase* into an individual thing already envelops a certain thought about seeing and a certain thought about the tree. It is, in short, in so far as I do not merely encounter the tree, am not simply confronted with it, but discover in this existent before me a certain nature, the notion of which I actively evolve. In so far as I find things round about me, this cannot be because they are actually there, for, *ex hypothesi*, I can know nothing of this factual existence. The fact that I am capable of recognizing it is attributable to my actual contact with the thing, which awakens within me a primordial knowledge of all things, and to my finite and determinate perceptions' being partial manifestations of a power of knowing which is coextensive with the world and unfolds it in its full extent and depth. If we imagine a space in itself with which the perceiving subject contrives to coincide, for example, if I imagine that my hand perceives the distance between two points as it spans it, how could the angle formed by my fingers, and indicative of that distance, come to be judged, unless it were so to speak measured out by the inner operation of some power residing in neither object, a power which, *ipso facto*, becomes able to know, or rather effect, the relation existing between them? If it be insisted that the 'sensation in my thumb' and that in my first finger are at any rate 'signs' of the distance, how could these sensations come to have in themselves any means of signifying the relationship between points in space, unless they were already situated on a path running from one to the other, and unless this path in its turn were not only traversed by my fingers as they open, but also 'aimed at' by my thought pursuing its intelligible purpose? 'How could the mind know the significance of a sign which it has not itself constituted as a sign?' For the picture of knowledge at which we arrived in describing the subject situated in this world, we must, it seems, substitute a second, according to which it constructs or constitutes this world itself, and this one is more authentic than the first, since the transactions between the subject and the things round about it are possible only provided that the subject first of all causes them to exist for itself, actually arranges them round about itself, and extracts them from its own core. The same applies with greater force in acts of spontaneous thought. The Cartesian *cogito*, which is the theme of my reflection, is always beyond what I bring to mind at the moment. It has a horizon of significance made up of a great number of thoughts which occurred to me as I was reading Descartes and which are not now present, along with others which I feel stirring within me, which I might have, but never have developed. But the fact that it is enough to utter these three syllables in my presence for me to be immediately directed towards a certain set of ideas, shows that in some way all possible developments and clarifications are at once present to me. 'Whoever tries to limit the spiritual light to what is at present before the mind always runs up against the Socratic problem. "How will you set about looking for that thing, the nature of which is totally unknown to you? Which, among the things you do not know, is the one which you propose to look for? And if by chance you should stumble upon it, how will you know that it is indeed that thing, since you are in ignorance of it?" (*Meno*, 80D.) A thought really transcended by its objects would find them proliferating in its path without ever being able to grasp their relationships to each other, or finding its way through to their truth. It is I who reconstitute the historical *cogito*, I who read Descartes's text, I who recognize in it an undying truth, so that finally the Cartesian *cogito* acquires its significance only through my own *cogito*, and I should have no thought of it, had I not within myself all that is needed to invent it. It is I who assign to my thought the objective of resuming the action of the *cogito*, and I who constantly verify my thought's orientation towards this objective, therefore my thought must forestall itself in the pursuit of this aim, and must already have found what it seeks, otherwise it would not seek it. We must define thought in terms of that strange power which it possesses of being ahead of itself, of launching itself and being at home everywhere, in a word, in terms of its autonomy. Unless thought itself had put into things what it subsequently finds in them, it would have no hold upon things, would not think of them, and would be an 'illusion of thought'. A sensible perception or a piece of reasoning cannot be facts which come about in me and of which I take note. When I consider them after the event, they are dispersed and distributed each to its due place. But all this is merely what is left in the wake of reasoning and perception which, seen contemporaneously, must necessarily, on pain of ceasing to hang together, take in simultaneously everything necessary to their realization, and consequently be present to themselves with no intervening distance, in one indivisible intention. All thought of something is at the same time self-consciousness, failing which it could have no object. At the root of all our experiences and all our reflections, we find, then, a being which immediately recognizes itself, because it is its knowledge both of itself and of all things, and which knows its own existence, not by observation and as a given fact, nor by inference from any idea of itself, but through direct contact with that existence. Self-consciousness is the very being of mind in action. The act whereby I am conscious of something must itself be apprehended at the very moment at which it is carried out, otherwise it would collapse. Therefore it is inconceivable that it should be triggered off or brought about by anything whatsoever; it must be *causa sui*. To revert with Descartes from things to thought about things is to take one of two courses: it is either to reduce experience to a collection of psychological events, of which the *I* is merely the overall name or the hypothetical cause, in which case it is not clear how my existence is more certain than that of any thing, since it is no longer immediate, save at a fleeting instant; or else it is to recognize as anterior to events a field and a system of thoughts which is subject neither to time nor to any other limitation, a mode of existence owing nothing to the event and which is existence as consciousness, a spiritual act which grasps at a distance and compresses into itself everything at which it aims, an 'I think' which is, by itself and without any adjunct, an 'I am'. 'The Cartesian doctrine of the *cogito* was therefore bound to lead logically to the assertion of the timelessness of mind, and to the acceptance of a consciousness of the eternal: *experimur nos aeternos esse.*' Accordingly eternity, understood as the power to embrace and anticipate temporal developments in a single intention, becomes the very definition of subjectivity.

Consequences: the impossibility of finitude and the other

Before questioning this interpretation of the *cogito* in terms of eternity, let us carefully observe what follows from it, as this will show the need of some rectification. If the *cogito* reveals to me a new mode of existence owing nothing to time, and if I discover myself as the universal constituent of all being accessible to me, and as a transcendental field with no hidden corners and no outside, it is not enough to say that my mind, 'when it is a question of the form of all the objects of sense . . . is the God of Spinoza', for the distinction between form and matter can no longer be given any ultimate value, therefore it is not clear how the mind, reflecting on itself, could in the last analysis find any meaning in the notion of receptivity, or think of itself in any valid way as undergoing modification: for if it is the mind itself which thinks of itself as affected, it does *not* think of itself thus, since it affirms its activity afresh simultaneously with appearing to restrict it: in so far, on the other hand, as it is the mind which places itself in the world, it is *not* there, and the self-positing is an illusion. It must then be said, with no qualification, that my mind is God. How can M. Lachièze-Rey, for example, have avoided this consequence? 'If, having suspended thinking, I resume it again, I return to life, I reconstitute, in its indivisibility, and by putting myself back at the source whence it flows, the movement which I carry on. . . . Thus, whenever he thinks, the subject makes himself his point of support, and takes his place, beyond and behind his various representations, in that unity which, being the principle of all recognition, is not there to be recognized, and he becomes once more the absolute because that is what he eternally is.' But how could there be several absolutes? How in the first place could I ever recognize other (my)selves? If the sole experience of the subject is the one which I gain by coinciding with it, if the mind, by definition, eludes 'the outside spectator' and can be recognized only from within, my *cogito* is necessarily unique, and cannot be 'shared in' by another. Perhaps we can say that it is 'transferable' to others. But then how could such a transfer ever be brought about? What spectacle can ever validly induce me to posit outside myself that mode of existence the whole significance of which demands that it be grasped from within? Unless I learn within myself to recognize the junction of the *for itself* and the *in itself*, none of those mechanisms called other bodies will ever be able to come to life; unless I have an exterior others have no interior. The plurality of consciousness is impossible if I have an absolute consciousness of myself. Behind the absolute of my thought, it is even impossible to conjecture a divine absolute. If it is perfect, the contact of my thought with itself seals me within myself, and prevents me from ever feeling that anything eludes my grasp; there is no opening, no 'aspiration' towards an Other for this self of mine, which constructs the totality of being and its own presence in the world, which is defined in terms of 'self-possession', and which never finds anything outside itself but what it has put there. This hermetically sealed self is no longer a finite self. 'There is ... a con-sciousness of the universe only through the previous consciousness of organization in the active sense of the word, and consequently, in the last analysis, only through an inner communion with the very working of godhead.' It is ultimately with God that the *cogito* brings me into coincidence. While the intelligible and identifiable structure of my experience, when recognized by me in the *cogito*, draws me out of the event and establishes me in eternity, it frees me simultaneously from all limiting attributes and, in fact, from that fundamental event which is my private existence. Hence the same reasoning which necessarily leads from the event to the act, from thoughts to the *I*, equally neces-sarily leads from the multiplicity of *I*'s to one sole constituting con-sciousness, and prevents me from entertaining any vain hope of sal-vaging the finiteness of the subject by defining it as a 'monad'. The constituting consciousness is necessarily unique and universal. If we try to maintain that what it constitutes in each one of us is merely a microcosm, if we keep, for the *cogito*, the meaning of 'existential experience', and if it reveals to me, not the absolute transparency of thought wholly in possession of itself, but the blind act by which I take up my destiny as a thinking nature and follow it out, then we are introducing another philosophy, which does not take us *out of* time. What is brought home to us here is the need to find a middle course between eternity and the atomistic time of empiricism, in order to resume the interpretation of the *cogito* and of time. We have seen once and for all that our relations with things cannot be eternal ones, nor our consciousness of ourself the mere recording of psychic events. We perceive a world only provided that, before being facts of which we take cognizance, that world and that perception are thoughts of our own. What remains to be understood precisely is the way the world comes to belong to the subject and the subject to himself, which is that *cogitatio* which makes experience possible; our hold on things and on our 'states of consciousness'. We shall see that this does not leave the event and time out of account, but that it is indeed the fundamental mode of the event and *Geschichte*, from which objective and impersonal events are derived forms, and finally that any recourse we have to eternity is necessitated solely by an objective conception of time.

The cogito *and perception*

There can therefore be no doubt at all that I think. I am not sure that there is over there an ash-tray or a pipe, but I am sure that I think I see an ash-tray or a pipe. Now is it in fact as easy as is generally thought to dissociate these two assertions and hold, independently of any judgement concerning the thing seen, the evident certainty of my 'thought about seeing'? On the contrary, it is impossible. Perception is precisely that kind of act in which there can be no question of setting the act itself apart from the end to which it is directed. Perception and the perceived necessarily have the same existential modality, since perception is inseparable from the consciousness which it has, or rather is, of reaching the thing itself. Any contention that the perception is indubitable, whereas the thing perceived is not, must be ruled out. If I see an ash-tray, *in the full sense of the word see*, there must be an ash-tray there, and I cannot forego this assertion. To see is to see something. To see red, is to see red actively in existence. Vision can be reduced to the mere presumption of seeing only if it is represented as the contemplation of a shifting and anchorless *quale*. But if, as we have shown above, the very quality itself, in its specific texture, is the suggestion of a certain way of existing put to us, and responded to by us, in so far as we have sensory fields; and if the perception of a colour, endowed with a definite structure (in the way of superficial colour or area of colour), at a place or distance away either definite or vague, presupposes our opening on to a reality or a world, how can we possibly dissociate the certainty of our perceptual existence from that of its external counterpart? It is of the essence of my vision to refer not only to an alleged visible entity, but also to a being actually seen. Similarly, if I feel doubts about the presence of the thing, this doubt attaches to vision itself, and if there is no red or blue there, I say that I have not *really seen* these colours, and concede that at no time has there been created that parity between my visual intentions and the visible which constitutes the genuine act of seeing. We are therefore faced with a choice: either I enjoy no certainty with regard to things themselves, in which case neither can I be certain about my own perception, taken as a mere thought, since, taken even in this way, it involves the assertion of a thing. Or else I grasp my thought with certainty, which involves the simultaneous assumption of the existence towards which it is projected. When Descartes tells us that the existence of visible things is doubtful, but that our vision, when considered as a mere thought of seeing is not in doubt, he takes up an untenable position. For thought about seeing can have two meanings. It can in the first place be understood in the restricted sense of alleged vision, or 'the impression of seeing', in which case it offers only the certainty of a possibility or a probability, and the 'thought of seeing' implies that we have had, in certain cases, the experience of genuine or actual vision to which the idea of seeing bears a resemblance and in which the certainty of the thing was, on those occasions, involved. The certainty of a possibility is no more than the possibility of a certainty, the thought of seeing is no more than seeing mentally, and we could not have any such thought unless we had on other occasions really seen. Now we may understand 'thought about seeing' as the consciousness we have of our constituting power. Whatever be the case with our empirical perceptions, which may be true or false, these perceptions are possible only if they are inhabited by a mind able to recognize, identify and sustain before us their intentional object. But if this constituting power is not a myth, if perception is really the mere extension of an inner dynamic power with which I can coincide, my certainty concerning the transcendental premises of the world must extend to the world itself, and, my vision being in its entirety thought about seeing, then the thing seen is in itself what I think about it, so that transcendental idealism becomes absolute realism. It would be contradictory to assert[1] both that the world is constituted by me and that, out of this constitutive operation, I can grasp no more than the outline and the essential structures; I must see the existing world appear at the end of the constituting process, and not only the world as an idea, otherwise I shall have no more than an abstract construction, and not a concrete consciousness, of the world. Thus, in whatever sense we take 'thought about seeing', it is certain only so long as actual sight is equally so. When Descartes tells us that sensation reduced to itself is always true, and that error creeps in through the transcendent interpretation of it that judgement provides, he makes an unreal distinction: it is no less difficult for me to know whether or not I have felt something than it is to know whether there is really something there, for the victim of hysteria feels yet does not know what it is that he feels, as he perceives external objects without being aware of that perception. When, on the other hand, I am sure of having felt, the certainty of some external thing is involved in the very way in which the sensation is articulated and unfolded before me: it is a pain *in the leg*, or it is *red*, and this may be an opaque red on one plane, or a reddish three-dimensional atmosphere. The 'interpretation' of my sensations which I give must necessarily be motivated, and be so only in terms of the structure of those sensations, so that it can be said with equal validity either that there is no transcendent interpretation and no judgement which does not spring from the very configuration of the phenomena – or that there is no sphere of immanence, no realm in which my consciousness is fully at home and secure against all risk of error. The acts of the *I* are of such a nature that they outstrip themselves leaving no interiority of consciousness. Consciousness is transcendence through and through, not transcendence undergone – we have already said that such a transcendence would bring consciousness to a stop – but active transcendence. The consciousness I have of seeing or feeling is no passive noting of some psychic event hermetically sealed upon itself, an event leaving me in doubt about the reality of the thing seen or felt. Nor is it the activation of some constituting power superlatively and eternally inclusive of every possible sight or sensation, and linking up with the object without ever having to be drawn away from itself. It is the actual effecting of vision. I reassure myself that I see by seeing this or that, or at least by bringing to life around me a visual surrounding, a visible world which is ultimately vouched for only by the sight of a particular thing. Vision is an action, not, that is, an eternal operation (which is a contradiction in terms) but an operation which fulfils more than it promises, which constantly outruns its premises and is inwardly prepared only by my primordial opening upon a field of transcendence, that is, once again, by an *ek-stase*. Sight is achieved and fulfils itself in the thing seen. It is of its essence to take a hold upon itself, and indeed if it did not do so it would not be the sight of anything, but it is none the less of its essence to take a hold upon itself in a kind of ambiguous and obscure way, since it is not in possession of itself and indeed escapes from itself into the thing seen. What I discover and recognize through the *cogito* is not psychological immanence, the inherence of all phenomena in 'private states of consciousness', the blind contact of sensation with itself. It is not even transcendental immanence, the belonging of all phenomena to a constituting consciousness, the possession of clear thought by itself. It is the deep-seated momentum of transcendence which is my very being, the simultaneous contact with my own being and with the world's being.

The cogito *and affective intentionality*

And yet is not the case of perception a special one? It throws me open to a world, but can do so only by outrunning both me and itself. Thus the perceptual 'synthesis' has to be incomplete; it cannot present me with a 'reality' otherwise than by running the risk of error. It is absolutely necessarily the case that the thing, if it is to be a thing, should have sides of itself hidden from me, which is why the distinction between appearance and reality straightway has its place in the perceptual 'synthesis'. It would seem, on the other hand, that consciousness comes back into its rights and into full possession of itself, if I consider my awareness of 'psychic facts'. For example, love and will are inner operations; they forge their own objects, and it is clear that in doing so they may be sidetracked from reality and, in that sense, mislead us; but it seems impossible that they should mislead us about themselves. From the moment I feel love, joy or sadness, it is the case that I love, that I am joyful or sad, even when the object does not in fact (that is, for others or for myself at other times) have the value that I now attribute to it. Appearance is, within me, reality, and the being of consciousness consists in appearing to itself. What is willing, if it is not being conscious of an object as valid (or as valid precisely in so far as it is invalid, in the case of perverse will), and what is loving other than being conscious of an object as lovable? And since the consciousness of an object necessarily involves a knowledge of itself, without which it would escape from itself and fail even to grasp its object, to will and to know that one wills, to love and know one loves are one and the same act; love is consciousness of loving, will is consciousness of willing. A love or a will unaware of itself would be an unloving love, or an unwilling will, as an unconscious thought would be an unthinking one. Will or love would seem to be the same whether their object be artificial or real and, considered independently of the object to which they actually refer, they would appear to constitute a sphere of absolute certainty in which truth cannot elude us. Everything is, then, truth within consciousness. There can never be illusion other than with regard to the external object. A feeling, considered in itself, is always true once it is felt. Let us, however, look at the matter more closely.

False or illusory feelings

It is, in the first place, quite clear that we are able to discriminate, within ourselves, between 'true' and 'false' feelings, that everything felt by us as within ourselves is not *ipso facto* placed on a single footing of existence, or true in the same way, and that there are degrees of reality within us as there are, outside of us, 'reflections', 'phantoms' and 'things'. Besides true love, there is false or illusory love. This last case must be distinguished from misinterpretations, and those errors in which I have deceitfully given the name of love to emotions unworthy of it. For in such cases there was never even a semblance of love, and never for a moment did I believe that my life was committed to that feeling. I conspired with myself to avoid asking the question in order to avoid receiving the reply which was already known to me; my 'love'-making was an attempt to do what was expected of me, or merely deception. In mistaken or illusory love, on the other hand, I was willingly united to the loved one, she was for a time truly the vehicle of my relationships with the world. When I told her that I loved her, I was not 'interpreting', for my life was in truth committed to a form which, like a melody, demanded to be carried on. It is true that, following upon disillusionment (the revelation of my illusion *about myself*), and when I try to understand what has happened to me, I shall find beneath this supposed love *something other* than love: the likeness of the 'loved' woman to another, or boredom, or force of habit, or a community of interests or of convictions, and it is just this which will justify me in talking about illusion. I loved only *qualities* (that smile that is so like another smile, that beauty which asserts itself like a fact, that youthfulness of gesture and behaviour) and not the individual manner of being which is that person herself. And, correspondingly, I was not myself wholly in thrall, for areas of my past and future life escaped the invasion, and I maintained within me corners set aside for other things. In that case, it will be objected, I was either unaware of this, in which case it is not a question of illusory love, but of a true love which is dying – or else I did know, in which case there was never any love at all, even 'mistaken'. But neither is the case. It cannot be said that this love, while it lasted, was indistinguishable from true love, and that it became 'mistaken love' when I repudiated it. Nor can it be said that a mystical crisis at fifteen is without significance, and that it *becomes*, when independently evaluated in later life, an incident of puberty or the first signs of a religious vocation. Even if I reconstruct my whole life on the basis of some incident of puberty, that incident does not lose its contingent character, so that it is my whole life which is 'mistaken'. In the mystical crisis itself as I experienced it, there must be discoverable in it some characteristic which distinguishes vocation from incident: in the first case the mystical attitude insinuates itself into my basic relationship to the world and other people; in the second case, it is within the subject as an impersonal form of behaviour, devoid of inner necessity: 'puberty'. In the same way, true love summons all the subject's resources and concerns him in his entire being, whereas mistaken love touches on only one persona: 'the man of forty' in the case of late love, 'the traveller' in the case of exotic appeal, 'the widower' if the misguided love is sustained by a memory, 'the child' where the mother is recalled. True love ends when I change, or when the object of affection changes; misguided love is revealed as such when I return to my own self. The difference is intrinsic. But as it concerns the place of feeling in my total being-in-the-world, and as mistaken love is bound up with the person I believe I am at the time I feel it, and also as, in order to discern its mistaken nature I require a knowledge of myself which I can gain only through disillusionment, ambiguity remains, which is why illusion is possible.

Let us return to the example of the hysterical subject. It is easy to treat him as a dissembler, but his deception is primarily self-deception, and this instability once more poses the problem we are trying to dispose of: how can the victim of hysteria not feel what he feels, and feel what he does not feel? He does not *feign* pain, sadness or anger, yet his fits of 'pain', 'sadness' or 'rage' are distinguishable from 'real' cases of these afflictions, because he is not wholly given over to them; at his core there is left a zone of tranquillity. Illusory or imaginary feelings are genuinely experienced, but experienced, so to speak, on the outer fringes of ourselves. Children and many grown people are under the sway of 'situational values', which conceal from them their actual feelings – they are pleased because they have been given a present, sad because they are at a funeral, gay or sad according to the countryside around them, and, on the hither side of any such emotions, indifferent and neutral. 'We experience the feeling itself keenly, but inauthentically. It is, as it were, the shadow of an authentic sentiment.' Our natural attitude is not to experience our own feelings or to adhere to our own pleasures, but to live in accordance with the emotional categories of the environment. 'The girl who is loved does not project her emotions like an Isolde or a Juliet, but feels the feelings of these poetic phantoms and infuses them into her own life. It is at a later date, perhaps, that a personal and authentic feeling breaks the web of her sentimental phantasies.' But until this feeling makes its appearance, the girl has no means of discovering the illusory and literary element in her love. It is the truth of her future feelings which is destined to reveal the misguidedness of her present ones, which are genuinely experienced. The girl 'loses her reality' in them as does the actor in the part he plays, so that we are faced, not with representations or ideas which give rise to real emotions, but artificial emotions and imaginary sentiments. Thus we are not perpetually in possession of ourselves in our whole reality, and we are justified in speaking of an inner perception, of an inward sense, an 'analyser' working from us to ourselves which, ceaselessly, goes some, but not all, the way in providing knowledge of our life and our being. What remains on the hither side of inner perception and makes no impression on the inward sense is not an unconscious. 'My life', my 'total being' are not dubious constructs, like the 'deep-seated self' of Bergson, but phenomena which are indubitably revealed to reflection. It is simply a question of what we *are doing*. I make the discovery that I am in love. It may be that none of those facts, which I now recognize as proof of my love, passed unnoticed by me; neither the quickened drive of my present towards my future, nor that emotion which left me speechless, nor my impatience for the arrival of the day we were to meet. Nevertheless I had not seen the thing as a whole, or, if I had, I did not realize that it was a matter of so important a feeling, for I now discover that I can no longer conceive my life without this love. Going back over the preceding days and months, I am made aware that my thoughts and actions were polarized, I pick out the course of a process of organization, a synthesis *in the making*. Yet it is impossible to pretend that I always knew what I now know, and to see as existing, during the months which have elapsed, a self-knowledge which I have only just come by. Quite generally, it is impossible to deny that I have much to learn about myself, as it is to posit ahead of time, in the very heart of me, a knowledge of myself containing in advance all that I am later destined to know of myself, after having read books and had experiences at present unsuspected by me. The idea of a form of consciousness which is transparent to itself, its existence being identifiable with its awareness of existing, is not so very different from the notion of the unconscious: in both cases we have the same retrospective illusion, since there is, introduced into me as an explicit object, everything that I am later to learn concerning myself. The love which worked out its dialectic through me, and of which I have just become aware, was not, from the start, a thing hidden in my unconscious, nor was it an object before my consciousness, but the impulse carrying me towards someone, the transmutation of my thoughts and behaviour – I was not unaware of it since it was I who endured the hours of boredom preceding a meeting, and who felt elation when she approached – it was lived, not known, from start to finish. The lover is not unlike the dreamer. The 'latent content' and the 'sexual significance' of the dream are undoubtedly present to the dreamer since it is he who dreams his dream. But, precisely because sexuality is the general atmosphere of the dream, these elements are not thematized as sexual, for want of any non-sexual background against which they may stand out. When we ask ourselves whether or not the dreamer is conscious of the sexual content of his dream, we are really asking the wrong question. If sexuality, as we have explained above, is indeed one of our ways of entering into a relationship with the world, then whenever our meta-sexual being is overshadowed, as happens in dreams, sexuality is everywhere and nowhere; it is, in the nature of the case, ambiguous and cannot emerge clearly as itself. The fire which figures in the dream is not, for the dreamer, a way of disguising the sexual drive beneath an acceptable symbol, since it is only in the waking state that it appears as a symbol; in the language of dreams, fire is the symbol of the sexual drive because the dreamer, being removed from the physical world and the inflexible context of waking life, uses imagery only in proportion as it has affective value. The sexual significance of the dream is neither unconscious nor 'conscious', because the dream does not 'signify', as does waking life, by relating one order of facts to another, and it is as great a mistake to see sexuality as crystallized in 'unconscious representations' as it is to see lodged in the depths of the dreamer a consciousness which calls it by its true name. Similarly, for the lover whose experience it is, love is nameless; it is not a thing capable of being circumscribed and designated, nor is it the love spoken of in books and newspapers, because it is the way in which he establishes his relations with the world; it is an existential signification. The criminal fails to see his crime, and the traitor his betrayal for what they are, not because they exist deeply embedded within him as unconscious representations or tendencies, but because they are so many relatively closed worlds, so many situations. If we are in a situation, we are surrounded and cannot be transparent to ourselves, so that our contact with ourselves is necessarily achieved only in the sphere of ambiguity.

I know that I think because, first, I think

But have we not overshot our mark? If illusion is possible in consciousness on some occasions, will it not be possible on all occasions? We said that there are imaginary sentiments to which we are committed sufficiently for them to be experienced, but insufficiently for them to be authentic. But are there any absolute commitments? Is it not of the essence of commitment to leave unimpaired the autonomy of the person who commits himself, in the sense that it is never complete, and does it not therefore follow that we have no longer any means of describing certain feelings as authentic? To define the subject in terms of existence, that is to say, in terms of a process in which he transcends himself, is surely by that very act to condemn him to illusion, since he will never be able to *be* anything. Through refraining, in consciousness, from defining reality in terms of appearance, have we not severed the links binding us to ourselves, and reduced consciousness to the status of a mere appearance of some intangible reality? Are we not faced with the dilemma of an absolute consciousness on the one hand and endless doubt on the other? And have we not by our rejection of the first solution, made the *cogito* impossible? This objection brings us to the crucial point. It is true neither that my existence is in full possession of itself, nor that it is entirely estranged from itself, because it is action or doing, and because action is, by definition, the violent transition from what I have to what I aim to have, from what I am to what I intend to be. I can effect the *cogito* and be assured of genuinely willing, loving or believing, provided that in the first place I actually do will, love or believe, and thus fulfil my own existence. If this were not so, an ineradicable doubt would spread over the world, and equally over my own thoughts. I should be for ever wondering whether my 'tastes', 'volitions', 'desires' and 'ventures' were really mine, for they would always seem artificial, unreal and unfulfilled. But then this doubt, not being an actual doubt, could no longer even manage to confer the absolute certainty of doubting. The only way out, and into 'sincerity', is by forestalling such scruples and taking a blind plunge into 'doing'. Hence it is not *because* I think I am that I am certain of my existence; on the contrary the certainty I enjoy concerning my thoughts stems from their genuine existence. My love, hatred and will are not certain as mere thoughts about loving, hating and willing; on the contrary the whole certainty of these thoughts is owed to that of the acts of love, hatred or will of which I am quite sure because I *perform* them. All inner perception is inadequate because I am not an object that can be perceived, because I make my reality and find myself only in the act. 'I doubt': there is no way of silencing all doubt concerning this proposition other than by actually doubting, involving oneself in the experience of doubting, and thus bringing this doubt into existence as the certainty of doubting. To doubt is always to doubt something, even if one 'doubts everything'. I am certain of doubting precisely because I take this or that thing, or even every thing and my own existence too, as doubtful. It is through my relation to 'things' that I know myself; inner perception follows afterwards, and would not be possible had I not already made contact with my doubt in its very object. What has been said of external can equally be said of internal perception: that it involves infinity, that it is a never-ending synthesis which, though always incomplete, is nevertheless self-affirming. If I try to verify my perception of the ashtray, my task will be endless, for this perception takes for granted more than I can know in an explicit way. Similarly, if I try to verify the reality of my doubt, I shall again be launched into an infinite regress, for I shall need to call into question my thought about doubting, then the thought about that thought, and so on. The certainty derives from the doubt itself as an act, and not from these thoughts, just as the certainty of the thing and of the world precedes any thetic knowledge of their properties. It is indeed true, as has been said, that to know is to know that one knows, not because this second order of knowing guarantees knowledge itself, but the reverse. I cannot reconstruct the thing, and yet there *are* perceived things. In the same way I can never coincide with my life which is for ever fleeing from itself, in spite of which there *are* inner perceptions. For the same reason I am open to both illusion and truth about myself: that is, there are acts in which I collect myself together in order to surpass myself. The *cogito* is the recognition of this fundamental fact. In the proposition 'I think, I am', the two assertions are to be equated with each other, otherwise there would be no *cogito*. Nevertheless we must be clear about the meaning of this equivalence: it is not the 'I am' which is pre-eminently contained in the 'I think,' not my existence which is brought down to the consciousness which I have of it, but conversely the 'I think,' which is re-integrated into the transcending process of the 'I am', and consciousness into existence.

Geometrical ideas and perceptual consciousness

It is true that it seems necessary to concede my absolute coincidence with myself, if not in the case of will and feeling, at least in acts of 'pure thought'. If this were the case, all that we have said would appear to be challenged, so that, far from appearing as a mere manner of existence, thought would truly monopolize us. We must now, therefore, consider the understanding. I think of the triangle, the three-dimensional space to which it is supposed to belong, the extension of one of its sides, and the line that can be drawn through its apex parallel to the opposite side, and I perceive that this line, with the apex, forms three angles the sum of which is equal to the sum of the angles of the triangle, and equal, moreover, to two right angles. I am sure of the result which I regard as proved; which means that my diagrammatic construction is not, as are the strokes arbitrarily added by the child to his drawing, each one of which completely transforms its meaning ('it's a house; no, it's a boat; no, it's a man'), a collection of lines fortuitously drawn by my hand. The process from start to finish has a triangle in view. The genesis of the figure is not only a real genesis, but an intelligible one; I make my construction according to rules, and cause *properties* to make their appearance in the figure – properties which are relations belonging to the essence of the triangle. I do not, like the child, reproduce those suggested by the ill-defined figure which is actually there on the paper. I am aware of presenting a proof, because I perceive a necessary link between the collection of data which constitute the hypothesis and the conclusion which I draw from them. It is this necessity which ensures that I shall be able to repeat the operation with an indefinite number of empirical figures, and the necessity itself stems from the fact that at each step in my demonstration, and each time I introduced new relationships, I remained conscious of the triangle as a stable structure conditioned, and left intact, by them. This is why we can say, if we want, that the proof consists in bringing the sum of the angles constructed into two different groupings, and seeing that sum alternately as equal to the sum of the angles of the triangle, and equal to two right angles, but it must be added that here we have not merely two successive configurations, the first of which eliminates the second (as is the case with the child sketching dreamily); the first survives for me while the second is in process of establishing itself, the sum of angles which I equate with two right angles *is* the same as I elsewhere equate with the sum of the angles of the triangle, all of which is possible only provided that I go beyond the order of phenomena or appearances and gain access to that of the *eidos* or of being. Truth would seem to be impossible unless one enjoys an absolute self-possession in active thought, failing which it would be unable to unfold in a set of successive operations, and to produce a permanently valid result.

There would be neither thought nor truth *but for* an act whereby I prevail over the temporal dispersal of the phases of thought, and the mere *de facto* existence of my mental events. The important thing, however, is fully to understand the nature of this act. The necessity of the proof is not an analytic necessity: the construction which enables the conclusion to be reached is not really contained in the essence of the triangle, but merely possible when that essence serves as a starting point. There is no definition of a triangle which includes in advance the properties subsequently to be demonstrated and the intermediate steps leading to that demonstration. Extending one side, drawing through the apex a line parallel to the opposite side, introducing the theorem relating to parallels and their secant, these steps are possible only if I consider the triangle itself as it is drawn on the paper, on the blackboard or in the imagination, with its physiognomy, the concrete arrangement of its lines, in short its *Gestalt*. Is not precisely this the essence or the idea of a triangle? Let us, at the outset, reject any idea of a formal essence of the triangle. Whatever one's opinion of attempts at formalization, it is in any case quite certain that they lay no claim to provide a logic of invention, and that no logical definition of a triangle could equal in fecundity the vision of the figure, or enable us to reach, through a series of formal operations, conclusions not already established by the aid of intuition. This, it will perhaps be objected, touches only on the psychological circumstances of discovery, so that in so far as, after the event, it is possible to establish, between the hypothesis and the conclusion, a link owing nothing to intution, it is because intuition is not the inevitable mediator of thought and has no place in logic. But the fact that formalization is always retrospective proves that it is never otherwise than apparently complete, and that formal thought feeds on intuitive thought. It reveals those unformulated axioms on which reason is said to rest, and seems to bring to reason a certain added rigour and to uncover the very foundations of our certainty; but in reality the place in which certainty arises and in which a truth makes its appearance is always intuitive thought, even though, or rather *precisely because*, the principles are tacitly assumed there. There would be no experience of truth, and nothing would quench our 'mental volubility' if we thought *vi formae*, and if formal relations were not first presented to us crystallized in some particular thing. We should not even be able to settle on a hypothesis from which to deduce the consequences, if we did not first hold it to be true. A hypothesis is what is presumed to be true, so that hypothetical thinking presupposes some experience of *de facto* truth. The construction relates, then, to the configuration of the triangle, to the way in which it occupies space, to the relations expressed by the words 'on', 'by', 'apex' and 'extend'. Do these relations constitute a kind of material essence of the triangle? If the words 'on', 'through', etc., are to retain any meaning, it is in virtue of my working on a perceptible or imaginary triangle, that is to say, one which is at least potentially situated in my perceptual field, orientated in relation to 'up' and 'down', 'right' and 'left', or again, as we pointed out earlier, implied in my general grip upon the world. The construction makes explicit the possibilities of the triangle, considered not in the light of its definition and as a pure idea, but as a configuration and as the pole towards which my movements are directed. The conclusion follows of necessity from the hypothesis because, in the act of constructing, the geometer has already experienced the possibility of the transition. Let us try to give a better description of this act. We have seen that what occurs is clearly not a purely manual operation, the actual movement of my hand and pen over the paper, for in that case there would be no difference between a construction and any arbitrary set of strokes, and no demonstration would accrue. The construction is a gesture, which means that the actual lines drawn are the outward expression of an intention. But then what is this intention? I 'consider' the triangle, which is for me a set of lines with a certain orientation, and if words such as 'angle' or 'direction' have any meaning for me, it is in so far as I place myself at a point, and from it tend towards another point, in so far as the system of spatial positions provides me with a field of possible movements. Thus do I grasp the concrete essence of the triangle, which is not a collection of objective 'characteristics', but the formula of an attitude, a certain modality of my hold on the world, a structure, in short. When I construct, I commit the first structure to a second one, the 'parallels and secant' structure. How is that possible? It is because my perception of the triangle was not, so to speak, fixed and dead, for the drawing of the triangle on the paper was merely its outer covering; it was traversed by lines of force, and everywhere in it new directions not traced out yet possible came to light. In so far as the triangle was implicated in my hold on the world, it was bursting with indefinite possibilities of which the construction actually drawn was merely one. The construction possesses a demonstrative value because I cause it to emerge from the dynamic formula of the triangle. It expresses my power to make apparent the sensible symbols of a certain hold on things, which is my perception of the triangle's structure. It is an act of the productive imagination and not a return to the eternal idea of the triangle. Just as the localization of objects in space, according to Kant himself, is not merely a mental operation, but one which utilizes the body's motility, movement conferring sensations at the particular point on its trajectory at which those sensations are produced, so the geometer, who, generally speaking, studies the objective laws of location, knows the relationships with which he is concerned only by describing them, at least potentially, with his body. The subject of geometry is a motor subject. This means in the first place that our body is not an object, nor is its movement a mere change of place in objective space, otherwise the problem would be merely shifted, and the movement of one's own body would shed no light on the problem of the location of things, since it would be itself nothing but a thing. There must be, as Kant conceded, a 'motion which generates space' which is our intentional motion, distinct from 'motion in space', which is that of things and of our passive body. But there is more to be said: if motion is productive of space, we must rule out the possibility that the body's motility is a mere 'instrument' for the constituting consciousness. If there is a constituting consciousness, then bodily movement is movement only in so far as that consciousness thinks of it in that light, the constructive power rediscovers in it only what it has put there, and the body is not even an instrument in this respect: it is an object among objects. There is no psychology in a philosophy of constituting consciousness. Or at least there can be nothing valid for such a psychology to say, for it can do nothing but apply the results of analytical reflection to each particular content, while nevertheless distorting them, since it deprives them of their transcendental significance. The body's motion can play a part in the perception of the world only if it is itself an original intentionality, a manner of relating itself to the distinct object of knowledge. The world around us must be, not a system of objects which we synthesize, but a totality of things, open to us, towards which we project ourselves. The 'motion which generates space' does not deploy the trajectory from some metaphysical point with no position in the real world, but from a certain here towards a certain yonder, which are necessarily interchangeable. The project towards motion is an act, which means that it traces out the spatio-temporal distance by actually covering it. The geometer's thought, in so far as it is necessarily sustained by this act, does not, therefore, coincide with itself: it is surely and simply transcendence. In so far as, by adding a construction, I can bring to light the properties of a triangle, and yet find that the figure thus transformed does not cease to be the same figure as I began with, and in so far, moreover, as I am able, to effect a synthesis retaining the character of necessity, this is not because my construction is upheld by a concept of the triangle in which all its properties are included, or because, starting from perceptual consciousness, I arrive at the *eidos*: it is because I perform the synthesis of the new property by means of my body, which immediately implants me in space, while its autonomous motion enables me, through a series of definite procedures, to arrive once more at an all-inclusive view of space. Far from its being the case that geometrical thinking transcends perceptual consciousness, it is from the world of perception that I borrow the notion of essence. I believe that the triangle has always had, and always will have, angles the sum of which equals two right angles, as well as all the other less obvious properties which geometry attributes to it, because I have had the experience of a real triangle, and because, as a physical thing, it necessarily *has* within itself everything that it has ever been able, or ever will be able, to display. Unless the perceived thing has for good and ever implanted within us the ideal notion of a being which is what it is, there would be no phenomenon of being, and mathematical thought would appear to us in the light of a creative activity. What I call the essence of the triangle is nothing but this presumption of a completed synthesis, in terms of which we have defined the thing.

Ideas and speech

Our body, to the extent that it moves itself about, that is, to the extent that it is inseparable from a view of the world and is that view itself brought into existence, is the condition of possibility, not only of the geometrical synthesis, but of all expressive operations and all acquired views which constitute the cultural world. When we say that thought is spontaneous, this does not mean that it coincides with itself; on the contrary it means that it outruns itself, and speech is precisely that act through which it immortalizes itself as truth. It is, indeed, obvious that speech cannot be regarded as a mere clothing for thought, or expression as the translation, into an arbitrary system of symbols, of a meaning already clear to itself. It is said again and again that sounds and phonemes have no meaning in themselves, and that all our consciousness can find in language is what it has put there. But it would follow from this that language can teach us nothing, and that it can at the most arouse in us new combinations of those meanings already possessed by us. But this is just what the experience of language refutes. It is true that communication presupposes a system of correspondences such as the dictionary provides, but it goes beyond these, and what gives its meaning to each word is the sentence. It is because it has been used in various contexts that the word gradually accumulates a significance which it is impossible to establish absolutely. A telling utterance or a good book impose their meaning upon us. Thus they carry it within them in a certain way. As for the speaking subject, he too must be enabled to outrun what he thought before and to find in his own words more than the thought he was putting into them, otherwise we should not see thought, even solitary thought, seeking expression with such perseverance. Speech is, therefore, that paradoxical operation through which, by using words of a given sense, and already available meanings, we try to follow up an intention which necessarily outstrips, modifies, and itself, in the last analysis, stabilizes the meanings of the words which translate it. Constituted language plays the same limited rôle in the work of expression as do colours in painting: had we not eyes, or more generally senses, there would be no painting at all for us, yet the picture 'tells' us more than the mere use of our senses can ever do. The picture over and above the sense-data, speech over and above linguistic data must, therefore, in themselves possess a signifying virtue, independently of any meaning that exists for itself, in the mind of the spectator or listener. 'By using words as the painter uses colours and the musician notes, we are trying to constitute, out of a spectacle or an emotion, or even an abstract idea, a kind of equivalent or *specie* soluble in the mind. Here the expression becomes the principal thing. We mould and animate the reader, we cause him to participate in our creative or poetic action, putting into the hidden mouth of his mind the message of a certain object or of a certain feeling.' In the painter or the speaking subject, picture and utterance respectively do not illustrate a ready-made thought, but make that thought their own. This is why we have been led to distinguish between a secondary speech which renders a thought already acquired, and an originating speech which brings it into existence, in the first place for ourselves, and then for others. Now all words which have become mere signs for a univocal thought have been able to do so only because they have first of all functioned as originating words, and we can still remember with what richness they appeared to be endowed, and how they were like a landscape new to us, while we were engaged in 'acquiring' them, and while they still fulfilled the primordial function of expression. Thus self-possession and coincidence with the self do not serve to define thought, which is, on the contrary, an outcome of expression and always an illusion, in so far as the clarity of what is acquired rests upon the fundamentally obscure operation which has enabled us to immortalize within ourselves a moment of fleeting life. We are invited to discern beneath thinking which basks in its acquisitions, and offers merely a brief resting-place in the unending process of expression, another thought which is struggling to establish itself, and succeeds only by bending the resources of constituted language to some fresh usage. This operation must be considered as an ultimate fact, since any explanation of it – whether empiricist, reducing new meanings to given ones; or idealist, positing an absolute knowledge immanent in the most primitive forms of knowledge – would amount to a denial of it. Language outruns us, not merely because the use of speech always presupposes a great number of thoughts which are not present, in the mind and which are covered by each word, but also for another reason, and a more profound one: namely, that these thoughts themselves, when present were not at any time 'pure' thoughts either, for already in them there was a surplus of the signified over the signifying, the same effort of thought already thought to equal thinking thought, the same provisional amalgam of both which gives rise to the whole mystery of expression. That which is called an idea is necessarily linked to an act of expression, and owes to it its appearance of autonomy. It is a cultural object, like the church, the street, the pencil or the Ninth Symphony. It may be said in reply that the church can be burnt down, the street and pencil destroyed, and that, if all the scores of the Ninth Symphony and all musical instruments were reduced to ashes, it would survive only for a few brief years in the memory of those who had heard it, whereas on the other hand the idea of the triangle and its properties are imperishable. In fact, the idea of the triangle with its properties, and of the quadratic equation, have their historical and geographical area, and if the tradition in which they have been handed down to us, and the cultural instruments which bear them on, were to be destroyed, fresh acts of creative expression would be needed to revive them in the world. What is true, however, is that once they have made their first appearance, subsequent 'appearances', if successful, add nothing and if unsuccessful, subtract nothing, from the quadratic equation, which remains an inexhaustible possession among us. But the same may be said of the Ninth Symphony, which lives on in its intelligible abode, as Proust has said, whether it is played well or badly; or rather which continues its existence in a more occult time than natural time. The time of ideas is not to be confused with that in which books appear and disappear, and musical works are printed or lost: a book which has always been reprinted one day ceases to be read, a musical work of which there were only a few copies extant is suddenly much sought after. The existence of the idea must not be confused with the empirical existence of the means of expression, for ideas endure or fall into oblivion, and the intelligible sky subtly changes colour. We have already drawn a distinction between empirical speech – the word as a phenomenon of sound, the fact that a certain word is uttered at a certain moment by a certain person, which may happen independently of thought – and transcendental or authentic speech, that by which an idea begins to exist. But if there had been no mankind with phonatory or articulatory organs, and a respiratory apparatus – or at least with a body and the ability to move himself, there would have been no speech and no ideas. What remains true is that in speech, to a greater extent than in music or painting, thought seems able to detach itself from its material instruments and acquire an eternal value. There is a sense in which all triangles which will ever exist through the workings of physical causality will always have angles the sum of which equals two right angles, even if a time comes when men have forgotten their geometry, and there is not a single person left who knows any. But in this case it is because speech is applied to nature, whereas music, and painting, like poetry, create their own object, and as soon as they become sufficiently aware of themselves, deliberately confine themselves within the cultural world. Prosaic, and particularly scientific, utterance is a cultural entity which at the same time lays claim to translate a truth relating to nature in itself. Now we know that this is not the case, for modern criticism of the sciences has clearly shown the constructive element in them. 'Real', i.e. perceived, triangles, do not necessarily have, for all eternity, angles the sum of which equals two right angles, if it is true that the space in which we live is no less amenable to non-Euclidean than to Euclidean geometry. Thus there is no fundamental difference between the various modes of expression, and no privileged position can be accorded to any of them on the alleged ground that it expresses a truth in itself. Speech is as dumb as music, music as eloquent as speech. Expression is everywhere creative, and what is expressed is always inseparable from it. There is no analysis capable of making language crystal clear and carraying it before us as if it were an object. The act of speech is clear only for the person who is actually speaking or listening; it becomes obscure as soon as we try to bring explicitly to light those reasons which have led us to understand thus and not otherwise. We can say of it what we have said of perception, and what Pascal says about opinions: in all three cases we have the same miracle of an immediately apprehended clarity, which vanishes as soon as we try to break it down to what we believe to be its component elements. I speak, and I understand myself and am understood quite unamaguously; I take a new grip on my life, and others take a new grip on it too. I may say that 'I have been waiting for a long time', or that someone 'is dead', and I think I know what I am saying. Yet if I question myself on time or the experience of death, which were supplied in my words, there is nothing clear in my mind. This is because I have tried to speak about speech, to re-enact the act of expression which gave significance to the words 'dead' and 'time', to extend the brief hold on my experience which they ensure for me. These second or third order acts of expression, like the rest, have indeed in each case their convincing clarity, without, however, ever enabling me to dispel the fundamental obscurity of what is expressed, or to eliminate the distance separating my thought from itself. Must we conclude from this that, born and developed in obscurity, yet capable of clarity, language is nothing but the obverse of an infinite Thought, and the message of that Thought as communicated to us? This would mean losing contact with the analysis which we have just carried out, and reaching a conclusion in conflict with what has been established as we have gone along. Language transcends us and yet we speak. If we are led to conclude from this that there exists a transcendent thought spelt out by our words, we are supposing that an attempt at expression is brought to completion, after saying that it can never be so, and invoking an absolute thought, when we have just shown that any such thought is beyond our conception. Such is the principle of Pascal's apologetics; but the more it is shown that man is without absolute power, the more any assertion of an absolute is made, not probable, but on the contrary suspect. In fact analysis demonstrates, not that there is behind language a transcendent thought, but that language transcends itself in speech, that speech itself *brings about* that concordance between me and myself, and between myself and others, on which an attempt is being made to base that thought. The phenomenon of language, in the double sense of primary fact and remarkable occurrence, is not explained, but eliminated, if we duplicate it with some transcendent thought, since it consists in this: that an act of thought, once expressed, has the power to outlive itself. It is not, as is often held, that the verbal formula serves us as a mnemonic means: merely committed to writing or to memory, it would be useless had we not acquired once and for all the inner power of interpreting it. To give expression is not to substitute, for new thought, a system of stable signs to which unchangeable thoughts are linked, it is to ensure, by the use of words already used, that the new intention carries on the heritage of the past, it is at a stroke to incorporate the past into the present, and weld that present to a future, to open a whole temporal cycle in which the 'acquired' thought will remain present as a dimension, without our needing henceforth to summon it up or reproduce it. What is known as the non-temporal in thought is what, having thus carried forward the past and committed the future, is presumptively of all time and is therefore anything but transcendent in relation to time. The non-temporal is the acquired.

The non-temporal is the acquired

Time itself presents us with the prime model of this permanent acquisition. If time is the dimension in accordance with which events drive each other successively from the scene, it is also that in accordance with which each one of them wins its unchallengeable place. To say that an event *takes place* is to say that it will always be true that it has taken place. Each moment of time, in virtue of its very essence, posits an existence against which the other moments of time are powerless. After the construction is drawn, the geometrical relation is acquired; even if I then forget the details of the proof, the mathematical gesture establishes a tradition. Van Gogh's paintings have their place in me for all time, a step is taken from which I cannot retreat, and, even though I retain no clear recollection of the pictures which I have seen, my whole sub-sequent aesthetic experience will be that of someone who has become acquainted with the painting of Van Gogh, exactly as a middle class man turned workman always remains, even in his manner of being a work-man, a middle-class-man-turned-workman, or as an act confers a certain quality upon us for ever, even though we may afterwards repudiate it and change our beliefs. Existence always carries forward its past, whether it be by accepting or disclaiming it. We are, as Proust declared, perched on a pyramid of past life, and if we do not see this, it is because we are obsessed by objective thought. We believe that our past, for ourselves, is reducible to the express memories which we are able to contemplate. We sever our existence from the past itself, and allow it to pick up only those threads of the past which are present. But how are these threads to be recognized as threads of the past unless we enjoy in some other way a direct opening upon that past? Acquisition must be accepted as an irreducible phenomenon. What we have experienced is, and remains, permanently ours; and in old age a man is still in contact with his youth. Every present as it arises is driven into time like a wedge and stakes its claim to eternity. Eternity is not another order of time, but the atmosphere of time. It is true that a false thought, no less than a true one, possesses this sort of eternity: if I am mistaken at this moment, it is for ever true that I am mistaken. It would seem necessary, therefore, that there should be, in true thought, a different fertility, and that it should remain true not only as a past actually lived through, but also as a perpetual present for ever carried forward in time's succession. This, however, does not secure any essential difference between truths of fact and truths of reason. For there is not one of my actions, not one of even my fallacious thoughts, once it is adhered to, which has not been dir-ected towards a value or a truth, and which, in consequence, does not retain its permanent relevance in the subsequent course of my life, not only as an indelible fact, but also as a necessary stage on the road to the more complete truths or values which I have since recognized. My truths have been built out of these errors, and carry them along in their eternity. Conversely, there is not one truth of reason which does not retain its coefficient of facticity: the alleged transparency of Euclidean geometry is one day revealed as operative for a certain period in the history of the human mind, and signifies simply that, for a time, men were able to take a homogeneous three-dimensional space as the 'ground' of their thoughts, and to assume unquestioningly what generalized science will come to consider as a contingent account of space. Thus every truth of fact is a truth of reason, and *vice versa*. The relation of reason to fact, or eternity to time, like that of reflection to the unreflective, of thought to language or of thought to perception is this two-way relationship that phenomenology has called *Fundierung*: the founding term, or originator – time, the unreflective, the fact, language, perception – is primary in the sense that the originated is presented as a determinate or explicit form of the originator, which prevents the latter from reabsorbing the former, and yet the originator is not primary in the empiricist sense and the originated is not simply derived from it, since it is through the originated that the originator is made manifest. It is for this reason that it is a matter of indifference whether we say that the present foreshadows eternity or that the eternity of truth is merely a sublimation of the present. This ambiguity cannot be resolved, but it can be understood as ultimate, if we recapture the intuition of real time which preserves everything, and which is at the core of both proof and expression. 'Reflection on the creative power of the mind,' says Brunschvicg, 'implies, in every certainty of experience, the feeling that, in any determinate truth that one may have managed to demonstrate, there exists a soul of truth which outruns it and frees itself from it, a soul which can detach itself from the particular expression of that truth in order to adumbrate a deeper and more comprehensive expression, although this drive forward in no way impairs the eternity of the true.' What is this eternally true that no one possesses? What is this thing expressed which lies beyond all expression, and, if we have the right to posit it, why is it our constant concern to arrive at a more precise expression? What is this One round which minds and truths are disposed, as if they tended towards it, while it is maintained at the same time that they tend towards no pre-established term? The idea of a transcendent Being had at least the advantage of not stultifying the actions through which, in an ever difficult process of carrying forward, each consciousness and intersubjectivity themselves forge their own unity. It is true that, if these actions belong to that most intimate part of ourselves accessible to us, the positing of God contributes nothing to the elucidation of our life. We experience, not a genuine eternity and a participation in the One, but concrete acts of taking up and carrying forward by which, through time's accidents, we are linked in relationships with ourselves and others. In short, we experience a *participation in the world*, and 'being-in-truth' is indistinguishable from being in the world.

Evidence, like perception, is a fact

We are now in a position to make up our minds about the question of evidence, and to describe the experience of truth. There are truths just as there are perceptions: not that we can ever array before ourselves in their entirety the reasons for any assertion – there are merely motives, we have merely a hold on time and not full possession of it – but because it is of the essence of time to take itself up as it leaves itself behind, and to draw itself together into visible things, into firsthand evidence. All consciousness is, in some measure, perceptual consciousness. If it were possible to lay bare and unfold all the presuppositions in what I call my reason or my ideas at each moment, we should always find experiences which have not been made explicit, large-scale contributions from past and present, a whole 'sedimentary history' which is not only relevant to the *genesis* of my thought, but which determines its *significance*. For an absolute evidence, free from any presupposition, to be possible, and for my thought to be able to pierce through to itself, catch itself in action, and arrive at a pure 'assent of the self to the self', it would, to speak the language of the Kantians, have to cease to be an event and become an act through and through: in the language of the Schoolmen, its formal reality would have to be included in its objective reality; in the language of Malebranche, it would have to cease to be 'perception', 'sentiment' or 'contact' with truth, to become pure 'idea' and 'vision' of the truth. It would be necessary, in other words, that instead of being myself, I should become purely and simply one who knows myself, and that the world should have ceased to exist around me in order to become purely and simply an object before me. In relation to what we are by reason of our acquisitions and this pre-existent world, we have a power of placing in abeyance, and that suffices to ensure our freedom from determinism. I may well close my eyes, and stop up my ears, I shall nevertheless not cease to see, if it is only the blackness before my eyes, or to hear, if only silence, and in the same way I can 'bracket' my opinions or the beliefs I have acquired, but, whatever I think or decide, it is always against the background of what I have previously believed or done. *Habemus ideam veram*, we possess a truth, but this experience of truth would be absolute knowledge only if we could thematize every motive, that is, if we ceased to be in a situation. The actual possession of the true idea does not, therefore, entitle us to predicate an intelligible abode of adequate thought and absolute productivity, it establishes merely a 'teleology[2] of consciousness which, from this first instrument, will forge more perfect ones, and these in turn more perfect ones still, and so on endlessly. 'Only through an eidetic intuition can the essence of eidetic intuition be elucidated,' says Husserl. The intuition of some particular essence necessarily precedes, in our experience, the essence of intuition. The only way to think of thought is in the first place to think of something, and it is therefore essential to that thought not to take itself as an object. To think of thought is to adopt in relation to it an attitude that we have initially learned in relation to 'things'; it is never to eliminate, but merely to push further back the opacity that thought presents to itself. Every halt in the forward movement of consciousness, every focus on the object, every appearance of a 'something' or of an idea presupposes a subject who has suspended self-questioning at least in that particular respect. Which is why, as Descartes maintained, it is true both that certain ideas are presented to me as irresistibly self-evident *de facto*, and that this fact is never valid *de jure*, and that it never does away with the possibility of doubt arising as soon as we are no longer in the presence of the idea. It is no accident that self-evidence itself may be called into question, because *certainty is doubt*, being the carrying forward of a tradition of thought which cannot be condensed into an evident 'truth' without my giving up all attempts to make it explicit. It is for the same reasons that a self-evident truth is irresistible in fact, yet always questionable, which amounts to two ways of saying the same thing: namely, that it is irresistible because I take for granted a certain acquisition of experience, a certain field of thought, and precisely for this reason it appears to me as self-evident for a certain thinking nature, the one which I enjoy and perpetuate, but which remains contingent and given to itself. The consistency of a thing perceived, of a geometrical relationship or of an idea, is arrived at only provided that I give up trying by every means to make it more explicit, and instead allow myself to come to rest in it. Once launched, and committed to a certain set of thoughts, Euclidean space, for example, or the conditions governing the existence of a certain society, I discover evident truths, but these are not unchallengeable, since perhaps this space or this society are not the only ones possible. It is therefore of the essence of certainty to be established only with reservations; there is an *opinion* which is not a provisional form of knowledge destined to give way later to an absolute form, but on the contrary, both the oldest or most rudimentary, and the most conscious or mature form of knowledge – an opinion which is primary in the double sense of 'original' and 'fundamental'. This is what calls up before us *something in general*, to which positing thought – doubt or demonstration – can subsequently relate in affirmation or denial. There is significance, something and not nothing, there is an indefinite train of concordant experiences, to which this ash-tray in its permanence testifies, or the truth which I hit upon yesterday and to which I think I can revert today.

This evidentness of the phenomenon, or again of the 'world', is no less misunderstood when we try to reach being without contact with the phenomenon, that is, when we make being necessary, as when we cut the phenomenon off from being, when we degrade it to the status of mere appearance or possibility. The first conception is Spinoza's. Primary opinion is here subordinated to absolute self-evidence, and the notion 'there is something' which is an amalgam of being and nothingness, to the notion 'Being exists'. One rejects as meaningless any questioning of being: it is impossible to ask why there is something rather than nothing, and why this world rather than a different one, since the shape of this world and the very existence of a world are merely consequences of necessary being. The second conception reduces self-evidence to appearance: all my truths are after all self-evident only for me, and for a thought fashioned like mine; they are bound up with my psycho-physiological constitution and the existence of this world. Other forms of thought functioning in accordance with other rules, and other possible worlds, can be conceived as having the same claim to reality as this one. And here the question why there is something rather than nothing seems apposite, and why this particular world has come into being, but the reply is necessarily out of our reach, since we are imprisoned in our psycho-physiological make-up, which is a simple fact like the shape of our face or the number of our teeth. This second conception is not so different from the first as it might appear: it implies a tacit reference to an absolute knowledge and an absolute being in relation to which our factual self-evidences, or synthetic truths, are considered inadequate. According to the phenomenological conception, this dogmatism on the one hand and scepticism on the other are both left behind. The laws of our thought and our self-evident truths are certainly facts, but they are not detachable from us, they are implied in any conception that we may form of being and the possible. It is not a question of confining ourselves to phenomena, of imprisoning consciousness in its own states, while retaining the possibility of another being beyond apparent being, nor of treating our thought as one fact among many, but of defining being as that which appears, and consciousness as a universal fact. I think, and this or that thought appears to me as true; I am well aware that it is not unconditionally true, and that the process of making it totally explicit would be an endless task; but the fact remains that at the moment I think, I think something, and that any other truth, in the name of which I might wish to discount this one, must, if it is to be called a truth for me, square with the 'true' thought of which I have experience. If I try to imagine Martians, or angels, or some divine thought outside the realm of my logic, this Martian, angelic or divine thought must figure in my universe without completely disrupting it.[3] My thought, my self-evident truth is not one fact among others, but a value-fact which envelops and conditions every other possible one. There is no other world possible in the sense in which mine is, not because mine is necessary as Spinoza thought, but because any 'other world' that I might try to conceive would set limits to this one, would be found on its boundaries, and would consequently merely fuse with it. Consciousness, if it is not absolute truth or $\dot{a}$-$\lambda\eta\theta\varepsilon\iota\alpha$, at least rules out all absolute falsity. Our mistakes, illusions and questions are indeed mistakes, illusions and questions. Error is not consciousness of error; it even excludes such consciousness. Our questions do not always admit of answers, and to say with Marx that man poses for himself only problems that he can solve is to revive a theological optimism and postulate the consummation of the world. Our errors become truths only once they are recognized, and there remains a difference between their revealed and their latent content of truth, between their alleged and their actual significance. The truth is that neither error nor doubt ever cut us off from the truth, because they are surrounded by a world horizon in which the teleology of consciousness summons us to an effort at resolving them. Finally, the contingency of the world must not be understood as a deficiency in being, a break in the stuff of necessary being, a threat to rationality, nor as a problem to be solved as soon as possible by the discovery of some deeper-laid necessity. That is ontic contingency, contingency within the bounds of the world. Ontological contingency, the contingency of the world itself, being radical, is, on the other hand, what forms the basis once and for all of our ideas of truth. The world is that reality of which the necessary and the possible are merely provinces.

Against psychologism and scepticism

To sum up, we are restoring to the *cogito* a temporal thickness. If there is not endless doubt, and if 'I think', it is because I plunge on into provisional thoughts and, by deeds, overcome time's discontinuity. Thus vision is brought to rest in a thing seen which both precedes and outlasts it. Have we got out of our difficulty? We have admitted that the certainty of vision and that of the thing seen are of a piece. Must we conclude from this that, since the thing seen is never absolutely certain, as illusions show, vision also is involved in this uncertainty, or, on the contrary, that, since vision on its own is absolutely certain, so is the thing seen, so that I am never really mistaken? The second solution would amount to reinstating the immanence which we have banished. But if we adopted the first, thought would be cut off from itself, there would no longer be anything but 'facts of consciousness' which might be called internal by nominal definition, but which, for me, would be as opaque as things; there would no longer be either inner experience or consciousness, and the experience of the *cogito* would be once more forgotten. When we describe consciousness as involved through its body in a space, through its language in a history, through its prejudices in a concrete form of thought, it is not a matter of setting it back in a series of objective events, even though they be 'psychic' events, and in the causal system of the world. He who doubts cannot, while doubting, doubt that he doubts. Doubt, even when generalized, is not the abolition of my thought, it is merely a pseudo-nothingness, for I cannot extricate myself from being; my act of doubting itself creates the possibility of certainty and is there for me, it occupies me, I am committed to it, and I cannot pretend to be nothing at the time I execute it. Reflection, which moves all things away to a distance, discovers itself as at least given to itself in the sense that it cannot think of itself as eliminated, or stand apart from itself. But this does not mean that reflection and thought are elementary facts there to be observed as such. As Montaigne clearly saw, one can call into question thought which is loaded with a sediment of history and weighed down with its own being, one can entertain doubts about doubt itself, considered as a definite modality of thought and as consciousness of a doubtful object, but the formula of radical reflection is not 'I know nothing' – a formula which it is all too easy to catch in flat contradiction with itself – but 'What do I know?' Descartes was not unmindful of this. He has frequently been credited with having gone beyond sceptical doubt, which is a mere state, and with making doubt into a method, an act, and with having thus provided consciousness with a fixed point and reinstated certainty. But, in fact, Descartes did not suspend doubt in the face of the certainty of doubt itself, as if the act of doubting were sufficient to sweep doubt away by entailing a certainty. He took it further. He does not say 'I doubt, therefore I am', but 'I think, therefore I am', which means that doubt itself is certain, not as actual doubt, but as pure thought about doubting and, since the same might be said in turn about this thought, the only proposition which is absolutely certain, and which halts doubt in its tracks because it is implied by that doubt, is 'I think,' or again, 'something appears to me'. There is no act, no particular experience which exactly fills my consciousness and imprisons my freedom, 'there is no thought which abolishes the power to think and brings it to a conclusion – no definite position of the bolt that finally closes the lock. No, there is no thought which is a resolution born of its own very development and, as it were, the final chord of this permanent dissonance.' No particular thought reaches through to the core of our thought in general, nor is any thought conceivable without another possible thought as a witness to it. And this is no imperfection from which we may imagine consciousness freed. If there must be consciousness, if something must appear to someone, it is necessary that behind all our particular thoughts there should lie a retreat of not-being, a Self. I must avoid equating myself with a series of 'consciousnesses', for each of these, with its load of sedimentary history and sensible implications, must present itself to a perpetual absentee. Our situation, then, is as follows: in order to know that we think, it is necessary in the first place that we actually should think. Yet this commitment does not dispel all doubts, for my thoughts do not deprive me of my power to question; a word or an idea, considered as events in my history, have meaning for me only if I take up this meaning from within. I know that I think through such and such particular thoughts that I have, and I know that I have these thoughts because I carry them forward, that is, because I know that I think in general. The aim at a transcendent objective and the view of myself aiming at it, the awareness of the connected and of connecting are in a circular relationship. The problem is how I can be the constituting agent of my thought in general, failing which it would not be thought by anybody, would pass unnoticed and would therefore not be thought at all – without ever being that agent of my particular thoughts, since I never see them come into being in the full light of day, but merely know myself through them. The question is how subjectivity can be both dependent yet irremovable.

Tacit cogito *and spoken* cogito

Let us tackle this by taking language as our example. There is a consciousness of myself which makes use of language and is humming with words. I read, let us say, the *Second Meditation*. It has indeed to do with me, but a me in idea, an idea which is, strictly speaking, neither mine nor, for that matter, Descartes's, but that of any reflecting man. By following the meaning of the words and the argument, I reach the conclusion that indeed because I think, I am; but this is merely a verbal *cogito*, for I have grasped my thought and my existence only through the medium of language, and the true formula of this *cogito* should be: 'One thinks, therefore one is.' The wonderful thing about language is that it promotes its own oblivion: my eyes follow the lines on the paper, and from the moment I am caught up in their meaning, I lose sight of them. The paper, the letters on it, my eyes and body are there only as the minimum setting of some invisible operation. Expression fades out before what is expressed, and this is why its mediating rôle may pass unnoticed, and why Descartes nowhere mentions it. Descartes, and *a fortiori* his reader, begin their meditation in what is already a universe of discourse. This certainty which we enjoy of reaching, beyond expression, a truth separable from it and of which expression is merely the garment and contingent manifestation, has been implanted in us precisely by language. It appears as a mere sign only once it has provided itself with a meaning, and the coming to awareness, if it is to be complete, must rediscover the expressive unity in which both signs and meaning appear in the first place. When a child cannot speak, or cannot yet speak the adult's language, the linguistic ritual which unfolds around him has no hold on him, he is near us in the same way as is a spectator with a poor seat at the theatre; he sees clearly enough that we are laughing and gesticulating, he hears the nasal tune being played, but there is nothing at the end of those gestures or behind those words, nothing *happens* for him. Language takes on a meaning for the child when it *establishes a situation* for him. A story is told in a children's book of the disappointment of a small boy who put on his grandmother's spectacles and took up her book in the expectation of being able himself to find in it the stories which she used to tell him. The tale ends with these words: 'Well, what a fraud! Where's the story? I can see nothing but black and white.' For the child the 'story' and the thing expressed are not 'ideas' or 'meanings', nor are speaking or reading 'intellectual operations'. The story is a world which there must be some way of magically calling up by putting on spectacles and leaning over a book. The power possessed by language of bringing the thing expressed into existence, of opening up to thought new ways, new dimensions and new landscapes, is, in the last analysis, as obscure for the adult as for the child. In every successful work, the significance carried into the reader's mind exceeds language and thought as already constituted and is magically thrown into relief during the linguistic incantation, just as the story used to emerge from Grandmother's book. In so far as we believe that, through thought, we are in direct communication with a universe of truth in which we are at one with others, in so far as Descartes's text seems merely to arouse in us thoughts already formed, and we seem never to learn anything from outside, and finally in so far as a philosopher, in a meditation purporting to be thoroughgoing, never even mentions language as the condition of the *reading* of the *cogito*, and does not more overtly invite us to pass from the idea to the practice of the *cogito*, it is because we take the process of expression for granted, because it figures among our acquisitions. The *cogito* at which we arrive by reading Descartes (and even the one which Descartes effects in relation to expression and when, looking back on his past life, he fastens it down, objectifies it and 'characterizes' it as indubitable) is, then, a spoken *cogito*, put into words and understood in words, and for this very reason not attaining its objective, since that part of our existence which is engaged in fixing our life in conceptual forms, and thinking of it as indubitable, is escaping focus and thought. Shall we therefore conclude that language envelops us, and that we are led by it, much as the realist believes he is subject to the determinism of the external world, or as the theologian believes he is led on by Providence? This would be to forget half the truth. For after all, words, 'cogito' and 'sum' for example, may well have an empirical and statistical meaning, for it is the case that they are not directed specifically to my own experience, but form the basis of a general and anonymous thought. Nevertheless, I should find them not so much derivative and inauthentic as meaningless, and I should be unable even to read Descartes's book, were I not, before any speech can begin, in contact with my own life and thought, and if the spoken *cogito* did not encounter within me a tacit *cogito*. This silent *cogito* was the one Descartes sought when writing his *Meditations*. He gave life and direction to all those expressive operations which, by definition, always miss their target since, between Descartes's existence and the knowledge of it which he acquires, they interpose the full thickness of cultural acquisitions. And yet Descartes would not even have tried to put these expressive operations into operation had he not in the first place caught a glimpse of his existence. The whole question amounts to gaining a clear understanding of the unspoken *cogito*, to putting into it only what is really there, and not making language into a product of consciousness on the excuse that consciousness is not a product of language.

Consciousness does not constitute language; it appropriates it

Neither the word nor the meaning of the word is, in fact *constituted* by consciousness. Let us make this clear. The word is certainly never reducible to one of its embodiments. The word 'sleet', for example, is not the set of characters which I have just written on the paper, nor that other set of signs that I once read in a book for the first time, nor again the sound that runs through the air when I pronounce it. Those are merely reproductions of the word, in which I recognize it but which do not exhaust it. Am I then to say that the word 'sleet' is the unified idea of these manifestations, and that it exists only for my consciousness and through a synthesis of identification? To do so would be to forget what psychology has taught us about language. To speak, as we have seen, is not to call up verbal images and articulate words in accordance with the imagined model. By undertaking a critical examination of the verbal image, and showing that the speaking subject plunges into speech without imagining the words he is about to utter, modern psychology eliminates the word as a representation, or as an object for conscious-ness, and reveals a motor presence of the word which is not the know-ledge of the word. The word 'sleet', when it is known to me, is not an object which I recognize through any identificatory synthesis, but a certain use made of my phonatory equipment, a certain modulation of my body as a being in the world. Its generality is not that of the idea, but that of a behavioural style 'understood' by my body in so far as the latter is a behaviour-producing power, in this case a phoneme-producing one. One day I 'caught on' to the word 'sleet', much as one imitates a gesture, not, that is, by analysing it and performing an articulatory or phonetic action corresponding to each part of the word as heard, but by hearing it as a single modulation of the world of sound, and because this acoustic entity presents itself as 'something to pronounce' in virtue of the all-embracing correspondence existing between my perceptual potentialities and my motor ones, which are elements of my indivisible and open existence. The word has never been inspected, analysed, known and constituted, but caught and taken up by a power of speech and, in the last analysis, by a motor power given to me along with the first experience I have of my body and its perceptual and practical fields. As for the meaning of the word, I learn it as I learn to use a tool, by seeing it used in the context of a certain situation. The word's meaning is not compounded of a certain number of physical characteristics belonging to the object; it is first and foremost the aspect taken on by the object in human experience, for example my wonder in the face of these hard, then friable, then melting pellets falling ready-made from the sky. Here we have a meeting of the human and the non-human and, as it were, a piece of the world's behaviour, a certain version of its style, and the generality of its meaning as well as that of the vocable is not the generality of the concept, but of the world as typical. Thus language presupposes nothing less than a consciousness of language, a silence of consciousness embracing the world of speech in which words first receive a form and meaning. This is why consciousness is never subordinated to any empirical language, why languages can be translated and learned, and finally, why language is not an attribute of external origin, in the sociologist's sense. Behind the spoken *cogito*, the one which is converted into discourse and into essential truth, there lies a tacit *cogito*, myself experienced by myself. But this subjectivity, albeit imperious, has upon itself and upon the world only a precarious hold. It does not constitute the world, it divines the world's presence round about it as a field not provided by itself; nor does it constitute the word, but speaks as we sing when we are happy, nor again the meaning of the word, which instantaneously emerges for it in its dealing with the world and other men living in it, being at the intersection of many lines of behaviour, and being, even once 'acquired', as precise and yet as indefinable as the significance of a gesture. The tacit *cogito*, the presence of oneself to oneself, being not less than existence, is anterior to any philosophy, and knows itself only in those extreme situations in which it is under threat: for example, in the dread of death or of another's gaze upon me. What is believed to be thought about thought, as pure feeling of the self, can not yet be thought and needs to be revealed. The consciousness which conditions language is merely a comprehensive and inarticulate grasp upon the world, like that of the infant at its first breath, or of the man about to drown and who is impelled towards life, and though it is true that all particular knowledge is founded on this primary view, it is true also that the latter waits to be won back, fixed and made explicit by perceptual exploration and by speech. Silent consciousness grasps itself only as a generalized 'I think' in face of a confused world 'to be thought about'. Any particular seizure, even the recovery of this generalized project by philosophy, demands that the subject bring into action powers which are a closed book to him and, in particular, that he should become a speaking subject. The tacit *cogito* is a *cogito* only when it has found expression for itself.

The subject as project of the world

Such formulations may appear puzzling: if ultimate subjectivity cannot think of itself the moment it exists, how can it ever do so. How can that which does not think take to doing so? And is not subjectivity made to amount to a thing or a force which produces its effects without being capable of knowing it? We do not mean that the primordial *I* completely overlooks itself. If it did, it would indeed be a thing, and nothing could cause it subsequently to become consciousness. We have merely withheld from it objective thought, a positing consciousness of the world and of itself. What do we mean by this? Either these words mean nothing at all, or else they mean that we refrain from assuming an explicit consciousness which duplicates and sustains the confused grasp of primary subjectivity upon itself and upon its world. My vision, for example, is certainly 'thinking that I see', if we mean thereby that it is not simply a bodily function like digestion or respiration, a collection of processes so grouped as to have a significance in a larger system, but that it is itself that system and that significance, that anteriority of the future to the present, of the whole to its parts. There is vision only through anticipation and intention, and since no intention could be a true intention if the object towards which it tends were given to it ready made and with no motivation, it is true that all vision assumes in the last resort, at the core of subjectivity, a total project or a logic of the world which empirical perceptions endow with specific form, but to which they cannot give rise. But vision is not thinking that one sees, if we understand thereby that it itself links up with its object, and that it becomes aware of itself as absolutely transparent, and as the originator of its own presence in the visible world. The essential point is clearly to grasp the project towards the world that we are. What we have said above about the world's being inseparable from our views of the world should here help us to understand subjectivity conceived as inherence in the world. There is no *hylé*, no sensation which is not in communication with other sensations or the sensations of other people, and *for this very reason* there is no *morphé*, no apprehension or apperception, the office of which is to give significance to a matter that has none, and to ensure the *a priori* unity of my experience, and experience shared with others. Suppose that my friend Paul and I are looking at a landscape. What precisely happens? Must it be said that we have both private sensations, that we know things but cannot communicate them to each other – that, as far as pure, lived-through experience goes, we are each incarcerated in our separate perspectives – that the landscape is not numerically the same for both of us and that it is a question only of a specific identity? When I consider my perception itself, before any objectifying reflection, at no moment am I aware of being shut up within my own sensations. My friend Paul and I point out to each other certain details of the landscape; and Paul's finger, which is pointing out the church tower, is not a finger-for-me that I *think of* as orientated towards a church-tower-for-me, it is Paul's finger which itself shows me the tower that Paul sees, just as, conversely, when I make a movement towards some point in the landscape that I can see, I do not imagine that I am producing in Paul, in virtue of some pre-established harmony, inner visions merely analogous to mine: I believe, on the contrary, that my gestures invade Paul's world and guide his gaze. When I think of Paul, I do not think of a flow of private sensations indirectly related to mine through the medium of interposed signs, but of someone who has a living experience of the same world as mine, as well as the same history, and with whom I am in communication through that world and that history. Are we to say, then, that what we are concerned with is an ideal unity, that my world is the same as Paul's, just as the quadratic equation spoken of in Tokyo is the same as the one spoken of in Paris, and that in short the ideal nature of the world guarantees its inter-subjective value? But ideal unity is not satisfactory either, for it exists no less between Mount Hymettus seen by the ancient Greeks and the same mountain seen by me. Now it is no use my telling myself, as I contemplate those russet mountainsides, that the Greeks saw them too, for I cannot convince myself that they are the same ones. On the other hand, Paul and I 'together' see this landscape, we are jointly present in it, it is the same for both of us, not only as an intelligible significance, but as a certain accent of the world's style down to its very thisness. The unity of the world crumbles and falls asunder under the influence of that temporal and spatial distance which the ideal unity traverses while remaining (in theory) unimpaired. It is precisely because the landscape makes its impact upon me and produces feelings in me, because it reaches me in my uniquely individual being, because it is my own view of the landscape that I enjoy possession of the landscape itself, and the landscape for Paul as well as for me. Both universality and the world lie at the core of individuality and the subject, and this will never be understood as long as the world is made into an object. It is understood immediately if the world is the *field* of our experience, and if we are nothing but a view of the world, for in that case it is seen that the most intimate vibration of our psycho-physical being already announces the world, the quality being the outline of a thing, and the thing the outline of the world. A world which, as Malebranche puts it, never gets beyond being an 'unfinished work', or which, as Husserl says of the body, is 'never completely constituted', does not require, and even rules out, a constituting subject. There must be corresponding to this adumbration of being which appears through the concordant aspects of my own experience, or of the experience I share with others – experience which I presume capable of being consummated through indefinite horizons, from the sole fact that my phenomena congeal into a thing, and display, as they occur, a certain consistency of style – there must be, then, corresponding to this open unity of the world, an open and indefinite unity of subjectivity. Like the world's unity, that of the *I* is invoked rather than experienced each time I perform an act of perception, each time I reach a self-evident truth, and the universal *I* is the background against which these effulgent forms stand out: it is through one present thought that I achieve the unity of all my thoughts. What remains, on the hither side of my particular thoughts, to constitute the tacit *cogito* and the original project towards the world, and what ultimately, am I in so far as I can catch a glimpse of myself independently of any particular act? I am a field, an experience. One day once and for all, something was set in motion which, even during sleep, can no longer cease to see or not to see, to feel or not to feel, to suffer or be happy, to think or rest from thinking, in a word to 'have it out' with the world. There then arose, not a new set of sensations or states of consciousness, not even a new monad or a new perspective, since I am not tied to any one perspective but can change my point of view, being under compulsion only in that I must always have one, and can have only one at once – let us say, therefore, that there arose a fresh *possibility of situations*. The event of my birth has not passed completely away, it has not fallen into nothingness in the way that an event of the objective world does, for it committed a whole future, not as a cause determines its effect, but as a situation, once created, inevitably leads on to some outcome. There was henceforth a new 'setting', the world received a fresh layer of meaning. In the home into which a child is born, all objects change their significance; they begin to await some as yet indeterminate treatment at his hands; another and different person is there, a new personal history, short or long, has just been initiated, another account has been opened. My first perception, along with the horizons which surrounded it, is an ever-present event, an unforgettable tradition; even as a thinking subject, I still am that first perception, the continuation of that same life inaugurated by it. In one sense, there are no more acts of consciousness or distinct *Erlebnisse* in a life than there are separate things in the world. Just as, as we have seen, when I walk round an object, I am not presented with a succession of perspective views which I subsequently coordinate thanks to the idea of one single flat projection, there being merely a certain amount of 'shift' in the thing which, in itself, is journeying through time, so I am not myself a succession of 'psychic' acts, nor for that matter a nuclear *I* who brings them together into a synthetic unity, but one single experience inseparable from itself, one single 'living cohesion', one single temporality which is engaged, from birth, in making itself progressively explicit, and in confirming that cohesion in each successive present. It is this advent or again this event of transcendental kind that the *cogito* reveals. The primary truth is indeed 'I think', but only provided that we understand thereby 'I belong to myself' while belonging to the world. When we try to go deeper into subjectivity, calling all things into question and suspending all our beliefs, the only form in which a glimpse is vouchsafed to us of that non-human ground through which, in the words of Rimbaud, 'we are not of world', is as the horizon of our particular commitments, and as the potentiality of something in the most general sense, which is the world's phantom. Inside and outside are inseparable. The world is wholly inside and I am wholly outside myself. When I perceive this table, the perception of the top must not overlook that of the legs, otherwise the object would be thrown out of joint. When I hear a melody, each of its moments must be related to its successor, otherwise there would be no melody. Yet the table is there with its external parts, and succession is of the essence of melody. The act which draws together at the same time takes away and holds at a distance so that I touch myself only by escaping from myself. In one of his celebrated *pensées*, Pascal shows that in one way I understand the world, and in another it understands me. We must add that it is in the *same* way: I understand the world because there are for me things near and far, foregrounds and horizons, and because in this way it forms a picture and acquires significance before me, and this finally is because I am situated in it and it understands me. We do not say that the *notion* of the world is inseparable from that of the subject, or that the subject *thinks himself* inseparable from the idea of his body and the idea of the world; for, if it were a matter of no more than a conceived relationship, it would *ipso facto* leave the absolute independence of the subject as thinker intact, and the subject would not be in a situation. If the subject *is* in a situation, even if he is no more than a possibility of situations, this is because he forces his ipseity into reality only by actually being a body, and entering the world through that body. In so far as, when I reflect on the essence of subjectivity, I find it bound up with that of the body and that of the world, this is because my existence as subjectivity is merely one with my existence as a body and with the existence of the world, and because the subject that I am, when taken concretely, is inseparable from this body and this world. The ontological world and body which we find at the core of the subject are not the world or body as idea, but on the one hand the world itself contracted into a comprehensive grasp, and on the other the body itself as a knowing-body.

But, it will be asked, if the unity of the world is not based on that of consciousness, and if the world is not the outcome of a constituting effort, how does it come about that appearances accord with each other and group themselves together into things, ideas and truths? And why do our random thoughts, the events of our life and those of collective history, at least at certain times assume common significance and direction, and allow themselves to be subsumed under one idea? Why does my life succeed in drawing itself together in order to project itself in words, intentions and acts? This is the problem of rationality. The reader is aware that, on the whole, classical thought tries to explain the concordances in question in terms of a world in itself, or in terms of an absolute mind. Such explanations borrow all the forces of conviction which they can carry from the phenomenon of rationality, and therefore fail to explain that phenomenon, or ever to achieve greater clarity than it possesses. Absolute Thought is no clearer to me than my own finite mind, since it is through the latter that I conceive the former. We are in the world, which means that things take shape, an immense individual asserts itself, each existence is self-comprehensive and comprehensive of the rest. All that has to be done is to recognize these phenomena which are the ground of all our certainties. The belief in an absolute mind, or in a world in itself detached from us is no more than a rationalization of this primordial faith.

Notes

1   As Husserl, for example, does when he concedes that any transcendental reduction is at the same time an eidetic one. The necessity of proceeding by essences, and the stubborn opacity of existences, cannot be taken for granted as facts, but contribute to determining the significance of the *cogito* and of ultimate subjectivity. I am not a constituting thought, and my 'I think' is not an 'I am', unless by thought I can equal the world's concrete richness, and re-absorb facticity into it.

2   This notion recurs frequently in the later writings of Husserl.
3   See *Logical Investigations, I.* What is sometimes termed Husserl's rational-
    ism is in reality the recognition of subjectivity as an inalienable fact, and of
    the world to which it is directed as *omnitudo realitatis.*

CHAPTER 3: FREEDOM (*PP* 434–56 [504–530])

Merleau-Ponty begins this chapter, the final chapter of The Phenomenology
of Perception, *with a Sartrean reflection on freedom, that it has no limits
except those which it places upon itself. But having set out this position he
turns against it, arguing that it serves only as a* reductio ad absurdum *of
freedom, since it implies that freedom is equally present in the most trivial
activities as it is in the most important. Further, he objects, Sartre's position
rests on an incoherent voluntarist conception of ourselves, as choosing ourselves through a continuously renewed choice of our fundamental project; but
choice requires alternatives to which we are antecedently drawn, and Sartre's
theory rules out any such motivations prior to choice.*

*What Sartre has failed to grasp is that the possibility of freedom presup-
poses that we find ourselves in situations whose significance we have not
chosen. Our body and our habits give a shape to our life which is neither
freely chosen nor deterministically imposed; but it is precisely because of the
motivations inherent in our existence and our past that we can then stand
back and make a free choice of a new future. Merleau-Ponty puts the point
with a nice metaphor: my freedom as an individual to lever myself out of
my situation finds its 'fulcrum' in my general commitment to the world.
So my capacity for freedom as a unique individual and my generalised
engagement in the world are not two conceptions of myself between which, as
a philosopher, I have to choose; instead they are just the opposite sides of my
life as a 'concrete subject'. Sartre's philosophy of freedom rules out freedom
because he misses out our fundamental being in the world which is both
antecedent to personal freedom and the condition of its possibility. We can
achieve freedom only when we understand the world in which we have been
living and from which we can never completely escape.*

Freedom as all or nothing

Again, it is clear that no causal relationship is conceivable between
the subject and his body, his world or his society. Only at the cost of
losing the basis of all my certainties can I question what is conveyed
to me by my presence to myself. Now the moment I turn to myself in
order to describe myself, I have a glimpse of an anonymous flux,[1] a

comprehensive project in which there are so far no 'states of consciousness', nor, *a fortiori*, qualifications of any sort. For myself I am neither 'jealous', nor 'inquisitive', nor 'hunchbacked', nor 'a civil servant'. It is often a matter of surprise that the cripple or the invalid can put up with himself. The reason is that such people are not for themselves deformed or at death's door. Until the final coma, the dying man is inhabited by a consciousness, he is all that he sees, and enjoys this much of an outlet. Consciousness can never objectify itself into invalid-consciousness or cripple-consciousness, and even if the old man complains of his age or the cripple of his deformity, they can do so only by comparing themselves with others, or seeing themselves through the eyes of others, that is, by taking a statistical and objective view of themselves, so that such complaints are never absolutely genuine: when he is back in the heart of his own consciousness, each one of us feels beyond his limitations and thereupon resigns himself to them. They are the price which we automatically pay for being in the world, a formality which we take for granted. Hence we may speak disparagingly of our looks and still not want to change our face for another. No idiosyncrasy can, seemingly, be attached to the insuperable generality of consciousness, nor can any limit be set to this immeasurable power of escape. In order to be determined (in the two senses of that word) by an external factor, it is necessary that I should be a thing. Neither my freedom nor my universality can admit of any eclipse. It is inconceivable that I should be free in certain of my actions and determined in others: how should we understand a dormant freedom that gave full scope to determinism? And if it is assumed that it is snuffed out when it is not in action, how could it be rekindled? If *per impossible* I had once succeeded in *making myself into* a thing, how should I subsequently reconvert myself to consciousness? Once I am free, I am not to be counted among things, and I must then be uninterruptedly free. Once my actions cease to be mine, I shall never recover them, and if I lose my hold on the world, it will never be restored to me. It is equally inconceivable that my liberty should be attenuated; one cannot be to some extent free, and if, as is often said, motives incline me in a certain direction, one of two things happens: either they are strong enough to force me to act, in which case there is no freedom, or else they are not strong enough, and then freedom is complete, and as great in the worst torments as in the peace of one's home. We ought, therefore, to reject not only the idea of causality, but also that of motivation.² The alleged motive does not burden my decision; on the contrary my decision lends the motive its force. Everything that I 'am' in virtue of nature or history –

---

hunchbacked, handsome or Jewish – I never am completely for myself, as we have just explained: and I may well be these things for other people, nevertheless I remain free to posit another person as a consciousness whose views strike through to my very being, or on the other hand merely as an object. It is also true that this option is itself a form of constraint: if I am ugly, I have the choice between being an object of disapproval or disapproving of others. I am left free to be a masochist or a sadist, but not free to ignore others. But this dilemma, which is given as part of the human lot, is not one for me as pure consciousness; it is still I who makes another to be for me and makes each of us be as human beings. Moreover, even if existence as a human being were imposed upon me, the manner alone being left to my choice, and considering this choice itself and ignoring the small number of forms it might take, it would still be a free choice. If it is said that my temperament inclines me particularly to either sadism or masochism, it is still merely a manner of speaking, for my temperament exists only for the second order knowledge that I gain about myself when I see myself as others see me, and in so far as I recognize it, confer value upon it, and in that sense, choose it. What misleads us on this, is that we often look for freedom in the voluntary deliberation which examines one motive after another and seems to opt for the weightiest or most convincing. In reality the deliberation follows the decision, and it is my secret decision which brings the motives to light, for it would be difficult to conceive what the force of a motive might be in the absence of a decision which it confirms or to which it runs counter. When I have abandoned a project, the motives which I thought held me to it suddenly lose their force and collapse. In order to resuscitate them, an effort is required on my part to reopen time and set me back to the moment preceding the making of the decision. Even while I am deliberating, already I find it an effort to suspend time's flow, and to keep open a situation which I feel is closed by a decision which is already there and which I am holding off. That is why it so often happens that after giving up a plan I experience a feeling of relief: 'After all, I wasn't all that involved'; the debate was purely a matter of form, and the deliberation a mere parody, for I had decided against it from the start.

We often see the weakness of the will brought forward as an argument against freedom. And indeed, although I can will myself to adopt a course of conduct and act the part of a warrior or a seducer, it is not within my power to be a warrior or seducer with ease and in a way that 'comes naturally'; really to *be* one, that is. But neither should we seek freedom in the act of will, which is, in its very meaning, something short of an act. We have recourse to an act of will only in order to go against our true decision, and, as it were, for the purpose of proving our power-lessness. If we had really and truly made the conduct of the warrior or the seducer our own, then we should *be* one or the other. Even what are called obstacles to freedom are in reality deployed by it. An unclimbable rock face, a large or small, vertical or slanting rock, are things which have no meaning for anyone who is not intending to surmount them, for a subject whose projects do not carve out such determinate forms from the uniform mass of the *in itself* and cause an orientated world to arise – a significance in things. There is, then, ultimately nothing that can set limits to freedom, except those limits that freedom itself has set in the form of its various initiatives, so that the subject has simply the external world that he gives himself. Since it is the latter who, on com-ing into being, brings to light significance and value in things, and since no thing can impinge upon it except through acquiring, thanks to it, significance and value, there is no action of things on the subject, but merely a signification (in the active sense), a centrifugal *Sinngebung*. The choice would seem to lie between scientism's conception of causality, which is incompatible with the consciousness which we have of ourselves, and the assertion of an absolute freedom divorced from the outside. It is impossible to decide beyond which point things cease to be ἐφ᾽ ἥμιν. Either they all lie within our power, or none does.

But then there is no action, choice, or 'doing'

The result, however, of this first reflection on freedom would appear to be to rule it out altogether. If indeed it is the case that our freedom is the same in all our actions, and even in our passions, if it is not to be measured in terms of our conduct, and if the slave displays freedom as much by living in fear as by breaking his chains, then it cannot be held that there is such a thing as *free action*, freedom being anterior to all actions. In any case it will not be possible to declare: 'Here freedom makes its appearance', since free action, in order to be discernible, has to stand out against a background of life from which it is entirely, or almost entirely, absent. We may say in this case that it is everywhere, but equally nowhere. In the name of freedom we reject the idea of acquisition, since freedom has become a primordial acquisition and, as it were, our state of nature. Since we do not have to provide it, it is the gift granted to us of having no gift, it is the nature of consciousness which consists in having no nature, and in no case can it find external expression or a place in our life. The idea of action, therefore, disappears: nothing can pass from us to the world, since we are nothing that can be specified, and since the non-being which constitutes us could not possibly find its way into the world's plenum. There are merely intentions immediately followed by their effects, and we are very near to the Kantian idea of an intention which is tantamount to the act, which Scheler countered with the argument that the cripple who would like to be able to save a drowning man and the good swimmer who actually saves him do not have the same experience of autonomy. The very idea of choice vanishes, for to choose is to choose *something* in which freedom sees, at least for a moment, a symbol of itself. There is free choice only if freedom comes into play in its decision, and posits the situation chosen as a situation of freedom. A freedom which has no need to be exercised because it is already acquired could not commit itself in this way: it knows that the following instant will find it, come what may, just as free and just as indeterminate. The very notion of freedom demands that our decision should plunge into the future, that something should have been *done* by it, that the subsequent instant should benefit from its predecessor and, though not necessitated, should be at least required by it. If freedom is doing, it is necessary that what it does should not be immediately undone by a new freedom. Each instant, therefore, must not be a closed world; one instant must be able to commit its successors and, a decision once taken and action once begun, I must have something acquired at my disposal, I must benefit from my impetus, I must be inclined to carry on, and there must be a bent or propensity of the mind. It was Descartes who held that conservation demands a power as great as does creation; a view which implies a realistic notion of the instant. It is true that the instant is not a philosopher's fiction. It is the point at which one project is brought to fruition and another begun[3] – the point at which my gaze is transferred from one end to another, it is the *Augenblick*. But this break in time cannot occur unless each of the two spans is of a piece. Consciousness, it is said, is, though not atomized into instants, at least haunted by the spectre of the instant which it is obliged continually to exorcise by a free act. We shall soon see that we have indeed always the power to interrupt, but it implies in any case a power to *begin*, for there would be no severance unless freedom had taken up its abode somewhere and were preparing to move it. Unless there are cycles of behaviour, open situations requiring a certain completion and capable of constituting a background to either a confirmatory or transformatory decision, we never experience freedom. The choice of intelligible character is excluded, not only because there is no time anterior to time, but because choice presupposes a prior commitment and because the idea of an initial choice involves a contradiction. If freedom is to have *room*[4] in which to move, if it is to be describable as freedom, there must be something to hold it away from its objectives, it must have a *field*, which means that there must be for it special possibilities, or realities which tend to cling to being. As J.-P. Sartre himself observes, dreaming is incompatible with freedom because, in the realm of imagination, we have no sooner taken a certain significance as our goal than we already believe that we have intuitively brought it into being, in short, because there is no obstacle and nothing *to do*.[5] It is established that freedom is not to be confused with those abstract decisions of will at grips with motives or passions, for the classical conception of deliberation is relevant only to a freedom 'in bad faith' which secretly harbours antagonistic motives without being prepared to act on them, and so itself manufactures the alleged proofs of its impotence. We can see, beneath these noisy debates and these fruitless efforts to 'construct' ourselves, the tacit decisions whereby we have marked out round ourselves the field of possibility, and it is true that nothing is done as long as we cling to these fixed points, and everything is easy as soon as we have weighed anchor. This is why our freedom is not to be sought in spurious discussion on the conflict between a style of life which we have no wish to reappraise and circumstances suggestive of another: the real choice is that of whole character and our manner of being in the world. But either this total choice is never uttered, since it is the silent upsurge of our being in the world, in which case it is not clear in what sense it could be said to be ours, since this freedom glides over itself and is the equivalent of a fate – or else our choice of ourselves is truly a choice, a conversion involving our whole existence. In this case, however, there is presupposed a previous acquisition which the choice sets out to modify and it founds a new tradition: this leads us to ask whether the perpetual severance in terms of which we initially defined freedom is not simply the negative aspect of our universal commitment to a world, and whether our indifference to each determinate thing does not express merely our involvement in all; whether the ready-made freedom from which we started is not reducible to a power of initiative, which cannot be transformed into *doing* without taking up some proposition of the world, and whether, in short, concrete and actual freedom is not indeed to be found in this exchange. It is true that nothing has *significance* and value for anyone but *me* and through anyone but me, but this proposition remains indeterminate and is still indistinguishable from the Kantian idea of a consciousness which 'finds in things only what it has put into them', and from the idealist refutation of realism, as long as we fail to make clear how we understand significance and the self. By defining ourselves as a universal power of *Sinngebung*, we have reverted to the method of the 'thing without which' and to the analytical reflection of the traditional type, which seeks the conditions of possibility without concerning itself with the conditions of reality. We must therefore resume the analysis of the *Sinngebung*, and show how it can be both centrifugal and centripetal, since it has been established that there is no freedom without a field.

Implicit evaluation of the sensible world

When I say that this rock is unclimbable, it is certain that this attribute, like that of being big or little, straight and oblique, and indeed like all attributes in general, can be conferred upon it only by the project of climbing it, and by a human presence. It is, therefore, freedom which brings into being the obstacles to freedom, so that the latter can be set over against it as its bounds. However, it is clear that, one and the same project being given, one rock will appear as an obstacle, and another, being more negotiable, as a means. My freedom, then, does not so contrive it that this way there is an obstacle, and that way a way through, it arranges for there to be obstacles and ways through in general; it does not draw the particular outline of this world, but merely lays down its general structures. It may be objected that there is no difference; if my freedom conditions the structure of the 'there is', that of the 'here' and the 'there', it is present wherever these structures arise. We cannot distinguish the quality of 'obstacle' from the obstacle itself, and relate one to freedom and the other to the world in itself which, without freedom, would be merely an amorphous and unnameable mass. It is not, therefore, outside myself that I am able to find a limit to my freedom. But do I not find it in myself? We must indeed distinguish between my express intentions, for example the plan I now make to climb those mountains, and general intentions which evaluate the potentialities of my environment. Whether or not I have decided to climb them, these mountains appear high to me, because they exceed my body's power to take them in its stride, and, even if I have just read *Micromégas*, I cannot so contrive it that they are small for me. Underlying myself as a thinking subject, who am able to take my place at will on Sirius or on the earth's surface, there is, therefore, as it were a natural self which does not budge from its terrestrial situation and which constantly adumbrates absolute valuations. What is more, my projects as a thinking being are clearly modelled on the latter; if I elect to see things from the point of view of Sirius, it is still to my terrestrial experience that I must have recourse in order to do so; I may say, for example, that the Alps are *molehills*. In so far as I have hands, feet, a body, I sustain around me intentions which are not dependent upon my decisions and which affect my surroundings in a way which I do not choose. These intentions are general in a double sense: firstly in the sense that they constitute a system in which all possible objects are simultaneously included; if the mountain appears high and upright, the tree appears small and sloping; and furthermore in the sense that they are not simply mine, they originate from other than myself, and I am not surprised to find them in all psycho-physical subjects organized as I am. Hence, as Gestalt psychology has shown, there are for me certain shapes which are particularly favoured, as they are for other men, and which are capable of giving rise to a psychological science and rigorous laws. The grouping of dots

..   ..

is always perceived as six pairs of dots with two millimetres between each pair, while one figure is always perceived as a cube, and another as a plane mosaic. It is as if, on the hither side of our judgement and our freedom, someone were assigning such and such a significance to such and such a given grouping. It is indeed true that perceptual structures do not always force themselves upon the observer; there are some which are ambiguous. But these reveal even more effectively the presence within us of spontaneous evaluation: for they are elusive shapes which suggest constantly changing meanings to us. Now a pure consciousness is capable of anything except being ignorant of its intentions, and an absolute freedom cannot choose itself as hesitant, since that amounts to allowing itself to be drawn in several directions, and since, the possibilities being *ex hypothesi* indebted to freedom for all the strength they have, the weight that freedom gives to one is thereby withdrawn from the rest. We *can* break up a shape by looking at it awry, but this too is because freedom uses the gaze along with its spontaneous evaluations. Without the latter, we would not have a world, that is, a collection of things which emerge from a background of formlessness by presenting themselves to our body as 'to be touched', 'to be taken', 'to be climbed over'. We should never be aware of adjusting ourselves to things and reaching them where they are, beyond us, but would be conscious only of restricting our thoughts to the immanent objects of our intentions, and we should not be in the world, ourselves implicated in the spectacle and, so to speak, intermingled with things, we should simply enjoy the spectacle of a universe. It is, therefore, true that there are no obstacles in themselves, but the self which qualifies them as such is not some acosmic subject; it runs ahead of itself in relation to things in order to confer upon them the form of things. There is an autochthonous significance of the world which is constituted in the dealings which our incarnate existence has with it, and which provides the ground of every deliberate *Sinngebung*.

Sedimentation of being-in-the-world

This is true not only of an impersonal and, all in all, abstract function such as 'external perception'. There is something comparable present in all evaluations. It has been perceptively remarked that pain and fatigue can never be regarded as causes which 'act' upon my liberty, and that, in so far as I may experience either at any given moment, they do not have their origin outside me, but always have a significance and express my attitude towards the world. Pain makes me give way and say what I ought to have kept to myself, fatigue makes me break my journey. We all know the moment at which we decide no longer to endure pain or fatigue, and when, simultaneously, they become intolerable in fact. Tiredness does not halt my companion, because he likes the clamminess of his body, the heat of the road and the sun, in short, because he likes to feel himself in the midst of things, to feel their rays converging upon him, to be the cynosure of all this light, and an object of touch for the earth's crust. My own fatigue brings me to a halt because I dislike it, because I have chosen differently my manner of being in the world, because, for instance, I endeavour, not to be in nature, but rather to win the recognition of others. I am free in relation to fatigue to precisely the extent that I am free in relation to my being in the world, free to make my way by transforming it.[6] But here once more we must recognize a sort of sedimentation of our life: an attitude towards the world, when it has received frequent confirmation, acquires a favoured status for us. Yet since freedom does not tolerate any motive in its path, my habitual being in the world is at each moment equally precarious, and the complexes which I have allowed to develop over the years always remain equally soothing, and the free act can with no difficulty blow them sky-high. However, having built our life upon an inferiority complex which has been operative for twenty years, it is not *probable* that we shall change. It is clear what a summary rationalism might say in reply to such a hybrid notion: there are no degrees of possibility; either the free act is no longer possible, or it is still possible, in which case freedom is complete. In short, 'probable' is meaningless. It is a notion belonging to statistical thought, which is not thought at all, since it does not concern any particular thing actually existing, any moment of time, any concrete event. 'It is improbable that Paul will give up writing bad books' means nothing, since Paul may well decide to write no more such books. The probable is everywhere and nowhere, a reified fiction, with only a psychological existence; it is not an ingredient of the world. And yet we have already met it a little while ago in the perceived *world*. The mountain is great or small to the extent that, as a perceived thing, it is to be found in the field of my possible actions, and in relation to a level which is not only that of my individual life, but that of 'any man'. Generality and probability are not fictions, but phenomena; we must therefore find a phenomenological basis for statistical thought. It belongs necessarily to a being which is fixed, situated and surrounded by things in the world. 'It is improbable' that I should at this moment destroy an inferiority complex in which I have been content to live for twenty years. That means that I have committed myself to inferiority, that I have made it my abode, that this past, though not a fate, has at least a specific weight and is not a set of events over there, at a distance from me, but the atmosphere of my present. The rationalist's dilemma: either the free act is possible, or it is not – either the event originates in me or is imposed on me from outside, does not apply to our relations with the world and with our past. Our freedom does not destroy our situation, but gears itself to it: as long as we are alive, our situation is open, which implies both that it calls up specially favoured modes of resolution, and also that it is powerless to bring one into being by itself.

Evaluation of historical situations

We shall arrive at the same result by considering our relations with history. Taking myself in my absolute concreteness, as I am presented to myself in reflection, I find that I am an anonymous and pre-human flux, as yet unqualified as, for instance, 'a working man' or 'middle class'. If I subsequently think of myself as a man among men, a bourgeois among bourgeois, this can be, it would seem, no more than a second order view of myself; I am never in my heart of hearts a worker or a bourgeois, but a consciousness which freely evaluates itself as a middle class or proletarian consciousness. And indeed, it is never the case that my objective position in the production process is sufficient to awaken class consciousness. There was exploitation long before there were revolutionaries. Nor is it always in periods of economic difficulty that the working class movement makes headway. Revolt is, then, not the outcome of objective conditions, but it is rather the decision taken by the worker to will revolution that makes a proletarian of him. The evaluation of the present operates through one's free project for the future. From which we might conclude that history by itself has no significance, but only that conferred upon it by our will. Yet here again we are slipping into the method of 'the indispensable condition failing which . . .': in opposition to objective thought, which includes the subject in its deterministic system, we set idealist reflection which makes determinism dependent upon the constituting activity of the subject. Now, we have already seen that objective thought and analytical reflection are two aspects of the same mistake, two ways of overlooking the phenomena. Objective thought derives class consciousness from the objective condition of the proletariat. Idealist reflection reduces the proletarian condition to the awareness of it, which the proletarian arrives at. The former traces class-consciousness to the class defined in terms of objective characteristics, the latter on the other hand reduces 'being a workman' to the consciousness of being one. In each case we are in the realm of abstraction, because we remain torn between the *in itself* and the *for itself*. If we approach the question afresh with the idea of discovering, not the causes of the act of becoming aware, for there is no cause which can act from outside upon a consciousness – nor the conditions of its possibility, for we need to know the conditions which actually produce it – but class-consciousness itself, if, in short, we apply a genuinely existential method, what do we find? I am not conscious of being working class or middle class simply because, as a matter of fact, I sell my labour or, equally as a matter of fact, because my interests are bound up with capitalism, nor do I become one or the other on the day on which I elect to view history in the light of the class struggle: what happens is that 'I exist as working class' or 'I exist as middle class' in the first place, and it is this mode of dealing with the world and society which provides both the motives for my revolutionary or conservative projects and my explicit judgements of the type 'I am working class' or 'I am middle class', without its being possible to deduce the former from the latter, or *vice versa*. What makes me a proletarian is not the economic system or society considered as systems of impersonal forces, but these institutions as I carry them within me and experience them; nor is it an intellectual operation devoid of motive, but my way of being in the world within this institutional framework.

Let us suppose that I have a certain style of living, being at the mercy of booms and slumps, not being free to do as I like, receiving a weekly wage, having no control over either the conditions or the products of my work, and consequently feeling a stranger in my factory, my nation and my life. I have acquired the habit of reckoning with a *fatum*, or appointed order, which I do not respect, but which I have to humour. Or suppose that I work as a day-labourer, having no farm of my own, no tools, going from one farm to another hiring myself out at harvest time; in that case I have the feeling that there is some anonymous power hovering over me and making a nomad of me, even though I want to settle into a regular job. Or finally suppose I am the tenant of a farm to which the owner has had no electricity laid on, though the mains are less than two hundred yards away. I have, for my family and myself, only one habitable room, although it would be easy to make other rooms available in the house. My fellow workers in factory or field, or other farmers, do the same work as I do in comparable conditions; we co-exist in the same situation and feel alike, not in virtue of some comparison, as if each one of us lived primarily within himself, but on the basis of our tasks and gestures. These situations do not imply any express evaluation, and if there is a tacit evaluation, it represents the thrust of a freedom devoid of any project against unknown obstacles; one cannot in any case talk about a choice, for in all three cases it is enough that I should be born into the world and that I exist in order to experience my life as full of difficulties and constraints – I do not choose so to experience it. But this state of affairs can persist without my becoming class-conscious, understanding that I am of the proletariat and becoming a revolutionary. How then am I to make this change? The worker learns that other workers in a different trade have, after striking, obtained a wage-increase, and notices that subsequently wages have gone up in his own factory. The appointed order with which he was at grips is beginning to take on a clearer shape. The day-labourer who has not often seen workers in regular employment, who is not like them and has little love for them, sees the price of manufactured goods and the cost of living going up, and becomes aware that he can no longer earn a livelihood. He may at this point blame town workers, in which case class-consciousness will not make its appearance. If it does, it is not because the day-labourer has decided to become a revolutionary and consequently confers a value upon his actual condition; it is because he has perceived, in a concrete way, that his life is synchronized with the life of the town labourers and that all share a common lot. The small farmer who does not associate himself with the day-labourers, still less with the town labourers, being separated from them by a whole world of customs and value judgements, nevertheless feels that he is on the same side as the journeyman when he pays them an inadequate wage, and he even feels that he has something in common with the town workers when he learns that the farm owner is chairman of the board of directors of several industrial concerns. Social space begins to acquire a magnetic field, and a region of the exploited is seen to appear. At every pressure felt from any quarter of the social horizon, the process of regrouping becomes clearly discernible beyond ideologies and various occupations. Class is coming into being, and we say that a situation is revolutionary when the connection objectively existing between the sections of the proletariat (the connection, that is, which an absolute observer would recognize as so existing) is finally experienced in perception as a common obstacle to the existence of each and every one. It is not at all necessary that at any single moment a *representation* of revolution should arise. For example, it is doubtful whether the Russian peasants of 1917 expressly envisaged revolution and the transfer of property. Revolution arises day by day from the concatenation of less remote and more remote ends. It is not necessary that each member of the proletariat should think of himself as such, in the sense that a Marxist theoretician gives to the word. It is sufficient that the journeyman or the farmer should feel that he is on the march towards a certain crossroads, to which the road trodden by the town labourers also leads. Both find their journey's end in revolution, which would perhaps have terrified them had it been described and represented to them in advance. One might say at the most that revolution is at the end of the road they have taken and in their projects in the form of 'things must change', which each one experiences concretely in his distinctive difficulties and in the depths of his particular prejudices. Neither the appointed order, nor the free act which destroys it, is represented; they are lived through in ambiguity. This does not mean that workers and peasants bring about revolution without being aware of it, and that we have here blind, 'elementary forces' cleverly exploited by a few shrewd agitators. It is possibly in this light that the prefect of police will view history. But such ways of seeing things do not help him when faced with a genuine revolutionary situation, in which the slogans of the allged agitators are immediately understood, as if by some pre-established harmony, and meet with concurrence on all sides, because they crystallize what is latent in the life of all productive workers. The revolutionary movement, like the work of the artist, is an intention which itself creates its instruments and its means of expression. The revolutionary project is not the result of a deliberate judgement, or the explicit positing of an end. It is these things in the case of the propagandist, because the propagandist has been trained by the intellectual, or, in the case of the intellectual, because he regulates his life on the basis of his thoughts. But it does not cease to be the abstract decision of a thinker and become a historical reality until it is worked out in the dealings men have with each other, and in the relations of the man to his job. It is, therefore, true that I recognize myself as a worker or a bourgeois on the day I take my stand in relation to a possible revolution, and that this taking of a stand is not the outcome, through some mechanical causality, of my status as workman or bourgeois (which is why all classes have their traitors), but neither is it an unwarranted evaluation, instantaneous and unmotivated; it is prepared by some molecular process, it matures in co-existence before bursting forth into words and being related to objective ends. One is justified in drawing attention to the fact that it is not the greatest poverty which produces the most clear-sighted revolutionaries, but one forgets to ask why a return of prosperity frequently brings with it a more radical mood among the masses. It is because the easing of living conditions makes a fresh structure of social space possible: the horizon is not restricted to the most immediate concerns, there is economic play and room for a new project in relation to living. This phenomenon does not, then, go to prove that the worker makes himself into worker and revolutionary *ex nihilo*, but on the contrary that he does so on a certain basis of co-existence. The mistake inherent in the conception under discussion is, in general, that of disregarding all but intellectual projects, instead of considering the existential project, which is the polarization of a life towards a goal which is both determinate and indeterminate, which, to the person concerned, is entirely unrepresented, and which is recognized only on being attained. Intentionality is brought down to the particular cases of the objectifying acts, the proletarian condition is made an object of thought, and no difficulty is experienced in showing, in accordance with idealism's permanent method, that, like every other object of thought, it subsists only before and through the consciousness which constitutes it as an object. Idealism (like objective thought) bypasses true intentionality, which is *at* its object rather than positing it. Idealism overlooks the interrogative, the subjunctive, the aspiration, the expectation, the positive indeterminacy of these modes of consciousness, for it is acquainted only with consciousness in the present or future indicative, which is why it fails to account for class. For class is a matter neither for observation nor decree; like the appointed order of the capitalistic system, like revolution, before being thought it is lived through as an obsessive presence, as possibility, enigma and myth. To make class-consciousness the outcome of a decision and a choice is to say that problems are solved on the day they are posed, that every question already contains the reply that it awaits; it is, in short, to revert to immanence and abandon the attempt to understand history. In reality, the intellectual project and the positing of ends are merely the bringing to completion of an existential project. It is I who give a direction, significance and future to my life, but that does not mean that these are concepts; they spring from my present and past and in particular from my mode of present and past co-existence. Even in the case of the intellectual who turns revolutionary, his decision does not arise *ex nihilo*; it may follow upon a prolonged period of solitude: the intellectual is in search of a doctrine which shall make great demands on him and cure him of his subjectivity; or he may yield to the clear light thrown by a Marxist interpretation of history, in which case he has given knowledge pride of place in his life, and that in itself is understandable only in virtue of his past and his childhood. Even the decision to become a revolutionary without motive, and by an act of pure freedom would express a certain way of being in the natural and social world, which is typically that of the intellectual. He 'throws in his lot with the working class' from the starting point of his situation as an intellectual and from nowhere else (and this is why even fideism, in his case, remains rightly suspect). Now with the worker it is *a fortiori* the case that his decision is elaborated in the course of his life. This time it is through no misunderstanding that the horizon of a particular life and revolutionary aims coincide: for the worker revolution is a more immediate possibility, and one closer to his own interests than for the intellectual, since he is at grips with the economic system in his very life. For this reason there are, statistically, more workers than middle class people in a revolutionary party. Motivation, of course, does not do away with freedom. Working class parties of the most unmistakable kind have had many intellectuals among their leaders, and it is likely that a man such as Lenin identified himself with revolution and eventually transcended the distinction between intellectual and worker. But these are the virtues proper to action and commitment; at the outset, I am not an individual beyond class, I am situated in a social environment, and my freedom, though it may have the power to commit me elsewhere, has not the power to transform me instantaneously into what I decide to be. Thus to be a bourgeois or a worker is not only to be aware of being one or the other, it is to identify oneself as worker or bourgeois through an implicit or existential project which merges into our way of patterning the world and co-existing with other people. My decision draws together a spontaneous meaning of my life which it may confirm or repudiate, but not annul. Both idealism and objective thinking fail to pin down the coming into being of class consciousness, the former because it deduces actual existence from consciousness, the latter because it derives consciousness from *de facto* existence, and both because they overlook the relationship of motivation.

It will perhaps be objected, from the idealist side, that I am not, for myself, a particular project, but a pure consciousness, and that the attributes of bourgeois or worker belong to me only to the extent that I place myself among others, and see myself through their eyes, from the outside, as 'another'. Here we should have categories of For Others and not For Oneself. But if there were two sorts of categories, how could I have the experience of another, that is, of an *alter ego*? This experience presupposes that already my view of myself is halfway to having the quality of a possible 'other', and that in my view of another person is implied his quality as *ego*. It will be replied that the other person is given to me as a fact, and not as a possibility of my own being. What is meant by this? Is it that I should not have the experience of other men if there were none on the earth's surface? The proposition is self-evidently true, but does not solve our problem since, as Kant has already said, we cannot pass from 'All knowledge begins with experience' to 'All knowledge derives from experience'. If the other people who empirically exist are to be, for me, other people, I must have a means of recognizing them, and the structures of the For Another must, therefore, already be the dimensions of the For Oneself. Moreover, it is impossible to derive from the For Another all the specifications of which we are speaking. Another person is not necessarily, is not even ever quite an object for me. And, in sympathy for example, I can perceive another person as bare existence and freedom as much or as little as myself. The-other-person-as-object is nothing but an insincere modality of others, just as absolute subjectivity is nothing but an abstract notion of myself. I must, therefore, in the most radical reflection, apprehend around my absolute individuality a kind of halo of generality or a kind of atmosphere of 'sociality'. This is necessary if subsequently the words 'a bourgeois' and 'a man' are to be able to assume meaning for me. I must apprehend myself immediately as centred in a way outside myself, and my individual existence must diffuse round itself, so to speak, an existence in quality. The For Themselves – me for myself and the other for himself – must stand out against a background of For Others – I for the other and the other for me. My life must have a significance which I do not constitute; there must strictly speaking be an intersubjectivity; each one of us must be both anonymous in the sense of absolutely individual, and anonymous in the sense of absolutely general. Our being in the world is the concrete bearer of this double anonymity.

History has some meaning
Provided that this is so, there can be situations, a direction[7] of history, and a historical truth: three ways of saying the same thing. If indeed I made myself into a worker or a bourgeois by an absolute initiative, and if in general terms nothing ever courted our freedom, history would display no structure, no event would be seen to take shape in it, and anything might emerge from anything else. There would be no British Empire as a relatively stable historical form to which a name can be given, and in which certain probable properties are recognizable. There would not be, in the history of social progress, revolutionary situations or periods of set-back. A social revolution would be equally possible at any moment, and one might reasonably expect a despot to undergo conversion to anarchism. History would never move in any direction, nor would it be possible to say that even over a short period of time events were conspiring to produce any definite outcome. The states-man would always be an adventurer, that is to say, he would turn events to his own advantage by conferring upon them a meaning which they *did not have*. Now if it is true that history is powerless to complete anything independently of consciousnesses which assume it and thereby decide its course, and if consequently it can never be detached from us to play the part of an alien force using us for its own ends, then *precisely because it is always history lived through* we cannot withhold from it at least a fragmentary meaning. Something is being prepared which will perhaps come to nothing but which may, for the moment, conform to the adumbrations of the present. Nothing can so order it that, in the France of 1799, a military power 'above classes' should not appear as a natural product of the ebb of revolution, and that the rôle of military dictator should not here be 'a part that has to be played'. It is Bonaparte's project, known to us through its realization, which causes us to pass such a judgement. But before Bonaparte, Dumouriez, Custine and others had envisaged it, and this common tendency has to be accounted for. What is known as the significance of events is not an

idea which produces them, or the fortuitous result of their occurring together. It is the concrete project of a future which is elaborated within social coexistence and in the One[8] before any personal decision is made. At the point of revolutionary history to which class dynamics had carried it by 1799, when neither the Revolution could be carried forward nor the clock put back, the situation was such that, all due reservations as to individual freedom having been made, each individual, through the functional and generalized existence which makes a historical subject of him, tended to fall back upon what had been acquired. It would have been a historical mistake at that stage to suggest to them either a resumption of the methods of revolutionary government or a reversion to the social conditions of 1789, not because there is a truth of history independent of our projects and evaluations, which are always free, but because there is an average and statistical significance of these projects. Which means that we confer upon history its significance, but not without its putting that significance forward itself. The *Sinngebung* is not merely centrifugal which is why the subject of history is not the individual. There is an exchange between generalized and individual existence, each receiving and giving something. There is a moment at which the significance which was foreshadowed in the One, and which was merely a precarious possibility threatened by the contingency of history, is taken up by an individual. It may well happen that now, having taken command of history, he leads it, for a time at least, far beyond what seemed to comprise its significance, and involves it in a fresh dialectic, as when Bonaparte, from being Consul, made himself Emperor and conqueror. We are not asserting that history from end to end has only one meaning, any more than has an individual life. We mean simply that in any case freedom modifies it only by taking up the meaning which history *was offering* at the moment in question, and by a kind of unobtrusive assimilation. On the strength of this proposal made by the present, the adventurer can be distinguished from the statesman, historical imposture from the truth of an epoch, with the result that our assessment of the past, though never arriving at absolute objectivity, is at the same time never entitled to be arbitrary.

The Ego and its halo of generality

We therefore recognize, around our initiatives and around that strictly individual project which is oneself, a zone of generalized existence and of projects already formed, significances which trail between ourselves and things and which confer upon us the quality of man, bourgeois or worker. Already generality intervenes, already our presence to ourselves is mediated by it and we cease to be pure consciousness, as soon as the natural or social constellation ceases to be an unformulated *this* and crystallizes into a situation, as soon as it has a meaning – in short, as soon as we exist. Every thing appears to us through a medium to which it lends its own fundamental quality; this piece of wood is neither a collection of colours and tactile data, not even their total *Gestalt*, but something from which there emanates a woody essence; these 'sensory givens' modulate a certain theme or illustrate a certain style which is the wood itself, and which creates, round this piece of wood and the perception I have of it, a horizon of significance. The natural world, as we have seen, is nothing other than the place of all possible themes and styles. It is indissolubly an unmatched individual and a significance. Correspondingly, the generality and the individuality of the subject, subjectivity qualified and pure, the anonymity of the One and the anonymity of consciousness are not two conceptions of the subject between which philosophy has to choose, but two stages of a unique structure which is the concrete subject. Let us consider, for example, sense-experience. I lose myself in this red which is before me, without in any way qualifying it, and it seems that this experience brings me into contact with a pre-human subject. Who perceives this red? It is nobody who can be named and placed among other perceiving subjects. For, between this experience of red which I have, and that about which other people speak to me, no direct comparison will ever be possible. I am here in my own point of view, and since all experience, in so far as it derives from impression, is in the same way strictly my own, it seems that a unique and unduplicated subject enfolds them all. Suppose I formulate a thought, the God of Spinoza, for example; this thought as it is in my living experience is a certain landscape to which no one will ever have access, even if, moreover, I manage to enter into a discussion with a friend on the subject of Spinoza's God. However, the very individuality of these experiences is not quite unadulterated. For the thickness of this red, its thisness, the power it has of reaching me and saturating me, are attributable to the fact that it requires and obtains from my gaze a certain vibration, and imply that I am familiar with a world of colours of which this one is a particular variation. The concrete colour red, therefore, stands out against a background of generality, and this is why, even without transferring myself to another's point of view, I grasp myself in perception as *a* perceiving subject, and not as unclassifiable consciousness. I feel, all round my perception of red, all the regions of my being unaffected by it, and that region set aside for colours, 'vision', through which the perception finds its way into me. Similarly my thought about the God of Spinoza is only apparently a strictly unique experience, for it is the concretion of a certain cultural world, the Spinozist philosophy, or of a certain philosophic style in which I immediately recognize a 'Spinozist' idea. There is therefore no occasion to ask ourselves why the thinking subject or consciousness perceives itself as a man, or an incarnate or historical subject, nor must we treat this apperception as a second order operation which it some-how performs starting from its absolute existence: the absolute flow takes shape beneath its own gaze as '*a* consciousness', or a man, or an incarnate subject, because it is a field of presence – to itself, to others and to the world – and because this presence throws it into the natural and cultural world from which it arrives at an understanding of itself. We must not envisage this flux as absolute contact with oneself, as an absolute density with no internal fault, but on the contrary as a being which is in pursuit of itself outside. If the subject made a constant and at all times peculiar choice of himself, one might wonder why his experience always ties up with itself and presents him with objects and definite historical phases, why we have a general notion of time valid through all times, and why finally the experience of each one of us links up with that of others. But it is the question itself which must be ques-tioned: for what is given, is not one fragment of time followed by another, one individual flux, then another; it is the taking up of each subjectivity by itself, and of subjectivities by each other in the generality of a single nature, the cohesion of an intersubjective life and a world. The present mediates between the For Oneself and the For Others, between individuality and generality. True reflection presents me to myself not as idle and inaccessible subjectivity, but as identical with my presence in the world and to others, as I am now realizing it: I am all that I see, I am an intersubjective field, not despite my body and historical situation, but, on the contrary, by being this body and this situation, and through them, all the rest.

I do not choose myself, starting from nothing
What, then, becomes of the freedom we spoke about at the outset, if this point of view is taken? I can no longer pretend to be a cipher, and to choose myself continually from the starting point of nothing at all. If it is through subjectivity that nothingness appears in the world, it can equally be said that it is through the world that nothingness comes into being. I am a general refusal to be anything, accompanied

surreptitiously by a continual acceptance of such and such a qualified form of being. *For even this general refusal is still one manner of being, and has its place in the world.* It is true that I can at any moment interrupt my projects. But what *is* this power? It is the power to begin something else, for we never remain suspended in nothingness. We are always in a plenum, in being, just as a face, even in repose, even in death, is always doomed to express something (there are people whose faces, in death, bear expressions of surprise, or peace, or discretion), and just as silence is still a modality of the world of sound. I may defy all accepted form, and spurn everything, for there is no case in which I am utterly committed: but in this case I do not withdraw into my freedom, I commit myself elsewhere. Instead of thinking about my bereavement, I look at my nails, or have lunch, or engage in politics. Far from its being the case that my freedom is always unattended, it is never without an accomplice, and its power of perpetually tearing itself away finds its fulcrum in my universal commitment in the world. My actual freedom is not on the hither side of my being, but before me, in things. We must not say that I continually choose myself, on the excuse that I *might* continually refuse what I am. Not to refuse is not the same thing as to choose. We could identify drift and action only by depriving the implicit of all phenomenal value, and at every instant arraying the world before us in perfect transparency, that is, by destroying the world's 'worldliness'. Consciousness holds itself responsible for everything, and takes everything upon itself, but it has nothing of its own and makes its life in the world. We are led to conceive freedom as a choice continually remade as long as we do not bring in the notion of a generalized or natural time. We have seen that there is no natural time, if we understand thereby a time of things without subjectivity. There is, however, at least a generalized time, and this is what the common notion of time envisages. It is the perpetual reiteration of the sequence of past, present and future. It is, as it were, a constant disappointment and failure. This is what is expressed by saying that it is continuous: the present which it brings to us is never a present for good, since it is already over when it appears, and the future has, in it, only the appearance of a goal towards which we make our way, since it quickly comes into the present, whereupon we turn towards a fresh future. This time is the time of our bodily functions, which like it, are cyclic, and it is also that of nature with which we co-exist. It offers us only the adumbration and the abstract form of a commitment, since it continually erodes itself and undoes that which it has just done. As long as we place in opposition, with no mediator, the For Itself and the In Itself, and fail to perceive, between ourselves and the world, this natural foreshadowing of a subjectivity, this prepersonal time which rests upon itself, acts are needed to sustain the upsurge of time, and everything becomes equally a matter of choice, the respiratory reflex no less than the moral decision, conservation no less than creation. As far as we are concerned, consciousness attributes this power of universal constitution to itself only if it ignores the event which upholds it and is the occasion of its birth. A consciousness for which the world 'can be taken for granted', which finds it 'already constituted' and present even in consciousness itself, does not *absolutely* choose either its being or its manner of being.

What then is freedom? To be born is both to be born of the world and to be born into the world. The world is already constituted, but also never completely constituted; in the first case we are acted upon, in the second we are open to an infinite number of possibilities. But this analysis is still abstract, for we exist in both ways *at once*. There is, therefore, never determinism and never absolute choice, I am never a thing and never bare consciousness. In fact, even our own pieces of initiative, even the situations which we have chosen, bear us on, once they have been entered upon by virtue of a state rather than an act. The generality of the 'rôle' and of the situation comes to the aid of decision, and in this exchange between the situation and the person who takes it up, it is impossible to determine precisely the 'share contributed by the situation' and the 'share contributed by freedom'. Let us suppose that a man is tortured to make him talk. If he refuses to give the names and addresses which it is desired to extract from him, this does not arise from a solitary and unsupported decision: the man still feels himself to be with his comrades, and, being still involved in the common struggle, he is as it were incapable of talking. Or else, for months or years, he has, in his mind, faced this test and staked his whole life upon it. Or finally, he wants to prove, by coming through it, what he has always thought and said about freedom. These motives do not cancel out freedom, but at least ensure that it does not go unbuttressed in being. What withstands pain is not, in short, a bare consciousness, but the prisoner with his comrades or with those he loves and under whose gaze he lives; or else the awareness of his proudly willed solitude, which again is a certain mode of the *Mitsein*. And probably the individual in his prison daily reawakens these phantoms, which give back to him the strength he gave to them. But conversely, in so far as he has committed himself to this action, formed a bond with his comrades or adopted this morality, it is because the historical situation, the comrades, the world around him seemed to him to expect that conduct from him. The analysis could be pursued endlessly in this way. We choose our world and the world chooses us. What is certain, in any case, is that we can at no time set aside within ourselves a redoubt to which being does not find its way through, without seeing this freedom, immediately and by the very fact of being a living experience, take on the appearance of being and become a motive and a buttress. Taken concretely, freedom is always a meeting of the inner and the outer – even the prehuman and prehistoric freedom with which we began – and it shrinks without ever disappearing altogether in direct proportion to the lessening of the *tolerance* allowed by the bodily and institutional data of our lives. There is, as Husserl says, on the one hand a 'field of freedom' and on the other a 'conditioned freedom', not that freedom is absolute within the limits of this field and non-existent outside it (like the perceptual field, this one has no traceable boundaries), but because I enjoy immediate and remote possibilities. Our commitments sustain our power and there is no freedom without some power. Our freedom, it is said, is either total or non-existent. This dilemma belongs to objective thought and its stable-companion, analytical reflection. If indeed we place ourselves within being, it must necessarily be the case that our actions must have their origin outside us, and if we revert to constituting consciousness, they must originate within. But we have learnt precisely to recognize the order of phenomena. We are involved in the world and with others in an inextricable tangle. The idea of situation rules out absolute freedom at the source of our commitments, and equally, indeed, at their terminus. No commitment, not even commitment in the Hegelian State, can make me leave behind all differences and free me for anything. This universality itself, from the mere fact of its being experienced, would stand out as a particularity against the world's background, for existence both generalizes and particularizes everything at which it aims, and cannot ever be finally complete.

My significance lies beyond myself

The synthesis of *in itself* and *for itself* which brings Hegelian freedom into being has, however, its truth. In a sense, it is the very definition of existence, since it is effected at every moment before our eyes in the phenomenon of presence, only to be quickly re-enacted, since it does not conjure away our finitude. By taking up a present, I draw together and transform my past, altering its significance, freeing and detaching myself from it. But I do so only by committing myself somewhere else. Psychoanalytical treatment does not bring about its cure by producing direct awareness of the past, but in the first place by binding the subject to his doctor through new existential relationships. It is not a matter of giving scientific assent to the psychoanalytical interpretation, and discovering a notional significance for the past; it is a matter of reliving this or that as significant, and this the patient succeeds in doing only by seeing his past in the perspective of his co-existence with the doctor. The complex is not dissolved by a non-instrumental freedom, but rather displaced by a new pulsation of time with its own supports and motives. The same applies in all cases of coming to awareness: they are real only if they are sustained by a new commitment. Now this commitment too is entered into in the sphere of the implicit, and is therefore valid only for a certain temporal cycle. The choice which we make of our life is always based on a certain givenness. My freedom can draw life away from its spontaneous course, but only by a series of unobtrusive deflections which necessitate first of all following its course – not by any absolute creation. All explanations of my conduct in terms of my past, my temperament and my environment are therefore true, provided that they be regarded not as separable contributions, but as moments of my total being, the significance of which I am entitled to make explicit in various ways, without its ever being possible to say whether I confer their meaning upon them or receive it from them. I am a psychological and historical structure, and have received, with existence, a manner of existing, a style. All my actions and thoughts stand in a relationship to this structure, and even a philosopher's thought is merely a way of making explicit his hold on the world, and what he is. The fact remains that I am free, not in spite of, or on the hither side of, these motivations, but by means of them. For this significant life, this certain significance of nature and history which I am, does not limit my access to the world, but on the contrary is my means of entering into communication with it. It is by being unrestrictedly and unreservedly what I am at present that I have a chance of moving forward; it is by living my time that I am able to understand other times, by plunging into the present and the world, by taking on deliberately what I am fortuitously, by willing what I will and doing what I do, that I can go further. I can miss being free only if I try to bypass my natural and social situation by refusing to take it up, in the first place, instead of assuming it in order to join up with the natural and human world. Nothing determines me from outside, not because nothing acts upon me, but, on the contrary, because I am from the start outside myself and open to the world. We are *true* through and through, and have with us, by the mere fact of belonging to the world, and not merely being in the world in the way that things are, all that we need to transcend ourselves. We need have no fear that our choices or actions restrict our liberty, since choice and action alone cut us loose from our anchorage. Just as reflection borrows its wish for absolute sufficiency from the perception which causes a thing to appear, and as in this way idealism tacitly uses that 'primary opinion' which it would like to destroy as opinion, so freedom flounders in the contradictions of commitment, and fails to realize that, without the roots which it thrusts into the world, it would not be freedom at all. Shall I make this promise? Shall I risk my life for so little? Shall I give up my liberty in order to save liberty? There is no theoretical reply to these questions. But there are these *things* which stand, irrefutable, there is before you this person whom you love, there are these men whose existence around you is that of slaves, and *your* freedom cannot be willed without leaving behind its singular relevance, and without willing freedom *for all*. Whether it is a question of things or of historical situations, philosophy has no other function than to teach us to see them clearly once more, and it is true to say that it comes into being by destroying itself as separate philosophy. But what is here required is silence, for only the hero lives out his relation to men and the world. 'Your son is caught in the fire; you are the one who will save him. . . . If there is an obstacle, you would be ready to give your shoulder provided only that you can charge down that obstacle. Your abode is your act itself. Your act is you. . . . You give yourself in exchange. . . . Your significance shows itself, effulgent. It is your duty, your hatred, your love, your steadfastness, your ingenuity. . . . Man is but a network of relationships, and these alone matter to him.'⁹

Notes

1 In the sense in which, with Husserl, we have taken this word.
2 See J.-P. Sartre, *Being and Nothingness*, pp. 435ff.
3 J.-P. Sartre, *Being and Nothingness*, p. 465.
4 'avoir du champ'; in this sentence there is a play on the word 'champ' = field (Translator's note).
5 J.-P. Sartre, *Being and Nothingness*, p. 482.
6 J.-P. Sartre, *Being and Nothingness*, pp. 453ff.
7 'sens' (Translator's note).
8 In the sense of *das Man*, the impersonal pronoun (Translator's note).
9 A. de Saint-Exupéry, *Pilote de Guerre*, pp. 171, 174, 176.

PART FOUR – SELECTION FROM *THE PROSE OF THE WORLD*

THE ALGORITHM AND THE MYSTERY OF LANGUAGE (pp. 115–29 in the 1973 translation)

As explained earlier (p. 34) this chapter comes from a manuscript that Merleau-Ponty abandoned in 1952, and that was only published post-humously in 1969. The chapter appears complete, though, unlike some of the other chapters, Merleau-Ponty did not publish it as a separate essay during his lifetime. His general aim here is to elucidate the way in which language gains meaning, and he starts from the 'mystery of language'. This is that, although language may appear to be nothing but a play of words, when we use it successfully it effaces itself as we reach through it to new meanings without thinking about our words at all. So to solve the mystery we have to find a way of understanding how speech can both be readily intelligible and yet 'pregnant' with a new meaning.

The case Merleau-Ponty then concentrates upon to elucidate this is, slightly surprisingly, a mathematical one, that of an algorithm. What he wants to show is that the Platonist conception of mathematical certainty as the discovery of timeless relations between abstract objects is a mistaken interpretation of a genuine phenomenon, namely the compulsion inherent in the construction and understanding of a new mathematical proof. For what this phenomenon reveals is that even mathematical language can be used to open out new possibilities for us, which, once they are manifest, strike us as truths that have always obtained and that demand our assent. Merleau-Ponty connects our attitude to this phenomenon to our attitude when perception reveals something new about the world; for in that case too, it is inherent in perception that its object should appear to us as something that was there already anyway. He does not, he insists, seek to reduce proof to perception, but only to observe that it is, like perception, creative, and thus that in this context truth is not correspondence to something already established, but a kind of 'anticipation, repetition and slippage of meaning' (p. 246). Language, or rather originating speech (of which each new proof is an instance), has here a role comparable to that of the body in perception, for 'speech is the vehicle of our movement toward truth, as the body is the vehicle of our being in the world' (p. 246).

On several occasions, we have questioned the view that language is tied to what it signifies only by habit and convention. The relation is much closer and much more distant. In a sense, language turns its back on signification, and does not give it a thought. It is far less a table of statements which satisfy well-formed thoughts than a swarm of gestures all occupied with differentiating themselves from one another and blending again. The phonologists have well observed this sublinguistic life whose whole effort is to differentiate signs and systematize them. This observation is true not only of the phonemes prior to words but also of words and all of language, which is not first of all the sign of certain significations but the rule-governed power of differentiating the verbal chain according to the characteristic dimensions of each language. In a sense, language never has anything to do with anything but itself. In the internal monologue, as in the dialogue, there are no "thoughts." It is words that words arouse and, to the degree that we "think" more fully, words so precisely fill our minds that they leave no empty corner for pure thoughts or for significations that are not the work of language. The mystery is that, in the very moment where language is thus obsessed with itself, it is enabled, through a kind of excess, to open us to a signification. One could say that it is a law of the spirit to find only that for which the spirit has looked. In an instant this flow of words annuls itself as noise, throwing us completely into what it means. If we still reply to it with words, it is without wanting to. We no more think of the *words* that we are saying or that are being said to us than of the very hand we are shaking. The hand is not a bundle of flesh and bone, it is the palpable presence of the other person. Language has, therefore, a peculiar signification which is the more evident the more we surrender ourselves to it, and the less equivocal the less we think of it. This signification resists any direct seizure but is docile to the incantation of language. It is always there when one starts to evoke it but always a bit beyond the point where we think we discern it. As Paulhan says perfectly, the signification of language consists in "rays sensible to him who sees them but hidden from him who watches them," while language is made of "gestures which are not accomplished without some negligence."[1] Paulhan is the first to have seen that in use speech is not content with designating thoughts the way a street number designates my friend Paul's house. Speech in use really undergoes "a metamorphosis through which words cease to be accessible to our senses and lose their weight, their noise, their lines, their space (to become thoughts). But on its side thought renounces (to become words) its rapidity or its slowness, its surprise, its invisibility, its time, the internal consciousness that we have of it."[2] This, indeed, is the mystery of language.

But does not the mystery condemn us to silence? If language is comparable to that point in the eye of which physiologists speak as what helps us to see everything, according to the evidence it cannot see itself and cannot be observed. If language hides from anyone who seeks it and surrenders to anyone who renounces it, then one cannot look it in the face. One can only "think of it obliquely," "mime," or "reveal" its mystery.[3] All that remains is to "be" language, to which Paulhan seems to resign himself. Yet that is not possible precisely because of his own principles. One can no longer simply *be* language after one has questioned it. One would be returning to language knowingly and, as Paulhan has said, it does not permit these measured obeisances. At the point of reflection reached by Paulhan, he could find the innocent use of language only in a second degree of language and *by speaking about it*, which is what we call philosophy. Even if we were only to "mime" or to "reveal" language, we would speak about language, and since what we would speak *about* would not be the same as we *who* speak about it, what we would say about it would be inadequate. The moment that we believe we are grasping the world as it is apart from us, it is no longer the world we are grasping, since we are there to grasp it. In the same way, there always remains, behind our talk about language, more living language than can ever be taken in by our view of it.

However, the situation is a dead end, the regressive movement in vain and philosophy in vain with it, only so long as it is a matter of explaining language, decomposing it, deducing it, grounding it, or operating in any other way to try to derive the clarity which belongs to a strange source. In this case, reflection, by virtue of being reflection and therefore speech, would always adopt whatever theme it chose and would in principle be incapable of achieving what it is seeking. But there are a philosophy and a mode of reflection which do not pretend to constitute their object, to be in rivalry with it, or to clarify it with a light that is not their own. People speak to me and I understand. When I have the feeling of dealing only with *words*, it is because expression has failed. When expression is successful, it seems to me that my thought is yonder, at the top of its voice, in those words that I have not spoken. Nothing is more convincing than this experience, and there is no need to look anywhere else than in it itself for what makes it evident, no need to replace the work of speech by some pure operation of spirit. All that is needed – and this is the whole of philosophy – is to cash in on this evidence, to confront it with the ready-made ideas we have of language and of the plurality of spirits. We need only reinstate this experience in its dignity as evidence, which it lost through the very use of language and because communication seems to us unproblematic. We need, finally, to restore what is paradoxical and even mysterious in this evidence, by providing it with an appropriate ground, from which it should be able to detach itself. We must conquer it as evidence, which is not just to use it, but quite the contrary. . . .

The best means of preserving the prodigious meaning we have found in language is not to silence it, to renounce philosophy, and to return to the immediate practice of language. Then the mystery would perish through familiarity. Language remains an enigma only to those who continue to question it, that is, to speak about it. Paulhan himself sometimes gets caught in this trap. He speaks of a "projection" of the self into the other, or of the other into me, which is the result of language.[4] But this implies a good deal of philosophy. The little word "projection" involves us in a theory of the relation between meaning and words. We may try to understand it as an analogous reasoning which would lead me to rediscover *my* thoughts in the other's words. But that is only pushing the problem farther back, since I am capable of understanding what I have never expressed. Thus we must have another idea of projection, according to which the other's speech not only awakes in me ready-made thoughts but also involves me in a movement of thought of which I would have been incapable alone and finally opens me to unfamiliar significations. Here, then, I would have to admit that I do not live just my own thought but that, in the exercise of speech, I *become* the one to whom I am listening. Finally, I would need to understand how speech can be pregnant with a meaning. Let us try, then, not to explain this but to establish more precisely the power of speaking, to get close to that signification which is nothing else than the unique movement of which signs are the visible trace.

Perhaps we shall see it better if we manage to rediscover it even in the cases where language restricts itself to saying nothing more than what has been decisively and precisely defined, to designating nothing but what language has already possessed. In other words, let us look where language denies its own past in order to reconstruct itself as an algorithm in which *in principle* the truth is no longer that floating spirit, ubiquitous but never with any location, which dwells in the language of literature and philosophy. There truth is instead an unmovable sphere of relations which were no less true prior to our formulations and would remain so even if all men and their language happened to disappear. As soon as integers appeared in human history, they announced themselves by certain properties which derive clearly from their definition. That is, if we find any new property in them, since it also derives from those which first served to delimit them, it appears equally old or contemporaneous with the integers themselves. Finally, if any still unknown property is revealed in the future, it seems that it already *belongs* to the integer. Even when it was not yet known that the sum of the n first integers is equal to the product of $\frac{n}{2}$ by $n + 1$, surely this relation existed between them? If it was an accident that led to the multiplication of $\frac{n}{2}$ by $n + 1$, would not a result equal to the sum of the n first integers have been found? Would not this coincidence have resulted here and now from the very structure of the series which would subsequently have grounded it? I had not yet noticed[5] that the series of the ten first integers is composed of five pairs of numbers whose sum is constant and equal to $10 + 1$. I had not yet understood that even this is demanded by the nature of the series, where the increase from 1 to 5 obeys exactly the same rhythm as the decrease from 10 to 6. But finally, even before I had recognized these relations, 10 increased by a unit was equal to 9 increased by 2, to 8 by 3, to 7 by 4, to 6 by 5, and the sum of these sums to that of the first ten integers. It seems that the changes of aspect which I introduced into the series by considering it from this new angle were contained in advance in the numbers themselves. When I *express* the relations unperceived until then, I limit myself to deducing them from a reservoir of truths which is the intelligible world of numbers.

When I introduce a new line into a drawing that changes its signification – for example, which results in the metamorphosis of a cube, seen in perspective, into a kitchen tile – there is no longer the same object before me. When the chimpanzee, wanting to get something beyond his reach, picks up a branch of a tree to use as a stick or borrows a stool to use as a ladder, his conduct shows that the branch in its new function is no longer a branch for him, that the stool ceases definitely to be a seat and becomes a ladder. The transformation is irreversible, and now it is not the *same* object which is treated each time from two perspectives. It is a branch which becomes a stick, it is a stool which becomes a ladder, the way a shake of a kaleidoscope makes a new pattern appear without my being able to recognize the old one in it. Between perceptual structures or structures of practical intelligence and the constructs of knowledge which open onto truth, there is a difference. The former, even when they resolve a problem and respond to a question of desire, recognize only blindly what they themselves contributed to the result. The latter arise from the *I can*, whereas the truth rises from an *I think*, from an inner recognition which traverses the length of the series of cognitive events, grounds its value, and posits it as an exemplar that is repeatable in principle by any consciousness placed in the same cognitive situation.

But if truth, to remain truth, presupposes this consorting of the self with itself, this inner unity through time, then the expressive operation which derives from Σn the formula $\frac{n}{2}(n + 1)$ should be guaranteed by the immanence of the new in the ancient. It is not enough that the mathematician treats given relations according to certain formulae to transform them into the meaning of found relationships, the way the chimpanzee treats the branch of the tree in terms of what is useful to him to achieve his end. If the operation is to escape the contingency of the event and reveal a truth, it must itself be legitimated by the mathematical being on which it works. It seems, therefore, that one cannot give an account of exact knowledge except on condition of admitting, at least in this domain, a thought which abolishes all distance between the self and itself, which envelopes the expressive operation of its sovereign clarity, and reabsorbs in the algorithm the congenital obscurity of language. Here, at least, signification ceases to have that ambiguous relation to signs about which we have spoken. In language signification is fused with the juncture of signs; it is simultaneously tied to their bodily composition and blossoms mysteriously behind them. Signification bursts out above the signs and yet it is only their vibration, the way a cry carries outside and makes present to everyone the very breathing and pain of the man crying out. In the purity of the algorithm, signification is disengaged from all interference with the unfolding of signs which it rules and legitimates. By the same token, the signs correspond to the algorithm so exactly that the expression leaves nothing wanting and appears to us to contain meaning its very self. The jumbled relations of transcendence give way to the clear relations of a system of signs which have no inner life and a system of significatins which do not descend into animal existence.

It is not our intention to question the character of *truth* which distinguishes the propositions of exact science or the incomparability of the moment where, in recognizing a truth, I touch on something that did not begin with me and will not cease to signify after me. This experience of an event which suddenly becomes hollow, losing its opacity, revealing a transparence, and becoming forever a meaning is a constant in culture and speech. If one wished to challenge the experience, he would not even know any more what he was seeking. All that can be done is to discover its implications, in particular whether, in relation to speech, it is originary or derivative. More precisely, one can discover whether, even in exact science, there exists, between the institutionalized signs and the *true* significations they designate, an instituting speech which is the vehicle of everything. When we say that the newly discovered properties of a mathematical entity are as old as it is, these very terms, "property" and "entity," already contain a whole interpretation of our experience of truth. Strictly, all we see is that certain supposedly given relations necessarily entail other relations. It is because we chose the first as principles and definitions that the others appear to us as *their* consequences. All we are entitled to say is that there is a solidarity of principle between them; that there are unbreakable ties such that, if certain relations are presupposed, so are others; that such and such relations are synonymous. This, of course, creates between given relations a relation of equivalence independent of its manifestation. This equivalence allows us to say that these relations constitute a system unaffected by time. But the new relations can have no other sense of existence than the relations from which they derive, and we never know whether these *are* anything more than mathematical entities – in other words, pure relations which we enjoy contemplating.

Henceforth we know that, although we are free to inquire into different objects (for example, different spaces), once an object is sufficiently determined we are no longer free to say anything whatsoever about it. This is, of course, a necessity which our mind encounters. However, the form in which it appears to us depends upon the starting point we have chosen. A proof is not a case of a certain mathematical entity imposing upon us properties which are its own. It is simply that there has to be a starting point and, once it has been determined, our freedom ends there, meeting its limit in the chain of consequences. Nothing reveals that the various forms that this limit to our freedom can take derive from the operation of an essence developing its own properties. Instead of saying that we establish certain *properties* of mathematical *entities*, we would be more exact if we said that we establish the possibility of the principle of enriching and making more precise the relations that served to define our object, of pursuing the construction of coherent mathematical wholes which our definitions merely outlined. To be sure, this possibility is not an empty thing, this coherence is not accidental, this validity is not illusory. But we cannot say that the new relations were true *before* they were revealed or that the first set of relations bring the later ones into existence. One could say so only if one were to hypothesize the first relations in some physical reality; the circle found in the sand already *had* equal radii, the triangle a sum of angles equal to two right angles ... and all the other properties deducible by geometry. If we could subtract, from our conception of mathematical entities, any substratum of this kind, we would perceive it not as timeless but more as a development of knowledge.

This development is not fortuitous. Each of the advances that I stake out is *legitimate*. It is not just any old event; it is prescribed, and it is in any case justified afterward by the preceding steps. If essence is not the principle of our science, it is nevertheless present in our science as its goal. The development of knowledge moves toward the totality of a meaning. That is true. But essence conceived as the future of knowledge is not an essence; it is what we call a structure. Its relation to effective knowledge is like the relation of the thing perceived to perception. Perception, which is an event, opens onto the thing perceived, which appeared to be prior to perception and to be true before it. And if perception always reaffirms the preexistence of the world, it is precisely *because* it is an event, because the subject who perceives is already at grips with being through the *perceptual fields*, the "senses." More generally, the subject of perception is a body made to explore the world. Whatever stimulates the perceiving apparatus awakes a primordial familiarity between it and the world that we express by saying that the perceived existed before perception. In a single stroke, the immediate data of perception signify well beyond their own content, finding an inordinate echo in the perceiving subject. This is what enables the data to appear to us as perspectives upon a present object, whereas the explication of this object would proceed to infinity and would never be completed. Mathematical truth, reduced to what we truly establish, is not of a different kind. If we are almost irresistibly tempted, in conceiving the essence of the circle, to imagine a circle traced in the sand which already *has* all *its properties*, it is because our very notion of essence is formed in contact with an imitation of the perceived object as it is presented to us in perception, namely, as more ancient than perception itself, a self-contained, pure being prior to the subject. And since, as regards perception, it is not contradictory but rather its very definition *to be* an event and to *open on* a truth, we must also understand that truth in the service of mathematics is available to a subject already immersed in it and benefits from the carnal ties which unite them both.

We are not reducing mathematical evidence to perceptual evidence. We are certainly not denying, as will be seen, the originality of the order of knowledge vis-à-vis the perceptual order. We are trying only to loose the intentional web which ties them to one another, to rediscover the paths of the sublimation which preserves and transforms the perceived world into the spoken world. But this is possible only if we describe the operation of speech as a repetition, a reconquest of the world-thesis, analogous in its order to perception and yet different from it. The fact is that every mathematical idea presents itself to us with the character of a construction after the fact, a reconquest. Cultural constructions never have the solidity of natural objects. They are never there in the same way. Each morning, after night has intervened, we must make contact with them again. They remain impalpable; they float in the air of the village but the countryside does contain them. If, nevertheless, in the fullness of thought, the truths of culture seem to us the measure of being, and if so many philosphies posit the world upon them, it is because knowledge continues upon the thrust of perception. It is because knowledge uses the world-thesis which is its fundamental sound. We believe truth is eternal because truth expresses the perceived world and perception implies a world which was functioning before it and according to principles which it discovers and does not posit. In one and the same movement knowledge roots itself in perception and distinguishes itself from perception. Knowledge is an effort to recapture, to internalize, truly to possess a meaning that escapes perception at the very moment that it takes shape there, because it is interested only in the echo that being draws from itself, not in this resonator, its own other which makes the echo possible. Perception opens us to a world already constituted and can only reconstitute it. This reduplication signifies both that the world offers itself as prior to perception and that we do not limit ourselves to registering the world but would like to engender it. The meaning of the perceived object already is the shadow cast by the operations we bring to bear upon things. It is nothing other than our viewpoint on them, our situation with respect to them. Each vector of the perceived spectacle posits, beyond its aspect at the moment, the principle of certain equivalences in the possible variations of the spectacle. It inaugurates on its own account a *style* of the explication of objects and a *style* of our movements with respect to them. This mute or operational language of perception begins a process of knowledge which it cannot itself accomplish. However firm my perceptive grasp of the world may be, it is entirely dependent upon a centrifugal movement which throws me toward the world. I can recapture my grasp only if I myself spontaneously posit new dimensions of its signification. Here is the beginning of speech, the style of knowledge, truth in the logician's sense. It is called forth from its first movement by perceptual evidence which it continues without being reducible to perceptual evidence.

Once there is a clear reference to the world-thesis – which is always *understood* by mathematical thought and is what enables mathematical thought to present itself as the reflection of an intelligible world – how are we to understand mathematical truth? Above all – that is our aim – how are we to understand the algorithmic expression yielded by mathematical thought? It is clear, first of all, that the "properties" of the series of integers are not "contained" in that series. Once the series is clear of the perceptual analogy which makes "something" (*etwas überhaupt*) of the mathematical expression, it is at each moment nothing but the ensemble of relations established within it *plus an open horizon of relations that can be constructed*. This horizon is not the mode of presentation of a self-contained mathematical entity; at every moment, there is really nothing in heaven or on earth but the known properties of the integer. One may say, if one wishes, that the unknown properties are already operative in the ensemble of objects which embody the numbers. But that is only a manner of speaking. One is trying to express by it that everything that will be revealed about numbers will also be true of numbered objects, which is quite certain but does not entail any preexistence of the truth.

The new relation, $\frac{n}{2}(n + 1)$, this new signification of the series of integers, appears in it only if one reconsiders and restructures Σn. I must notice that the progression from 1 to 5 is exactly symmetrical with the regression from 10 to 5, so that I can then conceive a constant value of the sums $10 + 1$, $9 + 2$, $8 + 3$, etc., and, finally, so that I can decompose the series into pairs each equal to $n + 1$, whose total can only be equal to

$\dfrac{n}{2}$. Of course, these transformations, which are the equivalent in the arithmetical object of a geometric construction, are always posible. I assure myself that they do not hold by some accident but derive from the structure which defines the series of numbers – and in this sense they are its result. But *they are not a part of it;* they emerge only when I address a certain question to the *structure* of the series of numbers, or rather when the structure poses a question to me insofar as it is an open and incomplete situation, as it offers itself as something *to be known.*

The operation through which I express Σn in the terms $\dfrac{n}{2}(n+1)$ is possible only if I perceive in the last formula the double function of n, first as a cardinal number, then as an ordinal number. It is not by any blind transformation that I am then able to pass to $\dfrac{n+1}{2}n$, or to $\dfrac{n(n+1)}{2}$, or to $\dfrac{n^2+n}{2}$. I see that $\dfrac{n}{2}(n+1)$ results from Σn by virtue of the structure of Σn. Then I understand what is involved in a mathematical truth. And, even if I proceed to exploit the formula I obtain by mechanical counting procedures, it is then only a question of a secondary and minor operation which teaches us nothing about what truth is.

Nothing in what we are saying would be changed if it were possible to constitute an algorithm which expressed the logical properties of the series of whole numbers. The moment these formal relations yielded – and this is the hypothesis – an exact equivalent of the structure of number, they, like the latter, would provide the occasion for the construction of a new relation rather than containing it. We are trying to show not that mathmatical thought rests upon the sensible but that it is creative. Creativity could also be shown for a formalized mathematics. Since the results are achieved through deduction and apply only to the definition of the integer, once I have arrived at the result I can as well say that the formula I obtain is derived strictly from the initial definitions or that the series itself determines its new significance. That is how my present knowledge views its own past; that is not how it happened, even behind the scene. The results were not immanent in the hypothesis. They were prefigured in the structure only as an open system and were caught in the development of my thought. When I vary this structure in terms of its own vectors, it is rather the new configuration which repeats and preserves the old one, contains it eminently, identifying with it, or recognizing it as indistinguishable from itself.

The synthesis is the result of the development of my knowledge and not its precondition. Non-Euclidean geometries contain Euclid's geometry as a particular case but not the inverse. What is essential to mathematical thought, therefore, lies in the moment where a structure is decentered, opens up to questioning, and reorganizes itself according to a new meaning which is nevertheless the meaning of this same structure. The truth of the result, its value independent of the content, consists in its not involving a *change* in which the initial relations dissolve, to be replaced by others in which they would be unrecognizable. Rather, the truth lies in a restructuring which, from one end to the other, is known to itself, is congruent with itself, a restructuring which was announced in the vectors of the initial structure by its style, so that each effective change is the fulfillment of an intention, and each anticipation receives from the structure the completion it needed.

We are dealing here with a veritable *development of meaning*. The *development* is not an objective succession, a transformation of fact, but a self-development, a development of meaning. When I say that there is truth here, I do not mean that, between the hypothesis and the conclusion, I experience a relation of identity that leaves nothing wanting or that I see the one's deriving from the other in an absolute transparence. There is no signification which is not surrounded by an horizon of naïve beliefs and is thus not in need of other clarifications. There is no expressive operation that exhausts its object. Euclid's demonstrations were rigorous, although they were always encumbered with a coefficient of facticity that rested upon a massive intuition of space which could be made thematic only later. In order for there to be truth, the restructuring which yields a new meaning must truly repeat the initial structure, even though it has its gaps and opacities. New thematizations subsequently will fill the gaps and dissolve the opacities but, apart from the fact that they themselves will be partial, they will not make a Euclidean triangle, for example, have properties other than those we know it has. The legitimate transformations which lead from the Euclidean universe to its properties will remain something that can be understood and needs only to be translated into a more general language. The proper domain of truth is therefore this repetition of the object of thought in its new signification, even if the object still retains in its crevices relations that we use without being aware of them. The fact is that at this moment something is acquired, there is a step toward truth, the structure propels itself toward its transformations.

The awareness of truth advances like a crab, turned toward its point of departure, toward that structure *whose* signification it expresses.

Such is the living operation that sustains the signs of the algorithm. If one considered the result alone, one could believe that nothing has been created. In the formula $\frac{n}{2}(n+1)$, only terms borrowed from the hypothesis, related through algebraic operations, enter. The new signification is represented by the initial signs and significations, and they are deflected from their original meaning, as happens in language. The algorithmic expression is *exact* because of the exact equivalence established between its initial relations and those that are derived from them. But the new formula is only a formula *of* the new signification and expresses it truly only if, for example, we gave to the term n first its ordinal meaning and then its cardinal meaning. This is possible only if we refer to the configuration of the series of numbers under the new aspect which our interrogation brings to it. But here there reappears the *shift* of restructuring which is characteristic of language. Once we have managed to find the formula, we then forget the shift, and so we believe in the preexistence of the world. But the shift is still there and it alone gives meaning to the formula. The algorithmic expression is therefore secondary. It is a special case of language. We believe that in this case signs repeat the intention exactly, that the signification is captured without remainder, and finally that the style which prescribed the structural transformations that we introduced is entirely ruled by us. But that is because we omitted mention of the structure's transcendence toward its transformations. To be sure, this transcendence is always possible in principle, since we consider only the invariants in our study of structure and not the accidental peculiarities of a line or a figure. But we are dealing with a transcendence and not a static identity, and here, as in language, truth is not an adequation but anticipation, repetition, and slippage of meaning. Truth allows itself to be reached only through a sort of distance. The thing thought is not the thing perceived. Knowledge is not perception, speech is not one gesture among all the other gestures. For speech is the vehicle of our movement toward truth, as the body is the vehicle of our being in the world.

Notes

1   Jean Paulhan, *Les Fleurs de Tarbes*, Paris: Gallimard, 1941, p. 177.
2   Jean Paulhan, *Clef de la poésie*, 2nd edn, Paris: Gallimard, 1944, p. 86.
3   *Ibid.*, p. 11.
4   Paulhan, *Les Fleurs de Tarbes*, pp. 115ff.
5   The example is given and analyzed in these terms by Max Wertheimer, *Productive Thinking*, New York and London: Harper, 1945.

PART FIVE – SELECTION FROM *THE VISIBLE AND THE INVISIBLE*

THE INTERTWINING – THE CHIASM (pp. 130–55 in the 1968 translation)

This chapter comes from a manuscript which was incomplete at Merleau-Ponty's death. In 1959 he converted his long-standing ambition to write a book about truth (see p. 34) into the project of a book about 'the visible and the invisible', in which he would move from a discussion of perception ('the visible') to one of language and thence truth ('the invisible'). The manuscript really addresses only the first part of this (though there are notes for the later parts); so it primarily represents his later thoughts about perception. In the first chapter Merleau-Ponty returns to his critique of realism and intellectualism. He then provides, in the second chapter, a decisive refutation of Sartre's Hegelian account in Being and Nothingness *of our being in the world (see p. 29). In the third chapter he discusses critically Bergson's conception of 'intuition' and then begins to set out his own thoughts about temporality and language. But it is in the fourth chapter, reproduced here, that he breaks new ground.*

The title of the chapter indicates his new conception of the body, as a 'chiasm' or crossing-over (the term comes from the Greek letter chi*) which combines subjective experience and objective existence. His term for this new conception of the body is 'flesh' (*chair*) and he insists that it is an 'ultimate notion', a 'concrete emblem of a general manner of being', which provides access both to subjective experience and objective existence. The phenomenon he concentrates upon is one he had discussed earlier in* The Phenomenology of Perception *(PP 92 [106]), that of touching one hand* with the other hand. This phenomenon, he suggests, reveals to us the two dimensions of our 'flesh', that it is both a form of experience (tactile experience) and something that can be touched. It is both 'touching' and 'tangible'. Furthermore the relationship is reversible: the hand that touches can be felt as touched, and vice versa, though never both at the same time, and it is this 'reversibility' that he picks out as the essence of flesh. It shows us the ambiguous status of our bodies as both subject and object. Thus Merleau-Ponty here qualifies his earlier view that gave priority to the 'phenomenal', subjective, body over the objective body. For he now regards these as but two aspects of a single fundamental phenomenon: our reversible 'flesh' (the influence of Husserl is perhaps apparent here: in Ideas II he had affirmed that 'the Body as Body presents, like Janus, two faces', p. 297, though the 'faces' in question are not Merleau-Ponty's alternatives).

Merleau-Ponty extends the application of this conception in two directions. First, he extends it from touch to sight, which he now models on touch – 'the look, we said, envelops, palpates, espouses visible things'. So sight has the same ambiguous nature as touch, and it is from its own 'objective' side that the objectivity of the visible world is generated. Second, taking the example of a handshake as exemplary, he extends his thesis to apply to our sense that others, like us, are both subjects and objects. Although these points are clear enough, and the chapter is not, as it stands, incomplete, it remains unclear how he intended to extend the line of thought further, since the manuscript ends at this point, and the notes that follow do not provide a connected discussion. Thus at this point there is a genuine sense of a thinker stopped in midair, and it is just not clear where the trajectory of his thought would have carried him.

If it is true that as soon as philosophy declares itself to be reflection or coincidence it prejudges what it will find, then once again it must recommence everything, reject the instruments reflection and intuition had provided themselves, and install itself in a locus where they have not yet been distinguished, in experiences that have not yet been "worked over," that offer us all at once, pell-mell, both "subject" and "object," both existence and essence, and hence give philosophy resources to redefine them. Seeing, speaking, even thinking (with certain reservations, for as soon as we distinguish thought from speaking absolutely we are already in the order of reflection), are experiences of this kind, both irrecusable and enigmatic. They have a name in all languages, but a name which in all of them also conveys significations in tufts, thickets of proper meanings and figurative meanings, so that, unlike those of science, not one of these names clarifies by attributing to what is named a circumscribed signification. Rather, they are the repeated index, the insistent reminder of a mystery as familiar as it is unexplained, of a light which, illuminating the rest, remains at its source in obscurity. If we could rediscover within the exercise of seeing and speaking some of the living references that assign them such a destiny in a language, perhaps they would teach us how to form our new instruments, and first of all to understand our research, our interrogation, themselves.

The visible about us seems to rest in itself. It is as though our vision were formed in the heart of the visible, or as though there were between it and us an intimacy as close as between the sea and the strand. And yet it is not possible that we blend into it, nor that it passes into us, for then the vision would vanish at the moment of formation, by disappearance of the seer or of the visible. What there is then are not things first identical with themselves, which would then offer themselves to the seer, nor is there a seer who is first empty and who, afterward, would open himself to them – but something to which we could not be closer than by palpating it with our look, things we could not dream of seeing "all naked" because the gaze itself envelops them, clothes them with its own flesh. Whence does it happen that in so doing it leaves them in their place, that the vision we acquire of them seems to us to come from them, and that to be seen is for them but a degradation of their eminent being? What is this talisman of color, this singular virtue of the visible that makes it, held at the end of the gaze, nonetheless much more than a correlative of my vision, such that it imposes my vision upon me as a continuation of its own sovereign existence? How does it happen that my look, enveloping them, does not hide them, and, finally, that, veiling them, it unveils them?[1]

We must first understand that this red under my eyes is not, as is always said, a *quale*, a pellicle of being without thickness, a message at the same time indecipherable and evident, which one has or has not received, but of which, if one has received it, one knows all there is to know, and of which in the end there is nothing to say. It requires a focusing, however brief; it emerges from a less precise, more general redness, in which my gaze was caught, into which it sank, before – as we put it so aptly – *fixing* it. And, now that I have fixed it, if my eyes penetrate into it, into its fixed structure, or if they start to wander round about again, the *quale* resumes its atmospheric existence. Its precise form is bound up with a certain wooly, metallic, or porous [?] configuration or texture, and the *quale* itself counts for very little compared with these participations. Claudel has a phrase saying that a certain blue of the sea is so blue that only blood would be more red. The color is yet a variant in another dimension of variation, that of its relations with the surroundings: this red is what it is only by connecting up from its place with other reds about it, with which it forms a constellation, or with other colors it dominates or that dominate it, that it attracts or that attract it, that it repels or that repel it. In short, it is a certain node in the woof of the simultaneous and the successive. It is a concretion of visibility, it is not an atom. The red dress a fortiori holds with all its fibers onto the fabric of the visible, and thereby onto a fabric of invisible being. A punctuation in the field of red things, which includes the tiles of roof tops, the flags of gatekeepers and of the Revolution, certain terrains near Aix or in Madagascar, it is also a punctuation in the field of red garments, which includes, along with the dresses of women, robes of professors, bishops, and advocate generals, and also in the field of adornments and that of uniforms. And its red literally is not the same as it appears in one constellation or in the other, as the pure essence of the Revolution of 1917 precipitates in it, or that of the eternal feminine, or that of the public prosecutor, or that of the gypsies dressed like hussars who reigned twenty-five years ago over an inn on the Champs-Elysées. A certain red is also a fossil drawn up from the depths of imaginary worlds. If we took all these participations into account, we would recognize that a naked color, and in general a visible, is not a chunk of absolutely hard, indivisible being, offered all naked to a vision which could be only total or null, but is rather a sort of straits between exterior horizons and interior horizons ever gaping open, something that comes to touch lightly and makes diverse regions of the colored or visible world resound at the distances, a certain differentiation, an ephemeral modulation of this world – less a color or a thing, therefore, than a difference between things and colors, a momentary crystallization of colored being or of visibility. Between the alleged colors and visibles, we would find anew the tissue that lines them, sustains them, nourishes them, and which for its part is not a thing, but a possibility, a latency, and a *flesh* of things.

If we turn now to the seer, we will find that this is no analogy or vague comparison and must be taken literally. The look, we said, envelops, palpates, espouses the visible things. As though it were in a relation of pre-established harmony with them, as though it knew them before knowing them, it moves in its own way with its abrupt and imperious style, and yet the views taken are not desultory – I do not look at a chaos, but at things – so that finally one cannot say if it is the look or if it is the things that command. What is this prepossession of the visible, this art of interrogating it according to its own wishes, this inspired exegesis? We would perhaps find the answer in the tactile palpation where the questioner and the questioned are closer, and of which, after all, the palpation of the eye is a remarkable variant. How does it happen that I give to my hands, in particular, that degree, that rate, and that direction of movement that are capable of making me feel the textures of the sleek and the rough? Between the exploration and what it will teach me, between my movements and what I touch, there must exist some relationship by principle, some kinship, according to which they are not only, like the pseudopods of the amoeba, vague and ephemeral deformations of the corporeal space, but the initiation to and the opening upon a tactile world. This can happen only if my hand, while it is felt from within, is also accessible from without, itself tangible, for my other hand, for example, if it takes its place among the things it touches, is in a sense one of them, opens finally upon a tangible being of which it is also a part. Through this crisscrossing within it of the touching and the tangible, its own movements incorporate themselves into the universe they interrogate, are recorded on the same map as it; the two systems are applied upon one another, as the two halves of an orange. It is no different for the vision – except, it is said, that here the exploration and the information it gathers do not belong "to the same sense." But this delimitation of the senses is crude. Already in the "touch" we have just found three distinct experiences which subtend one another, three dimensions which overlap but are distinct: a touching of the sleek and of the rough, a touching of the things – a passive sentiment of the body and of its space – and finally a veritable touching of the touch, when my right hand touches my left hand while it is palpating the things, where the "touching subject" passes over to the rank of the touched, descends into the things, such that the touch is formed in the midst of the world and as it were in the things. Between the massive sentiment I have of the sack in which I am enclosed, and the control from without that my hand exercises over my hand, there is as much difference as between the movements of my eyes and the changes they produce in the visible. And as, conversely, every experience of the visible has always been given to me within the context of the movements of the look, the visible spectacle belongs to the touch neither more nor less than do the "tactile qualities." We must habituate ourselves to think that every visible is cut out in the tangible, every tactile being in some manner promised to visibility, and that there is encroachment, infringement, not only between the touched and the touching, but also between the tangible and the visible, which is encrusted in it, as, conversely, the tangible itself is not a nothingness of visibility, is not without visual existence. Since the same body sees and touches, visible and tangible belong to the same world. It is a marvel too little noticed that every movement of my eyes – even more, every displacement of my body – has its place in the same visible universe that I itemize and explore with them, as, conversely, every vision takes place somewhere in the tactile space. There is double and crossed situating of the visible in the tangible and of the tangible in the visible; the two maps are complete, and yet they do not merge into one. The two parts are total parts and yet are not superposable.

Hence, without even entering into the implications proper to the seer and the visible, we know that, since vision is a palpation with the look, it must also be inscribed in the order of being that it discloses to us; he who looks must not himself be foreign to the world that he looks at. As soon as I see, it is necessary that the vision (as is so well indicated by the double meaning of the word) be doubled with a complementary vision or with another vision: myself seen from without, such as another would see me, installed in the midst of the visible, occupied in considering it from a certain spot. For the moment we shall not examine how far this identity of the seer and the visible goes, if we have a complete experience of it, or if there is something missing, and what it is. It suffices for us for the moment to note that he who sees cannot possess the visible unless he is possessed by it, unless he *is of it*,[2] unless, by principle, according to what is required by the articulation of the look with the things, he is one of the visibles, capable, by a singular reversal, of seeing them – he who is one of them.[3]

We understand then why we see the things themselves, in their places, where they are, according to their being which is indeed more than their being-perceived – and why at the same time we are separated from them by all the thickness of the look and of the body; it is that this distance is not the contrary of this proximity, it is deeply consonant with it, it is synonymous with it. It is that the thickness of flesh between the seer and the thing is constitutive for the thing of its visibility as for the seer of his corporeity; it is not an obstacle between them, it is their means of communication. It is for the same reason that I am at the heart of the visible and that I am far from it: because it has thickness and is thereby naturally destined to be seen by a body. What is indefinable in the *quale*, in the color, is nothing else than a brief, peremptory manner of giving in one sole something, in one sole tone of being, visions past, visions to come, by whole clusters. I who see have my own depth also, being backed up by this same visible which I see and which, I know very well, closes in behind me. The thickness of the body, far from rivaling that of the world, is on the contrary the sole means I have to go unto the heart of the things, by making myself a world and by making them flesh.

The body interposed is not itself a thing, an interstitial matter, a connective tissue, but a *sensible for itself,* which means, not that absurdity: color that sees itself, surface that touches itself – but this paradox [?]: a set of colors and surfaces inhabited by a touch, a vision, hence an *exemplar sensible,* which offers to him who inhabits it and senses it the wherewithal to sense everything that resembles himself on the outside, such that, caught up in the tissue of the things, it draws it entirely to itself, incorporates it, and, with the same movement, communicates to the things upon which it closes over that identity without superposition, that difference without contradiction, that divergence between the within and the without that constitutes its natal secret.[4] The body unites us directly with the things through its own ontogenesis, by welding to one another the two outlines of which it is made, its two laps: the sensible mass it is and the mass of the sensible wherein it is born by segregation and upon which, as seer, it remains open. It is the body and it alone, because it is a two-dimensional being, that can bring us to the things themselves, which are themselves not flat beings but beings in depth, inaccessible to a subject that would survey them from above, open to him alone that, if it be possible, would coexist with them in the same world. When we speak of the flesh of the visible, we do not mean to do anthropology, to describe a world covered over with all our own projections, leaving aside what it can be under the human mask. Rather, we mean that carnal being, as a being of depths, of several leaves or several faces, a being in latency, and a presentation of a certain absence, is a prototype of Being, of which our body, the sensible sentient, is a very remarkable variant, but whose constitutive paradox already lies in every visible. For already the cube assembles within itself incompossible *visibilia,* as my body is at once phenomenal body and objective body, and if finally it is, it, like my body, is by a tour de force. What we call a visible is, we said, a quality pregnant with a texture, the surface of a depth, a cross section upon a massive being, a grain or corpuscle borne by a wave of Being. Since the total visible is always behind, or after, or between the aspects we see of it, there is access to it only through an experience which, like it, is wholly outside of itself. It is thus, and not as the bearer of a knowing subject, that our body commands the visible for us, but it does not explain it, does not clarify it, it only concentrates the mystery of its scattered visibility; and it is indeed a paradox of Being, not a paradox of man, that we are dealing with here. To be sure, one can reply that, between the two "sides" of our body, the body as sensible and the body as sentient (what in the past we called objective body and phenomenal body), rather than a spread, there is the abyss that separates the In Itself from the For Itself. It is a problem – and we will not avoid it – to determine how the sensible sentient can also be thought. But here, seeking to form our first concepts in such a way as to avoid the classical impasses, we do not have to honor the difficulties that they may present when confronted with a *cogito*, which itself has to be re-examined. Yes or no: do we have a body – that is, not a permanent object of thought, but a flesh that suffers when it is wounded, hands that touch? We know: hands do not suffice for touch – but to decide for this reason alone that our hands do not touch, and to relegate them to the world of objects or of instruments, would be, in acquiescing to the bifurcation of subject and object, to forego in advance the understanding of the sensible and to deprive ourselves of its lights. We propose on the contrary to take it literally to begin with. We say therefore that our body is a being of two leaves, from one side a thing among things and otherwise what sees them and touches them; we say, because it is evident, that it unites these two properties within itself, and its double belongingness to the order of the "object" and to the order of the "subject" reveals to us quite unexpected relations between the two orders. It cannot be by incomprehensible accident that the body has this double reference; it teaches us that each calls for the other. For if the body is a thing among things, it is so in a stronger and deeper sense than they: in the sense that, we said, it *is of them*, and this means that it detaches itself upon them, and, accordingly, detaches itself from them. It is not simply a thing *seen* in fact (I do not see my back), it is visible by right, it falls under a vision that is both ineluctable and deferred. Conversely, if it touches and sees, this is not because it would have the visibles before itself as objects: they are about it, they even enter into its enclosure, they are within it, they line its looks and its hands inside and outside. If it touches them and sees them, this is only because, being of their family, itself visible and tangible, it uses its own being as a means to participate in theirs, because each of the two beings is an archetype for the other, because the body belongs to the order of the things as the world is universal flesh. One should not even say, as we did a moment ago, that the body is made up of two leaves, of which the one, that of the "sensible," is bound up with the rest of the world. There are not in it two leaves or two layers; fundamentally it is neither thing seen only nor seer only, it is Visibility sometimes wandering and sometimes reassembled.

And as such it is not in the world, it does not detain its view of the world as within a private garden: it sees the world itself, the world of everybody, and without having to leave "itself," because it is wholly – because its hands, its eyes, are nothing else than – this reference of a visible, a tangible-standard to all those whose resemblance it bears and whose evidence it gathers, by a magic that is the vision, the touch themselves. To speak of leaves or of layers is still to flatten and to juxtapose, under the reflective gaze, what coexists in the living and upright body. If one wants metaphors, it would be better to say that the body sensed and the body sentient are as the obverse and the reverse, or again, as two segments of one sole circular course which goes above from left to right and below from right to left, but which is but one sole movement in its two phases. And everything said about the sensed body pertains to the whole of the sensible of which it is a part, and to the world. If the body is one sole body in its two phases, it incorporates into itself the whole of the sensible and with the same movement incorporates itself into a "Sensible in itself." We have to reject the age-old assumptions that put the body in the world and the seer in the body, or, conversely, the world and the body in the seer as in a box. Where are we to put the limit between the body and the world, since the world is flesh? Where in the body are we to put the seer, since evidently there is in the body only "shadows stuffed with organs," that is, more of the visible? The world seen is not "in" my body, and my body is not "in" the visible world ultimately: as flesh applied to a flesh, the world neither surrounds it nor is surrounded by it. A participation in and kinship with the visible, the vision neither envelops it nor is enveloped by it definitively. The superficial pellicle of the visible is only for my vision and for my body. But the depth beneath this surface contains my body and hence contains my vision. My body as a visible thing is contained within the full spectacle. But my seeing body subtends this visible body, and all the visibles with it. There is reciprocal insertion and intertwining of one in the other. Or rather, if, as once again we must, we eschew the thinking by planes and perspectives, there are two circles, or two vortexes, or two spheres, concentric when I live naïvely, and as soon as I question myself, the one slightly decentered with respect to the other. . . .

We have to ask ourselves what exactly we have found with this strange adhesion of the seer and the visible. There is vision, touch, when a certain visible, a certain tangible, turns back upon the whole of the visible, the whole of the tangible, of which it is a part, or when suddenly it finds itself *surrounded* by them, or when between it and them, and through their commerce, is formed a Visibility, a Tangible in itself, which belong properly neither to the body qua fact nor to the world qua fact – as upon two mirrors facing one another where two indefinite series of images set in one another arise which belong really to neither of the two surfaces, since each is only the rejoinder of the other, and which therefore form a couple, a couple more real than either of them. Thus since the seer is caught up in what he sees, it is still himself he sees: there is a fundamental narcissism of all vision. And thus, for the same reason, the vision he exercises, he also undergoes from the things, such that, as many painters have said, I feel myself looked at by the things, my activity is equally passivity – which is the second and more profound sense of the narcissim: not to see in the outside, as the others see it, the contour of a body one inhabits, but especially to be seen by the outside, to exist within it, to emigrate into it, to be seduced, captivated, alienated by the phantom, so that the seer and the visible reciprocate one another and we no longer know which sees and which is seen. It is this Visibility, this generality of the Sensible in itself, this anonymity innate to Myself that we have previously called flesh, and one knows there is no name in traditional philosophy to designate it. The flesh is not matter, in the sense of corpuscles of being which would add up or continue on one another to form beings. Nor is the visible (the things as well as my own body) some "psychic" material that would be – God knows how – brought into being by the things factually existing and acting on my factual body. In general, it is not a fact or a sum of facts "material" or "spiritual." Nor is it a representation for a mind: a mind could not be captured by its own representations; it would rebel against this insertion into the visible which is essential to the seer. The flesh is not matter, is not mind, is not substance. To designate it, we should need the old term "element," in the sense it was used to speak of water, air, earth, and fire, that is, in the sense of a *general thing*, midway between the spatio-temporal individual and the idea, a sort of incarnate principle that brings a style of being wherever there is a fragment of being. The flesh is in this sense an "element" of Being. Not a fact or a sum of facts, and yet adherent to *location* and to the *now*. Much more: the inauguration of the *where* and the *when*, the possibility and exigency for the fact; in a word: facticity, what makes the fact be a fact. And, at the same time, what makes the facts have meaning, makes the fragmentary facts dispose themselves about "something." For if there is flesh, that is, if the hidden face of the cube radiates forth somewhere as well as does the face I have under my eyes, and coexists with it, and if I who see the cube also belong to the visible, I am visible from elsewhere, and if I and the cube are together caught up in one same "element" (should we say of the seer, or of the visible?), this cohesion, this visibility by principle, prevails over every momentary discordance. In advance every vision or very partial visible that would here definitively come to naught is not nullified (which would leave a gap in its place), but, what is better, it is replaced by a more exact vision and a more exact visible, according to the principle of visibility, which, as though through a sort of abhorrence of a vacuum, already invokes the true vision and the true visible, not only as substitutes for their errors, but also as their explanation, their relative justification, so that they are, as Husserl says so aptly, not erased, but "crossed out." . . . Such are the extravagant consequences to which we are led when we take seriously, when we question, vision. And it is, to be sure, possible to refrain from doing so and to move on, but we would simply find again, confused, indistinct, non-clarified, scraps of this ontology of the visible mixed up with all our theories of knowledge, and in particular with those that serve, desultorily, as vehicles of science. We are, to be sure, not finished ruminating over them. Our concern in this preliminary outline was only to catch sight of this strange domain to which interrogation, properly so-called, gives access. . . .

But this domain, one rapidly realizes, is unlimited. If we can show that the flesh is an ultimate notion, that it is not the union or compound of two substances, but thinkable by itself, if there is a relation of the visible with itself that traverses me and constitutes me as a seer, this circle which I do not form, which forms me, this coiling over of the visible upon the visible, can traverse, animate other bodies as well as my own. And if I was able to understand how this wave arises within me, how the visible which is yonder is simultaneously my landscape, I can understand a fortiori that elsewhere it also closes over upon itself and that there are other landscapes besides my own. If it lets itself be captivated by one of its fragments, the principle of captation is established, the field open for other Narcissus, for an "intercorporeity." If my left hand can touch my right hand while it palpates the tangibles, can touch it touching, can turn its palpation back upon it, why, when touching the hand of another, would I not touch in it the same power to espouse the things that I have touched in my own? It is true that "the things" in question are my own, that the whole operation takes place (as we say) "in me," within my landscape, whereas the problem is to institute another landscape. When one of my hands touches the other, the world of each opens upon that of the other because the operation is reversible at will, because they both belong (as we say) to one sole space of consciousness, because one sole man touches one sole thing through both hands. But for my two hands to open upon one sole world, it does not suffice that they be given to one sole *consciousness* – or if that were the case the difficulty before us would disappear: since other bodies would be known by me in the same way as would be my own, they and I would still be dealing with the same world. No, my two hands touch the same things because they are the hands of one same body. And yet each of them has its own tactile experience. If nonetheless they have to do with one sole tangible, it is because there exists a very peculiar relation from one to the other, across the corporeal space – like that holding between my two eyes – making of my hands one sole organ of experience, as it makes of my two eyes the channels of one sole Cyclopean vision. A difficult relation to conceive – since one eye, one hand, are capable of vision, of touch, and since what has to be comprehended is that these visions, these touches, these little subjectivities, these "consciousnesses of . . .," could be assembled like flowers into a bouquet, when each being "consciousness of," being For Itself, reduces the others into objects. We will get out of the difficulty only by renouncing the bifurcation of the "consciousness of" and the object, by admitting that my synergic body is not an object, that it assembles into a cluster the "consciousnesses" adherent to its hands, to its eyes, by an operation that is in relation to them lateral, transversal; that "my consciousness" is not the synthetic, uncreated, centrifugal unity of a multitude of "consciousnesses of . . ." which would be centrifugal like it is, that it is sustained, subtended, by the prereflective and preobjective unity of my body. This means that while each monocular vision, each touching with one sole hand has its own visible, its tactile, each is bound to every other vision, to every other touch; it is bound in such a way as to make up with them the experience of one sole body before one sole world, through a possibility for reversion, reconversion of its language into theirs, transfer, and reversal, according to which the little private world of each is not juxtaposed to the world of all the others, but surrounded by it, levied off from it, and all together are a Sentient in general before a Sensible in general. Now why would this generality, which constitutes the unity of my body, not open it to other bodies? The handshake too is reversible; I can feel myself touched as well and at the same time as touching, and surely there does not exist some huge animal whose organs our bodies would be, as, for each of our bodies, our hands, our eyes are the organs. Why would not the synergy exist among different organisms, if it is possible within each? Their landscapes interweave, their actions and their passions fit together exactly: this is possible as soon as we no longer make belongingness to one same "consciousness" the primordial definition of sensibility, and as soon as we rather understand it as the return of the visible upon itself, a carnal adherence of the sentient to the sensed and of the sensed to the sentient. For, as overlapping and fission, identity and difference, it brings to birth a ray of natural light that illuminates all flesh and not only my own. It is said that the colors, the tactile reliefs given to the other, are for me an absolute mystery, forever inaccessible. This is not completely true; for me to have not an idea, an image, nor a representation, but as it were the imminent experience of them, it suffices that I look at a landscape, that I speak of it with someone. Then, through the concordant operation of his body and my own, what I see passes into him, this individual green of the meadow under my eyes invades his vision without quitting my own, I recognize in my green his green, as the customs officer recognizes suddenly in a traveler the man whose description he had been given. There is here no problem of the *alter ego* because it is not *I* who sees, not *he* who sees, because an anonymous visibility inhabits both of us, a vision in general, in virtue of that primordial property that belongs to the flesh, being here and now, of radiating everywhere and forever, being an individual, of being also a dimension and a universal.

What is open to us, therefore, with the reversibility of the visible and the tangible, is – if not yet the incorporeal – at least an inter-corporeal being, a presumptive domain of the visible and the tangible, which extends further than the things I touch and see at present.

There is a circle of the touched and the touching, the touched takes hold of the touching; there is a circle of the visible and the seeing, the seeing is not without visible existence;[5] there is even an inscription of the touching in the visible, of the seeing in the tangible – and the con-verse; there is finally a propagation of these exchanges to all the bodies of the same type and of the same style which I see and touch – and this by virtue of the fundamental fission or segregation of the sentient and the sensible which, laterally, makes the organs of my body communicate and founds transitivity from one body to another.

As soon as we see other seers, we no longer have before us only the look without a pupil, the plate glass of the things with that feeble reflec-tion, that phantom of ourselves they evoke by designating a place among themselves whence we see them: henceforth, through other eyes we are for ourselves fully visible; that lacuna where our eyes, our back, lie is filled, filled still by the visible, of which we are not the titulars. To believe that, to bring a vision that is not our own into account, it is to be sure inevitably, it is always from the unique treasury of our own vision that we draw, and experience therefore can teach us nothing that would not be outlined in our own vision. But what is proper to the visible is, we said, to be the surface of an inexhaustible depth: this is what makes it able to be open to visions other than our own. In being realized, they therefore bring out the limits of our factual vision, they betray the solipsist illusion that consists in thinking that every going beyond is a surpassing accomplished by oneself. For the first time, the seeing that I am is for me really visible; for the first time I appear to myself completely turned inside out under my own eyes. For the first time also, my movements no longer proceed unto the things to be seen, to be touched, or unto my own body occupied in seeing and touching them, but they address themselves to the body in general and for itself (whether it be my own or that of another), because for the first time, through the other body, I see that, in its coupling with the flesh of the world, the body contributes more than it receives, adding to the world that I see the treasure necessary for what the other body sees. For the first time, the body no longer couples itself up with the world, it clasps another body, applying [itself to it]⁶ carefully with its whole extension, forming tirelessly with its hands the strange statute which in its turn gives everything it receives; the body is lost outside of the world and its goals, fascinated, by the unique occupation of floating in Being with another life, of making itself the outside of its inside and the inside of its outside. And henceforth movement, touch, vision, applying themselves to the other and to themselves, return toward their source and, in the patient and silent labor of desire, begin the paradox of expression.

Yet this flesh that one sees and touches is not all there is to flesh, nor this massive corporeity all there is to the body. The reversibility that defines the flesh exists in other fields; it is even incomparably more agile there and capable of weaving relations between bodies that this time will not only enlarge, but will pass definitively beyond the circle of the visible. Among my movements, there are some that go nowhere – that do not even go find in the other body their resemblance or their archetype: these are the facial movements, many gestures, and especially those strange movements of the throat and mouth that form the cry and the voice. Those movements end in sounds and I hear them. Like crystal, like metal and many other substances, I am a sonorous being, but I hear my own vibration from within; as Malraux said, I hear myself with my throat. In this, as he also has said, I am incomparable; my voice is bound to the mass of my own life as is the voice of no one else. But if I am close enough to the other who speaks to hear his breath and feel his effervescence and his fatigue, I almost witness, in him as in myself, the awesome birth of vociferation. As there is a reflexivity of the touch, of sight, and of the touch-vision system, there is a reflexivity of the movements of phonation and of hearing; they have their sonorous inscription, the vociferations have in me their motor echo. This new reversibility and the emergence of the flesh as expression are the point of insertion of speaking and thinking in the world of silence.[7]

At the frontier of the mute or solipsist world where, in the presence of other seers, my visible is confirmed as an exemplar of a universal visibility, we reach a second or figurative meaning of vision, which will be the *intuitus mentis* or idea, a sublimation of the flesh, which will be mind or thought. But the factual presence of other bodies could not produce thought or the idea if its seed were not in my own body. Thought is a relationship with oneself and with the world as well as a relationship with the other; hence it is established in the three dimensions at the same time. And it must be brought to appear directly in the infrastructure of vision. Brought to appear, we say, and not brought to birth: for we are leaving in suspense for the moment the question whether it would not be already implicated there. Manifest as it is that feeling is dispersed in my body, that for example my hand touches, and that consequently we may not in advance ascribe feeling to a thought of which it would be but a mode – it yet would be absurd to conceive the touch as a colony of assembled tactile experiences. We are not here proposing any empiricist genesis of thought: we are asking precisely what is that central vision that joins the scattered visions, that unique touch that governs the whole tactile life of my body as a unit, that *I think* that must be able to accompany all our experiences. We are proceeding toward the center, we are seeking to comprehend how there is a center, what the unity consists of, we are not saying that it is a sum or a result; and if we make the thought appear upon an infrastructure of vision, this is only in virtue of the uncontested evidence that one must see or feel in some way in order to think, that every thought known to us occurs to a flesh.

Once again, the flesh we are speaking of is not matter. It is the coiling over of the visible upon the seeing body, of the tangible upon the touching body, which is attested in particular when the body sees itself, touches itself seeing and touching the things, such that, simultaneously, *as* tangible it descends among them, *as* touching it dominates them all and draws this relationship and even this double relationship from itself, by dehiscence or fission of its own mass. This concentration of the visibles about one of them, or this bursting forth of the mass of the body toward the things, which makes a vibration of my skin become the sleek and the rough, makes me *follow with my eyes* the movements and the contours of the things themselves, this magical relation, this pact between them and me according to which I lend them my body in order that they inscribe upon it and give me their resemblance, this fold, this central cavity of the visible which is my vision, these two mirror arrangements of the seeing and the visible, the touching and the touched, form a close-bound system that I count on, define a vision in general and a constant style of visibility from which I cannot detach myself, even when a particular vision turns out to be illusory, for I remain certain in that case that in looking closer I would have had the true vision, and that in any case, whether it be this one or another, *there is a true vision*. The flesh (of the world or my own) is not contingency, chaos, but a texture that returns to itself and conforms to itself. I will never see my own retinas, but if one thing is certain for me it is that *one* would find at the bottom of my eyeballs those dull and secret membranes. And finally, I believe it – I believe that I have a man's senses, a human body – because the spectacle of the world that is my own, and which, to judge by our confrontations, does not notably differ from that of the others, with me as with them refers with evidence to typical dimensions of visibility, and finally to a virtual focus of vision, to a detector also typical, so that at the joints of the opaque body and the opaque world there is a ray of generality and of light. Conversely, when, starting from the body, I ask how it makes itself a seer, when I examine the critical region of the aesthesiological body, everything comes to pass (as we have shown in an earlier work[8]) as though the visible body remained incomplete, gaping open; as though the physiology of vision did not succeed in closing the nervous functioning in upon itself, since the movements of fixation, of convergence, are suspended upon the advent to the body of a visible world for which they were supposed to furnish the explanation; as though, therefore, the vision came suddenly to give to the material means and instruments left here and there in the working area a convergence which they were waiting for; as though, through all these channels, all these prepared but unemployed circuits, the current that will traverse them was rendered probable, in the long run inevitable: the current making of an embryo a newborn infant, of a visible a seer, and of a body a mind, or at least a flesh. In spite of all our substantialist ideas, the seer is being premediated in counterpoint in the embryonic development; through a labor upon itself the visible body provides for the hollow whence a vision will come, inaugurates the long maturation at whose term suddenly it will see, that is, will be visible for itself, will institute the interminable gravitation, the indefatigable metamorphosis of the seeing and the visible whose principle is posed and which gets underway with the first vision. What we are calling flesh, this interiorly worked-over mass, has no name in any philosophy. As the formative medium of the object and the subject, it is not the atom of being, the hard in itself that resides in a unique place and moment: one can indeed say of my body that it is not *elsewhere*, but one cannot say that it is *here* or *now* in the sense that objects are; and yet my vision does not soar over them, it is not the being that is wholly knowing, for it has its own inertia, its ties. We must not think the flesh starting from substances, from body and spirit – for then it would be the union of contradictories – but we must think it, as we said, as an element, as the concrete emblem of a general manner of being. To begin with, we spoke summarily of a reversibility of the seeing and the visible, of the touching and the touched. It is time to emphasize that it is a reversibility always imminent and never realized in fact. My left hand is always on the verge of touching my right hand touching the things, but I never reach coincidence; the coincidence eclipses at the moment of realization, and one of two things always occurs: either my right hand really passes over to the rank of touched, but then its hold on the world is interrupted; or it retains its hold on the world, but then I do not really touch *it* – my right hand touching, I palpate with my left hand only its outer covering. Likewise, I do not hear myself as I hear the others, the sonorous existence of my voice is for me as it were poorly exhibited; I have rather an echo of its articulated existence, it vibrates through my head rather than outside. I am always on the same side of my body; it presents itself to me in one invariable perspective. But this incessant escaping, this impotency to superpose exactly upon one another the touching of the things by my right hand and the touching of this same right hand by my left hand, or to superpose, in the exploratory movements of the hand, the tactile experience of a point and that of the "same" point a moment later, or the auditory experience of my own voice and that of other voices – this is not a failure. For if these experiences never exactly overlap, if they slip away at the very moment they are about to rejoin, if there is always a "shift," a "spread," between them, this is precisely because my two hands are part of the same body, because it moves itself in the world, because I hear myself both from within and from without. I experience – and as often as I wish – the transition and the metamorphosis of the one experience into the other, and it is only as though the hinge between them, solid, unshakeable, remained irremediably hidden from me. But this hiatus between my right hand touched and my right hand touching, between my voice heard and my voice uttered, between one moment of my tactile life and the following one, is not an ontological void, a nonbeing: it is spanned by the total being of my body, and by that of the world; it is the zero of pressure between two solids that makes them adhere to one another. My flesh and that of the world therefore involve clear zones, clearings, about which pivot their opaque zones, and the primary visibility, that of the *quale* and of the things, does not come without a second visibility, that of the lines of force and dimensions, the massive flesh without a rarefied flesh, the momentary body without a glorified body. When Husserl spoke of the horizon of the things – of their exterior horizon, which everybody knows, and of their "interior horizon," that darkness stuffed with visibility of which their surface is but the limit – it is necessary to take the term seriously. No more than are the sky or the earth is the horizon a collection of things held together, or a class name, or a logical possibility of conception, or a system of "potentiality of consciousness": it is a new type of being, a being by porosity, pregnancy, or generality, and he before whom the horizon opens is caught up, included within it. His body and the distances participate in one same corporeity or visibility in general, which reigns between them and it, and even beyond the horizon, beneath his skin, unto the depths of being.

We touch here the most difficult point, that is, the bond between the flesh and the idea, between the visible and the interior armature which it manifests and which it conceals. No one has gone further than Proust in fixing the relations between the visible and the invisible, in describing an idea that is not the contrary of the sensible, that is its lining and its depth. For what he says of musical ideas he says of all cultural beings, such as *The Princess of Clèves* and *René*, and also of the essence of love which "the little phrase" not only makes present to Swann, but communicable to all who hear it, even though it is unbeknown to themselves, and even though later they do not know how to recognize it in the loves they only witness. He says it in general of many other notions which are, like music itself "without equivalents," "the notions of light, of sound, of relief, of physical voluptuousness, which are the rich possessions with which our inward domain is diversified and adorned."[9] Literature, music, the passions, but also the experience of the visible world are – no less than is the science of Lavoisier and Ampère – the exploration of an invisible and the disclosure of a universe of ideas.[10] The difference is simply that this invisible, these ideas, unlike those of that science, cannot be detached from the sensible appearances and be erected into a second positivity. The musical idea, the literary idea, the dialectic of love, and also the articulations of the light, the modes of exhibition of sound and of touch speak to us, have their logic, their coherence, their points of intersection, their concordances, and here also the appearances are the disguise of unknown "forces" and "laws." But it is as though the secrecy wherein they lie and whence the literary expression draws them were their proper mode of existence. For these truths are not only hidden like a physical reality which we have not been able to discover, invisible in fact but which we will one day be able to see facing us, which others, better situated, could already see, provided that the screen that masks it is lifted. Here, on the contrary, there is no vision without the screen: the ideas we are speaking of would not be better known to us if we had no body and no sensibility; it is then that they would be inaccessible to us. The "little phrase," the notion of the light, are not exhausted by their manifestations, any more than is an "idea of the intelligence"; they could not be given to us *as ideas* except in a carnal experience. It is not only that we would find in that carnal experience the *occasion* to think them; it is that they owe their authority, their fascinating, indestructible power, precisely to the fact that they are in transparency behind the sensible, or in its heart. Each time we want to get at it[11] immediately, or lay hands on it, or circumscribe it, or see it unveiled, we do in fact feel that the attempt is misconceived, that it retreats in the measure that we approach. The explicitation does not give us the idea itself; it is but a second version of it, a more manageable derivative. Swann can of course close in the "little phrase" between the marks of musical notation, ascribe the "withdrawn and chilly tenderness" that makes up its essence or its sense to the narrow range of the five notes that compose it and to the constant recurrence of two of them: while he is thinking of these signs and this sense, he no longer has the "little phrase" itself, he has only "bare values substituted for the mysterious entity he had perceived, for the convenience of his understanding."[12] Thus it is essential to this sort of ideas that they be "veiled with shadows," appear "under a disguise." They give us the assurance that the "great unpenetrated and discouraging night of our soul" is not empty, is not "nothingness"; but these entities, these domains, these worlds that line it, people it, and whose presence it feels like the presence of someone in the dark, have been acquired only through its commerce with the visible, to which they remain attached. As the secret blackness of milk, of which Valéry spoke, is accessible only through its whiteness, the idea of light or the musical idea doubles up the lights and sounds from beneath, is their other side or their depth. Their carnal texture presents to us what is absent from all flesh; it is a furrow that traces itself out magically under our eyes without a tracer, a certain hollow, a certain interior, a certain absence, a negativity that is not nothing, being limited very precisely to *these* five notes between which it is instituted, to that family of sensibles we call lights. We do not see, do not hear the ideas, and not even with the mind's eye or with the third ear: and yet they are there, behind the sounds or between them, behind the lights or between them, recognizable through their always special, always unique manner of entrenching themselves behind them, "perfectly distinct from one another, unequal among themselves in value and in significance."[13]

With the first vision, the first contact, the first pleasure, there is initiation, that is, not the positing of a content, but the opening of a dimension that can never again be closed, the establishment of a level in terms of which every other experience will henceforth be situated. The idea is this level, this dimension. It is therefore not a *de facto* invisible, like an object hidden behind another, and not an absolute invisible, which would have nothing to do with the visible. Rather it is the invisible *of* this world, that which inhabits this world, sustains it, and renders it visible, its own and interior possibility, the Being of this being. At the moment one says "light," at the moment that the musicians reach the "little phrase," there is no lacuna in me; what I live is as "substantial," as "explicit," as a positive thought could be – even more so: a positive thought is what it is, but, precisely, is only what it is and accordingly cannot hold us. Already the mind's volubility takes it elsewhere. We do not possess the musical or sensible ideas, precisely because they are negativity or absence circumscribed; they possess us. The performer is no longer producing or reproducing the sonata: he feels himself, and the others feel him to be at the service of the sonata; the sonata sings through him or cries out so suddenly that he must "dash on his bow" to follow it. And these open vortexes in the sonorous world finally form one sole vortex in which the ideas fit in with one another. "Never was the spoken language so inflexibly necessitated, never did it know to such an extent the pertinence of the questions, the evidence of the responses."[14] The invisible and, as it were, weak being is alone capable of having this close texture. There is a strict ideality in experiences that are experiences of the flesh: the moments of the sonata, the fragments of the luminous field, adhere to one another with a cohesion without concept, which is of the same type as the cohesion of the parts of my body, or the cohesion of my body with the world. Is my body a thing, is it an idea? It is neither, being the measurant of the things. We will therefore have to recognize an ideality that is not alien to the flesh, that gives it its axes, its depth, its dimensions.

But once we have entered into this strange domain, one does not see how there could be any question of *leaving* it. If there is an animation *of* the body; if the vision and the body are tangled up in one another; if, correlatively, the thin pellicle of the *quale*, the surface of the visible, is doubled up over its whole extension with an invisible reserve; and if finally, in our flesh as in the flesh of things, the actual, empirical, ontic visible, by a sort of folding back, invagination, or padding, exhibits a visibility, a possibility that is not the shadow of the actual but is its principle, that is not the proper contribution of a "thought" but is its condition, a style, allusive and elliptical like every style, but like every style inimitable, inalienable, an interior horizon and an exterior horizon between which the actual visible is a provisional partitioning and which, nonetheless, opens indefinitely only upon other visibles – then (the immediate and dualist distinction between the visible and the invisible, between extension and thought, being impugned, not that extension be thought or thought extension, but because they are the obverse and the reverse of one another, and the one forever behind the other) there is to be sure a question as to how the "ideas of the intelligence" are initiated over and beyond, how from the ideality of the horizon one passes to the "pure" ideality, and in particular by what miracle a created generality, a culture, a knowledge come to add to and recapture and rectify the natural generality of my body and of the world. But, however we finally have to understand it, the "pure" ideality already streams forth along the articulations of the aesthesiological body, along the contours of the sensible things, and, however new it is, it slips through ways it has not traced, transfigures horizons it did not open, it derives from the fundamental mystery of those notions "without equivalent," as Proust calls them, that lead their shadowy life in the night of the mind only because they have been divined at the junctures of the visible world. It is too soon now to clarify this type of surpassing that does not leave its field of origin. Let us only say that the pure ideality is itself not without flesh nor freed from horizon structures: it lives of them, though they be another flesh and other horizons. It is as though the visibility that animates the sensible world were to emigrate, not outside of every body, but into another less heavy, more transparent body, as though it were to change flesh, abandoning the flesh of the body for that of language, and thereby would be emancipated but not freed from every condition. Why not admit – what Proust knew very well and said in another place – that language as well as music can sustain a sense by virtue of its own arrangement, catch a meaning in its own mesh, that it does so without exception each time it is conquering, active, creative language, each time something is, in the strong sense, said? Why not admit that, just as the musical notation is a *facsimile* made after the event, an abstract portrait of the musical entity, language as a system of explicit relations between signs and signified, sounds and meaning, is a result and a product of the operative language in which sense and sound are in the same relationship as the "little phrase" and the five notes found in it afterwards? This does not mean that musical notation and grammar and linguistics and the "ideas of the intelligence" – which are acquired, available, honorary ideas – are useless, or that, as Leibniz said, the donkey that goes straight to the fodder knows as much about the properties of the straight line as we do; it means that the system of objective relations, the acquired ideas, are themselves caught up in something like a second life and perception, which make the mathematician go straight to entities no one has yet seen, make the *operative* language and algorithm make use of a second visibility, and make ideas be the other side of language and calculus. When I think they animate my interior speech, they haunt it as the "little phrase" possesses the violinist, and they remain beyond the words as it remains beyond the notes – not in the sense that under the light of another sun hidden from us they would shine forth but because they are that certain divergence, that never-finished differentiation, that openness ever to be reopened between the sign and the sign, as the flesh is, we said, the dehiscence of the seeing into the visible and of the visible into the seeing. And just as my body sees only because it is a part of the visible in which it opens forth, the sense upon which the arrangement of the sounds opens reflects back upon that arrangement. For the linguist language is an ideal system, a fragment of the intelligible world. But, just as for me to see it is not enough that my look be visible for X, it is necessary that it be visible for itself, through a sort of torsion, reversal, or specular phenomenon, which is given from the sole fact that I am born; so also, if my words have a meaning, it is not *because* they present the systematic organization the linguist will disclose, it is because that organization, like the look, refers back to itself: the operative Word is the obscure region whence comes the instituted light, as the muted reflection of the body upon itself is what we call natural light. As there is a reversibility of the seeing and the visible, and as at the point where the two metamorphoses cross what we call perception is born, so also there is a reversibility of the speech and what it signifies; the signification is what comes to seal, to close, to gather up the multiplicity of the physical, physiological, linguistic means of elocution, to contract them into one sole act, as the vision comes to complete the aesthesiological body. And, as the visible takes hold of the look which has unveiled it and which forms a part of it, the signification rebounds upon its own means, it annexes to itself the speech that becomes an object of science, it antedates itself by a retrograde movement which is never completely belied – because already, in opening the horizon of the nameable and of the sayable, the speech acknowledged that it has its place in that horizon; because no locutor speaks without making himself in advance allocutary, *be it only for himself*; because with one sole gesture he closes the circuit of his relation to himself and that of his relation to the others and, with the same stroke, also sets himself up as *delocutary*, speech of which one speaks: he offers himself and offers every word to a universal Word. We shall have to follow more closely this transition from the mute world to the speaking world. For the moment we want only to suggest that one can speak neither of a destruction nor of a conservation of silence (and still less of a destruction that conserves or of a realization that destroys – which is not to solve but to pose the problem). When the silent vision falls into speech, and when the speech in turn, opening up a field of the nameable and the sayable, inscribes itself in that field, in its place, according to its truth – in short, when it metamorphoses the structures of the visible world and makes itself a gaze of the mind, *intuitus mentis* – this is always in virtue of the same fundamental phenomenon of reversibility which sustains both the mute perception and the speech and which manifests itself by an almost carnal existence of the idea, as well as by a sublimation of the flesh. In a sense, if we were to make completely explicit the architectonics of the human body, its ontological framework, and how it sees itself and hears itself, we would see that the structure of its mute world is such that all the possibilities of language are already given in it. Already our existence as seers (that is, we said, as beings who turn the world back upon itself and who pass over to the other side, and who catch sight of one another, who see one another with eyes) and especially our existence as sonorous beings for others and for ourselves contain everything required for there to be speech from the one to the other, speech about the world. And, in a sense, to understand a phrase is nothing else than to fully welcome it in its sonorous being, or, as we put it so well, to *hear what it says* (*l'entendre*). The meaning is not on the phrase like the butter on the bread, like a second layer of "psychic reality" spread over the sound: it is the totality of what is said, the integral of all the differentiations of the verbal chain; it is given with the words for those who have ears to hear. And conversely the whole landscape is overrun with words as with an invasion, it is henceforth but a variant of speech before our eyes, and to speak of its "style" is in our view to form a metaphor. In a sense the whole of philosophy, as Husserl says, consists in restoring a power to signify, a birth of meaning, or a wild meaning, an expression of experience by experience, which in particular clarifies the special domain of language. And in a sense, as Valéry said, language is everything, since it is the voice of no one, since it is the very voice of the things, the waves, and the forests. And what we have to understand is that there is no dialectical reversal from one of these views to the other; we do not have to reassemble them into a synthesis: they are two aspects of the reversibility which is the ultimate truth.

Notes

1 Here in the course of the text itself, these lines are inserted: "it is that the look is itself incorporation of the seer into the visible, quest for itself, which *is of it*, within the visible – it is that the visible of the world is not an envelope of *quale*, but what is between the qualia, a connective tissue of exterior and interior horizons – it is as flesh offered to flesh that the visible has its aseity, and that it is mine – The flesh as *Sichtigkeit* and generality. → whence vision is question and response. . . . The openness through flesh: the two leaves of my body and the leaves of the visible world. . . . It is between these intercalated leaves that there is visibility. . . . My body model of the things and the things model of my body: the body bound to the world through all its parts, up against it → all this means: the world, the flesh not as fact or sum of facts, but as the locus of an inscription of truth: the false crossed out, not nullified" (Editor of 1968 translation).
2 The *Urpräsentierbarkeit* is the flesh.
3 The visible is not a tangible zero, the tangible is not a zero of visibility (relation of encroachment).
4 Here, in the course of the text itself, between brackets, these lines are inserted: "One can say that we perceive the things themselves, that we are the world that thinks itself – or that the world is at the heart of our flesh. In any case, once a body-world relationship is recognized, there is a ramification of my body and a ramification of the world and a correspondence between its inside and my outside, between my inside and its outside" (Editor of 1968 translation).
5 Here is inserted between brackets, in the course of the text itself, the note: "what are these adhesions compared with those of the voice and the hearing?" (Editor of 1968 translation).
6 These words, which we reintroduce into the text, had been erased apparently by error (Editor of 1968 translation).
7 Inserted here between brackets: "in what sense we have not yet introduced thinking: to be sure, we are not in the in itself. From the moment we said *seeing, visible*, and described the dehiscence of the sensible, we were, if one likes, in the order of thought. We were not in it in the sense that the thinking we have introduced was *there is*, and not *it appears to me that* . . . (appearing that would make up the whole of being, self-appearing). Our thesis is that this *there is* by inherence is necessary, and our problem to show that thought, in the restrictive sense (pure signification, thought of seeing and of feeling), is comprehensible only as the accomplishment by

other means of the will of the *there is*, by sublimation of the *there is* and realization of an invisible that is exactly the reverse of the visible, the power of the visible. Thus between sound and meaning, speech and what it means to say, there is still the relation of reversibility, and no question of priority, since the exchange of words is exactly the differentiation of which the thought is the integral" (Editor of 1968 translation).

8 *The Structure of Behavior*, trans. Alden L. Fisher, Boston, 1963.
9 *Du côté de chez Swann*, II, Paris, 1926, p. 190. (English translation by C. K. Scott Moncrieff, *Swann's Way*, New York, 1928, p. 503.)
10 *Ibid.*, p. 192. (English trans., p. 505.)
11 It: that is, the idea (Editor of 1968 translation).
12 *Du côté de chez Swann*, II, p. 189. (English trans., p. 503.)
13 *Ibid.*
14 *Ibid.*, p. 192. (English trans., p. 505.)

PART SIX – PAINTING

CÉZANNE'S DOUBT (from *Sense and Non-sense*, pp. 9–24 in the 1964 translation)

'Cézanne's doubt' was first published in 1945, and is therefore intellectually very close to The Phenomenology of Perception, *in which there are many brief references to Cézanne. Merleau-Ponty here spells out in more detail the way in which Cézanne's paintings seem to him to bear witness to his own account of visual experience. Cézanne, he says, 'wanted to depict matter as it takes on form', so that the apparent distortions in his paintings contribute, in the context of the painting as a whole, to 'the impression of an emerging order, of an object in the act of appearing'. Thus Cézanne anticipated his own phenomenology, and Cézanne's incomparable achievement is that he managed to express in his paintings 'the vibration of appearances which is the cradle of things'.*

Merleau-Ponty then turns to the question of the relation between Cézanne's life and his work. He holds that the two are inseparable, but that it would be a complete mistake to treat them as the realisation of a project freely chosen from the start. At this point, therefore, without any explicit reference but with language whose intent is unmistakable, Merleau-Ponty briefly reiterates his criticisms of Sartre's account of freedom from The Phenomenology of Perception *(see p. 209); and he ends the essay with a brief discussion of Leonardo da Vinci's life to reinforce the point. Leonardo's life may seem at first to have exemplified Sartrean freedom; but as soon as one looks to the detail of it one finds a complexity that requires a quite different explanatory framework, one that makes space for a kind of repression whereby an individual's later inability to relate closely to others manifests the situation of his birth and childhood.*

He needed one hundred working sessions for a still life, five hundred sittings for a portrait. What we call his work was, for him, only an essay, an approach to painting. In September, 1906, at the age of 67 – one month before his death – he wrote: "I was in such a state of mental agitation, in such great confusion that for a time I feared my weak reason would not survive. . . . Now it seems I am better and that I see more clearly the direction my studies are taking. Will I ever arrive at the goal, so intensely sought and so long pursued? I am still learning from nature, and it seems to me I am making slow progress." Painting was his world and his way of life. He worked alone, without students, without admiration from his family, without encouragement from the critics. He painted on the afternoon of the day his mother died. In 1870 he was painting at l'Estaque while the police were after him for dodging the draft. And still he had moments of doubt about this vocation. As he grew old, he wondered whether the novelty of his painting might not come from trouble with his eyes, whether his whole life had not been based upon an accident of his body. The uncertainty or stupidity of his contemporaries correspond to this effort and this doubt. "The painting of a drunken privy cleaner," said a critic in 1905. Even today, C. Mauclair finds Cézanne's admissions of powerlessness an argument against him. Meanwhile, Cézanne's paintings have spread throughout the world. Why so much uncertainty, so much labor, so many failures, and, suddenly, the greatest success?

Zola, Cézanne's friend from childhood, was the first to find genius in him and the first to speak of him as a "genius gone wrong." An observer of Cézanne's life such as Zola, more concerned with his character than with the meaning of his painting, might well consider it a manifestation of ill-health.

For as far back as 1852, upon entering the Collége Bourbon at Aix, Cézanne worried his friends with his fits of temper and depression. Seven years later, having decided to become an artist, he doubted his talent and did not dare to ask his father – a hatter and later a banker – to send him to Paris. Zola's letters reproach him for his instability, his weakness, and his indecision. When finally he came to Paris, he wrote: "The only thing I have changed is my location: my ennui has followed me." He could not tolerate discussions, because they wore him out and because he could never give arguments. His nature was basically anxious. Thinking that he would die young, he made his will at the age of 42; at 46 he was for six months the victim of a violent, tormented, overwhelming passion of which no one knows the outcome and to which he would never refer. At 51 he withdrew to Aix, where he found landscape best suited to his genius but where also he returned to the world of his childhood, his mother and his sister. After the death of his mother, Cézanne turned to his son for support. "Life is terrifying," he would often say. Religion, which he then set about practicing for the first time, began for him in the fear of life and the fear of death. "It is fear," he explained to a friend; "I feel I will be on earth for another four days – what then? I believe in life after death, and I don't want to risk roasting *in aeternum*." Although his religion later deepened, its original motivation was the need to put his life in order and to be relieved of it. He became more and more timid, mistrustful, and sensitive: on his occasional visits to Paris he motioned his friends, when still far away, not to approach him. In 1903, after his pictures had begun to sell in Paris at twice the price of Monet's and when young men like Joachim Gasquet and Emile Bernard came to see him and ask him questions, he unbent a little. But his fits of anger continued. (In Aix a child once hit him as he passed by; after that he could not bear any contact.) One day when Cézanne was quite old, Emile Bernard supported him as he stumbled. Cézanne flew into a rage. He could be heard striding around his studio and shouting that he wouldn't let anybody "get his hooks into me." Because of these "hooks" he pushed women who could have modeled for him out of his studio, priests, whom he called "sticky," out of his life, and Emile Bernard's theories out of his mind, when they became too insistent.

This loss of flexible human contact; this inability to master new situations; this flight into established habits, in an atmosphere which presented no problems; this rigid opposition in theory and practice of the "hook" versus the freedom of a recluse – all these symptoms permit one to speak of a morbid constitution and more precisely, as, for example, in the case of El Greco, of schizophrenia. The notion of painting "from nature" could be said to arise from the same weakness. His extremely close attention to nature and to color, the inhuman character of his paintings (he said that a face should be painted as an object), his devotion to the visible world: all of these would then only represent a flight from the human world, the alienation of his humanity.

These conjectures nevertheless do not give any idea of the positive side of his work; one cannot thereby conclude that his painting is a phenomenon of decadence and what Nietzsche called "impoverished" life or that it has nothing to say to the educated man. Zola's and Emile Bernard's belief in Cézanne's failure probably arises from their having put too much emphasis on psychology and their personal knowledge of

Cézanne. It is quite possible that, on the basis of his nervous weaknesses, Cézanne conceived a form of art which is valid for everyone. Left to himself, he could look at nature as only a human being can. The meaning of his work cannot be determined from his life.

This meaning will not become any clearer in the light of art history – that is, by bringing in the influences on Cézanne's methods (the Italian school and Tintoretto, Delacroix, Courbet and the Impressionists) – or even by drawing on his own judgment of his work.

His first pictures – up to about 1870 – are painted fantasies: a rape, a murder. They are therefore almost always executed in broad strokes and present the moral physiognomy of the actions rather than their visible aspect. It is thanks to the Impressionists, and particularly to Pissarro, that Cézanne later conceived painting not as the incarnation of imagined scenes, the projection of dreams outward, but as the exact study of appearances: less a work of the studio than a working from nature. Thanks to the Impressionists, he abandoned the baroque technique, whose primary aim is to capture movement, for small dabs placed close together and for patient hatchings.

He quickly parted ways with the Impressionists, however. Impressionism tries to capture, in the painting, the very way in which objects strike our eyes and attack our senses. Objects are depicted as they appear to instantaneous perception, without fixed contours, bound together by light and air. To capture this envelope of light, one had to exclude siennas, ochres, and black and use only the seven colors of the spectrum. The color of objects could not be represented simply by putting on the canvas their local tone, that is, the color they take on isolated from their surroundings; one also had to pay attention to the phenomena of contrast which modify local colors in nature. Furthermore, by a sort of reversal, every color we perceive in nature elicits the appearance of its complement; and these complementaries heighten one another. To achieve sunlit colors in a picture which will be seen in the dim light of apartments, not only must there be a green – if you are painting grass – but also the complementary red which will make it vibrate. Finally, the Impressionists break down the local tone itself. One can generally obtain any color by juxtaposing rather than mixing the colors which make it up, thereby achieving a more vibrant hue. The result of these procedures is that the canvas – which no longer corresponds point by point to nature – affords a generally true impression through the action of the separate parts upon one another. But at the same time, depicting the atmosphere and breaking up the tones submerges the object and causes it to lose its proper weight. The composition of Cézanne's palette leads one to suppose that he had another aim. Instead of the seven colors of the spectrum, one finds eighteen colors – six reds, five yellows, three blues, three greens, and black. The use of warm colors and black shows that Cézanne wants to represent the object, to find it again behind the atmosphere. Likewise, he does not break up the tone; rather, he replaces this technique with graduated colors, a progression of chromatic nuances across the object, a modulation of colors which stays close to the object's form and to the light it receives. Doing away with exact contours in certain cases, giving color priority over the outline – these obviously mean different things for Cézanne and for the Impressionists. The object is no longer covered by reflections and lost in its relationships to the atmosphere and to other objects: it seems subtly illuminated from within, light emanates from it, and the result is an impression of solidity and material substance. Moreover, Cézanne does not give up making the warm colors vibrate but achieves this chromatic sensation through the use of blue.

One must therefore say that Cézanne wished to return to the object without abandoning the Impressionist aesthetic which takes nature as its model. Emile Bernard reminded him that, for the classical artists, painting demanded outline, composition, and distribution of light. Cézanne replied: "They created pictures; we are attempting a piece of nature." He said of the old masters that they "replaced reality by imagination and by the abstraction which accompanies it." Of nature, he said that "the artist must conform to this perfect work of art. Everything comes to us from nature; we exist through it; nothing else is worth remembering." He stated that he wanted to make of Impressionism "something solid, like the art in the museums." His painting was paradoxical: he was pursuing reality without giving up the sensuous surface, with no other guide than the immediate impression of nature, without following the contours, with no outline to enclose the color, with no perspectival or pictorial arrangement. This is what Bernard called Cézanne's suicide: aiming for reality while denying himself the means to attain it. This is the reason for his difficulties and for the distortions one finds in his pictures between 1870 and 1890. Cups and saucers on a table seen from the side should be elliptical, but Cézanne paints the two ends of the ellipse swollen and expanded. The work table in his portrait of Gustave Geoffrey stretches, contrary to the laws of perspective, into the lower part of the picture. In giving up the outline Cézanne was abandoning himself to the chaos of sensations, which would upset the objects and constantly suggest illusions, as, for example, the illusion we have when we move our head that objects themselves are moving – if our judgment did not constantly set these appearances straight. According to Bernard, Cézanne "submerged his painting in ignorance and his mind in shadows." But one cannot really judge his painting in this way except by closing one's mind to half of what he said and one's eyes to what he painted.

It is clear from his conversations with Emile Bernard that Cézanne was always seeking to avoid the ready-made alternatives suggested to him: sensation versus judgment; the painter who sees against the painter who thinks; nature versus composition; primitivism as opposed to tradition. "We have to develop an optics," said Cézanne, "by which I mean a logical vision – that is, one with no element of the absurd." "Are you speaking of our nature?" asked Bernard. Cézanne: "It has to do with both." "But aren't nature and art different?" "I want to make them the same. Art is a personal apperception, which I embody in sensations and which I ask the understanding to organize into a painting."[1] But even these formulas put too much emphasis on the ordinary notions of "sensitivity" or "sensations" and "understanding" – which is why Cézanne could not convince by his arguments and preferred to paint instead. Rather than apply to his work dichotomies more appropriate to those who sustain traditions than to those men, philosophers or painters, who initiate these traditions, he preferred to search for the true meaning of painting, which is continually to question tradition. Cézanne did not think he had to choose between feeling and thought, between order and chaos. He did not want to separate the stable things which we see and the shifting way in which they appear; he wanted to depict matter as it takes on form, the birth of order through spontaneous organization. He makes a basic distinction not between "the senses" and "the understanding" but rather between the spontaneous organization of the things we perceive and the human organization of ideas and sciences. We see things; we agree about them; we are anchored in them; and it is with "nature" as our base that we construct our sciences. Cézanne wanted to paint this primordial world, and his pictures therefore seem to show nature pure, while photographs of the same landscapes suggest man's works, conveniences, and imminent presence. Cézanne never wished to "paint like a savage." He wanted to put intelligence, ideas, sciences, perspective, and tradition back in touch with the world of nature which they must comprehend. He wished, as he said, to confront the sciences with the nature "from which they came."

By remaining faithful to the phenomena in his investigations of perspective, Cézanne discovered what recent psychologists have come to formulate: the lived perspective, that which we actually perceive, is not a geometric or photographic one. The objects we see close at hand appear smaller, those far away seem larger than they do in a photograph. (This can be seen in a movie, where a train approaches and gets bigger much faster than a real train would under the same circumstances.) To say that a circle seen obliquely is seen as an ellipse is to substitute for our actual perception what we would see if we were cameras: in reality we see a form which oscillates around the ellipse without being an ellipse. In a portrait of Mme Cézanne, the border of the wallpaper on one side of her body does not form a straight line with that on the other: and indeed it is known that if a line passes beneath a wide strip of paper, the two visible segments appear dislocated. Gustave Geoffrey's table stretches into the bottom of the picture, and indeed, when our eye runs over a large surface, the images it successively receives are taken from different points of view, and the whole surface is warped. It is true that I freeze these distortions in repainting them on the canvas; I stop the spontaneous movement in which they pile up in perception and in which they tend toward the geometric perspective. This is also what happens with colors. Pink upon gray paper colors the background green. Academic painting shows the background as gray, assuming that the picture will produce the same effect of contrast as the real object. Impressionist painting uses green in the background in order to achieve a contrast as brilliant as that of objects in nature. Doesn't this falsify the color relationship? It would if it stopped there, but the painter's task is to modify all the other colors in the picture so that they take away from the green background its characteristics of a real color. Similarly, it is Cézanne's genius that when the over-all composition of the picture is seen globally, perspectival distortions are no longer visible in their own right but rather contribute, as they do in natural vision, to the impression of an emerging order, of an object in the act of appearing, organizing itself before our eyes. In the same way, the contour of an object conceived as a line encircling the object belongs not to the visible world but to geometry. If one outlines the shape of an apple with a continuous line, one makes an object of the shape, whereas the contour is rather the ideal limit toward which the sides of the apple recede in depth. Not to indicate any shape would be to deprive the objects of their identity. To trace just a single outline sacrifices depth – that is, the dimension in which the thing is presented not as spread out before us but as an inexhaustible reality full of reserves. That is why Cézanne follows the swelling of the object in modulated colors and indicates *several* outlines in blue. Rebounding among these, one's glance captures a shape that emerges from among them all, just as it does in perception. Nothing could be less arbitrary than these famous distortions which, moreover, Cézanne abandoned in his last period, after 1890, when he no longer filled his canvases with colors and when he gave up the closely-woven texture of his still lifes.

The outline should therefore be a result of the colors if the world is to be given in its true density. For the world is a mass without gaps, a system of colors across which the receding perspective, the outlines, angles, and curves are inscribed like lines of force; the spatial structure vibrates as it is formed. "The outline and the colors are no longer distinct from each other. To the extent that one paints, one outlines; the more the colors harmonize, the more the outline becomes precise. . . . When the color is at its richest, the form has reached plenitude." Cézanne does not try to use color to *suggest* the tactile sensations which would give shape and depth. These distinctions between touch and sight are unknown in primordial perception. It is only as a result of a science of the human body that we finally learn to distinguish between our senses. The lived object is not rediscovered or constructed on the basis of the contributions of the senses; rather, it presents itself to us from the start as the center from which these contributions radiate. We *see* the depth, the smoothness, the softness, the hardness of objects; Cézanne even claimed that we see their odor. If the painter is to express the world, the arrangement of his colors must carry with it this indivisible whole, or else his picture will only hint at things and will not give them in the imperious unity, the presence, the insurpassable plenitude which is for us the definition of the real. That is why each brushstroke must satisfy an infinite number of conditions. Cézanne sometimes pondered hours at a time before putting down a certain stroke, for, as Bernard said, each stroke must "contain the air, the light, the object, the composition, the character, the outline, and the style." Expressing what *exists* is an endless task.

Nor did Cézanne neglect the physiognomy of objects and faces: he simply wanted to capture it emerging from the color. Painting a face "as an object" is not to strip it of its "thought." "I realize that the painter interprets it," said Cézanne. "The painter is not an imbecile." But this interpretation should not be a reflection distinct from the act of seeing. "If I paint all the little blues and all the little maroons, I capture and convey his glance. Who gives a damn if they want to dispute how one can sadden a mouth or make a cheek smile by wedding a shaded green to a red." One's personality is seen and grasped in one's glance, which is, however, no more than a combination of colors. Other minds are given to us only as incarnate, as belonging to faces and gestures. Countering with the distinctions of soul and body, thought and vision is of no use here, for Cézanne returns to just that primordial experience from which these notions are derived and in which they are inseparable. The painter who conceptualizes and seeks the expression first misses the mystery – renewed every time we look at someone – of a person's appearing in nature. In *La Peau de chagrin* Balzac describes a "tablecloth white as a layer of newly fallen snow, upon which the place-settings rise symmetrically, crowned with blond rolls." "All through youth," said Cézanne, "I wanted to paint that, that tablecloth of new snow . . . Now I know that one must will only to paint the place-settings rising symmetrically and the blond rolls. If I paint 'crowned' I've had it, you understand? But if I really balance and shade my place-settings and rolls as they are in nature, then you can be sure that the crowns, the snow, and all the excitement will be there too."

We live in the midst of man-made objects, among tools, in houses, streets, cities, and most of the time we see them only through the human actions which put them to use. We become used to thinking that all of this exists necessarily and unshakeably. Cézanne's painting suspends these habits of thought and reveals the base of inhuman nature upon which man has installed himself. This is why Cézanne's people are strange, as if viewed by a creature of another species. Nature itself is stripped of the attributes which make it ready for animistic communions: there is no wind in the landscape, no movement on the Lac d'Annecy; the frozen objects hesitate as at the beginning of the world. It is an unfamiliar world in which one is uncomfortable and which forbids all human effusiveness. If one looks at the work of other painters after seeing Cézanne's paintings, one feels somehow relaxed, just as conversations resumed after a period of mourning mask the absolute change and give back to the survivors their solidity. But indeed only a human being is capable of such a vision which penetrates right to the root of things beneath the imposed order of humanity. Everything indicates that animals cannot *look at* things, cannot penetrate them in expectation of nothing but the truth. Emile Bernard's statement that a realistic painter is only an ape is therefore precisely the opposite of the truth, and one sees how Cézanne was able to revive the classical definition of art: man added to nature.

Cézanne's painting denies neither science nor tradition. He went to the Louvre every day when he was in Paris. He believed that one must learn how to paint and that the geometric study of planes and forms is a necessary part of this learning process. He inquired about the geological structure of his landscapes, convinced that these abstract relationships, expressed, however, in terms of the visible world, should affect the act of painting. The rules of anatomy and design are present in each stroke of his brush just as the rules of the game underlie each stroke of a tennis match. But what motivates the painter's movement can never be simply perspective or geometry or the laws governing color, or, for that matter, particular knowledge. Motivating all the movements from which a picture gradually emerges there can be only one thing: the landscape in its totality and in its absolute fullness, precisely what Cézanne called a "motif." He would start by discovering the geological foundations of the landscape; then, according to Mme Cézanne, he would halt and look at everything with widened eyes, "germinating" with the countryside. The task before him was, first to forget all he had ever learned from science and, second *through* these sciences to recapture the structure of the landscape as an emerging organism. To do this, all the partial views one catches sight of must be welded together; all that the eye's versatility disperses must be reunited; one must, as Gasquet put it, "join the wandering hands of nature." "A minute of the world is going by which must be painted in its full reality." His meditation would suddenly be consummated: "I have my *motif*," Cézanne would say, and he would explain that the landscape had to be centered neither too high nor too low, caught alive in a net which would let nothing escape. Then he began to paint all parts of the painting at the same time, using patches of color to surround his original charcoal sketch of the geological skeleton. The picture took on fullness and density; it grew in structure and balance; it came to maturity all at once. "The landscape thinks itself in me," he said, "and I am its consciousness." Nothing could be father from naturalism than this intuitive science. Art is not imitation, nor is it something manufactured according to the wishes of instinct or good taste. It is a process of expressing. Just as the function of words is to name – that is, to grasp the nature of what appears to us in a confused way and to place it before us as a recognizable object – so it is up to the painter, said Gasquet, to "objectify," "project," and "arrest." Words do not *look like* the things they designate; and a picture is not a *trompe-l'oeil*. Cézanne, in his own words, "wrote in painting what had never yet been painted, and turned it into painting once and for all." Forgetting the viscous, equivocal appearances, we go through them straight to the things they present. The painter recaptures and converts into visible objects what would, without him, remain walled up in the separate life of each consciousness: the vibration of appearances which is the cradle of things. Only one emotion is possible for this painter – the feeling of strangeness – and only one lyricism – that of the continual rebirth of existence.

Leonardo da Vinci's motto was persistent rigor, and all the classical works on the art of poetry tell us that the creation of art is no easy matter. Cézanne's difficulties – like those of Balzac or Mallarmé – are of a different nature. Balzac (probably taking Delacroix for his model) imagined a painter who wants to express life through the use of color alone and who keeps his masterpiece hidden. When Frenhofer dies, his friends find nothing but a chaos of colors and elusive lines, a wall of painting. Cézanne was moved to tears when he read *Le Chef-d'oeuvre inconnu* and declared that he himself was Frenhofer. The effort made by Balzac, himself obsessed with "realization," sheds light on Cézanne's. In *La Peau de chagrin* Balzac speaks of "a thought to be expressed," "a system to be built," "a science to be explained." He makes Louis Lambert, one of the abortive geniuses of the Comédie Humaine, say: "I am heading toward certain discoveries . . ., but how shall I describe the power which binds my hands, stops my mouth, and drags me in the opposite direction from my vocation?" To say that Balzac set himself to understand the society of his time is not sufficient. It is no superhuman task to describe the typical traveling salesman, to "dissect the teaching profession," or even to lay the foundations of a sociology. Once he had named the visible forces such as money and passion, once he had described the way they evidently work, Balzac wondered where it all led, what was the impetus behind it, what was the *meaning* of, for example, a Europe "whose efforts tend toward some unknown mystery of civilization." In short, he wanted to understand what interior force holds the world together and causes the proliferation of visible forms. Frenhofer had the same idea about the meaning of painting: "A hand is not simply part of the body, but the expression and continuation of a thought which must be captured and conveyed. . . . That is the real struggle! Many painters triumph instinctively, unaware of this theme of art. You draw a woman, but you do not see her." The artist is the one who arrests the spectacle in which most men take part without really seeing it and who makes it visible to the most "human" among them.

There is thus no art for pleasure's sake alone. One can invent pleasurable objects by linking old ideas in a new way and by presenting forms that have been seen before. This way of painting or speaking at second hand is what is generally meant by culture. Cézanne's or Balzac's artist is not satisfied to be a cultured animal but assimilates the culture down to its very foundations and gives it a new structure: he speaks as the first man spoke and paints as if no one had ever painted before.

What he expresses cannot, therefore, be the translation of a clearly defined thought, since such clear thoughts are those which have already been uttered by ourselves or by others. "Conception" cannot precede "execution." There is nothing but a vague fever before the act of artistic expression, and only the work itself, completed and understood, is proof that there was *something* rather than *nothing* to be said. Because he returns to the source of silent and solitary experience on which culture and the exchange of ideas have been built in order to know it, the artist launches his work just as a man once launched the first word, not knowing whether it will be anything more than a shout, whether it can detach itself from the flow of individual life in which it originates and give the independent existence of an identifiable *meaning* either to the future of that same individual life or to the monads coexisting with it or to the open community of future monads. The meaning of what the artist is going to say *does not exist* anywhere – not in things, which as yet have no meaning, nor in the artist himself, in his unformulated life. It summons one away from the already constituted reason in which "cultured men" are content to shut themselves, toward a reason which contains its own origins.

To Bernard's attempt to bring him back to human intelligence, Cézanne replied: "I am oriented toward the intelligence of the *Pater Omnipotens*." He was, in any case, oriented toward the idea or the project of an infinite Logos. Cézanne's uncertainty and solitude are not essentially explained by his nervous temperament but by the purpose of his work. Heredity may well have given him rich sensations, strong emotions, and a vague feeling of anguish or mystery which upset the life he might have wished for himself and which cut him off from men; but these qualities cannot create a work of art without the expressive act, and they can no more account for the difficulties than for the virtues of that act. Cézanne's difficulties are those of the first word. He considered himself powerless because he was not omnipotent, because he was not God and wanted nevertheless to portray the world, to change it completely into a spectacle, to make *visible* how the world *touches* us. A new theory of physics can be proven because calculations connect the idea or meaning of it with standards of measurement already common to all men. It is not enough for a painter like Cézanne, an artist, or a philosopher, to create and express an idea; they must also awaken the experiences which will make their idea take root in the consciousness of others. A successful work has the strange power to teach its own lesson. The reader or spectator who follows the clues of the book or painting, by setting up stepping stones and rebounding from side to side guided by the obscure clarity of a particular style, will end by discovering what the artist wanted to communicate. The painter can do no more than construct an image; he must wait for this image to come to life for other people. When it does, the work of art will have united these separate lives; it will no longer exist in only one of them like a stubborn dream or a persistent delirium, nor will it exist only in space as a colored piece of canvas. It will dwell undivided in several minds, with a claim on every possible mind like a perennial acquisition.

Thus, the "hereditary traits," the "influences" – the accidents in Cézanne's life – are the text which nature and history gave him to decipher. They give only the literal meaning of his work. But an artist's creations, like a man's free decisions, impose on this given a figurative sense which did not pre-exist them. If Cézanne's life seems to us to carry the seeds of his work within it, it is because we get to know his work first and see the circumstances of his life through it, charging them with a meaning borrowed from that work. If the givens for Cézanne which we have been enumerating, and which we spoke of as pressing conditions, were to figure in the web of projects which he was, they could have done so only by presenting themselves to him as *what* he had to live, leaving *how* to live it undetermined. An imposed theme at the start, they become, when replaced in the existence of which they are part, the monogram and the symbol of a life which freely interpreted itself.

But let us make no mistake about this freedom. Let us not imagine an abstract force which could superimpose its effects on life's "givens" or which cause breaches in life's development. Although it is certain that a man's life does not *explain* his work, it is equally certain that the two are connected. The truth is that *this work to be done called for this life*. From the very start, the only equilibrium in Cézanne's life came from the support of his future work. His life was the projection of his future work. The work to come is hinted at, but it would be wrong to take these hints for causes, although they do make a single adventure of his life and work. Here we are beyond causes and effects; both come together in the simultaneity of an eternal Cézanne who is at the same time the formula of what he wanted to be and what he wanted to do. There is a rapport between Cézanne's schizoid temperament and his work because the work reveals a metaphysical sense of the disease: a way of seeing the world reduced to the totality of frozen appearances, with all expressive values suspended. Thus the illness ceases to be an absurd fact and a fate and becomes a general possibility of human existence. It becomes so when this existence bravely faces one of its paradoxes, the phenomenon of expression. In this sense to be schizoid and to be Cézanne come to the same thing. It is therefore impossible to separate creative liberty from that behavior, as far as possible from deliberate, already evident in Cézanne's first gestures as a child and in the way he reacted to things. The meaning Cézanne gave to objects and faces in his paintings presented itself to him in the world as it appeared to him. Cézanne simply released this meaning: it was the objects and the faces themselves as he saw them which demanded to be painted, and Cézanne simply expressed what they *wanted* to say. How, then, can any freedom be involved? True, the conditions of existence can only affect consciousness by way of a detour through the *raisons d'être* and the justifications consciousness offers to itself. We can only see what we are by looking ahead of ourselves, through the lens of our aims, and so our life always has the form of a project or of a choice and therefore seems spontaneous. But to say that we are from the start our way of aiming at a particular future would be to say that our project has already stopped with our first ways of being, that the choice has already been made for us with our first breath. If we experience no external constraints, it is because we are our whole exterior. That eternal Cézanne whom we first saw emerge and who then brought upon the human Cézanne the events and influences which seemed *exterior* to him, and who planned all that happened to him – that attitude toward men and toward the world which was not chosen through deliberation – free as it is from external causes, is it free in respect to itself? Is the choice not pushed back beyond life, and can a choice exist where there is as yet no clearly articulated field of possibilities, only one probability and, as it were, only one temptation? If I am a certain project from birth, the given and the created are indistinguishable in me, and it is therefore impossible to name a single gesture which is merely hereditary or innate, a single gesture which is not spontaneous – but also impossible to name a single gesture which is absolutely new in regard to that way of being in the world which, from the very beginning, is myself. There is no difference between saying that our life is completely constructed and that it is completely given. If there is a true liberty, it can only come about in the course of our life by our going beyond our original situation and yet not ceasing to be the same: this is the problem. Two things are certain about freedom: that we are never determined and yet that we never change, since, looking back on what we were, we can always find hints of what we have become. It is up to us to understand both these things simultaneously, as well as the way freedom dawns in us without breaking our bonds with the world.

Such bonds are always there, even and above all when we refuse to admit they exist. Inspired by the paintings of Da Vinci, Valéry described a monster of pure freedom, without mistresses, creditors, anecdotes, or adventures. No dream intervenes between himself and the things themselves; nothing taken for granted supports his certainties; and he does not read his fate in any favorite image, such as Pascal's abyss. Instead of struggling against the monsters he has understood what makes them tick, has disarmed them by his attention, and has reduced them to the state of known things. "Nothing could be more free, that is, less human, than his judgments on love and death. He hints at them in a few fragments from his notebooks: 'In the full force of its passion,' he says more or less explicitly, 'love is something so ugly that the human race would die out (*la natura si perderebbe*) if lovers could see what they were doing.' This contempt is brought out in various sketches, since the leisurely examination of certain things is, after all, the height of scorn. Thus, he now and again draws anatomical unions, frightful cross-sections of love's very act."[2] He has complete mastery of his means, he does what he wants, going at will from knowledge to life with a superior elegance. Everything he did was done knowingly, and the artistic process, like the act of breathing or living, does not go beyond his knowledge. He has discovered the "central attitude," on the basis of which it is equally possible to know, to act, and to create because action and life, when turned into exercises, are not contrary to detached knowledge. He is an "intellectual power"; he is a "man of the mind."

Let us look more closely. For Leonardo there was no revelation; as Valéry said, no abyss yawned at his right hand. Undoubtedly true. But in "Saint Anne, the Virgin, and Child," the Virgin's cloak suggests a vulture where it touches the face of the Child. There is that fragment on the flight of birds where Da Vinci suddenly interrupts himself to pursue a childhood memory: "I seem to have been destined to be especially concerned with the vulture, for one of the first things I remember about my childhood is how a vulture came to me when I was still in the cradle, forced open my mouth with its tail, and struck me several times between the lips with it."[3] So even this transparent consciousness has its enigma, whether truly a child's memory or a fantasy of the grown man. It does not come out of nowhere, nor does it sustain itself alone. We are caught in a secret history, in a forest of symbols. One would surely protest if Freud were to decipher the riddle from what we know about the meaning of the flight of birds and about *fellatio* fantasies and their relation to the period of nursing. But it is still a fact that to the ancient Egyptians the vulture was the symbol of maternity because they believed all vultures were female and that they were impregnated by the wind. It is also a fact that the Church Fathers used this legend to refute, on the grounds of natural history, those who were unwilling to believe in a virgin birth, and it is probable that Leonardo came across the legend in the course of his endless reading. He found in it the symbol of his own fate: he was the illegitimate son of a rich notary who married the noble Donna Albiera the very year Leonardo was born. Having no children by her, he took Leonardo into his home when the boy was five. Thus Leonardo spent the first four years of his life with his mother, the deserted peasant girl; he was a child without a father, and he got to know the world in the sole company of that unhappy mother who seemed to have miraculously created him. If we now recall that he was never known to have a mistress or even to have felt anything like passion; that he was accused – but acquitted – of homosexuality; that his diary, which tells us nothing about many other, larger expenses, notes with meticulous detail the costs of his mother's burial, as well as the cost of linen and clothing for two of his students – then we are on the verge of saying that Leonardo loved only one woman, his mother, and that this love left no room for anything but the platonic tenderness he felt for the young boys surrounding him. In the four decisive years of his childhood he formed a basic attachment which he had to give up when he was recalled to his father's home and into which he had poured all his resources of love and all his power of abandon. His thirst for life could only be turned toward the investigation and knowledge of the world, and, since he himself had been "*detached*," he had to become that intellectual power, that man who was all mind, that stranger among men. Indifferent, incapable of any strong indignation, love or hate, he left his paintings unfinished to devote his time to bizarre experiments; he became a person in whom his contemporaries sensed a mystery. It was as if Leonardo had never quite grown up, as if all the places in his heart had already been spoken for, as if the spirit of investigation was a way for him to escape from life, as if he had invested all his power of assent in the first years of his life and had remained true to his childhood right to the end. His games were those of a child. Vasari tells how "he made up a wax paste and, during his walks, he would model from it very delicate animals, hollow and filled with air; when he breathed into them, they would float; when the air had escaped, they would fall to the ground. When the wine-grower from Belvedere found a very unusual lizard, Leonardo made wings for it out of the skin of other lizards and filled these wings with mercury so that they waved and quivered whenever the lizard moved; he likewise made eyes, a beard, and horns for it in the same way, tamed it, put it in a box, and used this lizard to terrify his friends."[4] He left his work unfinished, just as his father had abandoned him. He paid no heed to authority and trusted only nature and his own judgment in matters of knowledge, as is often the case with people who have not been raised in the shadow of a father's intimidating and protective power. Thus even this pure power of examination, this solitude, this curiosity – which are the essence of mind – became Leonardo's only in reference to his history. At the height of his freedom he was, *in that very freedom*, the child he had been; he was detached in one way only because he was attached in another. Becoming a pure consciousness is just another way of taking a stand about the world and other people; Leonardo learned this attitude in assimilating the situation which his birth and childhood had made for him. There can be no consciousness that is not sustained by its primordial involvement in life and by the manner of this involvement.

Whatever is arbitrary in Freud's *explanations* cannot in this context discredit *psychoanalytical intuition*. True, the reader is stopped more than once by the lack of evidence. Why this and not something else? The question seems all the more pressing since Freud often offers several interpretations, each symptom being "over-determined" according to him. Finally, it is obvious that a doctrine which brings in sexuality everywhere cannot, by the rules of inductive logic, establish its effectiveness anywhere, since, excluding all differential cases beforehand, it deprives itself of any counter-evidence. This is how one triumphs over psychoanalysis, but only on paper. For if the suggestions of the analyst can never be proven, neither can they be eliminated: how would it be possible to credit chance with the complex correspondences which the psychoanalyst discovers between the child and the adult? How can we deny that psychoanalysis has taught us to notice echoes, allusions, repetitions from one moment of life to another – a concatenation we would not dream of doubting if Freud had stated the theory behind it correctly? Unlike the natural sciences, psychoanalysis was not meant to give us necessary relations of cause and effect but to point to motivational relationships which are in principle simply possible. We should not take Leonardo's fantasy of the vulture, or the infantile past which it masks, for a force which determined his future. Rather, it is like the words of the oracle, an ambiguous symbol which applies in advance to several possible chains of events. To be more precise: in every life, one's birth and one's past define categories or basic dimensions which do not impose any particular act but which can be found in all. Whether Leonardo yielded to his childhood or whether he wished to flee from it, he could never have been other than he was. The very decisions which transform us are always made in reference to a factual situation; such a situation can of course be accepted or refused, but it cannot fail to give us our impetus nor to be for us, as a situation "to be accepted" or "to be refused," the incarnation for us of the value we give to it. If it is the aim of psychoanalysis to describe this exchange between future and past and to show how each life muses over riddles whose final meaning is nowhere written down, then we have no right to demand inductive rigor from it. The psychoanalyst's hermeneutic musing, which multiplies the communications between us and ourselves, which takes sexuality as the symbol of existence and existence as symbol of sexuality, and which looks in the past for the meaning of the future and in the future for the meaning of the past, is better suited than rigorous induction to the circular movement of our lives, where the future rests on the past, the past on the future, and where everything symbolizes everything else. Psychoanalysis does not make freedom impossible; it teaches us to think of this freedom concretely, as a creative repetition of ourselves, always, in retrospect, faithful to ourselves.

Thus it is true both that the life of an author can teach us nothing and that – if we know how to interpret it – we can find everything in it, since it opens onto his work. Just as we may observe the movements of an unknown animal without understanding the law which inhabits and controls them, so Cézanne's observers did not guess the transmutations which he imposed on events and experiences; they were blind to *his* significance, to that glow from out of nowhere which surrounded him from time to time. But he himself was never at the center of himself: nine days out of ten all he saw around him was the wretchedness of his empirical life and of his unsuccessful attempts, the leftovers of an unknown party. Yet it was in the world that he had to realize his freedom, with colors upon a canvas. It was on the approval of others that he had to wait for the proof of his worth. That is the reason he questioned the picture emerging beneath his hand, why he hung on the glances other people directed toward his canvas. That is the reason he never finished working. We never get away from our life. We never see our ideas or our freedom face to face.

Notes

1 Cézanne's conversations with Bernard are recorded in *Souvenirs sur Paul Cézanne*, Paris, 1912 (trans.).

2 "Introduction à la méthode de Léonard de Vinci," *Variété*, p. 185. (English translation by Thomas McGreevy, *Introduction to the Method of Leonardo da Vinci*, London, 1929.)

3 Sigmund Freud, *Un souvenir d'enfance de Léonard de Vinci*, p. 65. (English translation by A. A. Brill, *Leonardo da Vinci: A Study in Psychosexuality*, New York, 1947.)

4 *Ibid.*, p. 189.

EYE AND MIND (from *The Primacy of Perception*, pp. 159–90 in the 1964 translation)[1]

'Eye and mind' was the last paper Merleau-Ponty published (in 1961; it was written in 1960). Thus it dates from the same period as the chapter from The Visible and the Invisible *reproduced above ('The Intertwining – The Chiasm', pp. 248–71) and there are many connections between them; for example he writes here of the body as 'an intertwining of vision and movement' (p. 294). Indeed his main aim is to discuss what he calls the 'metaphysical significance' (p. 310) of painting in the context of his own account of perception as the 'dehiscence of Being' (p. 318), whereby the visible makes present a certain absence, its rear side, its inside, its past, etc. (at this point Merleau-Ponty's thought connects with a line of thought which, in a different idiom, Derrida has called 'différance'[1]).*

In the central section of the paper Merleau-Ponty discusses critically the account of images which Descartes advances. This is based upon a theory of vision which, in effect, treats vision as a mode of thought in which the soul deciphers the corporeal images given through the eyes. Similarly, therefore, painting is thought of as an intellectual operation, the production of drawings whose spatial structure resembles that of the things depicted. As Merleau-Ponty observes, for painting so conceived, depth is always a problem; but, more deeply, he observes, Descartes cannot explain how the soul is located in space without reference to its body, and in particular to the way in which the body organises this space, i.e. without reference to real vision, and not just to thought about visual images. At this point, then, even the Cartesian account points to the need for a new conception of space, one that starts out from our bodily sense fields.

We are now back with Merleau-Ponty's late account of the reversibility of our body, the touching which is tangible, the seeing which is visible (voyant-visible). How then does painting, and especially modern painting, fit on to this? Merleau-Ponty's thought is elusive, but his claim seems to be that

once we have banished Cartesian objectivism, we can make sense of paint-
ing as the attempt to express the ways in which the visible world forms itself
to our eyes, 'radiating' its shape, colour and even movement (Merleau-Ponty
notes that whereas the attempt to catch movement by still photographs
normally fails – though he does not consider the use of blurred images –
great painters can express the durée *in which movement takes place). So*
painting is the attempt to catch the ways in which the visible world shows
itself to us, almost looking back at us as it reverses our vision of it; and the
lesson to be learnt from painting is that the visible world is a world that
opens out indefinitely before our eyes, which lend themselves to its expres-
sion, just as the painter 'lends his body to the world to change it into a
painting' (p. 294).

The translator added many helpful comments as notes to his translation, and
these are retained here along with Merleau-Ponty's own notes.

Note

1 See J. Derrida, 'Differance', in *Speech and Phenomena*, trans. D. B. Allison,
   Evanston, IL: Northwestern University Press, 1973.

.. ..

What I am trying to translate to you is more mysterious; it is
entwined in the very roots of being, in the impalpable source of
sensations.

J. Gasquet, *Cézanne*

1

Science manipulates things and gives up living in them. It makes its
own limited models of things; operating upon these indices or variables
to effect whatever transformations are permitted by their definition, it
comes face to face with the real world only at rare intervals. Science is
and always has been that admirably active, ingenious, and bold way of
thinking whose fundamental bias is to treat everything as though it
were an object-in-general – as though it meant nothing to us and yet was
predestined for our own use.

But classical science clung to a feeling for the opaqueness of the
world, and it expected through its constructions to get back into the
world. For this reason classical science felt obliged to seek a transcendent or transcendental foundation for its operations. Today we find – not
in science but in a widely prevalent philosophy of the sciences –

an entirely new approach Constructive scientific activities see themselves and represent themselves to be autonomous, and their thinking deliberately reduces itself to a set of data-collecting techniques which it has invented. To think is thus to test out, to operate, to transform – on the condition that this activity is regulated by an experimental control that admits only the most "worked-out" phenomena, more likely produced by the apparatus than recorded by it. From this state of affairs arise all sorts of vagabond endeavors.

Today more than ever, science is sensitive to intellectual fads and fashions. When a model has succeeded in one order of problems, it is tried out everywhere else. At the present time, for example, our embryology and biology are full of "gradients." Just how these differ from what tradition called "order" or "totality" is not at all clear. This question, however, is not raised; it is not even permitted. The gradient is a net we throw out to sea, without knowing what we will haul back in it. Or again, it is the slender twig upon which unforeseeable crystallizations will form. Certainly this freedom of operation will serve well to overcome many a pointless dilemma – provided only that we ask from time to time why the apparatus works in one place and fails in others. For all its fluency, science must nevertheless understand itself; it must see itself as a construction based on a brute, existent world and not claim for its blind operations that constituting value which "concepts of nature" were able to have in an idealist philosophy. To say that the world is, by nominal definition, the object *x* of our operations is to treat the scientist's knowledge as if it were absolute, as if everything that is and has been was meant only to enter the laboratory. Thinking "operationally" has become a sort of absolute artificialism, such as we see in the ideology of cybernetics, where human creations are derived from a natural information process, itself conceived on the model of human machines. If this kind of thinking were to extend its reign to man and history; if, pretending to ignore what we know of them through our own situations, it were to set out to construct man and history on the basis of a few abstract indices (as a decadent psychoanalysis and a decadent culturalism have done in the United States) – then, since man really becomes the *manipulandum* he takes himself to be, we enter into a cultural regimen where there is neither truth nor falsity concerning man and history, into a sleep, or a nightmare, from which there is no awakening.

Scientific thinking, a thinking which looks on from above, and thinks of the object-in-general, must return to the "there is" which underlies it; to the site, the soil of the sensible and opened world such as it is in our life and for our body – not that possible body which we may legitimately think of as an information machine but that actual body I call mine, this sentinel standing quietly at the command of my words and my acts. Further, *associated bodies* must be brought forward along with my body – the "others," not merely as my congeners, as the zoologist says, but the others who haunt me and whom I haunt; the "others" along *with* whom I haunt a single, present, and actual Being as no animal ever haunted those beings of his own species, locale, or habitat. In this primordial historicity, science's agile and improvisatory thought will learn to ground itself upon things themselves and upon itself, and will once more become philosophy . . .

But art, especially painting, draws upon this fabric of brute meaning which activism [or operationalism – *Trans.*] would prefer to ignore. Art and only art does so in full innocence. From the writer and the philosopher, in contrast, we want opinions and advice. We will not allow them to hold the world suspended. We want them to take a stand; they cannot waive the responsibilities of men who speak. Music, at the other extreme, is too far beyond the world and the designatable to depict anything but certain outlines of Being – its ebb and flow, its growth, its upheavals, its turbulence.

Only the painter is entitled to look at everything without being obliged to appraise what he sees. For the painter, we might say, the watchwords of knowledge and action lose their meaning and force. Political regimes which denounce "degenerate" painting rarely destroy paintings. They hide them, and one senses here an element of "one never knows" amounting almost to a recognition. The reproach of escapism is seldom aimed at the painter; we do not hold it against Cézanne that he lived hidden away at Estaque during the war of 1870. And we recall with respect his "C'est effrayant, la vie," even when the lowliest student, ever since Nietzsche, would flatly reject philosophy if it did not teach how to live fully [à *être de grands vivants*]. It is as if in the painter's calling there were some urgency above all other claims on him. Strong or frail in life, he is incontestably sovereign in his own rumination of the world. With no other technique than what his eyes and hands discover in seeing and painting, he persists in drawing from this world, with its din of history's glories and scandals, *canvases* which will hardly add to the angers or the hopes of man – and no one complains.

What, then, is this secret science which he has or which he seeks? That dimension which lets Van Gogh say he must go "further on"? What is this fundamental of painting, perhaps of all culture?

2

The painter "takes his body with him," says Valéry. Indeed we cannot imagine how a *mind* could paint. It is by lending his body to the world that the artist changes the world into paintings. To understand these transubstantiations we must go back to the working, actual body – not the body as a chunk of space or a bundle of functions but that body which is an intertwining of vision and movement.

I have only to see something to know how to reach it and deal with it, even if I do not know how this happens in the nervous machine. My mobile body makes a difference in the visible world, being a part of it; that is why I can steer it through the visible. Conversely, it is just as true that vision is attached to movement. We see only what we look at. What would vision be without eye movement? And how could the movement of the eyes bring things together if the movement were blind? If it were only a reflex? If it did not have its antennae, its clairvoyance? If vision were not prefigured in it?

In principle all my changes of place figure in a corner of my landscape; they are recorded on the map of the visible. Everything I see is in principle within my reach, at least within reach of my sight, and is marked upon the map of the "I can." Each of the two maps is complete. The visible world and the world of my motor projects are each total parts of the same Being.

This extraordinary overlapping, which we never think about sufficiently, forbids us to conceive of vision as an operation of thought that would set up before the mind a picture or a representation of the world, a world of immanence and of ideality. Immersed in the visible by his body, itself visible, the see-er does not appropriate what he sees; he merely approaches it by looking, he opens himself to the world. And on its side, this world of which he is a part is not *in itself,* or matter. My movement is not a decision made by the mind, an absolute doing which would decree, from the depths of a subjective retreat, some change of place miraculously executed in extended space. It is the natural consequence and the maturation of my vision. I say of a thing that it is moved; but my body moves itself, my movement deploys itself. It is not ignorant of itself; it is not blind for itself; it radiates from a self . . .

The enigma is that my body simultaneously sees and is seen. That which looks at all things can also look at itself and recognize, in what it sees, the "other side" of its power of looking. It sees itself seeing; it touches itself touching; it is visible and sensitive for itself. It is not a self through transparence, like thought, which only thinks its object by assimilating it, by constituting it, by transforming it into thought. It is a self through confusion, narcissism, through inherence of the one who sees in that which he sees, and through inherence of sensing in the sensed – a self, therefore, that is caught up in things, that has a front and a back, a past and a future. . . .

This initial paradox cannot but produce others. Visible and mobile, my body is a thing among things; it is caught in the fabric of the world, and its cohesion is that of a thing. But because it moves itself and sees, it holds things in a circle around itself.[2] Things are an annex or prolongation of itself; they are incrusted into its flesh, they are part of its full definition; the world is made of the same stuff as the body. This way of turning things around [ces renversements], these antinomies,[3] are different ways of saying that vision happens among, or is caught in, things – in that place where something visible undertakes to see, becomes visible for itself by virtue of the sight of things; in that place where there persists, like the mother water in crystal, the undividedness [l'indivision] of the sensing and the sensed.

This interiority no more precedes the material arrangement of the human body than it results from it. What if our eyes were made in such a way as to prevent our seeing any part of our body, or if some baneful arrangement of the body were to let us move our hands over things, while preventing us from touching our own body? Or what if, like certain animals, we had lateral eyes with no cross blending of visual fields? Such a body would not reflect itself; it would be an almost adamantine body, not really flesh, not really the body of a human being. There would be no humanity.

But humanity is not produced as the effect of our articulations or by the way our eyes are implanted in us (still less by the existence of mirrors which could make our entire body visible to us). These contingencies and others like them, without which mankind would not exist, do not by simple summation bring it about that there is a single man.

The body's animation is not the assemblage or juxtaposition of its parts. Nor is it a question of a mind or spirit coming down from somewhere else into an automaton; this would still suppose that the body itself is without an inside and without a "self." There is a human body when, between the seeing and the seen, between touching and the touched, between one eye and the other, between hand and hand, a blending of some sort takes place – when the spark is lit between sensing and sensible, lighting the fire that will not stop burning until some accident of the body will undo what no accident would have sufficed to do. . . .

Once this strange system of exchanges is given, we find before us all the problems of painting. These exchanges illustrate the enigma of the body, and this enigma justifies them. Since things and my body are made of the same stuff, vision must somehow take place in them; their manifest visibility must be repeated in the body by a secret visibility. "Nature is on the inside," says Cézanne. Quality, light, color, depth, which are there before us, are there only because they awaken an echo in our body and because the body welcomes them.

Things have an internal equivalent in me; they arouse in me a carnal formula of their presence. Why shouldn't these [correspondences] in their turn give rise to some [external] visible shape in which anyone else would recognize those motifs which support his own inspection of the world? Thus there appears a "visible" of the second power, a carnal essence or icon of the first. It is not a faded copy, a *trompe-l'oeil*, or another *thing*. The animals painted on the walls of Lascaux are not there in the same way as the fissures and limestone formations. But they are not *elsewhere*. Pushed forward here, held back there, held up by the wall's mass they use so adroitly, they spread around the wall without ever breaking from their elusive moorings in it. I would be at great pains to say *where* is the painting I am looking at. For I do not look at it as I do at a thing; I do not fix it in its place. My gaze wanders in it as in the halos of Being. It is more accurate to say that I see according to it, or with it, than that I *see it*.

The word "image" is in bad repute because we have thoughtlessly believed that a design was a tracing, a copy, a second thing, and that the mental image was such a design, belonging among our private bric-a-brac. But if in fact it is nothing of the kind, then neither the design nor the painting belongs to the in-itself any more than the image does. They are the inside of the outside and the outside of the inside, which the duplicity of feeling [*le sentir*] makes possible and without which we would never understand the quasi presence and imminent visibility which make up the whole problem of the imaginary. The picture and the actor's mimicry are not devices to be borrowed from the real world in order to signify prosaic things which are absent. For the imaginary is much nearer to, and much farther away from, the actual – nearer because it is in my body as a diagram of the life of the actual, with all its pulp and carnal obverse [*son envers charnel*] exposed to view for the first time. In this sense, Giacometti[4] says energetically, "What interests me in all paintings is resemblance – that is, what is resemblance for me: something which makes me discover more of the world." And the imaginary is much farther away from the actual because the painting is an analogue or likeness only according to the body; because it does *not* present the *mind* with an occasion to rethink the constitutive relations of things; because, rather, it offers to our *sight* [*regard*], so that it might join with them, the inward traces of vision, and because it offers to vision its inward tapestries, the imaginary texture of the real.

Shall we say, then, that we look out from the inside, that there is a third eye which sees the paintings and even the mental images, as we used to speak of a third ear which grasped messages from the outside through the noises they caused inside us? But how would this help us when the real problem is to understand how it happens that our fleshly eyes are already much more than receptors for light rays, colors, and lines? They are computers of the world, which have the gift of the visible as it was once said that the inspired man had the gift of tongues. Of course this gift is earned by exercise; it is not in a few months, or in solitude, that a painter comes into full possession of his vision. But that is not the question; precocious or belated, spontaneous or cultivated in museums, his vision in any event learns only by seeing and learns only from itself. The eye sees the world, sees what inadequacies [*manques*] keep the world from being a painting, sees what keeps a painting from being itself, sees – on the palette – the colors awaited by the painting, and sees, once it is done, the painting that answers to all these inadequacies just as it sees the paintings of others as other answers to other inadequacies.

It is no more possible to make a restrictive inventory of the visible than it is to catalogue the possible usages of a language or even its vocabulary and devices. The eye is an instrument that moves itself, a means which invents its own ends; it is *that which* has been moved by some impact of the world, which it then restores to the visible through the offices of an agile hand.

In whatever civilization it is born, from whatever beliefs, motives, or thoughts, no matter what ceremonies surround it – and even when it appears devoted to something else – from Lascaux to our time, pure or impure, figurative or not, painting celebrates no other enigma but that of visibility.

What we have just said amounts to a truism. The painter's world is a visible world, nothing but visible: a world almost demented because it is complete when it is yet only partial. Painting awakens and carries to its highest pitch a delirium which is vision itself, for to see is *to have at a distance*; painting spreads this strange possession to all aspects of Being, which must in some fashion become visible in order to enter into the work of art. When, apropos of Italian painting, the young Berenson spoke of an evocation of tactile values, he could hardly have been more mistaken; painting evokes nothing, least of all the tactile. What it does is much different, almost the inverse. It gives visible existence to what profane vision believes to be invisible; thanks to it we do not need a "muscular sense" in order to possess the voluminosity of the world. This voracious vision, reaching beyond the "visual givens," opens upon a texture of Being of which the discrete sensorial messages are only the punctuations or the caesurae. The eye lives in this texture as a man lives in his house.

Let us remain within the visible in the narrow and prosaic sense. The painter, whatever he is, *while he is painting* practices a magical theory of vision. He is obliged to admit that objects before him pass into him or else that, according to Malebranche's sarcastic dilemma, the mind goes out through the eyes to wander among objects; for the painter never ceases adjusting his clairvoyance to them. (It makes no difference if he does not paint from "nature"; he paints, in any case, because he has seen, because the world has at least once emblazoned in him the ciphers of the visible.) He must affirm, as one philosopher has said, that vision is a mirror or concentration of the universe or that, in another's words, the *idios kosmos* opens by virtue of vision upon a *koinos kosmos*; in short, that the same thing is both out there in the world and here in the heart of vision – the same or, if one prefers, a *similar* thing, but according to an efficacious similarity which is the parent, the genesis, the metamorphosis of Being in his vision. It is the mountain itself which from out there makes itself seen by the painter; it is the mountain that he interrogates with his gaze.

What exactly does he ask of it? To unveil the means, visible and not otherwise, by which it makes itself a mountain before our eyes: Light, lighting, shadows, reflections, color, all the objects of his quest are not altogether real objects; like ghosts, they have only visual existence. In fact they exist only at the threshold of profane vision; they are not seen by everyone. The painter's gaze asks them what they do to suddenly cause something to be and to be *this* thing, what they do to compose this worldly talisman and to make us see the visible.

We see that the hand pointing to us in *The Nightwatch* is truly there only when we see that its shadow on the captain's body presents it simultaneously in profile. The spatiality of the captain lies at the meeting place of two lines of sight which are incompossible and yet together. Everyone with eyes has at some time or other witnessed this play of shadows, or something like it, and has been made by it to see a space and the things included therein. But it works in us without us; it hides itself in making the object visible. To see the object, it is necessary *not* to see the play of shadows and light around it. The visible in the profane sense forgets its premises; it rests upon a total visibility which is to be re-created and which liberates the phantoms captive in it. The moderns, as we know, have liberated many others; they have added many a blank note [*note sourde*] to the official gamut of our means of seeing. But the interrogation of painting in any case looks toward this secret and feverish genesis of things in our body.

And so it is not a question asked of someone who doesn't know by someone who does – the schoolmaster's question. The question comes from one who does not know, and it is addressed to a vision, a seeing, which knows everything and which we do not make, for it makes itself in us. Max Ernst (with the surrealists) says rightly, "Just as the role of the poet since [Rimbaud's] famous *Lettre du voyant* consists in writing under the dictation of what is being thought, of what articulates itself in him, the role of the painter is to grasp and project what is seen in him."[5] The painter lives in fascination. The actions most proper to him – those gestures, those paths which he alone can trace and which will be revelations to others (because the others do not lack what he lacks or in the same way) – to him they seem to emanate from the things themselves, like the patterns of the constellations.

Inevitably the roles between him and the visible are reversed. That is why so many painters have said that things look at them. As André Marchand says, after Klee: "In a forest, I have felt many times over that it was not I who looked at the forest. Some days I felt that the trees were looking at me, were speaking to me. . . . I was there, listening. . . . I think that the painter must be penetrated by the universe and not want to penetrate it. . . . I expect to be inwardly submerged, buried. Perhaps I paint to break out."[6]

We speak of "inspiration," and the word should be taken literally. There really is inspiration and expiration of Being, action and passion so slightly discernible that it becomes impossible to distinguish between what sees and what is seen, what paints and what is painted.

It can be said that a human is born at the instant when something that was only virtually visible, inside the mother's body, becomes at one and the same time visible for itself and for us. The painter's vision is a continued birth.

In paintings themselves we could seek a figured philosophy[7] of vision – its iconography, perhaps. It is no accident, for example, that frequently in Dutch paintings (as in many others) an empty interior is "digested" by the "round eye of the mirror."[8] This prehuman way of seeing things is the painter's way. More completely than lights, shadows, and reflections, the mirror image anticipates, within things, the labor of vision. Like all other technical objects, such as signs and tools, the mirror arises upon the open circuit [that goes] from seeing body to visible body. Every technique is a "technique of the body." A technique outlines and amplifies the metaphysical structure of our flesh. The mirror appears because I am seeing-visible [*voyant-visible*], because there is a reflexivity of the sensible: the mirror translates and reproduces that reflexivity. My outside completes itself in and through the sensible. Everything I have that is most secret goes into this *visage*, this face, this flat and closed entity about which my reflection in the water has already made me puzzle. Schilder[9] observes that, smoking a pipe before a mirror, I feel the sleek, burning surface of the wood not only where my fingers are but also in those ghostlike fingers, those merely visible fingers inside the mirror. The mirror's ghost lies outside my body, and by the same token my own body's "invisibility" can invest the other bodies I see.[10] Hence my body can assume segments derived from the body of another, just as my substance passes into them; man is mirror for man. The mirror itself is the instrument of a universal magic that changes things into a spectacle, spectacles into things, myself into another, and another into myself. Artists have often mused upon mirrors because beneath this "mechanical trick," they recognized, just as they did in the case of the trick of perspective,[11] the metamorphosis of seeing and seen which defines both our flesh and the painter's vocation. This explains why they have so often liked to draw themselves in the act of painting (they still do – witness Matisse's drawings), adding to what *they* saw then, what *things* saw of them. It is as if they were claiming that there is a total or absolute vision, outside of which there is nothing and which closes itself over them. Where in the realm of the understanding can we place these occult operations, together with the potions and idols they concoct? What can we call them? Consider, as Sartre did in *Nausea*, the smile of a long-dead king which continues to exist and to reproduce itself [*de se produire et de se reproduire*] on the surface of a canvas. It is too little to say that it is there as an image or essence; it is there as itself, as that which was always most alive about it, even now as I look at the painting. The "world's instant" that Cézanne wanted to paint, an instant long since passed away, is still thrown at us by his paintings.[12] His Mount Saint Victor is made and remade from one end of the world to the other in a way that is different from, but no less energetic than, that of the hard rock above Aix. Essence and existence, imaginary and real, visible and invisible – a painting mixes up all our categories in laying out its oneiric universe of carnal essences, of effective likenesses, of mute meanings.

3

How crystal clear everything would be in our philosophy if only we could exorcise these specters, make illusions or object-less perceptions out of them, keep them on the edge of a world that doesn't equivocate!

Descartes's *Dioptric* is an attempt to do just that. It is the breviary of a thought that wants no longer to abide in the visible and so decides to construct the visible according to a model-in-thought. It is worthwhile to remember this attempt and its failure.

Here there is no concern to cling to vision. The problem is to know "how it happens," but only so far as it is necessary to invent, whenever the need arises, certain "artificial organs"[13] which correct it. We are to reason not so much upon the light we see as upon the light which, from outside, enters our eyes and commands our vision. And for that we are to rely upon "two or three comparisons which help us to conceive it [light]" in such a way as to explain its known properties and to deduce others.[14] The question being so formulated, it is best to think of light as an action by contact – not unlike the action of things upon the blind man's cane. The blind, says Descartes, "see with their hands."[15] The Cartesian concept of vision is modeled after the sense of touch.

At one swoop, then, he removes action at a distance and relieves us of that ubiquity which is the whole problem of vision (as well as its peculiar virtue). Why should we henceforth puzzle over reflections and mirrors? These unreal duplications are a class of things; they are real effects like a ball's bouncing. If the reflection resembles the thing itself, it is because this reflection acts upon the eyes more or less as a thing would. It deceives the eye by engendering a perception which has no object but which does not affect our idea of the world. In the world there is the thing itself, and outside this thing itself there is that other thing which is only reflected light rays and which happens to have an ordered correspondence with the real thing; there are two individuals, then, bound together externally by causality. As far as the thing and its mirror image are concerned, their resemblance is only an external denomination; the resemblance belongs to thought. [What for us is] the "cross-eyed" [*louche*] relationship of resemblance is – in the things – a clear relationship of projection.

A Cartesian does not see *himself* in the mirror; he sees a dummy, an "outside," which, he has every reason to believe, other people see in the very same way but which, no more for himself than for others, is not a body in the flesh. His "image" in the mirror is an effect of the mechanics of things. If he recognizes himself in it, if he thinks it "looks like him," it is his thought that weaves this connection. The mirror image is nothing that belongs to him.

Icons lose their powers.[16] As vividly as an etching "represents" forests, towns, men, battles, storms, it does not resemble them. It is only a bit of ink put down here and there on the paper. A figure flattened down onto a plane surface scarcely retains the forms of things; it is a deformed figure that *ought* to be deformed – the square becomes a lozenge, the circle an oval – in order to represent the object. It is an image only as long as it does not resemble its object. If not through resemblance, how, then, does it act? It "excites our thought" to "conceive," as do signs and words "which in no way resemble the things they signify."[17] The etching gives us sufficient indices, unequivocal means for forming an idea of the thing represented that does not come from the icon itself; rather, it arises in us as it is "occasioned." The magic of intentional species – the old idea of effective resemblance as suggested by mirrors and paintings – loses its final argument if the entire potency of a painting is that of a text to be read, a text totally free of promiscuity between the seeing and the seen. We need no longer understand how a painting of things in the body could make them felt in the soul – an impossible task, since the very resemblance between this painting and those things would have to be seen in turn, since we would "have to have other eyes in our head with which to apperceive it,"[18] and since the problem of vision remains whole even when we have given ourselves these likenesses which wander between us and the real things. What the light designs upon our eyes, and thence upon our brain, does not resemble the visible world any more than etchings do. There is nothing more going on between the things and the eyes, and the eyes and vision, than between the things and the blind man's hands, and between his hands and thoughts.

Vision is not the metamorphosis of things themselves into the sight of them; it is not a matter of things' belonging simultaneously to the huge, real world and the small, private world. It is a thinking that deciphers strictly the signs given within the body. Resemblance is the result of perception, not its mainspring. More surely still, the mental image, the clairvoyance which renders present to us what is absent, is nothing like an insight penetrating into the heart of Being. It is still a thought relying upon bodily indices, this time insufficient, which are made to say more than they mean. Nothing is left of the oneiric world of analogy. . . .

What interests us in these famous analyses is that they make us aware of the fact that any theory of painting is a metaphysics. Descartes does not stay much about painting, and one might think it unfair on our part to make an issue out of a few pages on copper engravings. And yet even if he speaks of them only in passing, that in itself is significant. Painting for him is not a central operation contributing to the definition of our access to Being; it is a mode or a variant of thinking, where thinking is canonically defined according to intellectual possession and evidence. It is this option that is expressed within the little he does say, and a closer study of painting would lead to another philosophy. It is significant too that when he speaks of "pictures" he takes line drawings as typical. We shall see that all painting is present in each of its modes of expression; one drawing, even a single line, can embrace all its bold potential.

But what Descartes likes most in copper engravings is that they preserve the forms of objects, or at least give us sufficient signs of their forms. They present the object by its outside, or its envelope. If he had examined that other, deeper opening upon things given us by secondary qualities, especially color, then – since there is no ordered or projective relationship between them and the true properties of things and since we understand their message all the same – he would have found himself faced with the problem of a conceptless universality and a conceptless opening upon things. He would have been obliged to find out how the indecisive murmur of colors can present us with things, forests, storms – in short the world; obliged, perhaps, to integrate perspective, as a particular case, with a more ample ontological power. But for him it goes without saying that color is an ornament, mere coloring [*coloriage*], and that the real power of painting lies in design, whose power in turn rests upon the ordered relationship existing between it and space-in-itself as taught to us by perspective-projection. Pascal is remembered for speaking of the frivolity of paintings which attach us to images whose originals would not touch us; this is a Cartesian opinion. For Descartes it is unarguably evident that one can paint only existing things, that their existence consists in being extended, and that design, or line drawing, alone makes painting possible by making the representation of extension possible. Thus painting is only an artifice which presents to our eyes a projection similar to that which the things themselves in ordinary perception would and do inscribe in our eyes. A painting makes us see in the same way in which we actually see the thing itself, even though the thing is absent. Especially it makes us see a *space* where there is none.[19]

The picture is a flat thing contriving to give us what we would see in the [actual] presence of "diversely contoured" things, by offering sufficient diacritical signs of the missing dimension, according to height and width.[20] Depth is a *third dimension* derived from the other two.

It will pay us to dwell for a moment upon this third dimension. It has, first of all, something paradoxical about it. I see objects which hide each other and which consequently I do not see; each one stands behind the other. I see it [the third dimension] and it is not visible, since it goes toward things from, as starting point, this body to which I myself am fastened. But the mystery here is a false one. I don't really see it [the third dimension], or if I do, it is only another *size* [measured by height and width]. On the line which lies between my eyes and the horizon, the first [vertical] plane forever hides all the others, and if from side to side I think I see things spread out in order before me, it is because they do not completely hide each other. Thus I see each thing to be outside the others, according to some measure otherwise reckoned [*autrement compté*].[21] We are always on this side of space or beyond it entirely. It is never the case that things really *are* one behind the other. The fact that things overlap or are hidden does not enter into their definition, and expresses only my incomprehensible solidarity with one of them – my body. And whatever might be positive in these facts, they are only thoughts that I formulate and not attributes of the things. I know that at this very moment another man, situated elsewhere – or better, God, who is everywhere – could penetrate their "hiding place" and see them openly deployed. Either what I call depth is nothing, or else it is my participation in a Being without restriction, a participation primarily in the being of space beyond every [particular] point of view. Things encroach upon one another *because each is outside of the others*. The proof of this is that I can see depth in a painting which everyone agrees has none and which organizes for me an illusion of an illusion. . . . This two-dimensional being,[22] which makes me see another [dimension], is a being that is opened up [*troué*] – as the men of the Renaissance said, a window. . . .

But in the last analysis the window opens only upon those *partes extra partes*, upon height and width seen merely from another angle – upon the absolute positivity of Being.

It is this identity of Being, or this space without hiding places which in each of its points is only what it is, neither more nor less, that underlies the analysis of copper engravings. Space is in-itself; rather, it is the in-itself *par excellence*. Its definition is *to be* in itself. Every point of space is and is thought to be right where it is – one here, another there; space is the evidence of the "where." Orientation, polarity, envelopment are, in space, derived phenomena inextricably bound to my presence. *Space* remains absolutely in itself, every-where equal to itself, homogeneous; its dimensions, for example, are interchangeable.

Like all classical ontologies, this one builds certain properties of beings into a structure of Being. Reversing Leibniz's remark, we might say that in doing this, it is true and false: true in what it denies and false in what it affirms. Descartes's space is true over against a too empirical thought which dares not construct. It was necessary first to idealize space, to conceive of that being – perfect in its genus, clear, manageable, and homogeneous – which our thinking glides over without a vantage point of its own: a being which thought reports entirely in terms of three rectangular dimensions. This done, we were enabled eventually to find the limits of construction, to understand that space does not have three dimensions or more or fewer, as an animal has either four or two feet, and to understand that the three dimensions are taken by different systems of measurement from a single dimensionality, a polymorphous Being, which justifies all with-out being fully expressed by any. Descartes was right in setting space free. His mistake was to erect it into a positive being, outside all points of view, beyond all latency and all depth, having no true thick-ness [*épaisseur*].

He was right also in taking his inspiration from the perspectival techniques of the Renaissance; they encouraged painting to freely pro-duce experiences of depth and, in general, presentations of Being. These techniques were false only in so far as they pretended to bring an end to painting's quest and history, to found once and for all an exact and infallible art of painting. As Panofsky has shown concerning the men of the Renaissance,[23] this enthusiasm was not without bad faith. The theoreticians tried to forget the spherical visual field of the ancients, their angular perspective which relates the apparent size not to distance but to the angle from which we see the object. They wanted to forget what they disdainfully called the *perspectiva naturalis*, or *communis*, in favor of a *perspectiva artificialis* capable in principle of founding an exact construction. To accredit this myth, they went so far as to expurgate Euclid, omitting from their translations that eighth theorem which bothered them so much. But the painters, on the other hand, knew from experience that no technique of perspective is an exact solution and that there is no projection of the existing world which respects it in all aspects and deserves to become the fundamental law of painting. They knew too that linear perspective was so far from being an ultimate breakthrough that, on the contrary, it opens several pathways for painting. For example, the Italians took the way of representing the object, but the northern painters discovered and worked out the formal technique of *Hochraum, Nahraum,* and *Schrägraum.* Thus plane projection does not always provoke our thought to reach the true form of things, as Descartes believed. Beyond a certain degree of deformation, it refers back, on the contrary, to our own vantage point. And the painted objects are left to retreat into a remoteness out of reach of all thought. Something in space escapes our attempts to look at it from "above."

The truth is that no means of expression, once mastered, resolves the problems of painting or transforms it into a technique. For no symbolic form ever functions as a stimulus. Wherever it has been put to work and has acted, has *gone* to work, it has been put to work and has acted with the entire context of the *oeuvre,* and not in the slightest by means of a *trompe-l'oeil.* The *Stilmoment* never gets rid of the *Wermoment.*[24] The language of painting is never "instituted by nature"; it is to be made and remade over and over again. The perspective of the Renaissance is no infallible "gimmick." It is only a particular case, a date, a moment in a poetic information of the world which continues after it.

Yet Descartes would not have been Descartes if he had thought to *eliminate* the enigma of vision. There is no vision without thought. But *it is not enough* to think in order to see. Vision is a conditioned thought; it is born "as occasioned" by what happens in the body; it is "incited" to think by the body. It does not *choose* either to be or not to be or to think this thing or that. It has to carry in its heart that heaviness, that dependence which cannot come to it by some intrusion from outside. Such bodily events are "instituted by nature" in order to bring us to see this thing or that. The thinking that belongs to vision functions according to a program and a law which it has not given itself. It does not possess its own premises; it is not a thought altogether present and actual; there is in its center a mystery of passivity.

As things stand, then, everything we say and think of vision has to make a *thought* of it. When, for example, we wish to understand how we see the way objects are situated, we have no other recourse than to suppose the soul to be capable, knowing where the parts of its body are, of "transferring its attention from there" to all the points of space that lie in the prolongation of [i.e., beyond] the bodily members.[25] But so far this is only a "model" of the event. For the question is, how does the soul know this space, its own body's, which it extends toward things, this primary *here* from which all the *there's* will come? This space is not, like them, just another mode or specimen of the extended; it is the place of the body the soul calls "mine," a place the soul inhabits. The body it animates is not, for it, an object among objects, and it does not derive from the body all the rest of space as an implied premise. The soul thinks with reference to the body, not with reference to itself, and space, or exterior distance, is stipulated as well within the natural pact that unites them. If for a certain degree of accommodation and eye convergence the soul takes note of a certain distance, the thought which draws the second relationship from the first is as if immemorially enrolled in our internal "works" [*fabrique*]. "Usually this comes about without our reflecting upon it – just as, when we clasp a body with our hand, we conform the hand to the size and shape of the body and thereby sense the body, without having need to think of those movements of the hand."[26] For the soul, the body is both natal space and matrix of every other existing space. Thus vision divides itself. There is the vision upon which I reflect; I cannot think it except *as* thought, the mind's inspection, judgment, a reading of signs. And then there is the vision that really takes place, an honorary or instituted thought, squeezed into a body – its own body, of which we can have no idea except in the exercise of it and which introduces, between space and thought, the autonomous order of the compound of soul and body. The enigma of vision is not done away with; it is relegated from the "thought of seeing" to vision in act.

Still this *de facto* vision and the "there is" which it contains do not upset Descartes's philosophy. Being thought united with a body, it cannot, by definition, really be thought [conceived]. One can practice it, exercise it, and, so to speak, exist it; yet one can draw nothing from it which deserves to be called true. If, like Queen Elizabeth,[27] we want at all costs to think *something* about it, all we can do is go back to Aristotle and scholasticism, to conceive thought as a corporeal something which cannot be conceived but which is the only way to formulate, for our understanding, the union of soul and body. The truth is that it is absurd to submit to pure understanding the mixture of understanding and body. These would-be thoughts are the hallmarks of "ordinary usage," mere verbalizations of this union, and can be allowed only if they are not taken to be thoughts. They are indices of an order of existence – of man and world as existing – about which we do not have to think. For this order there is no *terra incognita* on our map of Being. It does not confine the reach of our thoughts, because it, just as much as they, is sustained by a truth which grounds its obscurity as well as our own lights.[28]

We have to push Descartes this far to find in him something like a metaphysics of depth [*de la profondeur*]. For we do not attend the birth of this truth; God's being for us is an abyss. An anxious trembling quickly mastered; for Descartes it is just as vain to plumb that abyss as it is to think the space of the soul and the depth of the visible. Our very position, he would say, disqualifies us from looking into such things. Here is the Cartesian secret of equilibrium: a metaphysics which gives us decisive reasons to be no longer involved with metaphysics, which validates our evidences while limiting them, which opens up our thinking without rending it.

The secret has been lost for good, it seems. If we ever again find a balance between science and philosophy, between our models and the obscurity of the "there is," it must be of a new kind. Our science has rejected the justifications as well as the restrictions which Descartes assigned to its domain. It no longer pretends to deduce its invented models from the attributes of God. The depth of the existing world and that of the unfathomable God come no longer to stand over against the platitudes [and flatness] of "technicized" thinking. Science gets along without the excursion into metaphysics which Descartes had to make at least once in his life; it takes off from the point he ultimately reached. Operational thought claims for itself, in the name of psychology, that domain of contact with oneself and with the world which Descartes reserved for a blind but irreducible experience. It is fundamentally hostile to philosophy as thought-in-contact, and if operational thought rediscovers the sense of philosophy it will be through the very excess of its ingenuousness [*sa désinvolture*]. It will happen when, having introduced all sorts of notions which for Descartes would have arisen from confused thought – quality, scalar structures, solidarity of observer and observed – it will suddenly become aware that one cannot summarily speak of all these beings as *constructs*. As we await this moment, philosophy maintains itself against such thinking, entrenching itself in that dimension of the compound of soul and body, that dimension of the existent world, of the abyssal Being that Descartes opened up and so quickly closed again. Our science and our philosophy are two faithful and unfaithful consequences of Cartesianism, two monsters born from its dismemberment.

Nothing is left for our philosophy but to set out toward the prospection of the actual world. We *are* the compound of soul and body, and so there must be a thought of it. To this knowledge of position or situation Descartes owes what he himself says of it [this compound] or what he says sometimes of the presence of the body "against the soul," or the exterior world "at the end" of our hands. Here the body is not the means of vision and touch but their depository.

Our organs are no longer instruments; on the contrary, our instruments are detachable organs. Space is no longer what it was in the *Dioptric*, a network of relations between objects such as would be seen by a witness to my vision or by a geometer looking over it and reconstructing it from outside. It is, rather, a space reckoned starting from me as the zero point or degree zero of spatiality. I do not see it according to its exterior envelope; I live in it from the inside; I am immersed in it. After all, the world is all around me, not in front of me. Light is viewed once more as action at a distance. It is no longer reduced to the action of contact or, in other words, conceived as it might be by those who do not see in it.[29] Vision reassumes its fundamental power of showing forth more than itself. And since we are told that a bit of ink suffices to make us see forests and storms, light must have its *imaginaire*. Light's transcendence is not delegated to a reading mind which deciphers the impacts of the light-thing upon the brain and which could do this quite as well if it had never lived in a body. No more is it a question of speaking of space and light; the question is to make space and light, which are *there*, speak to us. There is no end to this question, since the vision to which it addresses itself is itself a question. The inquiries we believed closed have been reopened.

What is depth, what is light, τί τὸ ὄν? What are they – not for the mind that cuts itself off from the body but for the mind Descartes says is suffused throughout the body? And what are they, finally, not only for the mind but for themselves, since they pass through us and surround us?

Yet this philosophy still to be done is that which animates the painter – not when he expresses his opinions about the world but in that instant when his vision becomes gesture, when, in Cézanne's words, he "thinks in painting."[30]

4

The entire modern history of painting, with its efforts to detach itself from illusionism and to acquire its own dimensions, has a metaphysical significance. This is not something to be demonstrated. Not for reasons drawn from the limits of objectivity in history and from the inevitable plurality of interpretations, which would prevent the linking of a philosophy and an event; the metaphysics we have in mind is not a body of detached ideas [*idées séparées*] for which inductive justifications could be sought in the experiential realm. There are, in the flesh of contingency, a structure of the event and a virtue peculiar to the scenario. These do not prevent the plurality of interpretations but in fact are the deepest reasons for this plurality. They make the event into a durable theme of historical life and have a right to philosophical status. In a sense everything that could have been said and that will be said about the French Revolution has always been and is henceforth within it, in that wave which arched itself out of a roil of discrete facts, with its froth of the past and its crest of the future. And it is always by looking more deeply into *how it came about* that we give and will go on giving new representations of it. As for the history of art works, if they are great, the sense we give to them later on has issued from them. It is the work itself that has opened the field from which it appears in another light. It changes *itself* and *becomes* what follows; the interminable reinterpretations to which it is *legitimately* susceptible change it only in itself. And if the historian unearths beneath its manifest content the surplus and thickness of meaning, the texture which held the promise of a long history, this active manner of being, then, this possibility he unveils in the work, this monogram he finds there – all are grounds for a philosophical meditation. But such a labor demands a long familiarity with history. We lack everything for its execution, both the competence and the place. Just the same, since the power or the fecundity of art works exceeds every positive causal or filial relation, there is nothing wrong with letting a layman, speaking from his memory of a few paintings and books, tell us how painting enters into his reflections; how painting deposits in him a feeling of profound discordance, a feeling of mutation within the relations of man and Being. Such feelings arise in him when he holds a universe of classical thought, en bloc, up against the explorations [*recherches*] of modern painting. This is a sort of history by contact, perhaps, never extending beyond the limits of one person, owing everything nevertheless to his frequentation of others. . . .

"I believe Cézanne was seeking depth all his life," says Giacometti.[31] Says Robert Delaunay, "Depth is the new inspiration."[32] Four centuries after the "solutions" of the Renaissance and three centuries after Descartes, depth is still new, and it insists on being sought, not "once in a lifetime" but all through life. It cannot be merely a question of an unmysterious interval, as seen from an airplane, between these trees nearby and those farther away. Nor is it a matter of the way things are conjured away, one by another, as we see happen so vividly in a perspective drawing. These two views are very explicit and raise no problems. The enigma, though, lies in their bond, in what is between them. The enigma consists in the fact that I see things, each one in its place, precisely because they eclipse one another, and that they are rivals before my sight precisely because each one is in its own place. Their exteriority is known in their envelopment and their mutual dependence in their autonomy. Once depth is understood in this way, we can no longer call it a third dimension. In the first place, if it were a dimension, it would be the *first* one; there are forms and definite planes only if it is stipulated how far from me their different parts are. But a *first* dimension that contains all the others is no longer a dimension, at least in the ordinary sense of a *certain relationship* according to which we make measurements. Depth thus understood is, rather, the experience of the reversibility of dimensions, of a global "locality" – everything in the same place at the same time, a locality from which height, width, and depth are abstracted, of a voluminosity we express in a word when we say that a thing is *there*. In search of depth Cézanne seeks this deflagration of Being, and it is all in the modes of space, in form as much as anything. Cézanne knows already what cubism will repeat: that the external form, the envelope, is secondary and derived, that it is not that which causes a thing to take form, that this shell of space must be shattered, this fruit bowl broken – and what is there to paint, then? Cubes, spheres, and cones (as he said once)? Pure forms which have the solidity of what could be defined by an internal law of construction, forms which all together, as traces or slices of the thing, let it appear between them like a face in the reeds? This would be to put Being's solidity on one side and its variety on the other. Cézanne made an experiment of this kind in his middle period. He opted for the solid, for space – and came to find that inside this space, a box or container too large for them, the things began to move, color against color; they began to modulate in instability.[33] Thus we must seek space and its content *as* together. The problem is generalized; it is no longer that of distance, of line, of form; it is also, and equally, the problem of color.

Color is the "place where our brain and the universe meet," he says in that admirable idiom of the artisan of Being which Klee liked to cite.[34] It is for the benefit of color that we must break up the form-spectacle. Thus the question is not of colors, "simulacra of the colors of nature."[35] The question, rather, concerns the dimension of color, that dimension which creates identities, differences, a texture, a materiality, a something – creates them from itself, for itself. . . .

Yet (and this must be emphasized) there is no one master key of the visible, and color alone is no closer to being such a key than space is. The return to color has the merit of getting somewhat nearer to "the heart of things,"[36] but this heart is beyond the color envelope just as it is beyond the space envelope. The *Portrait of Vallier* sets between the colors white spaces which take on the function of giving shape to, and setting off, a being more general than the yellow-being or green-being or blue-being. Also in the water colors of Cézanne's last years, for example, space (which had been taken to be evidence itself and of which it was believed that the question of *where* was not to be asked) radiates around planes that cannot be assigned to any place at all: "a superimposing of transparent surfaces," "a flowing movement of planes of color which overlap, which advance and retreat."[37]

Obviously it is not a matter of adding one more dimension to those of the flat canvas, of organizing an illusion or an objectless perception whose perfection consists in simulating an empirical vision to the maximum degree. Pictorial depth (as well as painted height and width) comes "I know not whence" to alight upon, and take root in, the sustaining support. The painter's vision is not a view upon the *outside*, a merely "physical-optical"[38] relation with the world. The world no longer stands before him through representation; rather, it is the painter to whom the things of the world give birth by a sort of concentration or coming-to-itself of the visible. Ultimately the painting relates to nothing at all among experienced things unless it is first of all "autofigurative."[39] It is a spectacle of something only by being a "spectacle of nothing,"[40] by breaking the "skin of things"[41] to show how the things become things, how the world becomes world. Apollinaire said that in a poem there are phrases which do not appear to have been *created*, which seem to have *formed themselves*. And Henri Michaux said that sometimes Klee's colors seem to have been born slowly upon the canvas, to have emanated from some primordial ground, "exhaled at the right place"[42] like a patina or a mold. Art is not construction, artifice, meticulous relationship to a space and a world existing outside. It is truly the "inarticulate cry," as Hermes Trismegistus said, "which seemed to be the voice of the light." And once it is present it awakens powers dormant in ordinary vision, a secret of preexistence. When through the water's thickness I see the tiling at the bottom of a pool, I do not see it *despite* the water and the reflections there; I see it through them and because of them. If there were no distortions, no ripples of sunlight, if it were without this flesh that I saw the geometry of the tiles, then I would cease to see it *as* it is and where it is – which is to say, beyond any identical, specific place. I cannot say that the water itself – the aqueous power, the sirupy and shimmering element – is *in* space; all this is not somewhere else either, but it is not in the pool. It inhabits it, it materializes itself there, yet it is not contained there; and if I raise my eyes toward the screen of cypresses where the web of reflections is playing, I cannot gainsay the fact that the water visits it, too, or at least sends into it, upon it, its active and living essence. This internal animation, this radiation of the visible is what the painter seeks under the name of depth, of space, of color.

Anyone who thinks about the matter finds it astonishing that very often a good painter can also make good drawings or good sculpture. Since neither the means of expression nor the creative gestures are comparable, this fact [of competence in several media] is proof that there is a system of equivalences, a Logos of lines, of lighting, of colors, of reliefs, of masses – a conceptless presentation of universal Being. The effort of modern painting has been directed not so much toward choosing between line and color, or even between the figuration of things and the creation of signs, as it has been toward multiplying the systems of equivalences, toward severing their adherence to the envelope of things. This effort might force us to create new materials or new means of expression, but it could well be realized at times by the reexamination and reinvestment of those which existed already.

There has been, for example, a prosaic conception of the line as a positive attribute and a property of the object in itself. Thus, it is the outer contour of the apple or the border between the plowed field and the meadow, considered as present in the world, such that, guided by points taken from the real world, the pencil or brush would only have to pass over them. But this line has been contested by all modern painting, and probably by all painting, as we are led to think by da Vinci's comment in his *Treatise on Painting*: "The secret of the art of drawing is to discover in each object the particular way in which a certain flexuous line, which is, so to speak, its generating axis, is directed through its whole extent. . . ."[43] Both Ravaisson and Bergson sensed something important in this, without daring to decipher the oracle all the way. Bergson scarcely looked for the "sinuous outline" [*serpentement*] outside living beings, and he rather timidly advanced the idea that the undulating line "could be no one of the visible lines of the figure," that it is "no more here than there," and yet "gives the key to the whole."[44] He was on the threshold of that gripping discovery, already familiar to the painters, that there are no lines visible in themselves, that neither the contour of the apple nor the border between field and meadow is in *this* place or that, that they are always on the near or the far side of the point we look at. They are always between or behind whatever we fix our eyes upon; they are indicated, implicated, and even very imperiously demanded by the things, but they themselves are not things. They were supposed to circumscribe the apple or the meadow, but the apple and the meadow "form themselves" from themselves, and come into the visible as if they had come from a prespatial world behind the scenes.

Yet this contestation of the prosaic line is far from ruling out all lines in painting, as the impressionists may have thought. It is simply a matter of freeing the line, of revivifying its constituting power; and we are not faced with a contradiction when we see it reappear and triumph in painters like Klee or Matisse, who more than anyone believed in color. For henceforth, as Klee said, the line no longer imitates the visible; it "renders visible"; it is the blueprint of a genesis of things. Perhaps no one before Klee had "let a line muse."[45] The beginning of the line's path establishes or installs a certain level or mode of the linear, a certain manner for the line to be and to make itself a line, "to go line."[46] Relative to it, every subsequent inflection will have a diacritical value, will be another aspect of the line's relationship to itself, will form an adventure, a history, a meaning of the line – all this according as it slants more or less, more or less rapidly, more or less subtly. Making its way in space, it nevertheless corrodes prosaic space and the *partes extra partes*; it develops a way of extending itself actively into that space which subtends the spatiality of a thing quite as much as that of a man or an apple tree. This is so simply because, as Klee said, to give the generating axis of a man the painter "would have to have a network of lines so entangled that it could no longer be a question of a truly elementary representation."[47]

In view of this situation two alternatives are open, and it makes little difference which one is chosen. First, the painter may, like Klee, decide to hold rigorously to the principle of the genesis of the visible, the principle of fundamental, indirect, or – as Klee used to say – absolute painting, and then leave it up to the *title* to designate by its prosaic name the entity thus constituted, in order to leave the painting free to function more purely as a painting. Or alternatively he may choose with Matisse (in his drawings) to put into a single line both the prosaic definition [*signalement*] of the entity and the hidden [*sourde*] operation which composes in it such softness or inertia and such force as are required to constitute it as *nude*, as *face*, as *flower*.

There is a painting by Klee of two holly leaves, done in the most figurative manner. At first glance the leaves are thoroughly indecipherable, and they remain to the end monstrous, unbelievable, ghostly, *on account of their exactness* [*à force d'exactitude*]. And Matisse's women (let us keep in mind his contemporaries' sarcasm) were not immediately women; they became women. It is Matisse who taught us to see their contours not in a "physical-optical" way but rather as structural filaments [*des nervures*], as the axes of a corporeal system of activity and passivity. Figurative or not, the line is no longer a thing or an imitation of a thing. It is a certain disequilibrium kept up within the indifference of the white paper; it is a certain process of gouging within the in-itself, a certain constitutive emptiness – an emptiness which, as Moore's statues show decisively, upholds the pretended positivity of the things. The line is no longer the apparition of an entity upon a vacant background, as it was in classical geometry. It is, as in modern geometries, the restriction, segregation, or modulation of a pre-given spatiality.

Just as it has created the latent line, painting has made itself a movement without displacement, a movement by vibration or radiation. And well it should, since, as we say, painting is an art of space and since it comes about upon a canvas or sheet of paper and so lacks the wherewithal to devise things that actually move. But the immobile canvas could suggest a change of place in the same way that a shooting star's track on my retina suggests a transition, a motion not contained in it. The painting itself would offer to my eyes almost the same thing offered them by real movements: a series of appropriately mixed, instantaneous glimpses along with, if a living thing is involved, attitudes unstably suspended between a before and an after – in short, the outsides of a change of place which the spectator would read from the imprint it leaves. Here Rodin's well-known remark reveals its full weight: the instantaneous glimpses, the unstable attitudes, petrify the movement, as is shown by so many photographs in which an athlete-in-motion is forever frozen. We could not thaw him out by multiplying the glimpses. Marey's photographs, the cubists' analyses, Duchamp's *La Mariée* do not move; they give a Zenonian reverie on movement. We see a rigid body as if it were a piece of armor going through its motions; it is here and it is there, magically, but it does not *go* from here to there. Cinema portrays movement, but *how?* Is it, as we are inclined to believe, by copying more closely the changes of place? We may presume not, since slow-motion shows a body floating among objects like an alga but not moving *itself.*

Movement is given, says Rodin,[48] by an image in which the arms, the legs, the trunk, and the head are each taken at a different instant, an image which therefore portrays the body in an attitude which it never at any instant really held and which imposes fictive linkages between the parts, as if this mutual confrontation of incompossibles could, and could alone, cause transition and duration to arise in bronze and on canvas. The only successful instantaneous glimpses of movement are those which approach this paradoxical arrangement – when, for example, a walking man is taken at the moment when both his feet are touching the ground; for then we almost have the temporal ubiquity of the body which brings it about that the man *bestrides* space. The picture makes movement visible by its internal discordance. Each member's position, precisely by virtue of its incompatibility with the others' (according to the body's logic), is otherwise dated or is not "in time" with the others; and since all of them remain visibly within the unity of a body, it is the body which comes to bestride time [*la durée*]. Its movement is something premeditated between legs, trunk, arms, and head in some virtual "control center," and it breaks forth only with a subsequent change of place. When a horse is photographed at that instant when he is completely off the ground, with his legs almost folded under him – an instant, therefore, when he must be moving – why does he look as if he were leaping in place? Then why do Gericault's horses really *run* on canvas, in a posture impossible for a real horse at the gallop? It is just that the horses in *Epsom Derby* bring me to see the body's grip upon the soil and that, according to a logic of body and world I know well, these "grips" upon space are also ways of taking hold of time [*la durée*]. Rodin said very wisely, "It is the artist who is truthful, while the photograph is mendacious; for, in reality, time never stops cold."[49] The photograph keeps open the instants which the onrush of time closes up forthwith; it destroys the overtaking, the overlapping, the "metamorphosis" [Rodin] of time. But this is what painting, in contrast, makes visible, because the horses have in them that "leaving here, going there,"[50] because they have a foot in each instant. Painting searches not for the outside of movement but for its secret ciphers, of which there are some still more subtle than those of which Rodin spoke. All flesh, and even that of the world, radiates beyond itself. But whether or not one is, depending on the times and the "school," attached more to manifest movement or to the monumental, the art of painting is never altogether outside time, because it is always within the carnal [dans le charnel].

Now perhaps we have a better sense of what is meant by that little verb "to see." Vision is not a certain mode of thought or presence to self; it is the means given me for being absent from myself, for being present at the fission of Being from the inside – the fission at whose termination, and not before, I come back to myself.

Painters always knew this. Da Vinci[51] invoked a "pictorial science" which does not speak with words (and still less with numbers) but with *oeuvres* which exist in the visible just as natural things do and which nevertheless communicate through those things "to all the generations of the universe." This silent science, says Rilke (apropos of Rodin), brings into the *oeuvre* the forms of things "whose seal has not been broken";[52] it comes from the eye and addresses itself to the eye. We must understand the eye as the "window of the soul." "The eye . . . through which the beauty of the universe is revealed to our contemplation is of such excellence that whoever should resign himself to losing it would deprive himself of the knowledge of all the works of nature, the sight of which makes the soul live happily in its body's prison, thanks to the eyes which show him the infinite variety of creation: whoever loses them abandons his soul in a dark prison where all hope of once more seeing the sun, the light of the universe, must vanish." The eye accomplishes the prodigious work of opening the soul to what is not soul – the joyous realm of things and their god, the sun.

A Cartesian can believe that the existing world is not visible, that the only light is that of the mind, and that all vision takes place in God. A painter cannot grant that our openness to the world is illusory or indirect, that what we see is not the world itself, or that the mind has to do only with its thoughts or with another mind. He accepts with all its difficulties the myth of the windows of the soul; it must be that what has no place is subjected to a body – even more, that what has no place be initiated *by* the body to all the others and to nature. We must take literally what vision teaches us: namely, that through it we come in contact with the sun and the stars, that we are everywhere all at once, and that even our power to imagine ourselves elsewhere – "I am in Petersburg in my bed, in Paris, my eyes see the sun" – or to intend [*viser*] real beings wherever they are, borrows from vision and employs means we owe to it. Vision alone makes us learn that beings that are different, "exterior," foreign to one another, are yet absolutely *together*, are "simultaneity"; this is a mystery psychologists handle the way a child handles explosives. Robert Delaunay says succinctly, "The rail road track is the image of succession which comes closest to the parallel: the parity of the rails." The rails converge and do not converge; they converge *in order* to remain equidistant down below. The world is in accordance with my perspective *in order to* be independent of me, is for me *in order to be* without me, and to be the world. The "visual quale"[53] gives me, and alone gives me, the presence of what is not me, of what *is* simply and fully. It does so because, like texture, it is the concretion of a universal visibility, of a unique space which separates and reunites, which sustains every cohesion (and even that of past and future, since there would be no such cohesion if they were not essentially relevant to the same space). Every visual something, as individual as it is, functions also as a dimension, because it gives itself as the result of a dehiscence of Being. What this ultimately means is that the proper essence [*le propre*] of the visible is to have a layer [*doublure*] of invisibility in the strict sense, which it makes present as a certain absence. "In their time, our bygone antipodes, the impressionists, were perfectly right in making their abode with the castaways and the undergrowth of daily life. As for us, our heart throbs to bring us closer to the depths.... These oddities will become ... realities ... because instead of being held to the diversely intense restoration of the visible, they will annex to it the proper share [*la part*] of the invisible, occultly apperceived."[54] There is that which reaches the eye directly [*de face*], the frontal properties of the visible; but there is also that which reaches it from below – the profound postural latency where the body raises itself to see – and that which reaches vision from above like the phenomena of flight, of swimming, of movement, where it participates no longer in the heaviness of origins but in free accomplishments.[55] Through it, then, the painter touches the two extremities. In the immemorial depth of the visible, something moved, caught fire, and engulfed his body; everything he paints is in answer to this incitement, and his hand is "nothing but the instrument of a distant will." Vision encounters, as at a crossroads, all the aspects of Being. "[A] certain fire pretends to be alive; it awakens. Working its way along the hand as conductor, it reaches the support and engulfs it; then a leaping spark closes the circle it was to trace, coming back to the eye, and beyond."[56]

There is no break at all in this circuit; it is impossible to say that nature ends here and that man or expression starts here. It is, therefore, mute Being which itself comes to show forth its own meaning. Herein lies the reason why the dilemma between figurative and nonfigurative art is badly posed; it is true and uncontradictory that no grape was ever what it is in the most figurative painting and that no painting, no matter how abstract, can get away from Being, that even Caravaggio's grape is the grape itself.[57] This precession of what is upon what one sees and makes seen, of what one sees and makes seen upon what is – this is vision itself. And to give the ontological formula of painting we hardly need to force the painter's own words, Klee's words written at the age of thirty-seven and ultimately inscribed on his tomb: "I cannot be caught in immanence."[58]

5

Because depth, color, form, line, movement, contour, physiognomy are all branches of Being and because each one can sway all the rest, there are no separated, distinct "problems" in painting, no really opposed paths, no partial "solutions," no cumulative progress, no irretrievable options. There is nothing to prevent a painter from going back to one of the devices he has shied away from – making it, of course, speak differently. Rouault's contours are not those of Ingres. Light is the "old sultana," says Georges Limbour, "whose charms withered away at the beginning of this century."[59] Expelled first by the painters of materials [les peintres de le matière], it reappears finally in Dubuffet as a certain texture of matter. One is never immune to this kind of turning back or to the least expected convergences; some of Rodin's fragments are almost statues by Germain Richier because they were both sculptors – that is to say, enmeshed in a single, identical network of Being. For the same reason nothing is ever finally acquired and possessed for good.

In "working over" a favorite problem, even if it is just the problem of velvet or wool, the true painter unknowingly upsets the givens of all the other problems. His quest is total even where it looks partial. Just when he has reached proficiency in some area, he finds that he has reopened another one where everything he said before must be said again in a different way. The upshot is that what he has found he does not yet have. It remains to be sought out; the discovery itself calls forth still further quests. The idea of a universal painting, of a totalization of painting, of a fully and definitively achieved painting is an idea bereft of sense. For painters the world will always be yet to be painted, even if it lasts millions of years ... it will end without having been conquered in painting.

Panofsky shows that the "problems" of painting which magnetize its history are often solved obliquely, not in the course of inquiries instigated to solve them but, on the contrary, at some point when the painters, having reached an impasse, apparently forget those problems and permit themselves to be attracted by other things. Then suddenly, altogether off guard, they turn up the old problems and surmount the obstacle. This unhearing [*sourde*] historicity, advancing through the labyrinth by detours, transgression, slow encroachments and sudden drives, does not imply that the painter does not know what he wants. It does imply that what he wants is beyond the means and goals at hand and commands from afar all our *useful* activity.

We are so fascinated by the classical idea of intellectual adequation that painting's mute "thinking" sometimes leaves us with the impression of a vain swirl of significations, a paralyzed or miscarried utterance. Suppose, then, that one answers that no thought ever detaches itself completely from a sustaining support; that the only privilege of speaking-thought is to have rendered its own support manageable; that the figurations of literature and philosophy are no more settled than those of painting and are no more capable of being accumulated into a stable treasure; that even science learns to recognize a zone of the "fundamental," peopled with dense, open, rent [*déchirés*] beings of which an exhaustive treatment is out of the question – like the cyberneticians' "aesthetic information" or mathematical-physical "groups of operations"; that, in the end, we are never in a position to take stock of everything objectively or to think of progress in itself; and that the whole of human history is, in a certain sense, stationary. *What*, says the understanding, like [Stendhal's] Lamiel, *is it only that*?

Is this the highest point of reason, to realize that the soil beneath our feet is shifting, to pompously name "interrogation" what is only a persistent state of stupor, to call "research" or "quest" what is only trudging in a circle, to call "Being" that which never fully *is*?

But this disappointment issues from that spurious fantasy[60] which claims for itself a positivity capable of making up for its own emptiness. It is the regret of not being everything, and a rather groundless regret at that. For if we cannot establish a hierarchy of civilizations or speak of progress – neither in painting nor in anything else that matters – it is not because some fate holds us back; it is, rather, because the very first painting in some sense went to the farthest reach of the future. If no painting comes to be *the* painting, if no work is ever absolutely completed and done with, still each creation changes, alters, enlightens, deepens, confirms, exalts, re-creates, or creates in advance all the others. If creations are not a possession, it is not only that, like all things, they pass away; it is also that they have almost all their life still before them.

Le Tholonet, July/August 1960

Notes

1 "L'Oeil et l'esprit" was the last work Merleau-Ponty saw published. It appeared in the inaugural issue of *Art de France*, vol. I, no. 1 (January, 1961). After his death it was reprinted in *Les Temps Modernes*, no. 184–5, along with seven articles devoted to him. It has now been published, in book form, by Editions Gallimard (1964). Both the *Art de France* article and the book contain illustrations chosen by Merleau-Ponty. According to Professor Claude Lefort, "L'Oeil et l'esprit" is a preliminary statement of ideas that were to be developed in the second part of the book Merleau-Ponty was writing at the time of his death – *Le Visible et l'invisible* (part of which was published posthumously by Gallimard in February, 1964). The translator [Carleton Dallery] wishes to acknowledge his immense debt to George Downing, who spent many long hours working over final revisions of the translation. Also, thanks are due to Michel Beaujour, Arleen B. Dallery, and Robert Reitter for their advice and encouragement (*Trans.*).

2 Cf. *Le Visible et l'invisible*, Paris, 1964, pp. 273, 308–11 (*Trans.*).

3 See *Signes*, Paris, 1960, pp. 210, 222–3, especially the footnotes, for a clarification of the "circularity" at issue here (*Trans.*).

4 G. Charbonnier, *Le Monologue du peintre*, Paris, 1959, p. 172.

5 Charbonnier, *Le Monologue*, p. 34.

6 *Ibid.*, pp. 143–5.

7 ". . . une philosophie figurée . . ." Cf. Bergson (Ravaisson), note 43 below (*Trans.*).

8 P. Claudel, *Introduction à la peinture hollandaise*, Paris, 1935.

9 P. Schilder, *The Image and Appearance of the Human Body*, London, 1935; New York, 1950, pp. 223–4. (". . . the body-image is not confined to the borderlines of one's own body. It transgresses them in the mirror. There is a

body-image outside ourselves, and it is remarkable that primitive peoples even ascribe a substantial existence to the picture in the mirror" (p. 278). Schilder's earlier, shorter study, *Das Körperschema* (Berlin, 1923), is cited several times in *The Structure of Behavior* and in *Phenomenology of Perception*. Schilder's later work is of especial interest with regard to Merleau-Ponty's own elaborations of the meaning of the human body; it is worth examining for that reason, as well as for the chance it provides to discern some fundamental coincidences between Merleau-Ponty and certain American pragmatists. *Trans.*)

10 Cf. Schilder, *Image*, pp. 281–2 (*Trans.*).

11 Robert Delaunay, *Du cubisme à l'art abstrait*, Paris, 1957.

12 "A minute in the world's life passes! to paint it in its reality! and forget everything for that. To become that minute, be the sensitive plate, . . . give the image of what we see, forgetting everything that has appeared before our time. . . ." Cézanne, quoted in B. Dorival, *Paul Cézanne*, trans. H. H. A. Thackthwaite, London, 1948, p. 101 (*Trans.*).

13 Descartes, *La Dioptrique*, Discours VII (conclusion). Édition Adam et Tannery, VI, p. 165.

14 *Ibid.*, Discours I. Adam et Tannery, p. 83. (*Oeuvres et lettres de Descartes*, ed. André Bridoux, Edition Pléiade, p. 181. Page references from the Bridoux selections have been added in the belief that this volume is more widely accessible today than the Adam and Tannery complete edition.)

15 *Ibid.*, Adam et Tannery, p. 84. (Bridoux, p. 182.)

16 This paragraph continues the exposition of the *Dioptric* (*Trans.*).

17 *Ibid.*, Discours IV. Adam et Tannery, pp. 112–14. (Bridoux, pp. 203–4; in English, *Descartes: Philosophical Writings*, ed. and trans. N. Kemp Smith, Modern Library Edition, pp. 143–7.)

18 *Ibid.*, p. 130. (Bridoux, p. 217; Smith, p. 148.)

19 The system of means by which painting makes us see is a scientific matter. Why, then, do we not methodically produce perfect images of the world, arriving at a universal art purged of personal art, just as the universal language would free us of all the confused relationships that lurk in existent languages?

20 *Dioptrique*, Discours IV, Adam et Tannery, pp. 112–14. (Note 17 above.)

21 Discours V of the *Dioptrique*, especially Descartes's diagrams, helps considerably to clarify this compressed passage (*Trans.*).

22 That is, the painting (*Trans.*).

23 E. Panofsky, *Die Perspektive als symbolische Form*, in *Vorträge der Bibliotek Warburg*, IV (1924–5).

24 *Ibid.*

25 Descartes, *Dioptrique*, Adam et Tannery, VI, p. 135. (Bridoux, p. 220; Smith, p. 154. Here is Smith's translation of the passage under discussion: "Our knowledge of it (the situation of an object) does not depend on any image or action which comes to us from the object, but solely on the situation of the small parts of the brain whence the nerves take their origin. For this situation – a situation which changes with every change however small in the points at which these nerve-fibers are located – is instituted by nature in order to secure, not only that the mind be aware of the location of each part of the body which it animates, relatively to all the others, but also that it be able to transfer its attention to all the positions contained in the

straight line that can be imaged as drawn from the extremity of each of these parts, and as prolonged to infinity." *Trans.*)

26 *Ibid.*, Adam et Tannery, p. 137. (Bridoux, p. 222; Smith, p. 155. Smith's translation is given here.)

27 No doubt Merleau-Ponty is speaking of Princess Elizabeth, Descartes's correspondent. Cf. *Phénoménologie de la perception*, pp. 230–2 (C. Smith translation, pp. 198–9), and Descartes's letter to Elizabeth of June 28, 1643 (Bridoux, pp. 1157–61) (*Trans.*).

28 That is, the obscurity of the "existential" order is just as necessary, just as grounded in God, as is the clarity of true thoughts ("nos lumières") (*Trans.*).

29 "those who do not see in it," i.e., the blind (note 15, above) (*Trans.*).

30 B. Dorival, *Paul Cézanne*, Paris, 1948, p. 103 *et seq.* (*trans.* Thackthwaite, pp. 101–3).

31 Charbonnier, *Le Monologue*, p. 176.

32 Delaunay, *Du cubisme*, p. 109.

33 F. Novotny, *Cézanne und das Ende der wissenschaftlichen Perspective*, Vienna, 1938.

34 W. Grohmann, *Paul Klee*, Paris, 1954, p. 141 (New York, 1956).

35 Delaunay, *Du cubisme*, p. 118.

36 Klee, *Journal . . .*, French trans. P. Klossowski, Paris, 1959.

37 George Schmidt, *Les aquarelles de Cézanne*, p. 21. (*The Watercolors of Cézanne*, New York, 1953).

38 Klee, *Journal.*

39 "The spectacle is first of all a spectacle of itself before it is a spectacle of something outside of it." (*Translator's note from Merleau-Ponty's 1961 lectures.*)

40 C. P. Bru, *Esthétique de l'abstraction*, Paris, 1959, pp. 99, 86.

41 Henri Michaux, *Aventures de lignes.*

42 *Ibid.*

43 Ravaisson, cited by Bergson, "La vie et l'oeuvre de Ravaisson," in *La pensée et le mouvant*, Paris, 1934, pp. 264–5. (The passage quoted here is from M. L. Andison's translation of that work, *The Creative Mind*, New York, 1946, p. 229. It remains moot whether these are Ravaisson's or da Vinci's words. *Trans.*)

44 Bergson, *ibid.*

45 Michaux, *Aventures* ("laissé rêver une ligne").

46 *Ibid.* ("d'aller ligne").

47 Grohmann, *Paul Klee*, p. 192.

48 Rodin, *L'Art.* Interviews collected by Paul Gsell, Paris, 1911.

49 *Ibid.*, p. 86.

50 Michaux, *Aventures.*

51 Cited by Delaunay, *Du cubisme*, p. 175.

52 Rilke, *Auguste Rodin*, French translation by Maurice Betz, Paris, 1928, p. 150. (English translation by Jessie Lamont and Hans Trausil (New York, 1919; republished 1945)).

53 Delaunay, *Du cubisme*, pp. 115, 110.

54 Klee, *Conférence d'Iena* (1924), according to Grohmann, *Paul Klee*, p. 365.

55 Klee, *Wege des Naturstudiums* (1923), as found in G. di San Lazzaro, *Klee.*

56 Klee, cited by Grohmann, *Paul Klee*, p. 99.

57 A. Berne-Joffroy, *Le dossier Caravage*, Paris, 1959, and Michel Butor, "La Corbeille de l'Ambrosienne," *Nouvelle Revue Française*, 1959, pp. 969–89.

58 Klee, *Journal* ("Je suis insaissable dans l'immanence.")

59 G. Limbour, *Tableau bon levain à vous de cuire la pâte: l'art brut de Jean Dubuffet*, Paris, 1953, pp. 54–5.

60 "Mais cette deception est celle du faux imaginaire, qui . . ."

PART SEVEN – HISTORY

THE CRISIS OF UNDERSTANDING (from *Adventures of the Dialectic*, pp. 9–29 in the 1973 translation)

This essay opens the collection of essays Les Aventures de la dialectique *which Merleau-Ponty published in 1955, after his break with Sartre. The collection also includes three essays on Marxism and ends with his attack on Sartre ('Sartre and ultrabolshevism'). But it is this essay on Weber which shows the new direction of Merleau-Ponty's historical and political thought, away from a concentration upon Marxism and towards a more reflective view of history (in his lectures 'Materials for a theory of history' at the Collège de France he returns to Weber[1]). I think this interest in Weber may also have come from a personal identification with him, as an intellectual who, despite strong political convictions, decided to stand back from active politics in Wilhelmine Germany.*

In the essay Merleau-Ponty's main aim is to explore and discuss the way in which Weber searches out the meaning of capitalism by looking back to Calvinism and the development of Protestant faith by thinkers such as Benjamin Franklin.[2] He explains Weber's hypothesis that Calvinist doctrines of predestination gave rise to an unanswerable anxiety concerning individual salvation, and that this anxiety motivated a new Puritan work ethic which was ideally suited for exploitation by early entrepreneurs. But Merleau-Ponty's main aim is not to expound Weber, but, assuming that his account is broadly correct, to reflect on the conception of history it expresses. What Merleau-Ponty finds in Weber is a way of discerning an objective truth in history which is neither a dull chronicle of events nor the application of an abstract Hegelian formula. This objective truth is a meaning which arises from the fact that our freedom 'comprehends all the uses of freedom', and that, in achieving this, we can adopt the standpoint of others in order to understand ourselves better. So we arrive at objectivity by means of a dialogue with the past, in which we neither accept the past at face value nor impose ourselves on it. In doing this we draw on the 'metaphysical fact' that our own life is only present to us in ambiguity, with a past and alongside others. The kind of objectivity we can gain concerning the past is no different from that which we can gain concerning ourselves.

Merleau-Ponty does not draw explicitly here on his earlier discussions of our common bodily intentionality, nor on our capacity for cultural sedimentation, whereby old meanings accumulate in our practices without our being aware of them. But it is easy to see how these themes inform his discussion, and thus how he remains true to his programmatic claims in The Phenomenology of Perception:

> My life must have a significance which I do not constitute; there must strictly speaking be an intersubjectivity; each one of us must be both anonymous in the sense of absolutely individual and absolutely general. Our being in the world is the concrete bearer of this double anonymity.
>
> Provided that this is so, there can be situations, a direction of history, and a historical truth. (p. 225; PP 448–9 [521])

Notes

1 See 'Themes from the lectures at the Collège de France 1952–60', in *In Praise of Philosophy and Other Essays*, trans. J. O'Neill, Evanston, IL: Northwestern University Press, 1988.

2 Merleau-Ponty draws primarily on Weber's work, *The Protestant Ethic and the Spirit of Capitalism*, trans. T. Parsons, New York: Free Press, 1958.

.. ..

Max Weber's feeling toward freedom and truth was extremely exacting and distrustful. But he also knew that they appear only in certain cultures, provided that certain historical choices are made, that they are not fully realized there, and that they never assimilate the confused world from which they sprang. They have, therefore, no claim to divine right and no other justifications than those which they effectively bring to man, no other titles than those acquired in a struggle where they are in principle at a disadvantage, since they are unable to exhaust all possible means. Truth and freedom are of another order than strife and cannot subsist without strife. It is equally essential to them to legitimize their adversaries and to confront them. Because he remains faithful to

---

knowledge and to the spirit of investigation, Weber is a liberal. His liberalism is brand new, because he admits that truth always leaves a margin of doubt, that it does not exhaust the reality of the past and still less that of the present, and that history is the natural seat of violence. Contrary to previous liberalism, it does not ingenously consider itself to be the law of things; rather it perseveres in becoming such a law, through a history in which it is not predestined.

In the first place, Weber thinks it possible to juxtapose the order of truth and that of violence. We know history in the same way that Kant says we know nature, which is to say that the historian's understanding, like that of the physicist's, forms an "objective" truth to the degree that it constructs, and to the degree that the object is only an element in a coherent representation, which can be indefinitely corrected and made more precise but which never merges with the thing in itself. The historian cannot look at the past without giving it a meaning, without putting into perspective the important and the subordinate, the essential and the accidental, plans and accomplishments, preparations and declines. And already these vectors which are traced through the dense whole of the facts distort the original reality, in which everything is equally real, and cause our own interests to crystallize on its surface. One cannot avoid the invasion of the historian into history; but one can see to it that, like the Kantian subject, the historical understanding constructs according to certain rules which assure an intersubjective value to its representation of the past. The meanings, or, as Weber says, the ideal types, which it introduces into facts must not be taken as keys to history. They are only fixed guideposts for determining the difference between what we think and what has been and for making evident what has been left out by any interpretation. Each perspective is there only to prepare for others. It is well founded only if we understand that it is partial and that the real is still beyond it. Knowledge is never categorical; it is always open to revision. Nothing can make us be the past: it is only a spectacle before us which is there for us to question. As the questions come from us, the answers in principle cannot exhaust historical reality, since it does not depend on them for existence.

The present, on the contrary, is us: it depends on our consent or our refusal. Suspension of judgment, which is the rule with respect to the past, is here impossible; to wait for things to take shape before deciding is to decide to let them go their own way. But the proximity of the present, which makes us responsible for it, nevertheless does not give us access to the thing itself. This time it is lack of distance which allows us to see only one side of it. Knowledge and practice confront the same infinity of historical reality, but they respond to it in opposite ways: knowledge, by multiplying views, confronts it through conclusions that are provisional, open, and justifiable (that is to say, conditional), while practice confronts it through decisions which are absolute, partial, and not subject to justification.

But how can we hold to this dualism of past and present, which is evidently not absolute? Tomorrow I will have to construct an image of that which I am now living; and I cannot, at the time when I live it, ignore it. The past that I contemplate has been lived; and as soon as I want to enter into its genesis, I cannot be unaware that it has been a present. Because of the fact that the order of knowledge is not the only order, because it is not closed in on itself, and because it contains at least the gaping blank of the present, the whole of history is still action, and action is already history. History is one, whether we contemplate it as spectacle or assume it as responsibility. The historian's condition is not so different from that of the man of action. He puts himself in the place of those whose action has been decisive, reconstitutes the horizon of their decisions, and does again what they have done, with this difference: he knows the context better than they, and he is already aware of the consequences. This is not to say that history consists in penetrating the state of mind of great men. Even the search for motives, says Weber, involves ideal types. It is not a question of coinciding with what has been lived but rather of deciphering the total meaning of what has been done. To understand an action, it is necessary to restore the horizon, which is to say, not only the perspective of the agent but also the "objective" content. One could thus say that history is action in the realm of the imaginary, or even the spectacle that one gives oneself of an action. Conversely, action consults history, which teaches us, says Weber, certainly not what must be willed, but the true meaning of our volitions. Knowledge and action are two poles of a single existence. Our relationship to history is not only one of understanding – a relationship of the spectator to the spectacle. We would not be spectators if we were not involved in the past, and action would not be serious if it did not conclude the whole enterprise of the past and did not give the drama its last act. History is a strange object, an object which is ourselves. Our irreplaceable life, our fierce freedom, find themselves already prefigured, already compromised, already played out in other freedoms, which today are past. Weber is obliged to go beyond the domain of the double truth, the dualism of the objectivity of understanding and of moral feeling, to look beyond it for the formula of this singular situation.

*

He has nowhere given this formula. His methodological writings post-date his scientific applications. We must look in his historical works to see how he comes to terms with this object which adheres to the subject, how he forges a method out of this difficulty, and how he tries, by going beyond the past as spectacle, to understand the past itself by making it enter into our own lives. We cannot be content with the past as it saw itself; and it is understood that the very attempt to discover the past as it actually was always implies a spectator, and there is a danger that we will discover the past only as it is for us. But is it perhaps in the nature of history to be undefined so long as it remains in the present and to become completely real only when it has once been given as a spectacle to a posterity which passes judgment upon it? Is it perhaps the case that only successive generations ("générations appélantes," as Péguy called them) are in a position to see whether what has been brought about really deserved to be, to correct the deceptions of recorded history, and to reinstate other possibilities? Is our image of the past preceded only by sequences of events, which form neither a system nor even perspectives and whose truth is held in abeyance? Is it perhaps a definition of history to exist fully only through that which comes after, to be in this sense suspended into the future? If this is true, the historian's intervention is not a defect of historical understanding. That facts interest the historian, that they speak to the man of culture, that they may be taken up again in his own intentions as a historical subject – all this threatens historical knowledge with subjectivity but also promises it a superior objectivity, if only one succeeds in distinguishing between "comprehension" and arbitrariness and in determining the close relationship which our "metamorphoses" violate but without which they would be impossible.

Let us, for example, attempt to understand the relationship between Protestantism and the capitalistic spirit. The historian intervenes initially by abstracting these two historical identities. Weber does not consider speculative or venture capitalism, which depends upon venture politics. He takes as his object an economic system within which one can expect continuous return from a durable and profitable enterprise, a system which therefore involves a minimum of accountancy and organization, encourages free labor, and tends toward a market economy. In the same way he limits his discussion of the Protestant ethic to Calvinism, and more especially to the Calvinism of the sixteenth and seventeenth centuries, considered more as collective fact than in its original form as set forth by Calvin. These facts are chosen as interesting and historically important because they reveal a certain logical structure which is the key to a whole series of other facts. How does the historian know this when he begins? Strictly speaking, he does not know. His abstraction anticipates certain results that he has an inkling of, and it will be justified to the degree that it brings to light facts which had not contributed to the initial definitions. He is therefore not sure that they designate essences; they are not developed by proximate genus and specific difference and do not represent, as geometric definitions do, the genesis of an ideal being. They give only, as Weber says, a provisional illustration of the point of view chosen, and the historian chooses this point of view in the same way that one remembers a word of an author, or someone's gesture: in one's first encounter with it, one becomes aware of a certain style. It was a passage from one of Franklin's works that gave Weber this initial view of the relationship between Calvinism and capitalism. Dating from the age of the maturity of Puritanism and preceding the adult age of capitalism, Franklin's text shows the transition from one to the other. These famous words are striking and illuminating because they express a work ethic. We have a duty to augment our capital, to earn always more, without enjoying what we have earned. Production and accumulation are in themselves holy. One would miss the essential point if one thought that Franklin attempts here to disguise interest as virtue. On the contrary, he goes so far as to say that God uses interest to bring him back to faith. If he writes that time is money, it is first of all because he has learned from the Puritan tradition that time is spiritually precious and that we are in the world to bear witness to the glory of God at each moment. The useful could become a value only after having been sanctified. What inspired the pioneers of capitalism was not the philosophy of enlightenment and immanence, the joy of life, which will come later. The "righteous, strict, and formalistic" character that brought them success can be understood only in terms of their sense of a worldly calling and in terms of the economic ethic of Puritanism. Many of the elements of capitalism exist here and there in history; but if it is only in western Europe that one finds the rational capitalistic enterprise in the sense that Weber defines it, this is perhaps because no other civilization has a theology which sanctifies daily labor, organizes a worldly asceticism, and joins the glory of God to the transformation of nature. Franklin's text presents us with a vital choice in its pure state, a mode of *Lebensführung* which relates Puritanism to the capitalistic spirit and enables Calvinism to be defined as worldly asceticism and capitalism to be defined as "rationalization"; and finally, if the initial intution is confirmed, it enables us to discover an intelligible transition from one to the other. If, in extending the work ethic back to its Calvinistic origins and toward its capitalistic consequences, Weber succeeds in understanding the basic structure of the facts, it is because he has discovered an objective meaning in them, has pierced the apperances in which reason is enclosed, and has gone beyond provisional and partial perspectives by restoring the anonymous intention, the dialectic of a whole.

Tracing worldly asceticism back to its premises, Weber finds in Calvinism the feeling of an infinite distance between God and his creatures. In themselves they merit only eternal death; they can do nothing and are worth nothing and have no control over their destiny: God decides who is to be among the elect and who is not. They do not even know that they truly are: God alone, seeing the hidden side of things, knows whether they are lost or saved. The Calvinist conscience oscillates between culpability and justification, both equally unmerited, between an anguish without limits and a security without conditions. This relationship to God is also a relationship to others and to the world. Because there is an infinite distance between God and man, no third party can intervene in the relationship. The ties which man has with others and with the world are of a different order from those he has with God. In essential matters he cannot expect any help from a church where sinners are as numerous as the righteous or any aid from sermons and sacraments which can do nothing to alter the *decretum horribile*. The church is not a place where man can find a sort of other natural life. It is an institution created by will and attached to predetermined ends. The Catholic lives in his church as if a running account were open to him, and it is not until the end of his life that the balance is struck between what he has and what he owes. The solitude of the Calvinist means that he confronts the absolute continually and that he does so futilely because he knows nothing of his destiny. At each instant he poses in full the whole question of his salvation or damnation, and this question remains unanswered. There is no gain in the Christian life; it can never be self-sufficient. "The glory of God and personal salvation remain always above the threshold of consciousness."[1] Summoned to break the vital alliance that we have with time, with others, and with the world, the Calvinist pushes to its limits a demystification that is also a depoetization or a disenchantment (*Entzauberung*). The sacraments, the church as the place of salvation, human friendships, which are always on the point of deifying creatures, are rejected as magic. This absolute anguish finds no relaxation in brotherly relations with created things. The created is the material upon which one works, the matter which one transforms and organizes to manifest the glory of God. The conscious control which is useless for salvation is transferred to a worldly enterprise that takes on the value of duty. Plans, methods, balance sheets are useless in dealing with God, since, from his perspective, everything is done, and we can know nothing. All that is left to us is to put the world in order, to change its natural aspect, and to rationalize life, this being the only means we have of bringing God's reign to earth. We are not able to make God save us. But the same anguish that we feel before that which we do not control, the same energy that we would expend to implement our salvation, even though we cannot do so, is expended in a worldly enterprise which depends on us and is under our control and which will become, even in Puritanism, a presumption of salvation. The terror of man in the face of a supernatural destiny over which he has no control weighs heavily upon the Puritan's activity in the world. By an apparent paradox, because he wishes to respect the infinite distance between God and man, he endows the useful and even the comfortable with dignity and religious meaning. He discredits leisure and even poverty and brings the rigors of asceticism into his dealings with the world. In the Calvinist's estimation, the relation to being and to the absolute is precipitated by and perpetuated in the goods of this world.

Let us now move forward from the Calvinist ethic to the spirit of capitalism. Weber cites one of Wesley's phrases that marks this transition: "Religion necessarily produces the spirit of industry and frugality, and these cannot but produce riches. But as wealth increases, so will pride, passion, and the love of worldly things. . . . So although the form of religion remains, the spirit gradually declines." Franklin's generation leaves to its successors the possibility of becoming rich in good conscience. They will forget the motive and concentrate on gaining the best of this world and the next. Once crystallized in the world by the Protestant ethic, capitalism will develop according to its own logic. Weber does not believe that it is sustained by the motive that brought it into existence, or that it is the truth of Calvinism:

> The capitalistic economy of the present day is an immense cosmos into which the individual is born, and which presents itself to him, at least as an individual, as an unalterable order of things in which he must live. It forces the individual, insofar as he is involved in the system of market relationships, to conform to capitalistic rules of action. . . . Thus the capitalism of today, which has come to dominate economic life, educates and selects the economic subjects which it needs through a process of economic survival of the fittest. But here one can easily see the limits of the concept of

selection as a means of historical explanation. In order that a manner of life [*Lebensführung*] so well adapted to the peculiarities of capitalism could be selected at all, i.e., should come to dominate others, it had to originate somewhere, and not in isolated individuals alone, but as a way of life common to whole groups of men. This origin is what really needs explanation.[2]

There is thus a religious efficacy and an economic efficacy. Weber describes them as interwoven, exchanging positions so that now one, now the other, plays the role of tutor. The effect turns back on its cause, carrying and transforming it in its turn. Furthermore, Weber does not simply integrate spiritual motives and material causes; he renews the concept of historical matter itself. An economic system is, as he says, a cosmos, a human choice become a situation; and that is what allows it to rise from worldly asceticism to religious motives, as well as to descend toward its capitalistic decay: everything is woven into the same fabric. History has meaning, but there is no pure development of ideas. Its meaning arises in contact with contingency, at the moment when human initiative founds a system of life by taking up anew scattered givens. And the historical understanding which reveals an interior to history still leaves us in the presence of empirical history, with its density and its haphazardness, and does not subordinate it to any hidden reason. Such is the philosophy without dogmatism which one discerns all through Weber's studies. To go beyond this, we must interpret freely. Let us do this without imputing to Weber more than he would have wished to say.

These intelligible nuclei of history are typical ways of treating natural being, of responding to others and to death. They appear at the point where man and the givens of nature or of the past meet, arising as symbolic matrices which have no preexistence and which can, for a longer or a shorter time, influence history itself and then disappear, not by external forces but through an internal disintegration or because one of their secondary elements becomes predominant and changes their nature. The "rationalization" by which Weber defines capitalism is one of these seminal structures that can also be used to explain art, science, the organization of the State, mysticism, or Western economy. It emerges here and there in history and, like historical types, is confirmed only through the encounter of these givens, when, each confirming the other, they organize themselves into a system. For Weber, capitalism presupposes a certain technology of production and therefore presupposes science in the Western sense. But it also presupposes a certain sort of law, a government based on certain rules, without which bourgeois enterprise cannot exist, though venture or speculative capitalism may. To these conditions Weber adds a "rational conduct of life," which has been the historical contribution of Protestantism. In law, science, technology, and Western religion we see prime examples of this "rationalizing" tendency. But only after the fact. Each of these elements acquires its historical meaning only through its encounter with the others. History has often produced one of them in isolation (Roman law; the fundamental principles of calculus in India), without its being developed to the degree that it would have to be in capitalism. The encounter of these elements confirms in each one of them the outline of rationality which it bore. As interactions accumulate, the development of the system in its own sense becomes more likely. Capitalistic production pushes more and more in the direction of a development of technology and the applied sciences. At the start, however, it is not an all-powerful idea; it is a sort of *historical imagination* which sows here and there elements capable one day of being integrated. The meaning of a system in its beginnings is like the pictorial meaning of a painting, which not so much directs the painter's movements but is the result of them and progresses with them. Or again, it can be compared to the meaning of a spoken language which is not transmitted in conceptual terms in the minds of those who speak, or in some ideal model of language, but which is, rather, the focal point of a series of verbal operations which converge almost by chance. Historians come to talk of "rationalization" or "capitalism" when the affinity of these products of the historical imagination becomes clear. But history does not work according to a model; it is, in fact, the advent of meaning. To say that the elements of rationality were related to one another before crystallizing into a system is only a manner of saying that, taken up and developed by human intentions, they ought to confirm one another and form a whole. Just as, before the coming of the bourgeois enterprise, the elements which it joins did not belong to the same world, each must be said to be drawn by the others to develop in a way which is common to them all but which no one of them embodies. Worldly asceticism, whose principles have been established by Calvinism, is finished by capitalism, finished in both senses of the word: it is realized because, as activity in the world, capitalism surpasses it; it is destroyed as asceticism because capitalism strives to eliminate its own transcendent motives. There is, Weber says, an *elective affinity* between the elements of a historical totality:

In view of the tremendous confusion of interdependent influences between the material basis, the forms of social and political organization, and the ideas current in the time of the Reformation, we can only proceed by investigating whether and at what points certain correlations (*Wahlverwandtschaften*) between forms of religious belief and practical ethics can be worked out. At the same time, we shall as far as possible clarify the manner and the general *direction* in which, by virtue of those relationships, the religious movements have influenced the development of material culture. Only when this has been determined with reasonable accuracy can the attempt be made to estimate to what extent the historical development of modern culture can be attributed to those religious forces and to what extent to others.[3]

This relationship is supple and reversible. If the Protestant ethic and capitalism are two institutional ways of stating the relationship of man to man, there is no reason why the Protestant ethic should not for a time carry within itself incipient capitalism. Nor is there anything to prevent capitalism from perpetuating certain typically Protestant modes of behavior in history or even from displacing Protestantism as the driving force of history and substituting itself for it, allowing certain motives to perish and asserting others as its exclusive theme. The ambiguity of historical facts, their *Vielseitigkeit*, the plurality of their aspects, far from condemning historical knowledge to the realm of the provisional (as Weber said at first), is the very thing that agglomerates the dust of facts, which allows us to read in a religious fact the first draft of an economic system or read, in an economic system, positions taken with regard to the absolute. Religion, law, and economy make up a single history because any fact in any one of the three orders arises, in a sense, from the other two. This is due to the fact that they are all embedded in the unitary web of human choices.

This is a difficult position to hold and one which is threatened on two sides. Since Weber tries to preserve the individuality of the past while still situating it in a developmental process, perhaps even in a hierarchy, he will be reproached, sometimes for concluding too little and at other times for presuming too much. Does he not leave us without means for criticizing the past? Does he not in principle give the same degree of reality and the same value to all civilizations, since the system of real and imaginary methods by which man has organized his relations with the world and with other men has always managed, somehow or other, to function? If one wishes to go so far as to understand the past even in its phantasms, is one not inevitably led to justify it and thus be rendered unable to judge it? On the other hand, when Weber presents us with a logic of history, one can always object that, as Malraux has shown, the decision to investigate and understand all civilizations is the act of a civilization which is different from them, which transforms them. It transforms the crucifix into a work of art, so that what had been a means of capturing the holy becomes an object of knowledge. Finally, the objection can be made that historical consciousness lives off this indefensible paradox: fragments of human life, each of which has been lived as absolute, and whose meaning thus in principle eludes the disinterested onlooker, are brought together in the imagination in a single act of attention, are compared and considered as moments in a single developmental process. It is necessary, therefore, to choose between a history which judges, situates, and organizes – at the risk of finding in the past only a reflection of the troubles and problems of the present – and an indifferent, agnostic history which lines up civilizations one after another like unique individuals who cannot be compared. Weber is not unaware of these difficulties; indeed, it is these difficulties which have set his thought in action. The path which he seeks lies precisely between history considered as a succession of isolated facts and the arrogance of a philosophy which lays claim to have grasped the past in its categories and which reduces it to our thoughts about it. What he opposes to both of them is our *interest* in the past: it is ours, and we are its. The dramas which have been lived inevitably remind us of our own, and of ourselves; we must view them from a single perspective, either because our own acts present us with the same problems in a clearer manner or, on the contrary, because our own difficulties have been more accurately defined in the past. We have just as much right to judge the past as the present. The past, moreover, comes forward to meet the judgments we pass upon it. It has judged itself; having been lived by men, it has introduced values into history. This judgment and these values are part of it, and we cannot describe it without either confirming or annulling them. In most past mystifications those involved were to a certain extent aware of the deception. Objectivity asks only that one approach the past with the past's own criteria. Weber reconciles evaluative history with objective history by calling upon the past to testify concerning itself. Wesley enables him to discern the moment when religion becomes mystification. Ideology is never mystification completely unawares; it requires a great deal of complacency to justify the capitalistic world by means of Calvinistic principles; if these principles are fully articulated, they will expose the ruse of attempting to turn them to one's own purposes. The men of the past could not completely hide the truth of their era from themselves; they did not need us in order to catch a glimpse of it. It is there, ready to appear; we have only to make an effort to reveal it. Thus the very attempt to understand the past completely would oblige us to order the facts, to place them in a hierarchy, in a progression or a regression. In so doing we recapture the very movement of the past. It is true that the *Kulturmensch* is a modern type. History appears as a spectacle only to those who have decided to consider all the solutions and who place themselves before the solutions, freely disposed toward all. History thus stands in contrast to both the narrow and the profound passions which it considers. Truth, says Weber, "is that which *seeks* to be recognized by all those who *seek* the truth."[4] The decision to question each epoch concerning a fundamental choice that is diffused in its thoughts, its desires, and its actions, and of which it has perhaps never made an accounting, is the result of living in an epoch that has tasted of the tree of knowledge. Scientific history is in principle the exact opposite of naïve history, which it would, however, like to recapture. It presupposes itself in what it constructs. But this is not a vicious circle of thought; it is the postulate of all historical thought. And Weber consciously enters into it. As Karl Löwith shows, Weber well knows that scientific history is itself a product of history, a moment of "rationalization," a moment of the history of capitalism.[5] It is history turning back upon itself, presuming that we are theoretically and practically able to take possession of our life and that clarification is possible. This presumption cannot be demonstrated. It will be justified or not according to whether it will or will not give us a coherent image of "the universal history of culture"; and nothing guarantees in advance that the attempt will be successful. In order to try, it is enough to know that to make any other hypothesis is to choose chaos and that the truth which is sought is not, in principle, beyond our grasp. Of that we are certain. We discover that we possess a power of radical choice by which we give meaning to our lives, and through this power we become sensitive to all the uses that humanity has made of it. Through it other cultures are opened up to us and made understandable. All that we postulate in our attempt to understand history is that freedom comprehends all the uses of freedom. What we contribute ourselves is only the prejudice of not having any prejudices, the fact that we belong to a cultural order where our own choices, even those which are opposed to each other, tend to be complementary:

> Culture is a closed segment abstracted from the infinity of events which is endowed with meaning and signification only for man. . . . The transcendental condition of all cultural science is not that we find this or that culture valuable but the fact that we are "cultural men," endowed with the capacity consciously to take a position with regard to the world and to give meaning to it. Whatever this meaning might be, its consequence is that in living we abstract certain phenomena of human coexistence and in order to judge them we take a position (positive or negative) with regard to their significance.[6]

Historical understanding thus does not introduce a system of categories arbitrarily chosen; it only presupposes the possibility that we have a past which is ours and that we can recapture in our freedom the work of so many other freedoms. It assumes that we can clarify the choices of others through our own and ours through theirs, that we can rectify one by the other and finally arrive at the truth. There is no attitude more respectful, no objectivity more profound, than this claim of going to the very source of history. History is not an external god, a hidden reason of which we have only to record the conclusions. It is the metaphysical fact that the same life, our own, is played out both within us and outside us, in our present and in our past, and that the world is a system with several points of access, or, one might say, that we have fellow men.

Because a given economy, a given type of knowledge, a given law, and a given religion all arise from the same fundamental choice and are historical accomplices, we can expect, circumstances permitting, that the facts will allow themselves to be ordered. Their development will manifest the logic of an initial choice, and history will become an experience of mankind. Even if the Calvinistic choice has transcendent motives which capitalism is unaware of, we can still say that in tolerating certain ambiguities capitalism assumed responsibility for what followed, and thus we can treat this sequence as a logical development. Calvinism confronted and juxtaposed the finite and the infinite, carried to the extreme the consciousness we have of not being the source of our own being, and organized the obsession with the beyond at the same time that it closed the routes of access to it. In so doing it paved the way for the fanaticism of the bourgeois enterprise, authorized the work ethic, and eliminated the transcendent. Thus the course of history clarifies the errors and the contradictions of the fundamental choice, and its historical failure bears witness against Calvinism. But in factual sciences there is no proof by absurdity, no crucial experiment. We know, then, that certain solutions are impossible. We do not gain from the working operations of history that comprehensive understanding which would reveal the true solution. At best we rectify errors which occur along the way, but the new scheme is not immune to errors which will have to be rectified anew. History eliminates the irrational; but the rational remains to be created and to be imagined, and it does not have the power of replacing the false with the true. A historical solution of the human problem, an end of history, could be conceived only if humanity were a thing to be known – if, in it, knowledge were able to exhaust being and could come to a state that really contained all that humanity had been and all that it could ever be. Since, on the contrary, in the density of social reality each decision brings unexpected consequences, and since, moreover, man responds to these surprises by inventions which transform the problem, there is no situation without hope; but there is no choice which terminates these deviations or which can exhaust man's inventive power and put an end to his history. There are only advances. The capitalist rationalization is one of them, since it is the resolve to take our given condition in hand through knowledge and action. It can be demonstrated that the appropriation of the world by man, the demystification, is better because it faces difficulties that other regimes have avoided. But this progress is bought by regressions, and there is no guarantee that the progressive elements of history will be separated out from experience and be added back in later. Demystification is also depoetization and disenchantment. We must keep the capitalistic refusal of the sacred as external but renew within it the demands of the absolute that it has abolished. We have no grounds for affirming that this redress will be made. Capitalism is like a shell that the religious animal has secreted for his domicile, and it survives him:

> No one knows who will live in this cage [shell] in the future, or whether at the end of this tremendous development entirely new prophets will arise, or there will be a great rebirth of old ideas and ideals, or, if neither, mechanized petrification, embellished with a sort of convulsive self-importance. For of the last stage of this cultural development, it might well be truly said: "Specialists without spirit, sensualists without heart; this nullity imagines that it has attained a level of civilization never before achieved."[7]

If the system comes to life again, it will be through the intervention of new prophets or by a resurrection of past culture, by an invention or reinvention which does not come from something in that system. Perhaps history will eliminate, together with false solutions to the human problem, certain valid acquisitions as well. It does not locate its errors precisely in a total system. It does not accumulate truths; it works on a question that is confusedly posed and is not sheltered from regressions and setbacks. Projects change so much in the course of things that the lessons taught by events are not reaped, since the generations of men who make the accounting are not those who began the experiment. Weber's phenomenology is not systematic like Hegel's. It does not lead to an absolute knowledge. Man's freedom and the contingency of history exclude, definitively,

> the idea that the goal of the cultural sciences, even their remote goal, is to construct a closed system of concepts in which reality will be confined according to a definitive order . . . and from which it can be deduced. The course of unforeseeable events is transformed endlessly, stretching to eternity. The cultural problems that move men are constantly posed anew and from other aspects. That which becomes meaningful and significant in the infinite flow of individual data constantly changes the field, and it becomes a historical concept, just as the relations of thought are variable under which it is considered and posited as an object of science. The principles of the cultural sciences will keep changing in a future without limits as long as a sclerosis of life and of spirit does not disaccustom humanity, as in China, to posing new questions to an inexhaustible life. A system of the cultural sciences, even if confined to an area which is systematic and objectively valid for questions and for the domains which these questions are called upon to treat, will be nonsense in itself. An attempt of this type could only reassemble pell-mell the multiple, specific, heterogeneous, disparate points of view under which reality is presented to us each time as "culture," i.e., each time it is made significant in its specificity.[8]

The intelligible wholes of history never break their ties with contingency, and the movement by which history turns back on itself in an attempt to grasp itself, to dominate itself, to justify itself, is also without guarantee. History includes dialectical facts and adumbrative significations; it is not a coherent system. Like a distracted interlocutor, it allows the debate to become side-tracked; it forgets the data of the problem along the way. Historical epochs become ordered around a questioning of human possibility, of which each has its formula, rather than around an immanent solution, of which history would be the manifestation.

Because its aim is to recover the fundamental choices of the past, Weber's science is a methodical extension of his experience of the present. But have this experience and its practical options benefited in turn from historical understanding? For only if they have would Weber have reconciled theory and practice.

Weber is not a revolutionary. It is true that he writes that Marxism is "the most important instance of the construction of ideal types" and that all those who have employed its concepts know how fruitful they are – on condition that they take as *meanings* what Marx describes as *forces*. But for him this transposition is incompatible with both Marxist theory and practice. As historical materialism, Marxism is a causal explanation through economics; and in its revolutionary practices Weber never sees the fundamental choice of the proletariat appear. It thus happens that, as has been said, this great mind judges the revolutionary movements which he witnessed in Germany after 1918 as if he were a provincial, bourgeois German. The Munich riot had placed at the head of the revolutionary government the most moralistic of his students ("God, in his wrath, has made him a politician," Weber will say when defending him before the tribunal at the time of the repression).[9] Weber confines himself to these minor facts and never sees a new historical significance in the revolutions after 1917. He is against the revolution because he does not consider it to be revolution – that is to say, the creation of a historical whole. He describes it as essentially a military dictatorship and, for the rest, as a carnival of intellectuals dressed up as politicians.

Weber is a liberal. But, as we said at the beginning, his is a different kind of liberalism from those which preceded him. Raymond Aron writes that his politics is, like that of Alain, a "politics of the understanding." Only, from Alain to Weber, the understanding has learned to doubt itself. Alain recommended a policy which is not quite adequate: do each day what is just, and do not worry about the consequences. However, this maxim is inoperative every time we approach a critical situation, and understanding is then, against its principles, sometimes revolutionary, sometimes submissive. Weber himself well knows that understanding functions easily only within certain critical limits, and he consciously gives it the task of keeping history within the region where history is free from antinomies. He does not make an isolated instance of it. Since we cannot even be sure that the history within which we find ourselves is, in the end, rational, those who choose truth and freedom cannot convince those who, make other choices that they are guilty of absurdity, nor can they even flatter themselves with having "gone beyond" them:

> It is the destiny of a cultural epoch which has tasted of the tree of knowledge to know that we cannot decipher the meaning of world events, regardless of how completely we may study them. We must, rather, be prepared to create them ourselves and to know that world views can never be the product of factual knowledge. Thus the highest ideals, those which move us most powerfully, can become valid only by being in combat with the ideals of other men, which are as sacred to them as ours are to us.[10]

Weber's liberalism does not demand a political empyrean, it does not consider the formal universe of democracy to be an absolute; he admits all politics is violence – even, in its own fashion, democratic politics. His liberalism is militant, even suffering, heroic. It recognizes the rights of its adversaries, refuses to hate them, does not try to avoid confronting them, and, in order to refute them, relies only upon their own contradictions and upon discussions which expose these. Though he rejects nationalism, Communism, and pacifism, he does not want to out law them; he does not renounce the attempt to understand them. Weber, who under the Empire decided against submarine warfare and in favor of a white peace, declared himself jointly responsible with the patriot who had killed the first Pole to enter Danzig. He opposed the pacifist left, which made Germany alone responsible for the war and which exonerated in advance the foreign occupation, because he thought that these abuses of self-accusation paved the way for a violent nationalism in the future. Still, he testified in favor of his students who were involved in pacifist propaganda. Though he did not believe in revolution, he made public his esteem for Liebknecht and Rosa Luxemburg. Weber is against political discrimination within the university. Perhaps, he says, anarchist opinions might allow a scholar to see an aspect of history of which he would otherwise have been unaware. Though he scrupulously left out of his teaching anything which might have favored some cause or have exhibited his personal beliefs, he is in favor of professors who become engaged in politics. However, they should do this outside the classroom – in essays, which are open to discussion, and in public gatherings, where the adversary can respond. The academic soliloquy should not be fraudulently used for the purposes of propaganda. Thus he holds both ends of the chain. Thus he makes truth work together with decision, knowledge with struggle. Thus he makes sure that repression is never justified in the name of freedom.[11]

Is this better than a compromise? Has he succeeded in uniting, except in his own person, the meanings of force and freedom? Is there any other way of satisfying them both except through alternation? When he wished to found a political party on these bases, Weber was so easily expelled and returned so quickly to his studies that it was thought that he did not adhere to these ideas too strongly, that he felt there was an insurmountable obstacle in them, and that a party which did not play according to the rules of the game would be a utopia. However, this failure is perhaps only of Weber the man. Perhaps it leaves intact the political wisdom which he at least sketched out once, even if he did not know how to put this wisdom into practice. For he did not content himself with setting values and efficacy, feelings and responsibility, in opposition to each other. He tried to show how one must go beyond these alternatives. The taste for violence, he says, is a hidden weakness; the ostentation of virtuous feelings is a secret violence. These are two sorts of histrionics or neurosis, but there is a *force*, that of the true politician, which is beyond these. The true politician's secret is to not try to form an image of himself and of his life. Because he has put a certain distance between himself and his success, he does not take pleasure in his intentions alone, nor does he accept the judgment of others as final. Because his action is a "work," a devotedness to a "thing" (*Sache*) which grows outside him, it has a rallying power which is always lacking in undertakings which are done out of vanity. "Lack of distance" from oneself, from things, and from others is the professional disease of academic circles and of intellectuals. With them, action is only a flight from oneself, a decadent mode of self-love. By contrast, having once and for all decided to "bear the irrationality of the world," the politician is patient or intractable when he must be – that is to say, when he has compromised as much as he will allow himself and when the very sense of what he is doing is involved. Precisely because he is not a man of the ethics of ultimate ends [*la morale du coeur*], when he says no to others and to things, even this is an action, and it is he who gratifies the sterile wishes of the politics of ultimate ends [*la politique du coeur*]:

> If in these times, which, in your opinion, are not times of "sterile" excitation – excitation is not, after all, genuine passion – if now

suddenly the *Weltanschauungs*-politicians crop up *en masse* and pass the watchword, "The world is stupid and base, not I," "The responsibility for the consequences does not fall upon me but upon the others whom I serve and whose stupidity or baseness I shall eradicate," then I declare frankly that I would first inquire into the degree of inner poise backing this ethic of ultimate ends. I am under the impression that in nine out of ten cases I deal with windbags who do not fully realize what they take upon themselves but who intoxicate themselves with romantic sensations. From a human point of view this is not very interesting to me, nor does it move me profoundly. However, it is immensely moving when a *mature* man – no matter whether old or young in years – is aware of a responsibility for the consequences of his conduct and really feels such responsibility with heart and soul. He then acts by following an ethic of responsibility, and somewhere he reaches the point where he says: "Here I stand; I can do no other." That is something genuinely human and moving. And every one of us who is not spiritually dead must realize the possibility of finding himself at some time in that position. Insofar as this is true, an ethic of ultimate ends and an ethic of responsibility are not absolute contrasts but rather supplements, which only in unison constitute a genuine man – a man who *can* have the calling for politics.[12]

It will be said that this talisman is a small thing, that it is only a question of ethics, that a major political viewpoint prolongs the history of a time, and that it should therefore give it its formula. But this objection perhaps ignores the most certain conclusion Weber establishes. If history does not have a direction, like a river, but has a meaning, if it teaches us, not a truth, but errors to avoid, if its practice is not deduced from a dogmatic philosophy of history, then it is not superficial to base a politics on the analysis of the political man. After all, once the official legends have been put aside, what makes a politics important is not the philosophy of history which inspires it and which in other hands would produce only upheavals. What makes it important is the human quality that causes the leaders truly to animate the political apparatus and makes their most personal acts everyone's affair. It is this rare quality that elevates Lenin and Trotsky above the other authors of the 1917 revolution. The course of things is meaningful only to those who know how to read it, and the principles of a philosophy of history are dead letters if they are not recreated in contact with the present. To succeed in this, one must possess the capacity of which Weber speaks, the capacity to live history. In politics, truth is perhaps only this art of inventing what will later appear to have been required by the time. Certainly Weber's politics will have to be elaborated. It is not by chance that the art of politics is found in some places and not in others. One can think of it more as a symptom of the "intentions" of history than as a cause. One can seek to read the present more attentively than Weber did, to perceive "elective affinities" that escaped him. But what he has shown definitively is that a philosophy of history that is not a historical novel does not break the circle of knowledge and reality but is rather a meditation upon that circle.

We wanted to begin this study with Weber because, at a time when events were about to bring the Marxist dialectic to the fore, Weber's effort demonstrates under what conditions a historical dialectic is serious. There were Marxists who understood this, and they were the best. There developed a rigorous and consistent Marxism which, like Weber's approach, was a theory of historical comprehension, of *Vielseitigkeit*, and of creative choice, and was a philosophy that questioned history. It is only by beginning with Weber, and with this Weberian Marxism, that the adventures of the dialectic of the past thirty-five years can be understood.

Notes

1 Max Weber, "Die Protestantische Ethik und der Geist des Kapitalismus," *Archiv für Sozialwissenschaft und Sozialpolitik, neue Folge des Archivs für soziale Gesetzgebung und Statistik*, III (1905), p. 13. English translation by Talcott Parsons, *The Protestant Ethic and the Spirit of Capitalism*, New York, 1958, p. 223. (The English translation will be referred to as "ET.")
2 *Ibid.*, II (1904), pp. 17–18; ET, pp. 54–5.
3 *Ibid.*, p. 54; ET, pp. 91–2.
4 Max Weber, *Gesammelte Aufsätze zur Wissenschaftslehre*, Tübingen, 1922, p. 184.
5 Karl Löwith, "Max Weber und Karl Marx," *Archiv für Sozialwissenschaft und Sozialpolitik*, LVII (1932).
6 Weber, *Gesammelte Aufsätze*, pp. 180–1.
7 *Ibid.*, p. 240. (The passage Merleau-Ponty here refers to also appears in "Die Protestantische Ethik," *Archiv für Sozialwissenschaft und Sozialpolitik*, III (1905), p. 109; ET, p. 182 (*Trans.*)).
8 *Ibid.*, p. 185.
9 Marianne Weber, *Max Weber, ein Lebensbild*, Tübingen, 1926.
10 Max Weber, *Gesammelte Aufsätze*, p. 154.
11 On all these points see Marianne Weber, *Max Weber*.
12 Max Weber, *Politik als Beruf*, Munich, 1919, p. 66. English translation, "Politics as a Vocation," by H. H. Gerth and C. Wright Mills, in *From Max Weber: Essays in Sociology*, New York, 1958, p. 127.

BIBLIOGRAPHY

MAURICE MERLEAU-PONTY: MAIN WORKS

Monographs

La Structure du comportement, Paris: Presses Universitaires de France, 1942.
> Translated by A. L. Fisher as *The Structure of Behavior*, Boston, MA: Beacon Press, 1963.

Phénoménologie de la perception, Paris: Gallimard, 1945.
> Translated by C. Smith as *The Phenomenology of Perception*, London: Routledge and Kegan Paul, 1962; translation revised by F. Williams, London: Routledge, 1974; new edition, London: Routledge Classics, 2002.

Humanisme et terreur, Paris: Gallimard, 1947.
> Translated by J. O'Neill as *Humanism and Terror*, Boston, MA: Beacon Press, 1969.

Eloge de la philosophie, Paris: Gallimard, 1953.
> Translated by J. Wild and J. Edie as 'In praise of philosophy', in *In Praise of Philosophy and Other Essays*, Evanston, IL: Northwestern University Press, 1988.

L'Oeil et l'esprit, Paris: Gallimard, 1964.
> Translated by C. Dallery as 'Eye and mind', in *The Primacy of Perception and Other Essays*, edited by J. Edie, Evanston, IL: Northwestern University Press, 1964.

Le Visible et l'invisible, edited by C. Lefort, Paris: Gallimard, 1964.
> Translated by A. Lingis as *The Visible and the Invisible*, Evanston, IL: Northwestern University Press, 1968.

Collections of essays (originally in French)

Sens et non-sens, Paris: Nagel, 1948.
> Translated by H. L. Dreyfus and P. A. Dreyfus as *Sense and Non-sense*, Evanston, IL: Northwestern University Press, 1964.

Les Aventures de la dialectique, Paris: Gallimard, 1955.
> Translated by J. Bien as *Adventures of the Dialectic*, Evanston, IL: Northwestern University Press, 1973; London Heinemann, 1974.

Signes, Paris: Gallimard, 1960.
> Translated by R. C. McCleary as *Signs*, Evanston, IL: Northwestern University Press, 1964.

Résumés de cours, Collège de France, 1952–1960, Paris: Gallimard, 1968.
> Translated by J. O'Neill as 'Themes from the lectures at the Collège de France, 1952–1960', in *In Praise of Philosophy and Other Essays*, Evanston, IL: Northwestern University Press, 1988.

La Prose du monde, ed. C. Lefort, Paris: Gallimard, 1969.
> Edited by Claude Lefort and translated by J. O'Neill as *The Prose of the World*, Evanston, IL: Northwestern University Press, 1973; London: Heinemann, 1974.

Causeries 1948, ed. S. Ménasé, Paris: Seuil, 2002.

Collections of essays (originally in English)

The Primacy of Perception and Other Essays, ed. J. Edie, Evanston, IL: Northwestern University Press, 1964.

In Praise of Philosophy and Other Essays, Evanston, ILL: Northwestern University Press, 1988.

FURTHER READING

This is divided into sections which, after the general commentaries, match the ways in which in the extracts from Merleau-Ponty's writings are grouped together.

General commentaries on Merleau-Ponty's work

Bannan, J. F. (1967) *The Philosophy of Merleau-Ponty*, New York: Harcourt, Brace and World. (Very well-informed discussion of the central themes of Merleau-Ponty's work, though a bit dated by now.)

Dillon, M. C. (1988) *Merleau-Ponty's Ontology*, Evanston, IL: Northwestern University Press. (Generally helpful discussion of themes of Merleau-Ponty's work.)

Langan, T. (1966) *Merleau-Ponty's Critique of Reason*, New Haven, CT: Yale University Press. (A useful general introduction, if a bit dated by now.)

Langer, M. (1989) *Merleau-Ponty's Phenomenology of Perception*, Part I, London: Macmillan. (Helpful though largely uncritical.)

Matthews, E. (2002) *The Philosophy of Merleau-Ponty*, Chesham: Acumen. (Excellent discussion.)

Priest, S. (1998) *Merleau-Ponty*, London: Routledge. (Scholarly but resolutely analytical in style; thus, arguably, somewhat at odds with Merleau-Ponty's mode of thought.)

Rabil, A. (1967) *Merleau-Ponty: Existentialist of the Social World*, New York: Columbia University Press. (Especially useful as a discussion of Merleau-Ponty's later work.)

Schmidt, J. (1985) *Maurice Merleau-Ponty*, London: Macmillan. (A short but useful discussion of the social aspects of Merleau-Ponty's philosophy.)

Where these books have chapters that are specially relevant to the themes of the following sections, they are listed below, along with other works about or by Merleau-Ponty.

Merleau-Ponty's life and the context of his work

Bannan (1967) Introduction; Langan (1966) ch. 1; Matthews (2002) ch. 1; Priest (1998) ch. 1; Rabil (1967) Part I; Schmidt (1985) ch. 2.

Madison, G. B. (1993) 'Merleau-Ponty in retrospect', in P. Burke and J. van der Veken (eds), *Merleau-Ponty in Contemporary Perspective*, Dordrecht: Kluwer, pp. 183–95. (A helpful survey of Merleau-Ponty's work.)

Mirvish, A. M. (1983) 'Merleau-Ponty and the nature of philosophy', *Philosophy and Phenomenological Research* 43, pp. 449–76. (A reflective, sympathetic assessment.)

O'Neill, J. (1970) *Perception, Expression and History*, Evanston, IL: Northwestern University Press. (A general survey, with emphasis on social and political philosophy.)

The Structure of Behavior

Bannan (1967) ch. 1; Matthews (2002) ch. 4.

Goldstein, K. (1934) *Der Aufbau der Organismus*, The Hague: Martinus Nijhof. Trans. as *The Organism*, New York: American Book, 1938. (A key source for Merleau-Ponty's discussion of physiology, and still well worth reading.)

Kohler, W. (1930) *Gestalt Psychology*, London: Bell. (A classic introduction to gestalt psychology by one of the founders of the school.)

The Phenomenology of Perception, Preface: 'What is phenomenology?'

Merleau-Ponty, M. (1959) 'Le Philosophe et son ombre', in H. L. Van Breda and J. Taminiaux (eds), *Phenomenologica no. 4; Edmund Husserl: 1859–1959*, The Hague: Martinus Nijhof. Trans. by R. McCleary as 'The philosopher and his shadow', in *Signs*, Evanston, IL: Northwestern University Press, 1964. (Merleau-Ponty's later reflections on Husserl and phenomenology.)

Matthews (2002) ch. 2; Priest (1998) ch. 2; Rabil (1967) ch. 3.

Bell, D. (1990) *Husserl*, London: Routledge. (Part II is an excellent critical discussion of Husserl's later phenomenology and thereby provides a good introduction to Merleau-Ponty's conception of phenomenology.)

Heinemaa, S. (1999) 'Merleau-Ponty's modification of phenomenology', *Synthèse* 118, pp. 49–68. (Contrasts Merleau-Ponty with Husserl.)

Husserl, E. (1931) *Méditations cartésiennes*, Paris: Colin. Repr. (German text) as *Husserliana* I, The Hague: Martinus Nijhof, 1950. Trans. by D. Cairns as *Cartesian Meditations*, The Hague: Martinus Nijhof, 1973. (In his preface Merleau-Ponty appears to have this text very much in mind.)

Reuter, M. (1999) 'Merleau-Ponty's notion of pre-reflective intentionality', *Synthèse* 118, pp. 69–88. (Clarifies Merleau-Ponty's conception of intentionality.)

Toadvine, T. (ed.) (2002) *Merleau-Ponty's Reading of Husserl*, Dordrecht: Kluwer. (A good collection of essays exploring the relationship between Husserl and Merleau-Ponty.)

The Phenomenology of Perception, Part I: The body
Bannan (1967) ch. 2; Rabil (1967) ch. 2.

Gallagher, S. (1995) 'Bodily schema and intentionality', in J. L. Bermudez, N. Eilan and A. Marcel (eds), *The Body and the Self*, Cambridge, MA: MIT Press. (Discusses Merleau-Ponty's conception of the body in the light of recent work in psychology.)

Gallagher, S. and Meltzoff, A. (1996) 'The earliest sense of self and others', *Philosophical Psychology* 9, pp. 211–33. (Critical discussion of Merleau-Ponty's psychological presumptions in the light of recent work in developmental psychology.)

Gelb, A. and Goldstein, K. (1920) *Psychologische Analysen hirnpathologischer Fälle*, Leipzig: Barth. (Merleau-Ponty takes the details of Schneider's case from this work and others by Gelb and Goldstein.)

Herbenick, R. (1973) 'Merleau-Ponty and the primacy of reflection', in G. Gillan (ed.), *The Horizons of the Flesh*, Carbondale and Edwardsville, IL: Southern Illinois University Press. (A discussion of bodily intentionality.)

Husserl, E. (1952) 'Ideen II', *Husserliana* IV, The Hague: Martinus Nijhof. Trans. by R. Rojciewicz and A. Schuwer as *Ideas II*, The Hague: Martinus Nijhof, 1989. (Husserl's discussion of the 'constitution' of the *Leib* which greatly impressed Merleau-Ponty.)

Lhermitte, J. (1939) *L'Image de notre corps*, Paris: Nouvelle Revue Critique. (Merleau-Ponty relies a good deal on this work, especially the conception of the 'body-image' that Lhermitte here introduces.)

Sartre, J.-P. (1943) *L'Être et le néant*, Paris: Gallimard. Trans. by H. Barnes as *Being and Nothingness*, London: Methuen, 1958. (Merleau-Ponty draws critically on Sartre's long discussion of the body in part III, ch. 2.)

Taylor, C. (1989) 'Embodied agency', in H. Pietersma (ed.), *Merleau-Ponty: Critical Essays*, Washington, DC: University Press of America, pp. 1–21. (A discussion of Merleau-Ponty's conception of the body.)

The Phenomenology of Perception, Part II: The world as perceived
Bannan (1967) ch. 3; Dillon (1988) chs 3, 4, 7; Langer (1989) part II; Matthews (2002) ch. 3; Priest (1998) chs 5, 11; Schmidt (1985) ch. 3.

Compton, J. T. (1989) 'Merleau-Ponty's thesis of the primacy of perception and the meaning of scientific objectivity', in H. Pietersma (ed.), *Merleau-Ponty: Critical Essays*, Washington, DC: University Press of America, pp. 133–48. (This paper discusses the implications of Merleau-Ponty's account of perception for the philosophy of science.)

Dreyfus, H. and Todes, S. (1962) 'The three worlds of Merleau-Ponty', *Philosophy and Phenomenological Research* 22, pp. 559–65. (An important criticism of Merleau-Ponty's conception of the perceived world.)

Heidegger, M. (1927) *Sein und Zeit*, Tübingen: Max Niemayer. Trans. by J. Macquarrie and E. Robinson as *Being and Time*, Oxford: Blackwell, 1973. (Merleau-Ponty's account of intersubjectivity draws on Heidegger's account here of *Mitsein* (being-with-others); see ch. 4 of division 1.)

Husserl, E. (1954) 'Die Krisis der europäischen Wissenschaften', *Husserliana* VI, The Hague: Martinus Nijhof. Trans. by D. Carr as *The Crisis of European Sciences*, Evanston, IL: Northwestern University Press, 1968. (Merleau-Ponty's account of the natural sciences is much influenced by this work.)

Madison, G. B. (1992) 'Did Merleau-Ponty have a theory of perception?', in T. W. Busch and S. Gallagher (eds), *Merleau-Ponty, Hermeneutics and Postmodernism*, Albany, NY: SUNY Press, pp. 83–106. (An interesting discussion from a postmodern perspective.)

Olafson, F. A. (1969) 'A central theme of Merleau-Ponty's philosophy', in E. Lee and M. Mandelbaum (eds), *Phenomenology and Existentialism*, Baltimore, MD: Johns Hopkins University Press. (An early discussion of Merleau-Ponty's account of perception.)

Sartre, J.-P. (1943) *L'Être et le néant*, Paris: Gallimard. Trans. by H. Barnes, as *Being and Nothingness*, London: Methuen, 1958. (Merleau-Ponty criticises the account of our relationships with others that Sartre sets out in part III.)

Smith, M. B. (1999) 'Transcendence in Merleau-Ponty', in D. Olkowski and J. Morley (eds), *Merleau-Ponty, Interiority and Exteriority, Psychic Life and the World*, Albany, NY: SUNY Press, pp. 35–46. (Discusses the notion of 'transcendence' in Merleau-Ponty's account of the perceived world.)

Strawson, P. (1959) *Individuals: An Essay in Descriptive Metaphysics*, London: Methuen. (In ch. 3, 'Persons', Strawson argues for our essential dependence upon each other for our understanding of ourselves and hence for the primacy of the conception of ourselves as embodied persons; it is worthwhile to compare this argument with Merleau-Ponty's account of intersubjectivity.)

The Phenomenology of Perception, Part III: Being-for-itself and Being-in-the-world

Bannan (1967) ch. 4; Langan (1966) ch. 3; Langer (1989) part III; Matthews (2002) ch. 5.

Descartes, R. (1641) *Meditationes de prima philosophia*. Trans. by J. Cottingham, R. Stoothof and D. Murdoch as 'Meditations on first philosophy', in *The Philosophical Writings of Descartes* II, Cambridge: Cambridge University Press, 1984. (Merleau-Ponty discusses themes from Descartes's *Meditations* in his chapter on the *cogito*.)

Lachièze-Rey, P. (1932) *L'Idéalisme kantien*, Paris: Alcan. (Merleau-Ponty briefly expounds and then criticises the position of Lachièze-Rey at the start of the chapter on the *cogito*.)

Sartre, J.-P. (1943) *L'Être et le néant*, Paris: Gallimard. Trans. by H. Barnes as *Being and Nothingness*, London: Methuen, 1958. (Merleau-Ponty's discussion of the *cogito* includes an implicit criticism of Sartre's conception of consciousness, especially as set out in the 'Introduction'; and the discussion of freedom is an explicit critique of Sartre's account of freedom as set out in part IV.)

Stewart, J. (1995) 'Merleau-Ponty's criticisms of Sartre's theory of freedom', *Philosophy Today* 39, pp. 311–24. (Seeks to defend Sartre from Merleau-Ponty's criticisms.)

Williams, L. (1990) 'Merleau-Ponty's tacit cogito', *Man and World* 23, pp. 101–11. (A useful critical comparison between Descartes and Merleau-Ponty.)

The Prose of the World

Merleau-Ponty, M. (2002) [1945] *The Phenomenology of Perception*, Part I, ch. 6: 'The body as expression and speech'. (A discussion that complements well the chapter printed here.)

——(1964) [1951] 'On the phenomenology of language', in *Signs*, pp. 84–97. (A discussion in which Merleau-Ponty presents his position specifically from a phenomenological perspective.)

Bannan (1967) ch. 5; Langan (1966) ch. 5; Priest (1998) ch. 10; Schmidt (1985) ch. 4.

Dillon, M. C. (1993) 'The unconscious: language and world', in P. Burke and J. van der Veken (eds), *Merleau-Ponty in Contemporary Perspective*, Dordrecht: Kluwer, pp. 69–84. (Uses Merleau-Ponty's account of language to clarify his account of the unconscious.)

Low, D. (1992) 'The continuity between Merleau-Ponty's early and late philosophy of language', *Journal of Philosophical Research* 17, pp. 287–311. (A very helpful comparison of Merleau-Ponty's early and late discussions of language.)

Spurling, L. (1977) *Phenomenology and the Social World*, London: Routledge, ch. 2. (A good account of Merleau-Ponty's treatment of language.)

The Visible and the Invisible

Dillon (1988) chs 8, 9; Matthews (2002) ch. 8; Priest (1998) ch. 14.

Dillon, M. C. (1989) 'Merleau-Ponty and the reversibility thesis', in H. Pietersma (ed.), *Merleau-Ponty: Critical Essays*, Washington, DC: University Press of America, pp. 77–100. (A good discussion of a central theme of Merleau-Ponty's late thought.)

Irigary, L. (1993) 'The invisible of the flesh: a reading of Merleau-Ponty, "The Intertwining – The Chiasm" ', in C. Burke and G. Gill (trans.), *An Ethics of Sexual Difference*, New York: Cornell University Press, pp. 151–84. Reprinted 2000 in C. Caseaux (ed.), *The Continental Aesthetics Reader*, London: Routledge. (An important paper, which provides both a sympathetic exposition of Merleau-Ponty's line of thought and a well-argued challenge to it from a feminist perspective.)

Johnson, G. A. and Smith, M. B. (eds) (1990) *Ontology and Alterity in Merleau-Ponty*, Part I (papers by Lefort, Dillon, Madison), Evanston, IL: Northwestern University Press. (A helpful debate on Merleau-Ponty's conception of 'flesh'.)

Yount, M. (1990) 'Two reversibilities: Merleau-Ponty and Derrida', *Philosophy Today* 34, pp. 129–40. (A useful comparison, which shows well the connections between phenomenology and deconstruction.)

Painting

Matthews (2002) ch. 7.

Bernard, E. (1926) *Souvenirs sur Paul Cézanne; et une conversation avec Cézanne*, Paris: R. G. Michael. (Merleau-Ponty draws a good deal on Bernard's account of his conversations with Cézanne.)

Crowther, P. (1991) *Critical Aesthetics and Postmodernism*, Oxford: Clarendon Press, ch. 2. (A well-informed and sensitive critical discussion.)

——(1993) *Art and Embodiment*, Oxford, Clarendon Press, ch. 6. (More of the same.)

Freud, S. (1910) *Eine Kinderheitserinnerung des Leonardo da Vinci*, Leipzig: Deuticke. Trans. by A. Brill as *Leonardo da Vinci: A Study in Psychosexuality*, New York, 1947. (Merleau-Ponty discusses Freud's interpretation critically in 'Cézanne's doubt'.)

Valéry, P. (1919) *Introduction à la méthode de Léonard de Vinci*, Paris. Trans. by T. McGreevy as *Introduction to the Method of Leonardo da Vinci*, London, 1929. (Merleau-Ponty alludes to this in 'Cézanne's doubt' and in *The Phenomenology of Perception*.)

History

Merleau-Ponty, M. (1973, 1974) [1955] ' "Western" Marxism', in *Adventures of the Dialectic*, pp. 30–58. (A careful discussion of Lukács and the history of Marxism, which complements his treatment of Weber.)

Bannan (1967) ch. 7; Rabil (1967) ch. 6; Schmidt (1985) ch. 4.

Bien, J. (1973) 'Merleau-Ponty's conception of history', in G. Gillan (ed.), *The Horizons of the Flesh*, Carbondale and Edwardsville, IL: Southern Illinois University Press, pp. 127–42. (An account that connects Merleau-Ponty's account of history with his ontology.)

Nagel, C. (1997) 'Hegelianism in Merleau-Ponty's philosophy', *Philosophy Today* 41, pp. 288–98. (A Hegelian reading of Merleau-Ponty.)

Weber, M. (1905) *The Protestant Ethic and the Spirit of Capitalism*, trans. T. Parsons, New York: Free Press, 1958. (Merleau-Ponty discusses this work in 'The crisis of understanding'.)

INDEX

Note: Page numbers followed by *n* indicate information is in a note. The abbreviation M-P stands for Merleau-Ponty.

Bernard, Emile 141, 274–5, 276–7, 279, 280, 283
biology 7, 44; evolutionary theory 9
body in perception 2, 34–6, 50, 79–125, 142–3, 143–4; Bergson's image theory 24; body image 101, 102–6, 126; as chiasm 247–8; and experience 12, 15, 18; Husserl's phenomenology 25–6; ideality of 6; intentionality of 122–4, 326; objective body 25, 85–101, 149–50; of others 147–52, 248; and painting 294–321; psychological disorder and movement 16–18; spatial relations 36, 38; status of 15; and subject 207–8, 209–11; vision 79–84, 253–5, 267, 268; *see also* phantom limb phenomenon
Bonaparte's project 225–6
Brunschvicg, L. 12, 23, 193

Calvinism 325, 329–41
capitalism 325, 329–30, 332–41
Carnap, Rudolf 12
Cartesianism 150; *see also* Descartes
Cassirer, Ernst 39, 116
categorical attitude 59
causality 44, 45, 85–6, 89; subject/ body relationship 209–11, 212
cenethesis 103
cerebral localization 35
certainty 167, 182, 195, 199
Cézanne, Paul 37, 77, 137, 140–1, 293, 296, 300, 309, 311; 'Cézanne's Doubt' 38, 272–90
child development 55–7, 153–4; language 200–1
Chomsky, Noam 18
cinema 316
civilization 146–7, 336
class consciousness 218–25
Claudel, Paul 250
co-existence 147–54, 156
cogito 66, 69–70, 73, 124, 164, 166, 167–209; and eternity 172–3; and false feelings 176–80; and Heidegger 27; of others 151–2, 154–8; and perception 173–5; 'spoken' and 'tacit' cogito 167, 200–2, 203–4, 206

colour: in art 140–1, 276, 278–9, 311–12, 314; sensitivity 86
commitment 180–1, 229, 231
common sense realism 14, 19, 21
communication: of meaning 38, 39–40; with others 152–4; *see also* language; speech
computational psychology 6
concrete movements 16, 101, 107–10, 114–16
consciousness 43–4, 47–8; and abstract movement 113–16; and being 28–9, 66; of children 55–6; essence of 72–3; evolvement of meaning 71–2; of human order 52–61; intentional arc 120–2; and language 201–4; nature of 44–5; of other people 148–50, 171–2, 224, 248; of reality 58–60, 67, 72–3; of self *see cogito*; symbolic consciousness 116–19; and vision 173–5; *see also* perceptual consciousness
constituted speech/language 167, 188, 202
constituting consciousness 186, 202
constitution in Husserl's phenomenology 25, 26, 206
creativity 244
cubism 311, 316
cultural world 146–7, 153–4; expression of 282–3; and speech 187, 189, 190
culture 7, 41, 50; and history 337–9, 340
cybernetics 292

Da Vinci *see* Leonardo da Vinci
Dasein 26, 27
deep structures 18
Delaunay, Robert 311, 318
demystification 339
depth in art 311, 312–13
Derrida, Jacques 290
Descartes, René 23, 27, 125n, 150, 154, 200, 201, 213; consciousness 66, 166; doubt 195, 198–9; soul 36; theory of vision 290, 301–9; *see also cogito*
desire 56–7
determinism 10

167, 200–2, 203–4, 206; and
thought 169–70, 171;
transcendental subjectivity 23,
66–7, 69, 160; *see also cogito*
substitutions 89–90
surrealism 299
symbolic function 114, 116–19
synthesis, perceptual 132–5, 176, 182

'tacit' cogito 167, 200–2, 203–4, 206
tangible 251–2, 255–67, 290
temporality 27, 81–3; and *cogito*
172–3; generalized time 229–30;
and history 327–8; and illness 120;
individual past 163; instant 213;
mendacity of photography 316–
17; non-temporal thought 191–4;
perceptual synthesis 132–5;
prepersonal time 230; and
repression 94–6
Temps Modernes, Les (journal) 2,
28
theism 13
thing and the natural world 135–45,
146
thought: about seeing 173–4; in art
320; and language 39, 235; and
speech 187–91; and subjectivity
169–70, 171; *see also*
consciousness; idealism; objective
thought
Tilquin, A. 45–6*n*
time *see* temporality
tiredness 217
touch 247–8, 251–2, 254–67, 290
transcendence 162–4, 175, 338
transcendental field 15
transcendental idealism 4–5, 6,
10–11, 12, 13, 66–7, 68, 70, 72, 163
transcendental man 41–2
transcendental reflection 133
transcendental subjectivity 23, 66–7,
69, 160
triangle 182–7, 189
Trismegistus, Hermes 313
true love 176–7
truth: acquired thought 192–3;

evidence 194–7; mathematical
truth 166, 183–4, 192, 234, 238,
240–6; objective truth 325–6, 327;
perception of 73; theory of 38

unity of things 137–8

Valéry, Paul 9, 77, 135*n*, 265, 270, 286,
294
Van Gogh, Vincent 192, 293
Vasari, Giorgio 287
Vienna Circle 71
violence 327, 342, 343
Visible and the invisible, The 34,
247–71
vision 79–84, 150; colour sensitivity
86; and consciousness 121, 173–5;
Descartes's theory of 290, 301–9;
'Eye and mind' 290–324; symbolic
function 118–19; visible 247–64,
290–1, 296–301, 314–15, 317–19;
visual field 131, 136, 137
vital order 6, 16, 49, 50

Wahl, Jean 72
Watson, John B. 3, 45, 46*n*
Weber, Max 28, 325, 326–45; politics
of 341–5
Weltlichkeit der Welt 73
Wertheimer, Max 3
Wesley, John 332, 336
will 176; and freedom 211–12
Wittgenstein, Ludwig 21, 22, 23
wonder at the world 70, 77–8
work ethic 325, 329, 330–1, 332, 335
world as perceived 36–8, 41–2,
126–65; implicit evaluation of
215–17; other selves and human
world 145–65, 171–2, 224, 248;
sense experience 14, 126–35, 227;
subject as project of 204–8; things
in the natural world 135–45
World Spirit 41
world-thesis 242–6
worldly asceticism 330–1, 332, 334

Zola, Emile 273, 274–5

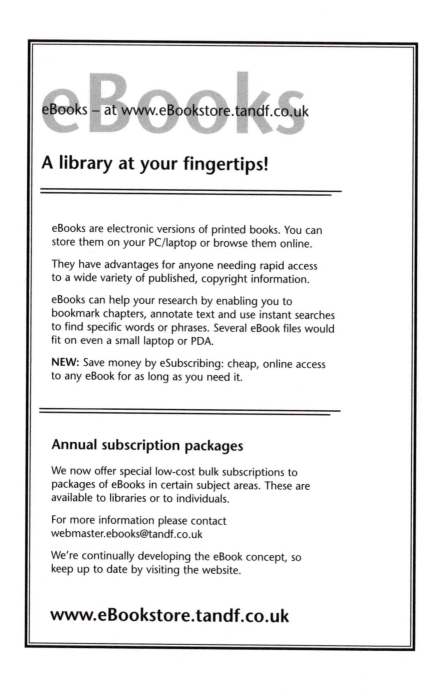